Family Law
PRACTICE AND PROCEDURE

FIFTH EDITION

VOLUME I

JoAnn Kurtz

 **emond** ▪ Toronto, Canada ▪ 2018

Emond Montgomery Publications Limited
60 Shaftesbury Avenue
Toronto ON M4T 1A3
http://www.emond.ca/highered

Printed in Canada.

We acknowledge the financial support of the Government of Canada.   Canadä

Emond Montgomery Publications has no responsibility for the persistence or accuracy of URLs for external or third-party Internet websites referred to in this publication, and does not guarantee that any content on such websites is, or will remain, accurate or appropriate.

Vice president, publishing: Anthony Rezek
Publisher: Lindsay Sutherland
Director, development and production: Kelly Dickson
Developmental editor: Joanne Sutherland
Production editor: Natalie Berchem
Copy editor: Margaret Henderson
Typesetter: SPi Global
Text designer: Tara Agnerian
Permissions editor: Alison Lloyd-Baker
Proofreader: Ann Lau
Indexer: Paula Pike
Cover image: Pavel_Klimenko/Shutterstock

Library and Archives Canada Cataloguing in Publication

Kurtz, JoAnn, 1951-, author
    Family law : practice and procedure / JoAnn Kurtz. -- Fifth edition.

(Working with the law)
Includes bibliographical references and indexes.
ISBN 978-1-77255-269-0 (v. 1 : softcover).--ISBN 978-1-77255-317-8 (v. 2 : softcover)

    1. Domestic relations--Ontario--Textbooks.   2. Textbooks.   I. Title.
I. Series: Working with the law
KEO213.K87 2018   346.71301'5   C2017-906819-9
KF505.ZB3K87 2018

To my (thankfully intact) family—my husband Daniel Henry,
and my three sons, Jacob, Max, and Ely

Brief Contents

PART I

INTRODUCTION

PART II

THE SUBSTANTIVE LAW OF MARRIAGE AND FAMILY BREAKDOWN

PART III

PROCEDURE IN FAMILY LAW MATTERS

PART IV

NEGOTIATION, VARIATION, AND ENFORCEMENT

Contents

PART I

INTRODUCTION

1 Overview of a Marriage Breakdown

2 A Brief History of Family Law in Ontario

7 Spousal Support

8 Child Support

9 Property Rights

PART III
PROCEDURE IN FAMILY LAW MATTERS

10 The Family Law Rules

13 Support and Custody Claims: A Fast Track Case and a Motion

14 Property Claims: A Standard Track Case and Conferences

PART IV

NEGOTIATION, VARIATION, AND ENFORCEMENT

15 Negotiation and Domestic Contracts

Preface to the Fifth Edition

For many years, my colleagues at Seneca College and I taught family law to students in our law clerk program using a patchwork of texts, statutes, rules, and precedents. No one text discussed both the substantive law and the practice and procedure in the area. I wrote this book so that my family law students could have the text I always wanted them to have.

The area of family law has been marked by ongoing change since the first edition of this book was published in 2004, and this book has been revised throughout the years to keep up with those changes.

In the less than two years between the publication of the first and second editions of this book, there were major developments in family law in both substantive law and practice. When the first edition was published, the *Family Law Rules* applied to proceedings in the Ontario Court of Justice and in the Family Court of the Superior Court of Justice. Procedure in family law matters in the Superior Court of Justice of Ontario, however, was governed by the *Rules of Civil Procedure*. Since July 1, 2004 the *Family Law Rules* govern procedure in all courts having jurisdiction over family law matters.

When the first edition was published, the legality of same-sex marriage had been upheld by the courts, but family law legislation at the federal and provincial level had not yet been amended to reflect that new reality. At the federal level, Parliament had not, as of the publication of the second edition, passed legislation to codify the legality of same-sex marriage, nor had it amended other federal legislation, including the *Divorce Act*, to recognize the spousal status of parties to a same-sex marriage. However, in November 2004, the Ontario Superior Court of Justice extended the right to divorce to same-sex married couples when it ruled that the existing definition of spouse as "either of a man or woman who are married to each other" contravenes the *Charter of Rights and Freedoms*, and should instead read "either of two persons who are married to one another." At the provincial level, the Province of Ontario passed Bill 171 in March 2005. Bill 171 amended a number of statutes to change the definition of spouse to include both opposite-sex and same-sex couples. The second edition addressed those significant changes in substantive law and procedure.

In the four years between the publication of the second and third editions of this book, much changed again. On July 20, 2005, the federal *Civil Marriage Act* became law and changed the definition of marriage, for civil purposes, to "the lawful union of two persons to the exclusion of all others," thus legalizing same-sex marriage throughout Canada. The same statute amended the definition of "spouse" in the *Divorce Act* to allow for same-sex divorce. In July 2008, a final revised version of the *Spousal Support Advisory Guidelines* (first released as a draft proposal in January 2005) was released. The third edition addressed these significant changes in substantive law, as well as the numerous changes in procedure that were instituted since the second edition.

In the almost five years between the publication of the third and fourth editions of this book, there were still more changes. After the *Civil Marriages Act* was passed in 2005, many same-sex couples came to Canada to be married. As time went by, some of these marriages failed and these non-Canadian couples found themselves unable to obtain divorces in their home jurisdictions because those jurisdictions did not recognize the validity of their Canadian-performed marriages. In the summer of 2013, the *Civil Marriages Act* was amended to allow these couples to be divorced in Canada. Among other substantive law changes, the Child Support Tables under the *Child Support Guidelines* were revised as of December 31, 2011. In addition, the *Children's Law Reform Act* was amended to require an applicant to provide information respecting his or her current or previous involvement in any family proceedings or in any criminal proceedings; a non-parent applicant is also required to provide a police records check and a Children's Aid Society records search.

There were also numerous significant changes to practice and procedure. The *Family Law Rules* were amended to reflect the changes to the *Children's Law Reform Act* by the addition of a new Rule 35.1 (and accompanying Form 35.1) that deals with the practice in cases involving a claim for custody or access. Also, in March 2010, the financial disclosure forms required under Rule 13 were substantially revised.

And now here we are almost three years since the publication of the fourth edition of this book and, as the saying goes, the only constant is change. As a result of amendments to the *Children's Law Reform Act,* the determination of parentage has been clarified to address the parental rights and obligations of the parties involved in the use of various methods of reproductive technology, and the law recognizes the existence of family units that include more than two parents. In the area of child support, the child support tables of the *Child Support Guidelines* were updated effective November 22, 2017 to reflect more recent tax rules. In addition, amendments to the *Family Law Act* created an online Child Support Calculation Service that allows separated parents to establish support payments in the first instance, or to vary existing support payments, using an online portal rather than going to court. There have also been changes to family law practice and procedure. Rule 13 has been amended again to expand financial disclosure, including the requirement of a certificate of financial disclosure and supporting documents. Finally, a number of the forms under the *Family Law Rules* have been revised.

This text covers all of the material that we teach in our two family law courses at Seneca College, separated into clearly defined parts. Part I is an introduction to family law. It starts with an overview of a marriage breakdown, to place the study of family law in a practical context, and a brief history of family law, to place the study of family law in a historical context. Part II—The Substantive Law of Marriage and Family Breakdown—contains chapters discussing the substantive law of marriage, annulment, divorce, custody and access, spousal support, and child support. Part III—Procedure in Family Law Matters—starts with an overview of the *Family Law Rules* and then covers the practice and procedure in a variety of family law proceedings by examining the relevant *Family Law Rules* and forms in the context of client fact situations. Part IV—Negotiation, Variation, and Enforcement—covers negotiation and domestic contracts, the substantive law and practice regarding variation and indexing of family law orders and agreements, and the substantive law and practice of the enforcement of family law orders and agreements.

This edition has been expanded to provide additional examples throughout, including a complete financial statement and a complete separation agreement. There are also now additional questions at the end of each chapter: review questions recap the topics covered, discussion questions expand on principles and concepts, exercises provide calculation questions, and drafting questions require the completion of court forms.

This book is designed to be as comprehensive as possible. It includes, in a separate volume, the text of the federal *Marriage Act*, *Civil Marriage Act*, and *Divorce Act* and the following provincial statutes:

- the *Child, Youth and Family Services Act, 2017*;
- the *Children's Law Reform Act*;
- the *Family Law Act*; and
- the *Family Responsibility and Support Arrears Enforcement Act, 1996*.

It also contains the federal *Child Support Guidelines* (including all tables), the *Family Law Rules*, the "Formal Requirements of the Continuing Record Under the Family Law Rules," and excerpts from the *Spousal Support Advisory Guidelines*. This legislation was current at the date of publication, but all legislation is subject to change and readers should verify the currency of any statute or regulation before relying on it. For a complete understanding of the area, students will also need access to a precedent separation agreement.

The text is not meant to serve as a blueprint for the teaching of a family law course. It is not necessary, nor is it even recommended, that the chapters be taught or studied in sequence. Rather, the professor and students should move between the substantive law and procedure in the different areas.

Acknowledgments

I would like to thank my friends and colleagues Gilda Berger, Arlene Blatt, Joan Emmans, and Camille Sherman for their ongoing help in correcting, updating, and improving this book.

The publisher also wishes to thank the following reviewers of the fourth edition for their valuable feedback: Kristy Babcock (St. Lawrence College), Shane Ellis (Georgian College), Sharon Norris (Algonquin College), Stacey Pipicelli (Fanshawe College), and Kamini Steinberg (Humber College).

JoAnn Kurtz
December 2017

About the Author

JoAnn Kurtz carried on a general practice with an emphasis on family law and real estate before joining Seneca College where she is the program coordinator for the Law Clerk Diploma program of the School of Legal and Public Administration. She has taught various topics, including contract law, family law, residential tenancy law and advocacy, and is the author or co-author of many general interest and academic texts. She attended New York University and holds a JD from Osgoode Hall Law School.

PART I

Introduction

Overview of a Marriage Breakdown

1

LEARNING OUTCOMES

After completing this chapter, you should be able to:

- Identify the most commonly encountered legal issues in a marriage breakdown situation.

- Identify the sources of family law in Ontario.

- Explain the division of jurisdiction over family law between the federal and provincial governments.

- Name the key statutes governing marriage breakdown in Ontario.

- Name the courts with jurisdiction over family law in Ontario, and explain the jurisdiction of each court.

- Understand the role a law clerk plays in a family law matter.

Introduction

Harold and Wendy have been married for five years. They have two children—Sam, age three, and Deb, age six—and a cat and a dog. Harold is a partner in a small and successful accounting firm. Wendy gave up the practice of law to be a full-time mother. The couple owns a house, a cottage, a sailboat, and a variety of investments. Harold has just told Wendy that he is leaving her for a Canada Revenue Agency investigator whom he met when one of his clients was audited. Wendy is emotionally devastated, but she is also a lawyer and realizes the issues that have to be resolved with Harold:

- Who will get custody of the children?
- How much child support will the other spouse be required to pay?
- Will Harold have to pay her spousal support; if so, how much and for how long?
- How will their property be divided?
- Will they divorce and, if so, when?

If Harold and Wendy are like the majority of separating couples, they will negotiate a settlement of all these issues and incorporate the terms of their settlement into a separation agreement without going to court, except to get a divorce. At some point after the separation agreement is signed, Harold, Wendy, or the two of them together will start divorce proceedings, and a divorce will be granted by the court without a trial.

If Harold and Wendy cannot agree on a settlement, either of them can start a court proceeding. They can ask the court to deal with the issues of support, custody, and property in a divorce proceeding, or they can ask the court to deal with support, custody, and property issues without seeking a divorce.

In this book, we will be studying the substantive law and procedure involved in resolving the issues that arise when domestic relationships break down. In this chapter, we will look at

- the law that governs these issues,
- the courts' jurisdiction over these issues, and
- the role of a law clerk in a family law matter.

Sources of Family Law

Whether Harold and Wendy settle their outstanding issues themselves or leave them for the courts to decide, both must know their legal rights and responsibilities. In Ontario, family law is governed by both statute law and case law.

Because of Canadian constitutional law, some family law issues are governed by federal legislation, some are governed by provincial legislation, and some are governed by both.

Sections 91 and 92 of the *Constitution Act, 1867*,[1] divide statute-making power between the federal and the provincial governments. The Act gives jurisdiction over marriage and divorce to the federal government, and jurisdiction over the

---

1   30 & 31 Vict, c 3 (UK).

solemnization of marriage and property rights to the provincial governments. As a result, the legislation that governs divorce is federal, while the legislation that governs the division of property is provincial. Custody and support (both spousal and child) are addressed in both federal and provincial statutes.

The jurisdiction over family law is divided between the federal and provincial governments, as set out in Table 1.1.

If a claim for custody and/or support is made in a divorce proceeding, the federal divorce legislation governs. If a claim for custody and/or support is made while the marriage continues, it is dealt with under the provincial legislation.

Table 1.2 sets out the relevant federal and provincial family law statutes that deal with divorce, property division, custody, and support.

There have been many court decisions that have interpreted and applied the provisions of these statutes. These decisions form a part of Ontario family law as well.

TABLE 1.1   Jurisdiction Over Family Law in Canada

	Federal jurisdiction	Provincial jurisdiction
Divorce	X	
Division of property		X
Custody	X	X
Child support	X	X
Spousal support	X	X

TABLE 1.2   Relevant Family Law Legislation

Federal	*Divorce Act*,[2] which deals with dissolution of marriage, custody, and support.
Provincial	• *Family Law Act*,[3] which deals with division of property and support. • *Children's Law Reform Act*,[4] which deals with custody.

Jurisdiction of the Courts

If Harold and Wendy cannot settle the issues that arise from the breakdown of their marriage on their own, a court proceeding must be started. Although Ontario is moving toward the creation of a unified family court across the province, for now there are three Ontario courts with jurisdiction over family law:

1. Family Court of the Superior Court of Justice,
2. Superior Court of Justice, and
3. Ontario Court of Justice.

---

2   RSC 1985, c 3 (2d Supp).

3   RSO 1990, c F.3.

4   RSO 1990, c C.12.

The party who starts the proceeding must know which court to use. In order to understand this jurisdictional division, it is helpful to examine the overall structure of the Ontario court system.

Constitutional Framework Governing the Ontario Courts

Jurisdiction over the courts is governed by the *Constitution Act*, and is divided between the federal and provincial governments.

Under section 92 of the Act, the provinces have the power to administer both civil and criminal courts in the province, while the federal government, under section 101, has the power to establish and operate the Supreme Court of Canada, the Federal Court, the Tax Court, and military courts.

Even though the provinces have the power to administer courts within the province, section 96 of the *Constitution Act* gives the federal government the power to appoint judges in the superior courts. The provinces have the power to appoint judges in lower level courts only, under section 92 of the Act.

In addition, section 92 of the Act gives the provincial governments the power to create procedural law for civil matters only, while section 91 gives the federal government the power to create procedural law for criminal matters.

Organization of the Ontario Courts

The *Courts of Justice Act*[5] is the Ontario statute that prescribes how the Ontario courts are established, operated, and administered. The rules of procedure for the various Ontario courts are regulations made under that statute.

There are three levels of courts in Ontario:

1. Court of Appeal for Ontario,
2. Superior Court of Justice, and
3. Ontario Court of Justice.

The nature of the case, civil or criminal, along with the monetary value of the case in civil matters, and the nature of charge, in criminal matters, determine which court will hear a particular case.

Court of Appeal for Ontario

The Court of Appeal is the highest court in Ontario, and hears appeals in civil and criminal matters from the Superior Court of Justice and the Ontario Court of Justice. Appeals are usually heard by a panel of either three or five judges. Its only location is in Toronto.

Judges of the Court of Appeal are appointed by the federal government.

---

5 RSO 1990 c C.43.

Superior Court of Justice

The Superior Court of Justice is a trial court of general jurisdiction, and can hear any case on any matter that is not required by statute to be heard in another court.

As a trial court, the Superior Court of Justice hears all civil proceedings involving claims over $25,000. It also has jurisdiction to hear family law matters of custody, support, division of property, and divorce. With respect to criminal matters, the court hears the more serious criminal cases under the *Criminal Code*.[6]

The Superior Court of Justice also administers three other courts:

1. Divisional Court—dealing mainly with appeals of Superior Court of Justice civil judgments involving less than $50,000; and of judgments from the Ontario Court of Justice in family law matters and summary conviction offences;
2. Family Court of the Superior Court of Justice—discussed below; and
3. Small Claims Court—a less-formal trial court dealing with civil matters involving less than $25,000.

Judges of the Superior Court of Justice are appointed by the federal government.

Ontario Court of Justice

The Ontario Court of Justice is also a trial court. However, unlike the Superior Court of Justice, it has jurisdiction to hear only those matters that are specifically given to it by statute. In the family law area, the Ontario Court of Justice has jurisdiction over adoption, child protection, custody, access, child support and spousal support. It does not have jurisdiction over divorce or property matters.

Judges of the Ontario Court of Justice are appointed by the provincial government.

Family Court of the Superior Court of Justice

Historically, jurisdiction over family law matters was split between the province's superior court (then called the Ontario Court (General Division)) and the province's provincial court. The superior court had jurisdiction over all family breakdown matters—divorce, property, custody, and support—while the provincial court's jurisdiction was limited to custody and support issues. (The provincial court also had jurisdiction over adoption, child protection, and young offenders.)

This split in jurisdiction was confusing, and for many years there was talk of consolidating jurisdiction over all family matters into one court. In 1977, a Unified Family Court was established in Hamilton-Wentworth as a three-year pilot project. The Hamilton court was made a permanent entity in 1982, and the province promised to create more unified family courts across the province. However, it was not until 1995 that the Unified Family Court was expanded to include four more sites.

As part of the most recent set of Ontario court reforms, the province committed itself to the creation of the Family Court of the Superior Court of Justice, a single family court at the superior court level across the province.

---

6 RSC 1985, c C-46.

At the time of printing, the Family Court of the Superior Court of Justice has 17 locations: Barrie, Bracebridge, Brockville, Cobourg, Cornwall, Hamilton, Kingston, L'Orignal, Lindsay, London, Napanee, Newmarket, Oshawa/Whitby, Ottawa, Perth, Peterborough, and St. Catharines, serving 18 of the province's 49 counties and judicial districts. In all other parts of the province, including the City of Toronto and the Regional Municipality of Peel, jurisdiction over family law matters continues to be divided between the Superior Court of Justice and the Ontario Court of Justice.

The province has committed itself to expanding the operation of the Family Court throughout the province. In addition, the federal government, as part of its child-centred family justice strategy announced in December 2002, pledged additional funding to the provinces to assist in the expansion of unified family courts such as the Family Court of the Superior Court of Justice. However, the number of unified family courts has not increased since the first edition of this book was published in 2004.

In those places where it has been established, the Family Court of the Superior Court of Justice has jurisdiction over all family law matters, including

- divorce,
- child support,
- support for spouses and common law partners,
- custody of and access to children,
- equalization of net family property,
- trust claims and claims for unjust enrichment,
- possession of the matrimonial home,
- adoption, and
- child protection.

The goal of the court is to deal with family problems in an integrated manner. Each Family Court site offers the following support services to litigants:

- a family law information centre,
- mediation services,
- legal support services (legal aid duty counsel),
- family law information meetings, and
- a supervised access and exchange centre.

Where There Is No Family Court of the Superior Court of Justice

In those areas of Ontario where the Family Court of the Superior Court of Justice does not exist, jurisdiction over family law matters continues to be divided between the Superior Court of Justice and the Ontario Court of Justice. Cases that include divorce or property claims must be brought before the Superior Court of Justice.

Cases that involve only custody and/or support claims may be brought before either the Superior Court of Justice or the Ontario Court of Justice.

The appendix to this chapter lists those provincial jurisdictions with the Family Court and those without.

The Role of the Law Clerk in a Family Law Matter

Law clerks work for or under the supervision of a lawyer, assisting the lawyer in his or her routine tasks. There is a great deal of work for a law clerk to do in a family law matter.

Expectations of a Law Clerk

A law clerk working in any area of law is expected to be able to work independently, communicate well with other staff and clients (orally and in writing), use analytic skills, and be a good problem solver. A law clerk is also expected to assist in maintaining the authority and dignity of the courts and the integrity of the legal profession and to conduct him or herself in a professional, diligent, and ethical manner.

A law clerk working in family law is expected to have a general knowledge of the law, practice and procedures involved within the family law field, and to carry out his or her tasks in accordance with the law firm's procedures and the individual lawyer's instructions.

Professional Conduct Considerations

Lawyers are governed by the Law Society of Ontario (LSO)[7] and are required to follow the By-Laws[8] and the *Rules of Professional Conduct*.[9] Law clerks are not members of the LSO, and are therefore not directly bound by those by-laws and professional conduct rules. However, a lawyer is responsible for the actions of a law clerk working under his or her supervision. As a result, a law clerk must be familiar with the relevant by-laws and rules.

Chapter 3 of the *Rules of Professional Conduct* sets out the obligations of a lawyer in his or her relationship with clients. Lawyers are expected to be competent in the areas of law in which they offer services, and to give honest and objective advice to their clients. Lawyers are also required to care for and safeguard any property or documents given to them by or on behalf of the client. Most importantly, a lawyer owes a duty of confidentiality to every client. This duty of confidentiality, known as solicitor and client privilege, is at the heart of the lawyer-client relationship.

By-Law 7.1 of the LSO and Chapter 6 of the *Rules of Professional Conduct* govern the circumstances in which a lawyer may assign work to a law clerk. The lawyer must directly supervise the law clerk, is required to review the law clerk's work at frequent intervals, and is required to assume complete professional responsibility for all tasks performed by the law clerk, including all documents prepared by the law clerk.

---

7   In November of 2017 the Law Society of Upper Canada's governing body voted to change the regulator's name to the Law Society of Ontario.

8   Law Society of Ontario, *By-Laws*, online: <https://www.lsuc.on.ca/by-laws/>.

9   Law Society of Ontario, *Rules of Professional Conduct*, (1 October, 2014; amendments current to June 2017), online: <https://www.lsuc.on.ca/lawyer-conduct-rules/>.

A law clerk is not permitted to

- accept new clients,
- give legal advice or opinions,
- give or accept undertakings without permission,
- exercise personal legal judgment,
- hold him/herself out as a lawyer,
- appear in court except in a support role,
- be named as a member of a firm,
- be paid on a sliding scale unless an employee, or
- conduct negotiations unless routine.

So, What Can a Law Clerk Do in a Family Law Matter?

The law clerk will be involved primarily in the preparation of the many documents discussed in this book, such as:

- applications (see Chapters 12, 13, and 14),
- financial statements (see Chapter 11),
- continuing records (see Chapter 10),
- notices of motion and affidavits (see Chapter 13),
- orders (see Chapters 12 and 13),
- conference notices and briefs (see Chapter 14),
- domestic contracts such as marriage contracts and separation agreements (see Chapter 15), and
- Family Responsibility Office forms (see Chapter 17).

As the law clerk gains experience, he or she may be asked to interview the client to obtain the information necessary to prepare these documents.

The law clerk may also be required to schedule motion and conference dates, to arrange for the service and filing of documents, and to attend to routine correspondence.

In addition, a more experienced law clerk may be asked to assist in various calculations, such as:

- net family property (see Chapter 9),
- spousal support under the Spousal Support Advisory Guidelines (see Chapter 7),
- indexing of spousal support payments (see Chapter 16), and
- child support under the Child Support Guidelines (see Chapter 8).

Appendix: Judicial Districts and Counties

Family Court Jurisdictions

1. Durham Regional Municipality—Oshawa/Whitby
2. Frontenac County—Kingston
3. Haliburton County—Perth
4. Hamilton-Wentworth Regional Municipality—Hamilton
5. Lanark County—Perth
6. Leeds and Grenville Counties—Brockville
7. Lennox and Addington Counties—Napanee
8. Middlesex County—London
9. Muskoka District Municipality—Bracebridge
10. Niagara Regional Municipality—St. Catharines, Welland
11. Northumberland County—Cobourg
12. Ottawa
13. Peterborough County—Peterborough
14. Prescott and Russell Counties—L'Orignal
15. Simcoe County—Barrie
16. Stormont, Dundas, and Glengarry Counties—Cornwall
17. Victoria County—Lindsay
18. York Regional Municipality—Newmarket

Non-Family Court Jurisdictions

1. Algoma District—Sault Ste. Marie
2. Brant County—Brantford
3. Bruce County—Walkerton
4. Chatham-Kent Municipality—Chatham
5. Cochrane District—Timmins, Cochrane
6. Dufferin County—Orangeville
7. Elgin County—St. Thomas
8. Essex County—Windsor
9. Grey County—Owen Sound
10. Haldimand County—Cayuga
11. Halton Regional Municipality—Milton
12. Hastings County—Belleville

13. Huron County—Goderich
14. Kenora District—Kenora
15. Lambton County—Sarnia
16. Manitoulin District—Gore Bay
17. Nipissing District—North Bay
18. Norfolk County—Simcoe
19. Oxford County—Woodstock
20. Parry Sound District—Parry Sound
21. Peel Regional Municipality—Brampton
22. Perth County—Stratford
23. Prince Edward County—Picton
24. Rainy River District
25. Renfrew County—Pembroke
26. Sudbury Regional Municipality—Sudbury
27. Thunder Bay District—Thunder Bay
28. Timiskaming District—Haileybury
29. Toronto
30. Waterloo Regional Municipality—Kitchener
31. Wellington County—Guelph

CHAPTER SUMMARY

When a marriage breaks down, there are many issues to be resolved, including those of child support and custody, division of property, spousal support, and divorce. If the parties cannot reach agreement on their own, the courts will have to resolve the matter.

The *Constitution Act, 1867*, divided statute-making power between the federal and the provincial governments. The federal government has exclusive jurisdiction over divorce, dealt with in the *Divorce Act*. The provincial government has exclusive jurisdiction over the division of property, dealt with in the *Family Law Act*. The two levels of government share jurisdiction over custody and support. If a divorce proceeding is started, those matters are also dealt with under the *Divorce Act*. If no divorce proceeding

is started, those matters are dealt with under the *Family Law Act* and the *Children's Law Reform Act*.

At present, the three courts with jurisdiction over family law in Ontario are the Family Court of the Superior Court of Justice, the Superior Court of Justice, and the Ontario Court of Justice.

In Ontario regions where the Family Court of the Superior Court of Justice has been established, that court has jurisdiction over all family law matters. In Ontario regions where the Family Court of the Superior Court of Justice does not exist, jurisdiction over family law matters remains divided between the Superior Court of Justice and the Ontario Court of Justice.

REVIEW QUESTIONS

1. What legal issues must a separating couple resolve?

2. How do the majority of separating couples resolve the issues between them?

3. What are the sources of family law in Ontario?

4. Why are some family law issues dealt with under federal legislation, some under provincial legislation, and some under both?

5. What family law issues are dealt with under federal legislation only?

6. What family law issues are dealt with under provincial legislation only?

7. What family law issues are dealt with under both federal and provincial legislation?

8. Name the federal family law statute. What issues does this statute deal with?

9. Name two provincial family law statutes. What issues do each of these statutes deal with?

10. What are the three Ontario courts with jurisdiction over family law matters?

DISCUSSION QUESTIONS

1. Alonzo and Gabriella lived together for five years and had two children. They never married. They have now separated. Gabriella wants to start a proceeding against Alonzo for custody of the children and child support.

   a. Under what statute or statutes would these proceeding be brought?

   b. If Gabriella and Alonzo live in Peterborough, in which court or courts can her proceeding be started?

   c. If Gabriella and Alonzo live in Toronto, in which court or courts can her proceeding be started?

2. Amar and Ashitha have been married for five years and have two children. They have now separated. Amar wants to start a proceeding against Ashitha for divorce, custody of the children, and child support.

   a. Under what statute or statutes would these proceeding be brought?

   b. If Amar and Ashitha live in Ottawa, in which court or courts can his proceeding be started?

   c. If Amar and Ashitha live in Brampton, in which court or courts can his proceeding be started?

A Brief History of Family Law in Ontario

2

LEARNING OUTCOMES

After completing this chapter, you should be able to explain how family law has evolved in the following areas:

- The legal status of the husband and wife.
- The physical relationship between the husband and wife.
- The property of the husband and wife.
- The custody of the children.
- The support of one spouse by the other.
- Divorce.

Introduction

Before beginning a study of contemporary family law in Ontario, it is important to realize that this law has been in effect for a relatively short time. Ontario's family law, like most of our law, has its origins in England during the late Middle Ages. The law has changed a great deal since that time as our society and its values have changed. Until recently, the history of family law has been the history of the relationship between husbands and wives. It was not until the latter part of the 20th century that the law began to recognize first the relationships between cohabiting couples of the opposite sex, and then those of the same sex. It is only in the last few years that the law has recognized the validity of same-sex marriages.[1]

In this chapter, we will look at how family law has evolved in the following areas:

- the legal status of the husband and wife,
- the physical relationship between the husband and wife,
- the property of the husband and wife,
- the custody of the children,
- the support of one spouse by the other, and
- divorce.

English Law Before the 19th Century

The family in pre-19th-century England was an important social and economic unit. It was the family, not society or government, that educated its children and cared for the sick, disabled, and old. The economy was largely rural, and all members of the family worked to provide for the family unit. The division of labour was based on gender and age. The husband and father, as the head of the family, made all decisions affecting family members and could enforce those decisions through the use of corporal punishment.

Marriages—at least among the middle and upper classes[2]—were usually arranged by the families of the bride and groom. The choice of a spouse was based largely on economic factors: Could the prospective husband provide financially for the wife? Would the prospective bride bring any money or property with her in the form of a dowry?

Romantic love, although it existed, was not thought of as a basis for marriage and was not expected in the marriage relationship. While it was hoped that a husband and wife would come to love each other, that love was not expected to be of a romantic

---

1   The validity of same-sex marriage was recognized in the case of *Halpern v Canada (Attorney General)* (2003), 65 OR (3d) 161 (CA) and by the *Civil Marriage Act*, SC 2005, c. 33. The changing definition of marriage is discussed in Chapter 3.

2   What we know about marriages of the time comes from written records such as journals, correspondence, marriage contracts, and land deeds. As a result, we don't know very much about marriage among the lower classes, who did not leave records of this kind.

nature. In fact, romantic love between husband and wife was not much heard of until the beginning of the 19th century, when it started to appear in literature.

Women had few prospects outside marriage. There were not many jobs available to them. Single women past marriageable age (referred to as spinsters) were pitied. If their families were unable to support them, they were forced to take one of the few low-paying jobs open to women, such as teacher, governess, or domestic help.

Marriage was based on Christian principles and was viewed as an oath taken before God. Marriage was for life: "Whom God hath joined together, let no man put asunder." According to Christian doctrine, the husband was considered the "head" of the marriage.

The legal aspects of the marriage relationship reflected the values of the time.

Legal Status of the Husband and Wife

A husband and a wife were considered to be one person in law—and that person was the husband. This doctrine was referred to as the **unity of legal personality**. A married woman had no right to enter into contracts on her own behalf, although she could enter into contracts on her husband's behalf for necessities for herself. She could neither sue nor be sued. Her husband was responsible for her debts and for any torts she might commit. Because a husband and wife were one person, spouses could not sue each other.

> **unity of legal personality**
> a doctrine by which a husband and wife were considered to be one person in law

Physical Relationship Between the Husband and Wife

Both husband and wife had a duty to have sexual relations with each other. This was both a legal and a religious duty that either the husband or wife could enforce in the church courts (called **ecclesiastical courts**). A wife had no legal right to refuse to have sex with her husband, and it was not considered rape if a man had sexual intercourse with his wife without her consent.

If a wife had sexual intercourse with a man other than her husband, her husband had the right to sue the man for damages in an action for **criminal conversation**. A man who enticed a wife away from her husband or who offered her shelter and support could also be sued for damages.

The husband, as head of the family, had the **right of physical chastisement**, in other words, the right to use physical force to discipline his wife.

> **ecclesiastical courts**
> a system of church courts in England

> **criminal conversation**
> a tort action by which a husband could claim damages against a man who had sexual intercourse with the husband's wife

> **right of physical chastisement**
> the right of a husband to use physical force to discipline his wife

Property of the Husband and Wife

In keeping with the view that the husband and the wife were one person—namely, the husband—on marriage, the wife's personal property became the husband's. The wife's real property became his to use; he had the right to use her land and buildings, including the right to mortgage them to raise money. Married women were not legally able to own property. On separation or divorce, the husband kept all property that was originally his or that had become his by virtue of the marriage.

To protect against this loss of property, a wealthy family would either give no property to a daughter or would make arrangements before marriage to keep the property in trust for her. That way, her husband would have access to the income from the property but would not be able to deal with the property itself.

Custody of the Children

Children were traditionally seen as property and, as with all other property of a married couple, they were the property of the husband. The husband had the absolute right to determine the children's religious training, general education, choice of career, and choice of marriage partner.

A woman had no right to custody of her children. If she left the marriage, the husband had the absolute right to custody.

Support of One Spouse by the Other

Support flowed only from the husband as supporter to the wife as dependant. It was based on principles of reward and punishment, not on financial need.

A husband was required to support his wife while the couple were living together, but a wife who left her husband was not entitled to receive any support from him. If the breakdown of the marriage relationship was caused by the husband, a wife could, in limited circumstances, bring a common law action for **alimony**.

A wife would be awarded alimony only if she could prove that

- the parties were living separate and apart;
- the husband
  - had committed adultery, or
  - was guilty of cruelty (physical or mental injury to the wife), or
  - had deserted the wife for two or more years; and
- the wife had not herself committed a matrimonial offence (adultery, cruelty, or desertion).

A wife was not entitled to alimony unless she was willing to take her husband back to live with her. However, if she actually took him back and resumed the marriage relationship with knowledge of his misconduct, she was considered to have **condoned** (forgiven) the misconduct and would also be disentitled to alimony.

Alimony, if awarded, was not designed to meet all of a wife's financial needs. Rather, the amount was meant to be sufficient only to allow her to live "modestly and in retirement." A wife was not awarded alimony if she had enough income to maintain herself. Alimony payments continued only so long as the wife remained chaste: she lost all right to support if she had sexual intercourse with another man.

Divorce

Originally, there was no divorce. A marriage ended only with the death of one party or with an **annulment** (a declaration that the marriage was never valid). In the latter case, the ecclesiastical courts issued a **divorce *a vinculo matrimonii*** (from the bonds of marriage).

alimony
a common law action by a wife for support from her husband

condonation
forgiveness of a matrimonial offence by continuing or resuming cohabitation with the guilty spouse, with knowledge of the offence

annulment
a declaration that the marriage was never valid

divorce *a vinculo matrimonii*
an order of the ecclesiastical courts, following a declaration that a marriage was not valid, by which the parties were released from the bonds of marriage

If the marriage was valid, either party could apply to the ecclesiastical courts for a **divorce *a mensa et thoro*** (from bed and board), which was granted for adultery, extreme cruelty, or desertion, but this decree did *not* terminate the marriage. The parties no longer had the duty to live together, but they remained married. The husband continued to have a duty to support the wife if the decree was issued at the wife's request and based on the husband's misconduct. If the decree was granted at the husband's request and based on the wife's misconduct, the husband was not obliged to support the wife.

Thanks to Henry VIII,[3] eventually it became possible to terminate a marriage by divorce. It was not possible, however, to obtain a divorce through civil court proceedings. Instead, a divorce was obtained through a combination of an ecclesiastical court proceeding and a private member's bill in Parliament.

A husband could obtain a divorce based on his wife's adultery. First, he had to sue the other man for damages for criminal conversation. Then he was required to apply to the ecclesiastical courts for a divorce *a mensa et thoro*, a judicial order permitting him to live separately from his wife. Finally, he had to get his member of Parliament to put through a private member's bill for divorce. In other words, the husband needed a law passed that divorced him from his wife. The process was long and expensive, and it was not available to those without money and connections. It was also not available to women. There was no remedy available to a wife to divorce her husband on any ground.

> **divorce *a mensa et thoro*** an order of the ecclesiastical courts by which the parties to a valid marriage were relieved of their obligation to cohabit, but were still legally married

19th-Century Reforms

The first major reforms in family law took place in the mid- to late-19th century as the economic and intellectual changes brought about by the Industrial Revolution led to a move toward greater rights for women.

Legal Status of the Husband and Wife

Reforms of the 19th century started to give a married woman a legal identity separate from that of her husband. A married woman became entitled to buy and own property and to sue and be sued in her own name, although spouses still could not sue each other.

Physical Relationship Between the Husband and Wife

During the 19th century, a husband's right to physically discipline his wife ended.

Property of the Husband and Wife

In the 1880s, both England and Ontario passed statutes called the *Married Women's Property Act*,[4] which provided that married women could own property separately from their husbands.

---

3 He founded his own church, separate from the Roman Catholic Church, so that he could divorce Catherine of Aragon and marry Anne Boleyn (whom he dispatched not long after by beheading).

4 Repealed.

presumption of advancement
the presumption, created by the *Married Women's Property Act*, that a husband who placed property in the name of his wife intended to make a gift of the property to her

presumption of resulting trust
an equitable principle under which it is presumed that a person who places property in the name of another person intends that person to hold the property in trust for the donor

The *Married Women's Property Act* also created the **presumption of advancement** between a husband and wife: if a husband placed property in the name of his wife, it was presumed that he intended to make a gift of the property to her. Before the *Married Women's Property Act*, transfers of property from a husband to a wife were treated like transfers of property between unrelated parties. It was presumed that a person who paid for property and placed it in the name of another person intended the other person to hold the property in trust for the donor. (This presumption is called the **presumption of resulting trust**.)

In the event of a marriage breakdown, property was divided between the spouses strictly on the basis of ownership. Under common law, that meant that a wife could keep only property that was registered in her name. Under the law of equity, she might also be given an interest in property if she had contributed money or money's worth directly to the creation, improvement, or acquisition of the property. There was no recognition of an interest based on indirect contributions that the wife may have made to the marriage. The result was that, ordinarily, the husband would get most of the property.

Custody of the Children

During the 19th century, there was a change in the way children were viewed by society. Whereas children had previously been thought of as miniature adults, now childhood began to be seen as a distinct stage in human development during which children needed special care and nurturing. There was also a growing recognition of the need to consider the best interests of the children in the event of a separation of their parents. Children were no longer viewed as the property of the father, and courts began to make decisions about custody on the basis of psychological and emotional factors.

In 1886, the *Infants Custody Act*[5] made "the best interests of the child" the basis on which custody was to be awarded. As a result, fathers no longer had an absolute right to custody, and mothers, as the parents responsible for raising children, were usually granted custody of young children ("children of tender years").

Support of One Spouse by the Other

Alimony continued through the 19th century and beyond, and continued to be tied to the conduct of the wife. There was no legislation passed in this area. However, judges effected changes in the common law through their decisions over time.

doctrine of constructive desertion
a doctrine related to alimony under which it was deemed that the husband had deserted the wife if a wife left her husband because of his misconduct

One judicial innovation was the **doctrine of constructive desertion**. Under the original alimony rules, if a wife left her husband for any reason, it was considered to be desertion. Desertion was a matrimonial offence that disentitled a wife to alimony. Under the doctrine of constructive desertion, if a wife left the marriage because of her husband's misconduct, the husband was deemed to have deserted the wife, and the wife did not lose her entitlement to alimony.

Another judicial innovation relaxed the requirement that a wife be willing to take her husband back in order to be entitled to alimony. Eventually, the courts decided that a wife was required to accept her husband's return only for a reasonable time.

---

5 Repealed.

Divorce

In England, judicial divorce (divorce through the civil courts) was established in 1857 by the *Divorce and Matrimonial Causes Act*.[6] The ecclesiastical courts were abolished, and private members' bills were no longer required. The action of criminal conversation was also abolished.

A husband could divorce his wife on the ground of her adultery. Until 1925, a wife could not divorce her husband unless she could prove that he had committed incestuous adultery, bigamy, sodomy, bestiality, rape, adultery with cruelty, or adultery coupled with desertion for at least two years. A husband's adultery alone was not a ground; neither was his desertion alone, nor his cruelty alone. The 1925 *Divorce Act* made the grounds for divorce the same for both spouses, thus allowing a wife to divorce her husband on the ground of adultery alone.

Canada did not follow suit, in large part because of the opposition of Roman Catholic Quebec. Judicial divorce and the abolition of the action of criminal conversation did not come to Canada until the 20th century.

20th-Century Changes

The 20th century brought major changes in the role of women in society, and in the way the law dealt with women and marriage. Ontario family law was drastically reformed in 1978 with the passage of the *Family Law Reform Act*[7] and was further reformed in 1986 by the *Family Law Act*.[8] The first Canada-wide *Divorce Act* was passed in 1968 and reformed in 1985.[9]

Legal Status of the Husband and Wife

The *Family Law Reform Act* abolished the unity of legal personality between husband and wife by stating that for all purposes a married person has a legal personality that is independent, separate, and distinct from that of his or her spouse. Husbands and wives were also given the right to sue each other in tort.

Physical Relationship Between the Husband and Wife

Before 1983, the *Criminal Code*[10] defined the offence of rape as involving sexual intercourse by a male person with "a female person who is not his wife." In 1983, this provision was replaced by a general sexual assault provision. A husband no longer has a special right to sexual intercourse with his wife, and either a husband or a wife can be charged with sexual assault against the other party.

---

6 Repealed.

7 Repealed.

8 RSO 1990, c F.3.

9 RSC 1985, c 3 (2d Supp).

10 RSC 1985, c C-46.

Property of the Husband and Wife

In 1975, the Supreme Court of Canada decided the case of *Murdoch v Murdoch*.[11] Mr. and Mrs. Murdoch were married from 1943 until 1968. During the course of the marriage, Mr. Murdoch bought and sold a series of ranches. Mrs. Murdoch worked on all of them. At the time of the separation, Mr. Murdoch owned a valuable ranch that was registered in his name only. Mrs. Murdoch claimed an interest in the ranch based on her contribution to the various ranches in the form of her labour over the years. The court decided that she had not made a substantial contribution to the acquisition of the ranch since the work she had done "was the work done by any ranch wife." Many people considered the decision unfair. Within several years, the Supreme Court of Canada took a different approach to the division of property on a marriage breakdown,[12] and the legislatures of most provinces, including Ontario, passed statutes reforming the law as it related to the property of a married couple.

The 1978 *Family Law Reform Act* recognized for the first time in Ontario that the division of property on a marriage breakdown should not be decided simply on the basis of ownership of or direct contribution to property. Instead, the Act acknowledged that marriage is a partnership to which both spouses make a contribution—whether by working outside the home or by assuming responsibility for child care and household management—and that by contributing to the partnership, the spouses were entitled to a share of the "partnership property." Under this Act, assets owned by the spouses were categorized as either "family assets" or "non-family assets," depending on how the assets were used by the family. On a marriage breakdown, family assets were divided equally between the parties. Non-family assets were not divided unless a court found that a division of only the family assets was inequitable.

The *Family Law Act*, which is the current legislation in Ontario, came into force on March 1, 1986. It continues to recognize the partnership aspect of marriage. However, it takes a different approach to property division. Property is no longer categorized on the basis of its use, and instead of dividing property, the Act divides the profits of the marriage. An accounting, called an **equalization of net family properties**, takes place in which both spouses calculate the value of the assets they have on leaving the marriage, as compared with the value of the assets they had on entering the marriage. If the value has gone up, the profit must be shared with the other party.

equalization of net family properties
a process under the *Family Law Act* under which spouses share equally in the value of most property acquired during the marriage

Custody of the Children

Custody continues to be decided on the basis of the best interests of the child. The current statute, the *Children's Law Reform Act*,[13] sets out a number of factors for the court to consider when deciding what those best interests might be. The biggest

---

11 [1975] 1 SCR 423.

12 In the case of *Rathwell v Rathwell*, [1978] 2 SCR 436, the court relied upon principles of unjust enrichment and constructive trust to give a wife a share in property acquired by her husband during the marriage.

13 RSO 1990, c C.12.

change in this area is more judicial than legislative, in that the courts have recently begun to grant custody, even of young children, to fathers.

Support of One Spouse by the Other

Starting with the *Family Law Reform Act* in 1978 and continuing with the *Family Law Act*, support is now based solely on the need of the dependent party and the ability of the other party to pay. Conduct is not an issue, except in the most unusual cases. Support can be paid by either a husband or a wife.

The term "alimony" is no longer used. Now the term "support" applies to payments ordered under the *Family Law Act* and the *Divorce Act*.

Divorce

In Ontario, there was no judicial divorce until 1930. Before then, a party seeking a divorce had to obtain a private member's bill in Parliament. The grounds for divorce were the same as those in England.

The *Divorce Act (Ontario)* of 1930 brought judicial divorce to Ontario. The only ground available to a husband was his wife's adultery. A wife could obtain a divorce on the grounds of adultery, rape, sodomy, bestiality, or bigamy.

The first Canada-wide divorce legislation, the *Divorce Act*, was passed in 1968. That Act allowed divorce on both fault and no-fault grounds. The fault grounds included adultery, physical or mental cruelty, sodomy, bestiality, rape, and homosexual acts. The no-fault grounds included three years of separation, although a deserting spouse had to wait five years before being able to start a divorce action based on separation. The same grounds were available to both husbands and wives. The Act also dealt with child custody and support on the basis of the needs of the spouses and children.

A new *Divorce Act* came into effect in June 1986. It also provides for fault and no-fault grounds. The only fault grounds are adultery and cruelty. The no-fault ground requires a separation of one year.

CHAPTER SUMMARY

Before the 19th century, marriages were typically arranged based on economic factors and ended only with the death of a spouse or by annulment. A husband was the head of the family, and a wife did not have an identity separate from that of her husband. Upon marriage, a wife's personal property, along with any children of the marriage, became the property of the husband. If a couple separated, it was difficult for a wife to qualify for alimony, which, if granted, would only be enough to allow her to live "modestly and in retirement."

Beginning in the 19th century, wives were granted a legal identity separate from that of their husbands. Married women could now buy and own property. Upon a marriage breakdown, property was divided between spouses based strictly on ownership. Custody decisions were now based on the "best interests of the child." It was not possible to obtain a judicial divorce.

Marriage laws changed significantly over the course of the 20th century. Judicial divorce, based solely on fault grounds, became available in Ontario for the first time in 1930. Canada-wide divorce became available in 1968, based on both fault and no-fault grounds. Ontario family law was drastically reformed with the passage of first the *Family Law Reform Act* (1978), and then the *Family Law Act* (1986), to recognize marriage as a partnership and to divide property on a marriage breakdown based not on ownership, but on contributions to that partnership. Both husbands and wives can be required to pay support to their spouses, based on the need of the dependant spouse and the ability of the other spouse to pay.

KEY TERMS

alimony, 18
annulment, 18
condonation, 18
criminal conversation, 17
divorce *a mensa et thoro*, 18
divorce *a vinculo matrimonii*, 18
doctrine of constructive desertion, 20

ecclesiastical courts, 17
equalization of net family properties, 22
presumption of advancement, 20
presumption of resulting trust, 20
right of physical chastisement, 17
unity of legal personality, 17

REVIEW QUESTIONS

1. What is the "unity of legal personality"?

2. Before the 19th century, what right did a married woman have to own property?

3. Before the 19th century, what right did a woman have to custody of her children?

4. Before the 19th century, under what circumstances would a wife be awarded alimony?

5. Before the 19th century, what right did a woman have to divorce her husband? What right did a husband have to divorce his wife?

6. What is the *Married Women's Property Act*?

7. What is the "presumption of advancement"?

8. What is the "presumption of resulting trust"?

9. What is the *Infants Custody Act*?

10. What is the doctrine of constructive desertion?

11. When was the first Canada-wide divorce legislation passed?

12. What is the *Family Law Reform Act*?

13. What is the *Family Law Act*?

14. What is the *Children's Law Reform Act*?

DISCUSSION QUESTIONS

1. Ontario's family law has its origins in England during the late Middle Ages. The law has changed a great deal since that time as our society and its values have changed. Discuss.

2. The 1978 *Family Law Reform Act* recognized for the first time in Ontario that the division of property on a marriage breakdown should not be decided simply on the basis of ownership of or direct contribution to property. Discuss.

PART II

The Substantive Law of Marriage and Family Breakdown

Marriage

3

LEARNING OUTCOMES

After completing this chapter, you should be able to:

- Give the legal definition of "marriage."

- Explain the division of jurisdiction over marriage between the federal and provincial governments.

- Explain what is meant by the legal capacity to marry.

- Explain what is meant by the formalities of marriage.

- Explain the difference between marriage and other forms of family arrangements.

- Explain how a spouse may assume the surname of the other spouse on marriage.

Introduction

Family law deals with the legal rights and responsibilities of family members, and focuses primarily on the legal consequences of family breakdown. Before we can examine what happens when there is a family breakdown, we have to look at how a family is created.

What is meant by the word "family"? Is marriage a necessary element? Certainly a man and a woman who marry form a family unit, but in Canada today, families take other forms as well. Throughout Canada, same-sex couples may also marry. Many unmarried couples of the same or opposite sex live together in "common law" relationships. The partners in all of these family relationships have certain legal rights and responsibilities, whose nature depends on a number of factors, the most significant of which is whether the parties are, in fact, married.

In this chapter, we will look at one of the ways that families are created—through marriage—and in particular

- the meaning of marriage,
- the requirements for a valid marriage, and
- the difference between marriage and other forms of family arrangements.

Definition of Marriage

The definition of marriage comes from English common law. Historically, marriage was defined in Canada as "the voluntary union for life of one man and one woman to the exclusion of all others." In other words, marriage required a man and a woman, and there was no valid same-sex marriage.

On June 10, 2003, in the case of *Halpern v Canada (Attorney General)*,[1] the Ontario Court of Appeal ruled that this common law definition of marriage is contrary to the *Canadian Charter of Rights and Freedoms*.[2] Courts in British Columbia and Quebec had already made similar rulings. One week later, the federal government announced that it would not be appealing these rulings, and would instead be proposing legislation to change the common law definition of marriage to allow for same-sex marriage.[3] The federal government then referred the draft legislation to the Supreme Court of Canada to ensure that it was within federal jurisdiction and consistent with the Charter. The Supreme Court ruled that it was. On July 20, 2005, the *Civil Marriage Act*[4] became law and changed the definition of marriage, for civil purposes, to "the lawful union of two persons to the exclusion of all others."

---

1   2003 CanLII 26403, 65 OR (3d) 161 (CA).

2   Part I of the *Constitution Act, 1982*, RSC 1985, App II, No 44.

3   Under the *Constitution Act, 1867*, the federal government has legislative authority over marriage. Therefore, federal legislation is required to change the common law definition of marriage.

4   SC 2005, c 33.

Marriage is a contract and, like any contract, confers legal rights and responsibilities on the parties. However, unlike other contracts, the rights and obligations of the parties are largely defined by statute, rather than by the parties themselves.

Marriage is subject to the same rules that govern all contracts, and so the parties to a marriage must have the **legal capacity** to enter into the contract and must comply with certain **legal formalities** for the contract to be valid.

legal capacity to marry
legal ability to enter into the contract of marriage

legal formalities of marriage
the form a marriage ceremony must take

Legal Jurisdiction Over Marriage

Under the *Constitution Act, 1867*,[5] the federal government has jurisdiction over marriage and divorce, including matters that relate to the capacity to marry, while the provinces have jurisdiction over the solemnization of marriage—in other words, the formal requirements of licensing and ceremony.

Legal Capacity to Marry

When we talk about the legal capacity to marry, we are talking about matters such as

- gender,
- age,
- mental capacity,
- consent,
- consanguinity (blood relationship), and
- marital status.

Whether or not the parties have the legal capacity to marry is determined according to the law of the **domicile** (permanent residence) of the parties at the time of the marriage.

domicile
permanent residence

Gender

Before the *Civil Marriage Act*[6] changed the definition of marriage, for civil purposes, to "the lawful union of two persons to the exclusion of all others," the parties to a marriage had to be one man and one woman. Now the parties must be "two persons."

Age

At common law, a female party to a marriage must be at least 12 years old and a male party at least 15 years old. If either party is under age, the marriage is voidable at the option of the underage party; if either party is under the age of 7, however, the marriage is void. Pursuant to the Ontario *Marriage Act*,[7] a person must be at least 18 years old to be married without the consent of his or her parents. A person who is 16

---

5 30 & 31 Vict, C 3 (UK).

6 SC 2005, c 33.

7 RSO 1990, c M.3.

or 17 years old may marry with the written consent of both parents. If the parents are not available or if they unreasonably withhold their consent to the marriage, the person may apply to a judge to dispense with parental consent. Lack of parental consent is not a matter of capacity, and does not affect the validity of the marriage.

Mental Capacity

A person entering a marriage must have the capacity to understand the nature of a marriage and its duties and responsibilities. A person who lacks this understanding at the time of the marriage as a result of an inherent lack of mental capacity cannot enter into a valid marriage, and the marriage is void. If a person lacks this understanding at the time of the marriage as a result of drugs or alcohol, the marriage is voidable.

Consent

duress
force or threats that cause a person to do something he or she would not ordinarily do

To be valid, a marriage must be entered into freely, without **duress** (force or threats). A person marries under duress if

- the person is so afraid as to remove the element of consent,
- the fear is reasonable, and
- the fear is caused by a circumstance for which the person is not responsible.

In addition, the marriage must be entered into without any mistake as to the identity of the other party at the time of the ceremony or the nature of the ceremony. For example, if a party goes through a ceremony in a foreign country without realizing that it is a marriage ceremony, the party is not married. However, a mistake about certain characteristics of the other party, such as wealth or background, does not make a marriage invalid.

If a person goes through a marriage ceremony knowing the identity of the other person and the nature of the ceremony, the person's motives for doing so are irrelevant. For example, a marriage entered into for the sole objective of immigration is a valid marriage.

Consanguinity

The parties to a marriage may not be too closely related to each other, either by blood (consanguinity) or by adoption. Under the federal *Marriage (Prohibited Degrees) Act*,[8] no person shall marry another person if they are related lineally (in other words, as parent, grandparent, daughter, or son), or as brother or sister or half-brother or half-sister, including by adoption.

These prohibitions apply to relationships by whole or half blood, or by adoption. Historically, marriage between parties closely related by marriage (affinity) was also prohibited. That is no longer the case.

---

8 SC 1990, c 46.

Marital Status

A party to a marriage may not already be married to someone else. Any previous marriage must have been ended by death, divorce, or annulment.

Formalities

The formalities of marriage involve such matters as

- the persons authorized to perform a marriage ceremony,
- the nature of the ceremony,
- licence requirements, and
- residency requirements (in some jurisdictions).

The formalities of a valid marriage are determined by the law of the jurisdiction in which the marriage takes place. In Ontario, the formalities required of marriages are set out in the *Marriage Act*.

Persons Authorized to Perform a Marriage Ceremony

A couple marrying in Ontario may have a civil marriage or a religious marriage. A civil marriage can be performed by a judge, a justice of the peace, or a clerk of a local municipality. A religious marriage can be performed by a person who is recognized by a religious body to perform marriages and who is registered to perform marriages in Ontario under the *Marriage Act*.

The person who performs a marriage, whether it is civil or religious, is required to send documentation to the Office of the Registrar General for registration.

Nature of the Ceremony

Under Ontario law, each of the parties to a civil marriage must at some point in the ceremony, in the presence of the person solemnizing the marriage and witnesses, declare: "I do solemnly declare that I do not know of any lawful impediment why I, AB, may not be joined in matrimony to CD," and must say to the other: "I call upon these persons here present to witness that I, AB, do take you CD, to be my lawful wedded wife (*or* to be my lawful wedded husband *or* to be my lawful wedded partner *or* to be my lawful wedded spouse)," after which the person solemnizing the marriage must say: "I, EF, by virtue of the powers vested in me by the *Marriage Act*, do hereby pronounce you AB and CD to be married."[9] Otherwise, no particular form is required for a civil marriage.

Any religious marriage performed by a properly registered person according to the rites, usages, and customs of the particular religion is valid.

---

9   The Ontario *Marriage Act*, RSA 2000, c M-5 was amended in March 2005 to include language appropriate for use at the marriages of same-sex couples.

Licence Requirements

A civil marriage can be performed only under the authority of a marriage licence. A religious marriage can be performed under the authority of a marriage licence or, depending on the religious denomination, the publication of banns,[10] provided that neither of the parties was previously in a marriage that ended in divorce or annulment.

A marriage licence can be obtained from the clerk of most cities, townships, towns, or villages.

Residency Requirements

In some jurisdictions, the parties must reside in the jurisdiction for a minimum period of time before they may be married in that jurisdiction. There are no residency requirements for marriage in Ontario.

Rights and Obligations of Marriage

Like all contracts, marriage confers rights and obligations on the parties. The main rights and obligations of the parties to a marriage involve support and property. In Ontario, each spouse has an obligation to provide financial support for himself or herself and for the other spouse, in accordance with the other spouse's need, to the extent that he or she is capable of doing so. Married couples in Ontario are also given the right to a share of the value of property acquired during the marriage and to possession of their matrimonial home (the home in which they live).[11] Married couples also have rights to share in each other's estates, as well as rights under various statutes regarding taxes, pensions, insurance, and benefits.

Same-Sex Marriage

As stated earlier, the parties to a marriage must have the legal capacity to enter into the contract and must comply with certain legal formalities for the contract to be valid. Legal capacity to marry is determined in accordance with the law of the domicile of the parties to the marriage, while the formalities of a valid marriage are determined by the law of the jurisdiction in which the marriage takes place. For a marriage to be valid, the parties must have the capacity to marry according to the law of their domicile, and must comply with the formalities required by the law where the marriage is performed.

Many same-sex couples have come to Canada to be married because same-sex marriage is not allowed in their home jurisdictions. Under international law, these marriages are arguably not valid because the parties lack the capacity to marry according to the law of their domicile. Parties to these marriages have been unable to obtain a divorce in their home jurisdictions because the marriage is not recognized

---

10 The publication of banns involves proclaiming the intention to marry during church services.

11 The *Family Law Act* was amended in March 2005 to extend the right to share in property to married couples of the same sex.

as valid in that jurisdiction. One such couple applied for a Canadian divorce in 2012.[12] The federal government, relying on these same principles of international law, initially took the position that the marriage was also not valid in Canada. The federal government soon withdrew that objection, but there was still a problem because the couple could not satisfy the residency requirements under the *Divorce Act*.[13] (These requirements are discussed in Chapter 5.)

The federal government passed the *Civil Marriage of Non-residents Act*[14] in June 2013, and it addresses both of these issues. Under that legislation, a marriage that is performed in Canada and that would be valid in Canada if the spouses were domiciled in Canada is valid for the purposes of Canadian law even though either or both of the spouses do not, at the time of the marriage, have the capacity to enter into it under the law of their respective states of domicile. The Act addresses the issue of divorce in these cases as well. Those provisions are discussed in Chapter 5.

Common Law Marriage

The term "common law marriage" is sometimes used to describe the relationship between people who live in a marital relationship but who have not gone through a marriage ceremony. Parties in these relationships may consider themselves married, and others may think of them as married, but they are not. No matter how long they live together, and whether or not they have children, people who have not gone through a formal marriage ceremony are not married and do not have all of the rights and obligations that married people have.

Under federal and provincial statutes, unmarried same-sex and opposite-sex couples who cohabit have been given many of the same rights as married couples when it comes to taxes and to pensions, insurance, and other benefits. After a certain period of time, they may also have the same obligation as married people to support each other and the same right to claim support from the estate of the deceased partner.

Parties who cohabit without being married do *not* have the same property rights as parties to a marriage. In fact, they do not have *any* statutory right to a share of their partner's property or to possession of the home in which the parties live. Parties in these non-marriage relationships can, however, choose to give each other these rights by entering into a cohabitation agreement (discussed in Chapter 15).

Change of Surname on Marriage/Divorce

Traditionally, a woman assumed her husband's surname on marriage. That surname was referred to as her "married name," and her surname at birth was referred to as her "maiden name." While many women still do assume their husband's surname, there is no legal requirement for a woman to do so. It is more and more common for

---

12 They were married in Toronto in 2005 and had since separated, one living in Britain and the other living in Florida, where same-sex marriage is not recognized. As a result, neither jurisdiction would grant them a divorce.

13 RSC 1985, c 3 (2d Supp).

14 SC 2013, c 30.

a woman to retain her own surname after marriage. Other couples decide to change the surnames of both spouses to a combination of their two names.

Under the *Change of Name Act*,[15] no formal change of name application is required. Instead, a spouse may simply elect, at any time while married, to change his or her surname to the surname of the other spouse or a surname that hyphenates or combines the surnames of both spouses. The spouse must apply in person at a Service-Ontario centre and present his or her marriage certificate and documentation to prove that he or she is a Canadian citizen and Ontario resident. There is no fee.

If the marriage subsequently ends by divorce, annulment or death, the former spouse may elect to resume the surname that he or she had immediately before the marriage by providing a divorce certificate, certificate of annulment, or death certificate, as the case may be. Again, there is no fee.

Similar provisions apply to parties who are cohabiting but not married. If the parties are cohabiting but not married, they must provide a joint declaration acknowledging that they live together in a conjugal relationship to assume the new surname. A party wishing to resume his or her previous surname must file a declaration that the relationship has ended.

---

15   RSO 1990, c C.7.

CHAPTER SUMMARY

Like all contracts, marriage confers rights and obligations on the parties. The main rights and obligations of the parties to a marriage involve support and property.

Under the *Constitution Act, 1867*, the federal government has jurisdiction over marriage and divorce, including matters relating to the capacity to marry. Whether or not parties have the legal capacity to marry is determined according to the law of the domicile of the parties at the time of the marriage. The provinces have jurisdiction over the formal requirements of licensing and ceremony. In Ontario, the *Marriage Act* sets out the formalities required of marriages.

Historically, marriage has required a man and a woman; however, the *Civil Marriage Act* (2005) changed the definition of marriage to "the lawful union of two persons to the exclusion of all others."

While the term "common law marriage" describes a relationship between two people who live in a marital relationship without having gone through a marriage ceremony, these couples do not have all of the rights and obligations of married couples. They do, however, have some of these rights (e.g., with respect to taxes and to pensions, insurance, and other benefits), and, after a certain period of time, they may also have the same obligation to support each other.

A spouse who wishes to assume the surname of the other spouse does not have to file a formal change of name application, but may apply in person at a ServiceOntario centre. There is no fee.

KEY TERMS

domicile, 29
duress, 30

legal capacity to marry, 29
legal formalities of marriage, 29

REVIEW QUESTIONS

1. Which level of government has jurisdiction over the legal capacity to marry?

2. Which level of government has jurisdiction over marriage licences and marriage ceremonies?

3. Describe how *Halpern v Canada (Attorney General)* affected the laws of marriage in Ontario.

4. How old must a person be to be married in Ontario without the consent of his or her parents?

5. What must a person have the capacity to understand in order to form a valid marriage?

6. By the law of which place are the formalities of a valid marriage determined?

7. What statute governs the formalities of marriage in Ontario?

8. Who may perform a civil marriage in Ontario? Who may perform a religious marriage?

9. Describe the form required for a civil and a religious marriage ceremony in Ontario.

10. Is a marriage licence always required?

11. Are there any residency requirements for marriage in Ontario?

12. What are the main rights and obligations of the parties to a marriage?

13. Do parties who cohabit without being married have the right to be supported by each other?

14. Do parties who cohabit without being married have a statutory right to a share of the other party's property?

DISCUSSION QUESTIONS

1. In the Bible, Jacob fell in love with Rachel and asked to marry her. At the ceremony, Rachel's father substituted her older sister Leah for Rachel. Leah was covered in a heavy veil, and Jacob, thinking he was marrying Rachel, was married to Leah instead. Would this be a valid marriage in Ontario?

2. Susan Sarandon and Tim Robinson lived together for many years and had several children together, but they never married. In Ontario, would either of them have a statutory right to share in each other's property?

3. Yoko and John decided to get married in Japan. Yoko is from Japan, but she and John reside permanently in Ontario. They planned a two-week trip to Japan, hoping to get married in a Shinto ceremony. When they got to Japan, they learned that there was a residency requirement of one month to get married. They went ahead with the ceremony any way. Will this marriage be recognized as valid in Ontario?

Dissolution of Marriage by Annulment

4

LEARNING OUTCOMES

After completing this chapter, you should be able to:

- Define "annulment."

- Explain the difference between a divorce and an annulment.

- Describe the grounds for an annulment.

- Explain the effect of an annulment.

- Explain the rights of the parties to an annulment.

- Briefly describe the procedure for obtaining an annulment.

Introduction

A marriage can be terminated in only three ways: annulment, divorce, or the death of one of the parties. While a divorce puts an end to a valid marriage, an annulment declares that a marriage is invalid and, therefore, void. Both divorce and annulment require a court judgment.

The law of annulment[1] developed when it was virtually impossible to get a divorce on any ground. It continued to be an important remedy when divorce was available only on fault grounds. Annulment is now a rarely used remedy, since divorce is available on the basis of a one-year separation.

In this chapter, we will look at

- the grounds for annulment, and
- the remedies available in an annulment proceeding.

What Is an Annulment?

void *ab initio*
void, or having no legal force, from the beginning

voidable
may be declared void but is otherwise not void

An annulment is a judgment that declares that a marriage is void. A marriage may be **void *ab initio*** or it may be **voidable**. In the latter case, the parties can choose whether to treat the marriage as void or as valid. If a marriage is void *ab initio*, it is as if the marriage had never taken place. A voidable marriage, however, is treated as a valid marriage unless and until it is annulled by a court.

Marriages That Are Void Ab Initio

A marriage is void *ab initio* if one of the parties did not have the legal capacity to marry. The factors affecting capacity, which are discussed more fully in Chapter 3, are the following:

- *Age*. A marriage is void *ab initio* if either of the parties was too young. Even though the *Marriage Act*[2] of Ontario states that a marriage licence cannot be issued to a minor without parental consent, a marriage that has been performed without parental consent is void *ab initio* only if one of the parties was younger than 7 years old. (If a female party is between the ages of 7 and 12 or a male party is between the ages of 7 and 14, the marriage, while not void, is voidable at the option of the underage party.)

- *Mental capacity*. A marriage is void *ab initio* if, at the time of the marriage ceremony, one of the parties was incapable of understanding the nature of a marriage and its obligations as a result of an inherent lack of mental capacity.

---

1 By virtue of the federal *Annulment of Marriages Act (Ontario)*, RSC 1970, c A-14, originally enacted in 1930, annulment is governed by the common law of England as it existed on July 15, 1870. It continues to be a common law remedy—that is, all of the law in this area comes from case decisions. As of the date of publication, the courts have not been called on to address the issue of annulment of a same-sex marriage.

2 RSO 2000, c M.3.

If a person lacks this understanding at the time of the marriage as a result of drugs or alcohol, the marriage is voidable.

- *Consent.* A marriage is void *ab initio* if either of the parties did not freely consent to the marriage because of mistake or fraud, and is voidable if either of the parties did not consent because of duress.
- *Consanguinity.* A marriage is void *ab initio* if the parties are too closely related to each other by blood or adoption.
- *Marital status.* A marriage is void *ab initio* if either of the parties was married to another person at the time of the marriage ceremony. This is the reason that most marriages are declared void *ab initio*. In some cases, one of the parties lies about his or her marital status at the time of the wedding, but, more commonly, a party enters into a marriage in the honest belief that his or her prior marriage has been terminated. For example, a party may have participated in a divorce proceeding that is not recognized as valid in Canada.

Marriages That Are Voidable

A marriage is voidable if one of the parties is unable to consummate the marriage after the ceremony.[3] Either party may apply to have the marriage annulled on this ground. (In other words, an applicant may rely on his or her own inability to consummate.)

The applicant must prove that either party to the marriage has an incurable inability or incapacity to consummate the marriage. The inability may be physical or mental, but a simple refusal to have sexual intercourse is not enough.

Effect of an Annulment

A marriage that is void *ab initio* was never valid, and the parties to a void marriage were never validly married. The judicial decree of nullity merely confirms the status of the parties as unmarried.

A marriage that is voidable continues to be valid, and the parties continue to be married unless and until the marriage is declared to be invalid by a court. Once a decree of nullity is granted, it is as if the marriage never took place.

Rights of the Parties

Under section 1(1) of the *Family Law Act*,[4] the definition of "spouse" includes "either of two persons who … have together entered into a marriage that is voidable or void, in good faith on the part of the person relying on this clause to assert any right." In

---

3 A marriage is consummated when ordinary and complete sexual intercourse takes place between the spouses after the marriage ceremony.

4 RSO 1990, c F.3.

other words, a person who entered into a void or voidable marriage in good faith can assert the same property and support claims as a person who is validly married.

Procedure

A party wishing to annul a marriage may do so by way of an application in the Family Court of the Superior Court of Justice or in the Superior Court of Justice. The proceeding may include claims for custody, support, and property rights.

CHAPTER SUMMARY

A marriage can be terminated in only three ways: annulment, divorce, or the death of one of the parties. While a divorce puts an end to a valid marriage, an annulment declares that a marriage is invalid and, therefore, void. A void marriage may be either void *ab initio* or voidable.

If a marriage is void *ab initio*, it is as if the marriage had never taken place; it will be void *ab initio* if one of the parties did not have the legal capacity to marry. A marriage that is void *ab initio* was never valid. The judicial decree of nullity merely confirms the status of the parties as unmarried.

If a marriage is voidable, the parties choose whether to treat the marriage as void or as valid. This may be the case if one of the parties is unable to consummate the marriage. A marriage that is voidable continues to be valid, and the parties continue to be married, unless and until the marriage is declared to be invalid by a court. Once a decree of nullity is granted, it is as if the marriage never took place.

Under section 1(1) of the *Family Law Act*, a person who entered into a void or voidable marriage in good faith can assert the same property and support claims as a person who is validly married.

To annul a marriage, a party may file an application in the Family Court of the Superior Court of Justice or in the Superior Court of Justice. The proceeding may include claims for custody, support, and property rights.

KEY TERMS

void *ab initio*, 38
voidable, 38

REVIEW QUESTIONS

1. What is an annulment?

2. What does void *ab initio* mean?

3. What marriages are void *ab initio*?

4. What marriages are voidable?

5. What is the effect of an annulment?

6. What type of proceeding is required to obtain an annulment?

DISCUSSION QUESTIONS

1. Jude loved Sue and so he married her. Unfortunately, he neglected to tell her that he was already married to Arabella. Is this a valid marriage? Does Sue have any property or support rights against Jude? Does Jude have any property or support rights against Sue?

2. Barry is gay but has never told his parents. Under pressure from his family, he married Angela, hoping that he would be able to make the marriage work. However, after three months it has become apparent to him that he will never be able to consummate the marriage, and he would like to have the marriage annulled. Can he do so?

Dissolution of Marriage by Divorce

5

LEARNING OUTCOMES

After completing this chapter, you should be able to:

■ Explain the legislative jurisdiction over divorce.

■ Determine which province has jurisdiction in a particular divorce matter.

■ State which Ontario court has jurisdiction to determine divorces.

■ Explain the grounds for divorce.

■ Explain the bars to divorce.

■ Explain the statutory duties regarding reconciliation.

■ State the effective date of a divorce.

■ State the legal effect of a divorce.

■ Explain the factors in the recognition of foreign divorce decrees.

■ Understand the statutory provisions regarding divorce by non-resident same-sex couples.

Introduction

A valid marriage may be terminated in only two ways: by the death of one of the parties or by divorce.

In this chapter, we will look at

- the legislative jurisdiction over divorce,
- the jurisdiction of the courts in divorce matters,
- the grounds for divorce,
- the bars to divorce,
- the statutory duties regarding reconciliation,
- the effective date of a divorce,
- the legal effect of a divorce,
- the recognition of foreign divorce decrees, and
- the jurisdiction to grant a divorce to a non-resident, same-sex couple.

The law relating to custody and support under the *Divorce Act*[1] and procedure in divorce proceedings are discussed later in this book.

Legislative Jurisdiction Over Divorce

Divorce is a matter of federal jurisdiction. The first Canada-wide statute dealing with divorce was passed in 1968. The current *Divorce Act* has been in effect since 1986.

Once a divorce proceeding is commenced, questions of spousal support, child support, and custody are dealt with under the *Divorce Act*. Issues relating to the property of the parties are dealt with under provincial legislation (and not under the *Divorce Act*).

Jurisdiction of the Courts in Divorce Matters

A party seeking a divorce must know which court has jurisdiction to deal with the matter. This involves two questions:

1. Which province has jurisdiction?
2. If Ontario has jurisdiction, which Ontario court has jurisdiction?

Which Province Has Jurisdiction?

The *Divorce Act* is a federal statute that governs divorce throughout Canada. The spouses may live anywhere in Canada, and may even be living in different provinces. The statute sets out which province has jurisdiction to deal with their divorce.

---

1   RSC 1985, c 3 (2d Supp).

Section 3(1) of the Act states that

A court in a province has jurisdiction to hear and determine a divorce proceeding if either spouse has been ordinarily resident in the province for at least one year immediately preceding the commencement of the proceeding.

In other words, if one spouse has lived in a province for at least *one* year immediately before the commencement of the divorce, then *either* spouse can start a divorce proceeding in that province.

Dharma and Greg were married in Ontario and lived there until their separation a little more than a year ago. Immediately after their separation, Dharma moved to British Columbia, while Greg stayed in Ontario.

Dharma can start a divorce action in British Columbia since she has resided in that province for at least one year, and Greg can start a divorce action in Ontario for the same reason. But Dharma can also start her divorce action in Ontario, and Greg can also start his divorce action in British Columbia.

Section 3(1) is very useful if the person who wants to start the divorce action has not lived in one province long enough to be able to rely on his or her own residency.

Fred and Ethel were married in Alberta and lived there until their separation a little more than one year ago. After the separation, Fred moved to British Columbia and stayed there. Ethel, however, decided to work her way across Canada, moving first to Manitoba, where she lived for three months, then to Ontario, where she lived for the next three months, then on to Quebec, where she lived for four months, and finally to Newfoundland, where she has lived ever since. Ethel now wants a divorce. What can she do?

Clearly, Fred can start a divorce action in British Columbia since he has resided in that province for at least one year. But what if Ethel wants to start the divorce action? She cannot start an action in any of the provinces she has lived in during the marriage or since the separation because she has not lived in any of them for the year leading up to the divorce action. But Ethel, like Fred, can start a divorce action in British Columbia, relying on the fact that Fred has resided there for at least one year before she commences the divorce action.

As you can see in the Dharma and Greg example, it is possible for more than one province to have jurisdiction to start a divorce proceeding. What happens if two spouses both start divorce proceedings in different provinces? Under section 3(2) of the Act, the divorce proceeding that was started first continues, while the one that was started second is deemed to be discontinued. If the proceedings are both started on the same day and neither spouse discontinues his or her action, the divorce is dealt with by the Federal Court under section 3(3) of the Act.

Which Ontario Court Has Jurisdiction?

In Ontario, the Superior Court of Justice (including the Family Court of the Superior Court of Justice) has jurisdiction over divorce actions.

Grounds for Divorce

The grounds for divorce are dealt with in section 8 of the *Divorce Act*. The Act speaks of one ground only: breakdown of the marriage (in section 8(1)), but there are three ways to establish marriage breakdown. One is a no-fault ground, and two are fault grounds.

No-Fault Ground

Spouses may divorce on the ground of separation. This ground involves no allegation of fault against either party.

Under section 8(2)(a), breakdown of a marriage is established if

the spouses have lived separate and apart for at least one year immediately preceding the determination of the divorce proceeding and were living separate and apart at the commencement of the proceeding.

Either spouse can start a divorce action any time after the parties have separated, but the parties must have been living separate and apart for at least one year by the time the matter is dealt with by the judge. In other words, a spouse can *start* a divorce proceeding on the day of separation, but a judge cannot *grant* a divorce until the parties have been separated for at least one year.

Spouses are considered to be living separate and apart only if they are both physically separated, and at least one of them has an intention to be separate and apart. Spouses who live in different places are not living separate and apart if they have an intention to remain married.

Lucy and Ricky were married and lived together in Toronto. Ricky got a job as a band leader in Cuba and set up an apartment there. Lucy and Ricky continued to consider themselves married. Lucy flew to Cuba twice a year, and Ricky returned to Toronto twice a year.

Lucy and Ricky are not living separate and apart under the *Divorce Act*.

Sometimes it is difficult for the courts to decide when spouses have separated.

Lynn and Keith were married in 1985. After many difficulties in the marriage, Lynn moved out in 1995, telling Keith she needed "some space." Over the next three and a half years, Lynn and Keith maintained separate households, cars, and bank accounts, but they also continued to have a sexual relationship and regularly went out, travelled, and spent weekends together. They never told Keith's parents that they had separated, and they spent Christmas with his family, pretending that they were still living together. One night in January 1998, Lynn and Keith had an argument. She told him that she did not want to have sex with him, and she realized that she wanted her marriage to end.

The judge who presided at the couple's divorce decided that Lynn's desire to end the marriage and the cessation of sexual relations marked the point at which the couple began to live separate and apart.

It is even possible for spouses to be living separate and apart under the same roof as long as there are two households or the spouses are living separate lives. It is not enough for the spouses simply to have ceased having a sexual relationship. There must be a mutual repudiation of the marriage relationship. Spouses living under the same roof who rarely communicate, eat separately, do not share social activities, and occupy separate bedrooms have been found to be living separate and apart.

Under section 8(3)(b)(ii) of the *Divorce Act*, if the spouses resume cohabitation, in an attempt at reconciliation, for a period of 90 days or periods not totalling more than 90 days, the period during which the spouses have lived separate and apart is not considered to have been interrupted or ended.

Fault Grounds

There are two grounds for divorce that involve an allegation of fault against one of the spouses: adultery and cruelty.

Adultery

Pursuant to section 8(2)(b)(i) of the Act, breakdown of a marriage can also be established if the spouse against whom the divorce action is brought has committed adultery. Historically, adultery was defined by the courts to mean voluntary sexual intercourse between a married person and another person of the opposite sex other than his or her spouse. In 2005, the British Columbia Supreme Court held that adultery may include same-sex sexual acts.[2] The adultery must be committed by the respondent spouse. The spouse who starts the divorce proceeding cannot rely on his or her own adultery as a ground for divorce.

Cruelty

Pursuant to section 8(2)(b)(ii) of the Act, breakdown of a marriage can also be established if the spouse against whom the divorce action is brought has treated the other spouse with physical or mental cruelty of such a kind as to render intolerable the continued cohabitation of the spouses.

A spouse who by his or her conduct "causes wanton, malicious or unnecessary infliction of pain or suffering upon the body, the feelings or emotions of the other" may be guilty of cruelty.[3] To constitute cruelty, the conduct must be of a grave and weighty nature; it cannot be trivial. At the same time, the test for cruelty is subjective.

---

2 *P (SE) v P (DD)*, 2005 BCSC 1290.

3 *Knoll v Knoll* (1970), 1 RFL 141 (Ont CA).

The question is whether particular conduct by a particular party against his or her spouse is cruelty. Isolated acts that do not themselves constitute cruelty can amount to cruelty if they are part of an ongoing course of conduct whose cumulative effect is to make continued cohabitation intolerable.[4]

Examples of conduct found to constitute cruelty include

- a series of assaults,
- one savage attack,
- persistent harassment and abuse,
- a husband's transvestism,
- a husband's pedophilia,
- a spouse's persistent refusal to have sexual relations with the other,
- a husband's forcing his wife to engage in fellatio against her will, and
- a wife's ongoing ridicule of her husband's sexual performance.

Bars to Divorce

There are certain circumstances in which a court will not grant a divorce, even if the spouse who started the proceeding proves that one or more of the grounds for divorce exist. The three major bars to divorce, which are dealt with in section 11 of the Act, are

- collusion,
- connivance, and
- condonation.

Collusion

Collusion is defined in section 11(4) of the Act as

> an agreement or conspiracy to which an applicant for a divorce is ... a party for the purpose of subverting the administration of justice, and includes any agreement, understanding or arrangement to fabricate or suppress evidence or to deceive the court.

Harry and Sally have just separated. They do not want to wait for a divorce until they've been separated for one year, so Sally suggests to Harry that he sue her for divorce based on adultery. They agree that Sally will give evidence that she committed adultery with a co-worker even though that is not the case. This agreement constitutes collusion.

It would also be collusion if Harry and Sally agreed to lie about the date on which they separated so that they could get a divorce early.

---

4   *Powell v Powell* (1971), 5 RFL 195 (Sask CA) and *Wittstock v Wittstock*, [1971] 2 OR 472 (CA).

It is the duty of the court to satisfy itself that there has been no collusion in relation to the application for a divorce. If the court finds collusion on the part of the applicant, the court must dismiss the divorce claim. Collusion is an absolute bar to a divorce whether the divorce is brought on a fault or a no-fault ground.

Connivance

Connivance is not defined in the Act, but it takes place when the spouse bringing the proceeding encourages the other spouse to commit a matrimonial offence so that there are grounds for a divorce.

> Harry and Sally have just separated. They don't want to wait until they've been separated for one year, so Sally suggests to Harry that he have sexual intercourse with a co-worker so that she can sue him for divorce based on adultery. Harry agrees. The couple's actions here constitute connivance.

Unlike collusion, connivance is not an absolute bar to divorce. Pursuant to section 11(1)(c), the court may grant a divorce notwithstanding connivance on the part of the spouse bringing the proceeding if, in its opinion, "the public interest would be better served by granting the divorce." Connivance applies only to a divorce brought on the fault grounds of adultery or cruelty.

Condonation

Condonation, which may also be a bar to a divorce, applies only to a divorce brought on the fault grounds of adultery or cruelty. Condonation is not defined in the Act, but at common law, condonation takes place when a spouse, with knowledge of the offence, forgives the offence and continues or resumes cohabitation with the guilty spouse.

In order to encourage spouses to attempt to reconcile before commencing divorce proceedings, section 11(3) provides that a continuation or resumption of cohabitation during a period or periods totalling no more than 90 days, with reconciliation as its primary purpose, is not considered to constitute condonation.

> Angelina and Billy Bob have been married for only a short time when Angelina discovers that Billy Bob has been having an affair with a co-worker. Angelina is furious and moves out, threatening to start divorce proceedings immediately. Billy Bob begs for forgiveness and promises to change. Angelina relents and moves back in with Billy Bob in an attempt at reconciliation. After two months, she notices him flirting with other women whenever they go out together, and she decides that he has not changed at all. She moves out again.
>
> Angelina can still rely on Billy Bob's affair as a ground for divorce. Even though she resumed cohabitation with him with full knowledge that he had committed adultery, her behaviour does not constitute condonation because of the exception

> in section 11(3). However, if the couple had resumed cohabitation for four months instead of two, Angelina could not rely on Billy Bob's original affair and would need new grounds for divorce.

Condonation, like connivance, is not an absolute bar to a divorce. Pursuant to section 11(1)(c), the court may grant a divorce notwithstanding condonation on the part of the spouse who brings the proceeding if, in its opinion, "the public interest would be better served by granting the divorce."

Failure to Make Reasonable Arrangements for Child Support

If the parties to the divorce have children, pursuant to section 11(1)(b), the court has a duty to satisfy itself that reasonable arrangements have been made for the support of the children. If arrangements have not been made, the court must stay the granting of the divorce until arrangements are made.

Encouragement of Reconciliation Under the Divorce Act

There are a number of provisions of the *Divorce Act* that are designed to encourage reconciliation by the spouses. We have examined two already:

- Under section 8(3)(b)(ii), the one-year period of separation is not interrupted by a resumption of cohabitation, with reconciliation as its primary purpose, for a period or periods totalling no more than 90 days.
- Under section 11(3), a resumption of cohabitation, with reconciliation as its primary purpose, for a period or periods totalling no more than 90 days does not constitute condonation of a matrimonial offence.

How do these provisions encourage reconciliation? It is presumed that spouses will be more willing to attempt to reconcile if they know that they have nothing to lose (in terms of their grounds for divorce) if the reconciliation fails.

In addition to these provisions, the Act imposes a duty on legal advisers and the court to encourage the parties to reconcile:

- Under section 9, except in cases where it would clearly not be appropriate to do so, it is the duty of every legal adviser who acts on behalf of a spouse in a divorce proceeding to draw the provisions in section 8(3) and section 11(3) to the attention of the spouse, to discuss with the spouse the possibility of reconciliation, and to advise the spouse about marriage counselling or guidance facilities. The legal adviser must certify that he or she has done this.

- Under section 10, except in cases where it would clearly not be appropriate to do so, it is the duty of the court, before hearing the evidence in the divorce proceeding, to satisfy itself that there is no possibility of the reconciliation of the spouses. If the court is of the opinion that there is a possibility of reconciliation, it must adjourn the proceedings to allow the spouses an opportunity to achieve a reconciliation.

Effective Date of Divorce

Under the provisions of section 12 of the Act, a divorce generally takes effect on the 31st day after the divorce judgment is granted. If the court is of the opinion that special circumstances exist, it can order that the judgment take effect earlier. In order for the court to grant this kind of order, the spouses must file a document with the court by which they agree and undertake not to appeal the judgment.

Because a divorce takes effect on the 31st day, a party who wishes to appeal a judgment granting a divorce must file his or her appeal (or an application to extend the appeal period) within the 31-day period. If no appeal is filed within the time limit, the divorce judgment becomes effective.

When a court grants a divorce, it signs a formal divorce judgment. The judgment document itself does not prove that the divorce has become effective because it does not indicate whether or not the judgment was appealed. As a result, the Act provides that once a divorce becomes effective, the court must issue on request a certificate that the divorce was effective as of a specified date. A party requires this certificate to prove that he or she is divorced.

Effect of Divorce

Pursuant to section 14 of the Act, on taking effect, a divorce dissolves the marriage of the spouses. According to section 13 of the Act, a divorce has legal effect throughout Canada.

Recognition of Foreign Divorces

Not all divorces granted by other jurisdictions are considered valid in Canada. "Quickie" foreign divorces are frowned upon. Canada requires some legitimate connection between the parties and the jurisdiction that granted the divorce before a foreign divorce judgment will be recognized.

Under the provisions of section 22(1) of the Act, a divorce granted by a foreign jurisdiction is recognized in Canada if either party was resident in the jurisdiction for at least one year immediately before the proceeding was commenced. (Note that this is the same basis on which jurisdiction of the Canadian courts is based.)

Another basis for recognizing foreign divorce judgments is found in section 22(3) of the Act, which provides that common law rules for recognition of foreign divorces are preserved. The common law test, which was stated in the 1969 House of Lords decision of *Indyka v Indyka*,[5] was adopted by the Canadian courts. In that case, it was decided that a foreign divorce is recognized if there is a real and substantial connection between the spouse bringing the proceeding and the jurisdiction granting the divorce, unless the divorce was obtained by fraud, or unless recognition of the divorce would offend the rules of natural justice.

Divorce for Non-Resident Same-Sex Couples

Many same-sex couples have come to Canada to be married because same-sex marriage is not allowed in their home jurisdictions. Parties to these marriages have been unable to obtain a divorce in their home jurisdictions because the marriage is not recognized as valid in that jurisdiction. As non-residents, neither party can satisfy the one-year residency requirement of the *Divorce Act*, and so they are ineligible for a divorce in Canada as well.

The federal government passed the *Civil Marriage of Non-residents Act*,[6] which addresses this issue. Under that legislation, the court of the province where the marriage was performed may, on application, grant the spouses a divorce if

- there has been a breakdown of the marriage as established by the spouses having lived separate and apart for at least one year before the making of the application;
- neither spouse resides in Canada at the time the application is made; and
- each of the spouses is residing—and for at least one year immediately before the application is made, has resided—in a state where a divorce cannot be granted because that state does not recognize the validity of the marriage.

The application for divorce must be made jointly by both spouses, or by one spouse with the consent of the other, or an order dispensing with consent.

---

5   [1969] 1 AC 33 (HL).

6   SC 2013 c 30.

CHAPTER SUMMARY

Divorce is a matter of federal jurisdiction under the *Divorce Act*, which also deals with spousal support, child support, and custody.

Either spouse can start a divorce proceeding in any province as long as one of them has lived there for at least one year immediately before the start of the proceedings. In Ontario, the Superior Court of Justice (including the Family Court of the Superior Court of Justice) has jurisdiction over divorce actions.

While the only ground for divorce is the breakdown of marriage, there are three ways to establish marriage breakdown: separation, a no-fault ground, and adultery and cruelty, both fault grounds.

There are certain circumstances in which a court will not grant a divorce, even if the spouse who started the proceeding proves that one or more of the grounds for divorce exist. The main bars for divorce are collusion, an absolute bar, and condonation and connivance, both discretionary bars.

Legal advisers have a duty to encourage reconciliation wherever appropriate before commencing a divorce proceeding.

Generally, a divorce takes effect on the 31st day after it is granted. A certificate stating the date the divorce takes effect is issued to prove that the parties are divorced. Once effective, a divorce dissolves the marriage throughout Canada.

Generally, a divorce granted by a foreign jurisdiction will not be recognized in Canada unless at least one of the parties resided in that jurisdiction for at least one year immediately before the divorce proceeding was started.

The *Civil Marriage of Non-residents Act* makes special provision allowing for non-resident, same-sex couples to obtain a divorce in Canada.

REVIEW QUESTIONS

1. What statute governs divorce? Is it a federal statute or a provincial statute?

2. Under what legislation are issues of spousal support, child support, and custody dealt with once a divorce proceeding is commenced?

3. Under what legislation are issues relating to property dealt with once a divorce proceeding is commenced?

4. How does a party determine which province has jurisdiction to deal with his or her divorce?

5. In the province of Ontario, which court has jurisdiction over divorce actions?

6. When may a spouse start a divorce on the grounds of separation? When may the divorce be granted?

7. Is it possible for spouses to live separate and apart under the same roof?

8. Can the spouse who starts a divorce proceeding rely on his or her own adultery as a ground for the divorce?

9. What is collusion?

10. What is connivance?

11. What is condonation?

12. What provisions of the *Divorce Act* encourage reconciliation of the spouses?

13. When does a divorce generally take effect?

14. What is a certificate of divorce, and why is one necessary?

15. Under what circumstances is a divorce granted by a foreign jurisdiction recognized in Canada?

DISCUSSION QUESTIONS

1. Helen caught her husband, Hank, in bed with her former best friend, Jamie. In an ensuing argument, Hank punches Helen in the eye, something that he has done several times before. Helen has just left Hank and wants a divorce. Name all possible grounds for divorce that are available to Helen. For each ground, state when Helen may commence divorce proceedings and when a divorce may be granted.

2. Adam and Behati were married for two years and lived in Ontario. They separated one year ago and Adam now wants to start divorce proceedings. He has lived in British Columbia for only five months, but Behati has lived in Ontario for five years. Can Adam start divorce proceedings? If so, in which province(s)?

3. Bradley and Irina were married in 2010 and separated on June 11, 2016. On August 1, they decided to see if they could work things out and resumed cohabitation. On September 1, they separated again. They gave it one more try over Christmas, resuming cohabitation on December 20, but separated again on January 3, 2017, at which time Irina started a divorce proceeding claim for a divorce based on separation. What is the earliest date on which a divorce can be granted?

Custody and Access

6

LEARNING OUTCOMES

After completing this chapter, you should be able to:

- State which legislation applies to a particular custody situation.
- Explain when an Ontario court has jurisdiction to determine a custody matter under the *Divorce Act*.
- Explain when an Ontario court has jurisdiction to determine a custody matter under the *Children's Law Reform Act*.
- Explain the basic principles applied in determining custody.
- Explain the importance of an interim custody order.

And, under both the *Divorce Act* and the *Children's Law Reform Act*, you should be able to:

- Define "custody" and "access."
- Explain who may apply for custody and access.
- Describe the custody and access orders that a court may make.
- Explain the factors to be considered by the court in determining custody and access.
- Describe custody assessments and when they may be ordered.
- Explain the role of mediation in custody and access matters.
- Describe the enforcement provisions for custody and access orders.
- Discuss the principles the courts apply in varying custody and access orders.

Introduction

When a two-parent family is intact, the children live with and are cared for by both parents. When the parents separate, a decision must be made as to which parent will live with and care for the children. If the parents cannot make this decision, a court will make it for them.

As we will discuss later in this chapter, the law now recognizes the existence of family units that include more than two parents. However, except as otherwise noted, this chapter discusses the legal situation of a two-parent family.

In this chapter, we will be looking at the law of custody and access, including:

- the applicable legislation,
- the jurisdiction of the Ontario courts,
- the meaning of custody and access,
- the relevant factors in determining custody,
- interim and permanent custody orders,
- custody under the *Divorce Act*,[1]
- custody under the *Children's Law Reform Act*,[2]
- custody assessments,
- mediation,
- enforcement of custody orders, and
- variation of custody orders.

Which Legislation Applies?

Custody and access are dealt with in both the provincial *Children's Law Reform Act* and the federal *Divorce Act*. Custody and access are determined under the *Divorce Act* if divorce proceedings have been commenced by either spouse. If a spouse has not started a divorce proceeding, custody and access are determined under Part III of the *Children's Law Reform Act*.

Jurisdiction of the Ontario Courts

Before an Ontario court considers the issue of custody, whether under the *Divorce Act* or under the *Children's Law Reform Act*, it must be satisfied that it is appropriate to assume jurisdiction.

---

1   RSC 1985, c 3 (2d Supp).

2   RSO 1990, c C.12.

Under the Divorce Act

As discussed in Chapter 5, a court has jurisdiction to hear a divorce proceeding if either spouse has been ordinarily resident in the province for at least one year immediately preceding the commencement of the divorce proceeding. A court that has jurisdiction to hear a divorce proceeding has jurisdiction over a custody application included in the proceeding. However, under section 6 of the *Divorce Act*, if the custody application is opposed, the court has the power to transfer the divorce proceeding to another province if it is of the opinion that the child is most substantially connected with the other province.

Under the Children's Law Reform Act

The provisions of the *Children's Law Reform Act* concerning the jurisdiction of the Ontario courts are designed to discourage child abduction and **jurisdiction shopping** in custody matters. To that end, the provisions of the Act require the return of any child to the appropriate jurisdiction if the court is of the opinion that the child has inappropriately come before the Ontario courts.

Under section 22 of the Act, Ontario courts may take jurisdiction only if

- the child is "habitually resident" in Ontario, or
- although the child is not habitually resident in Ontario,
  - the child is physically present in Ontario at the commencement of the proceedings,
  - substantial evidence concerning the best interests of the child is available in Ontario,
  - no application for custody or access is pending in a jurisdiction where the child is habitually resident,
  - no foreign custody or access order has been recognized by an Ontario court,
  - the child has a real and substantial connection with Ontario, and
  - on the balance of convenience, it is appropriate for jurisdiction to be exercised in Ontario.

"Habitual residence" is defined in section 22(2) as the place where the child resided with both parents, or, if the parents are separated, the place where the child has resided with one parent under a separation agreement or court order or, if there is no agreement or order, with the consent or acquiescence of the other parent. If the child is residing with a person other than a parent on a permanent basis for a significant period of time, the child's habitual residence is where he or she resided with that person. The child's habitual residence may not be changed by the abduction of the child (taking the child without the consent of the person having custody) unless the person having custody has acquiesced to the abduction or has unduly delayed in taking steps to have the child returned.

jurisdiction shopping
the practice of choosing a jurisdiction in which to start a proceeding based on a party's view of his or her chances of success in that jurisdiction rather than on the jurisdiction's connection with the subject matter of the proceeding

Section 23 of the Act also allows an Ontario court to assume jurisdiction, even though the criteria of section 22 have not been met, if the child is physically present in Ontario and the court is satisfied that the child would otherwise suffer serious harm.

On the flip side, section 25 of the Act allows an Ontario court to decline jurisdiction, even though the criteria of section 22 have been met, if the court is of the opinion that it would be more appropriate for jurisdiction to be exercised outside Ontario.

Meaning of Custody and Access

custody
the rights and responsibilities of a parent, including the right and responsibility to make decisions that will affect the well-being of the child

When the parents of a child reside together, both parents have **custody**: the right and responsibility to make decisions affecting the well-being of the child. It is only when the parents separate that custodial issues arise. Then the parties must answer questions such as the following:

- Where will the child reside (with one parent or both parents)?
- When will each parent see the child?
- Who has the right to make decisions affecting the child: one parent or both parents? If both parents, what happens if the parents disagree?
- If one parent leaves the child to be cared for by the other parent, how are the first parent's custody rights affected?

These issues have been addressed in the *Divorce Act*, the *Children's Law Reform Act*, and court decisions over the years. They will be discussed in detail later in this chapter.

Custody involves more than where a child lives. It involves the right to make decisions affecting the child's welfare on matters such as place of residence, health, education, and religion. **Access** is the right to visit with the child and to obtain information regarding the child's health, education, and welfare.

access
the right to visit with the child and to obtain information regarding the child's health, education, and welfare

Custody arrangements can take various forms. At one extreme, one parent may have total care of and decision-making power over the child, while the other parent is not allowed even to see the child. At the other extreme, both parents may share care and decision making equally. More commonly, however, the arrangements involve the child's residing primarily with one parent while spending some time, such as every weekend or alternate weekends, with the other parent.

sole custody
when one parent has total care of and decision-making power over the child

joint custody
when both parents share care of and decision-making power over the child

If we are told that one parent has total care and decision-making power, it is easy to determine that that parent has **sole custody**. If we are told that both parents share care and decision-making power, it is easy to determine that the parents have **joint custody**. But if we are told that a child lives primarily with one parent and spends weekends with the other parent, we do not have enough information to determine who has custody. Custody is not a matter of how much time is spent with the child. Rather, it is a matter of decision-making authority. If both parents share decision-making authority, the parents have joint custody, even though the child spends considerably more time with one parent than the other.

Principles in Determining Custody

When a court decides a custody case, the same principles apply whether the case is decided under the *Children's Law Reform Act* or the *Divorce Act*.

Under both statutes, the issue of custody is determined on the basis of the "best interests of the child." The *Children's Law Reform Act* lists a number of factors in section 24(2) that the court should consider when deciding what those best interests are; the *Divorce Act* does not.

Although each case is decided on its individual merits, a number of principles have emerged over the years:

- As a general rule, siblings are not separated.
- The wishes of the child, especially an older child, are considered.
- Past conduct of the parents is not relevant unless it has an impact on the parent's ability to be a parent to the child.

The most important factor in any custody dispute is the status quo. Generally, a judge will change existing custody arrangements only if it is clear that the status quo is not working.

Interim or Temporary Custody Orders

A decision must be made about the custody of children at the time the parents separate. If the parties cannot agree on the issue of custody, either of them can ask the court to decide the issue, either by starting a custody proceeding under the *Children's Law Reform Act* or by claiming custody in a divorce proceeding. However, the question of custody will not be finally decided until the matter comes to trial, which can take a year or more.

The decision regarding interim custody is extremely important in light of the courts' reluctance to interfere with the status quo when deciding custody at trial. Generally speaking, the parent who is awarded interim custody will win permanent custody at the trial (unless that parent has made a mess of things).

In fact, even at the interim custody stage, the courts will not, generally speaking, disturb the status quo. As a result, the person who has **de facto custody** (custody in fact) of a child at the time of the interim custody motion is generally allowed to keep the child until the trial.

de facto **custody**
actual custody, or custody in fact

Custody Under the Divorce Act

Application of the Act

The issues of custody and access are dealt with under the *Divorce Act* if divorce proceedings have been commenced by a spouse. The court may make an order respecting any "child of the marriage."

"Child of the marriage" is defined in section 2(1) of the Act to mean a child of two spouses or former spouses who, at the material time,

- is under the age of majority and who has not withdrawn from their charge, or
- is the age of majority or over, and is under their charge, but unable, by reason of illness, disability, or other cause, to withdraw from their charge or to obtain the necessaries of life.

Accordingly, the court has jurisdiction to make a custody order with respect to a disabled child over the age of 18 who is in the care of one or both parents.

Under section 2(2) of the Act, a child of two spouses or former spouses includes

- any child for whom the spouses both stand in the place of parents, and
- any child of whom one is the parent and for whom the other stands in the place of a parent.

Accordingly, a child of only one spouse is considered to be a child of the marriage if the other spouse acted as a parent to the child, even if that spouse never formally adopted the child.

Definition of Custody and Access

The *Divorce Act* gives a partial definition of custody in section 2(1), stating that custody "includes care, upbringing and any other incident of custody," and gives no definition of access. However, section 16(5) of the Act states that unless ordered otherwise, a spouse who is granted access to a child has the right to make inquiries and to be given information about the health, education, and welfare of the child.

Who May Apply for Custody?

Pursuant to sections 16(1) and (3) of the Act, an application for custody may be made by either or both spouses, or by any other person. However, a person other than a spouse may not make a custody application without leave of the court.

Orders That May Be Made

Under section 16(4) of the Act, the court may make an order granting custody of, or access to, any or all children of the marriage to any one or more persons. (This section authorizes the court to make an order granting joint custody.) Section 16(6) gives the court the power to impose terms, conditions, or restrictions as it thinks fit and just.

Pursuant to section 16(7), the court may require a person who has custody of a child to give at least 30 days' notice to any person who has access of an intention to change the child's place of residence. This notice period gives non-custodial parents and others with access time to take steps to prevent the move if they wish. (For a more complete discussion of the right of a custodial parent to change the child's place of residence, see the section entitled "Variation of Custody Orders," which can be found later in this chapter.)

Section 16(2) provides for the making of interim orders with respect to custody and access.

Factors in Deciding Custody

Section 16(8) of the Act states that, in making an order for custody or access,

> the court shall take into consideration only the best interests of the child of the marriage as determined by reference to the condition, means, needs and other circumstances of the child.

The Act does not give a definition of "best interests of the child," nor does it direct the court to any specific factors to consider. However, in section 16(9), the court is directed not to take into consideration the past conduct of any person unless the conduct is relevant to the ability of that person to act as a parent of a child.

In addition, in section 16(10), the court is directed to give effect to the principle that a child of the marriage should have as much contact with each spouse as is consistent with the best interests of the child and, for that purpose, to take into consideration the willingness of the person seeking custody to facilitate that contact. Accordingly, it is important for a parent seeking custody to demonstrate a willingness to provide access to the other parent.

Custody Under the Children's Law Reform Act

Application of the Act

If no divorce proceeding has been started, custody of a child is determined under Part III of the *Children's Law Reform Act*.

If a proceeding for custody is started under the *Children's Law Reform Act* and a divorce proceeding is subsequently commenced, any custody or access application that has not been determined is stayed except by leave of the court pursuant to section 27 of the *Children's Law Reform Act*.

A child is defined by section 18(2) of the Act to mean a child under the age of 18. Unlike the *Divorce Act*, the *Children's Law Reform Act* confers no jurisdiction on a court to make a custody order with respect to an adult child who is disabled.

Definition of Parent

The *Divorce Act* focuses on the custody rights and obligations of spouses. The *Children's Law Reform Act*, however, deals with the rights and obligations of parents rather than simply spouses. As a result of recent amendments to the statute, the determination of parentage has been clarified to address the parental rights and obligations of the parties involved in the use of various methods of reproductive technology.

While custody and access are dealt with in Part III of the Act, the determination of parentage is dealt with in Part I.

According to section 4(2) of the Act, a parent of a child is stated to be a parent under sections 6 to 13 of the Act. The effect of those sections is summarized below.

The following are parents of a child:

- The woman who gave birth to the child (the birth parent), unless she is surrogate (see below).
- The man whose sperm resulted in the conception of the child, if the child was conceived through sexual intercourse.
- The spouse of the birth parent of a child conceived through insemination by a sperm donor or through assisted reproduction, defined as a method of conceiving other than by sexual intercourse.
- The parties to a written pre-conception parentage agreement, who have agreed to be parents of the child (see below).
- The parties who have agreed to be the parents of a child under a surrogacy agreement (see below).

Under the Act, a spouse means a person to whom a person is married or with whom the person is living in a conjugal relationship outside marriage.

The following are not parents of a child:

- A third-party sperm donor if the child has been conceived through assisted reproduction.
- A third-party egg donor if the child has been conceived through assisted reproduction.
- A surrogate under a surrogacy agreement, provided that she relinquishes the entitlement to parentage of the child by consent in writing given after the child is seven days old.

Pre-Conception Parentage Agreement

According to section 9 of the Act, a pre-conception parentage agreement is "a written agreement between two or more parties in which they agree to be, together, the parents of a child yet to be conceived." There may be no more than four parties to the agreement, and the parties must include

- the intended birth parent (who must not be a surrogate),
- the person whose sperm is used if the child is to be conceived through sexual intercourse, or
- the spouse, if any, of the intended birth parent, unless he or she provides written confirmation that he or she does not consent to be a parent of the child if the child is to be conceived through assisted reproduction or through insemination by a sperm donor.

> Ellen and Portia are a married, same-sex couple, as are Neil and David. They are very good friends and decide to have a child together, and all wish to be parents to the child. They decide that Portia will be the birth parent through insemination by sperm donated by Neil.
>
> In the absence of a pre-conception agreement, Portia, as the birth parent, will be a parent of the child, and Ellen, as Portia's spouse, will also be recognized as a parent of the child, but neither Neil, as a sperm donor, nor David will be a parent of the child. However, if they enter into a pre-conception parentage agreement, on the birth of the child, they will all be recognized in law to be the parents.

On the birth of a child contemplated by a pre-conception agreement, all of the parties to the agreement are recognized in law to be the parents of the child.

Surrogacy Agreement

A surrogate is defined in section 1 of the Act as "a person who agrees to carry a child conceived through assisted reproduction if, at the time of conception, the person intends to relinquish entitlement to parentage of the child, once born, to one or more persons."

According to section 10 of the Act, a surrogacy agreement is "a written agreement between a surrogate and one or more persons, the intended parent(s), respecting a child to be carried by the surrogate, in which the surrogate agrees not to be a parent of the child, and each of the other parties to the agreement agrees to be a parent of the child." A surrogacy agreement must satisfy the following conditions:

- it is entered into before the child is conceived,
- each party receives independent legal advice,
- there are no more than four intended parents under the agreement, and
- the child will be conceived through assisted reproduction.

After the birth of the child, each intended parent is recognized in law to be a parent of the child, and the surrogate ceases to be a parent of the child if, not earlier than seven days after the birth of the child, the surrogate gives the intended parent(s) consent in writing relinquishing her entitlement to parentage. If the surrogate refuses to provide the consent, any party to the agreement may apply to the court for a declaration of parentage, to be determined by the court on the basis of the best interests of the child.

Definition of Custody and Access

As we've just seen, it is possible for a child to have more than two parents. However, for the purposes of our discussion, we will assume a two-parent family.

According to section 20(2) of the Act, a person entitled to custody of a child has the rights and responsibilities of a parent with respect to that child, and must exercise those rights and responsibilities in the best interests of the child.

The Act sets out the custody rights of the respective parents during cohabitation and following a separation. It starts in section 20(1) with the statement that the child's parents are equally entitled to custody. In section 20(3), it states that where more than one person is entitled to custody, any one of them may exercise the rights of custody on behalf of them. Accordingly, if both parents are residing together, they both have custody, and either one of them can make decisions with respect to the child.

Section 20(4) of the Act clarifies the rights of the parties after a separation and before any court order is made. If the child lives with one parent with the consent or acquiescence of the other parent, the right of that other parent to custody is suspended until a separation agreement or court order provides otherwise. A parent who leaves a child in the care of the other parent cannot unilaterally return and take the child away. That parent's custody rights are suspended unless he or she gets a court order or enters into a separation agreement giving him or her custody.

The term "access" is defined in section 20(5) to include the right to visit with and be visited by the child and the same right as a parent to make inquiries and to be given information as to the health, education, and welfare of the child.

Who May Apply for Custody?

Under section 21 of the Act, a parent of a child or any other person, including a grandparent, may apply to the court for custody or access. A non-parent does not require leave of the court to make an application as is necessary under the *Divorce Act*.

Orders That May Be Made

The powers of the court on an application are set out in section 28. The court may

- grant custody or access to one or more persons,
- determine any aspect of the incidents of the right to custody or access, and
- make any other order it considers necessary and proper in the circumstances.

Factors in Deciding Custody

Pursuant to section 24, an application for custody or access is to be determined on the basis of the best interests of the child. Unlike the *Divorce Act*, the *Children's Law Reform Act* lists a number of factors that the court should take into account. The court is directed to consider "all the needs and circumstances of the child," including:

- the love, affection, and emotional ties between the child and each person, including a grandparent, entitled to or claiming custody or access, other members of the child's family who reside with the child, and persons involved in the child's care and upbringing;
- the views and preferences of the child;
- the length of time the child has lived in a stable home environment;

- the ability and willingness of each person applying for custody to provide the child with guidance and education, the necessaries of life, and any special needs of the child;

- proposed plans for the care and upbringing of the child;

- the permanence and stability of the proposed custodial family unit;

- the ability of each person applying for custody of or access to the child to act as a parent; and

- any familial relationship between the child and the person applying for custody.

Under sections 24(3) to (5), the past conduct of the person applying for custody is not to be considered unless (a) the person has at any time committed violence or abuse against his or her spouse, a parent of the child, or a member of the person's household or any child, or (b) the court is satisfied that the conduct is otherwise relevant to the ability of the person to act as a parent of a child.

Custody Assessments

What is a court to do when presented with two parents who seek custody of a child? How is a court to decide who is the better parent and what arrangements will be in the best interests of the child?

Under the Children's Law Reform Act

Under section 30 of the *Children's Law Reform Act*, the court can appoint a person who has "technical or professional skill" (such as a psychiatrist, psychologist, or social worker) to assess and report to the court on the needs of the child and the "ability and willingness" of the parties to satisfy the needs of the child.

If an assessment is ordered, a professional meets with the parents and the child separately and in various combinations, and then writes a report for the court containing his or her observations, conclusions, and recommendations.

An assessment report can help a court in deciding the issue of custody. It can also encourage settlement by allowing a parent to withdraw a custody claim if that parent becomes satisfied that it would be in the best interests of the child for the other parent to have custody. An assessment report does not necessarily determine the issue. Parties have been known to fight on in the face of a negative report. It is the responsibility of the judge, not the assessor, to make the decision regarding custody. The judge is not bound to follow the recommendations in an assessment report, but it is an uphill battle to overcome an assessment report that has been made by a qualified and responsible professional.

Notwithstanding the usefulness of assessment reports, the court will not automatically order an assessment if one of the parties opposes it. For some time, the courts have held that the costs of an assessment and the length of time required to complete it are generally not warranted unless there are "clinical issues" to be determined.

The mechanics of getting an assessment are set out in section 30. The court can order an assessment on the request of either party or on its own motion. The court chooses the assessor, a person agreed upon by the parties if possible. The assessor must consent to the appointment. The court makes an order regarding payment for the assessment. The order may require the attendance of the parties, the child, or any other person. Adverse inferences may be drawn if a party fails to attend.

Once the report is prepared, the assessor is required to file it with the court, which then gives a copy to the parties. The report is admissible in the hearing of the custody application, and either party may require the assessor to testify. Either party is entitled to lead other expert evidence on the issue of custody.

Under the Divorce Act

There is no provision in the *Divorce Act* for the ordering of an assessment. However, the court has inherent jurisdiction to do so if it is of the opinion that an assessment is necessary.

Mediation

Mediation is a process in which a neutral third party meets with the parties to a dispute to help them reach an agreement. The mediator assists the parties in identifying the matters underlying their dispute and the possible solutions. It is up to the parties to arrive at a voluntary agreement. The mediator does not impose a solution.

Parties to a mediation decide in advance whether the mediation is to be open or closed. In an open mediation, the mediator is allowed to disclose to the court anything the parties say during the mediation. In a closed mediation, anything said by the parties is confidential, and the mediator can disclose to the court only whether or not an agreement was reached.

Under section 9 of the *Divorce Act*, every legal adviser who acts for a spouse in a divorce action has a duty to tell the spouse of the advisability of negotiating a settlement of custody (and support) matters, and to inform him or her of mediation facilities that might be able to assist the spouses to achieve a reconciliation.

Under section 31 of the *Children's Law Reform Act*, the court may appoint a mediator at the request of the parties. A court will make the order only if both parties agree to mediation and to the mediator, and if the mediator consents to act. Before entering into mediation, the parties decide whether the mediation is to be open or closed.

Enforcement of Custody Orders

Under the Children's Law Reform Act

Sections 34 to 39 deal with enforcement of custody and access orders.

Under section 34, the court may order that custody or access be supervised by a person, a children's aid society, or another body if there is a concern that a child will be harmed or abducted while in a party's custody, or while access is being exercised. The supervising party must consent to act before an order is made.

Under section 35, the court may make an order restraining a person from contacting or communicating with the applicant or the children in the applicant's lawful custody, or restraining the respondent from coming within a specified distance of one or more locations.

Under section 36, the court may direct the sheriff or the police force to locate, apprehend, and deliver a child to the person lawfully entitled to custody or access, if a court is satisfied that there are reasonable and probable grounds for believing that someone is unlawfully withholding the child from that person, or is proposing to remove the child from Ontario contrary to a separation agreement or court order.

Section 37 gives the court the power to make orders with respect to property, support payments, and passports in order to prevent a party from unlawfully removing a child from Ontario.

Section 38 gives the Ontario Court of Justice powers to punish willful contempt of custody or access orders by fine or imprisonment or both.

Under section 39, the court may make orders requiring any person or public body to provide the court with particulars of the address of the respondent, where the court is of the opinion that the information is necessary for the purpose of bringing a custody or access application or enforcing a custody or access order.

Under the Divorce Act

Pursuant to section 20 of the *Divorce Act*, a custody or access order has legal effect throughout Canada. It may be registered in any court in a province and enforced as an order of that court.

Variation of Custody Orders

A custody or access order, whether made under the *Divorce Act* or under the *Children's Law Reform Act*, is never final and is always subject to variation if the circumstances of the parties and/or the children change.

Under the Divorce Act

A custody order made under the *Divorce Act* must be varied under that Act by way of a variation proceeding. Variation of custody (and support) orders is dealt with under section 17 of the Act.

A variation proceeding may be commenced by either or both former spouses or any other person, although a person other than a former spouse requires leave of the court. The court has the power to vary, rescind, or suspend a custody order or any provision thereof. A court may include in a variation order any provisions that could be included in a custody order.

Section 17(5) sets out the factors that a court is to consider in a variation proceeding. It states that before a court makes a variation order, the court must satisfy itself that there has been a change in the condition, means, needs, or other circumstances of the child since the making of the custody order. The section also states that in making the variation order, the court shall take into consideration only the best interests of the child as determined by reference to that change.

As in the making of a custody order, the court may not take into consideration the past conduct of any person unless the conduct is relevant to the ability of that person to act as a parent of the child. The court is also directed to give effect to the principle that a child should have as much contact with each former spouse as is consistent with the best interests of the child. Where the variation order would grant custody of the child to a person who does not currently have custody, the court is directed to take into consideration the willingness of the person seeking custody to facilitate that contact.

Under the Children's Law Reform Act

A custody order made under the *Children's Law Reform Act* must be varied under that Act. Variation of custody orders is dealt with in section 29. According to that section, a court must not make an order that varies a custody or access order unless there has been a material change in circumstances that affects or is likely to affect the best interests of the child.

Principles Applied in Varying Custody Orders

While the language of the statutes differs, courts apply the same principles whether a case is decided under the *Children's Law Reform Act* or the *Divorce Act*.

Under either statute, the party who applies to vary the original order must show that a material change in circumstances that affects the best interests of the child has occurred since the original order was made. If the applicant meets this threshold test, the court will consider whether a variation in the existing order is necessary to meet the best interests of the child under these changed circumstances.

A variation application is not an appeal. It is not designed to correct an error made by the trial judge. A court hearing a variation application assumes that the original order was correctly made.

The Right of a Custodial Parent to Move the Child's Residence

Many variation applications arise because a parent who has been granted custody wishes to move with the child, but the other parent objects because the move will make it difficult or impossible for that parent to exercise access rights. An application to vary the custody order may be brought by the custodial parent to seek permission of the court to relocate, or it may be brought by the access parent to prevent the move.

Should the court give greater weight to the right of the custodial parent to get on with his or her life, even if that involves moving the child far away from the access parent? Should it give greater weight to the right of the access parent to continue an established pattern of access visits? In the case of *Gordon v Goertz*,[3] the Supreme Court of Canada made it clear that there is no legal presumption in favour of the

---

3   [1996] 2 SCR 27.

custodial parent. In fact, the issue does not involve the parents' rights. The primary concern is the best interests of the child in the particular circumstances of the case. The court should consider, among other things,

- the relationship between the child and the custodial parent;
- the existing access arrangement and the relationship between the child and the access parent;
- the desirability of maximizing contact between the child and both parents;
- the views of the child;
- the custodial parent's reason for moving only if it is relevant to that parent's ability to meet the needs of the child;
- the disruption that would be caused to the child if custody were changed; and
- the disruption that would be caused to the child if the child were moved away from family, schools, and community.

Ultimately, the court must weigh the benefits of the child's remaining in the care of the custodial parent in a new location against the benefits of a change in custody that maintains contact with the access parent, extended family, and community.

A court has at least two options:

- The parent wishing to move keeps custody and is given permission to move.
- The parent wishing to move is given an option: either stay and keep custody or move and lose custody.

Public Policy Concerns About Custody and Access

There have been various proposals over the years for legislative changes designed to reduce the adversarial aspects in resolving custody and access issues between separating parents.

In December 2002, the federal government announced a child-centred family justice strategy whose objective is to help parents focus on the needs of their children following separation and divorce, and thereby minimize the potentially negative impact of separation and divorce.

As part of this strategy, in late 2002, the government proposed amendments to the *Divorce Act* that would eliminate the terms "custody" and "access" from the Act. It was proposed that the Act instead use the term "parenting arrangements," under which the parties allocate "parenting time" and "decision-making responsibilities," and the term "parenting order" instead of "custody order." The bill containing these proposed amendments died on the order paper. However, some lawyers now use this new terminology in their separation agreements.

CHAPTER SUMMARY

If separating parents cannot decide which of them will live with and care for their children, a court will decide for them. If a spouse has started a divorce proceeding, custody and access are determined under the *Divorce Act*. If not, custody and access are determined under the *Children's Law Reform Act*.

The *Divorce Act* says that custody "includes care, upbringing and any other incident of custody," but gives no definition of access. Under the *Children's Law Reform Act*, "access" means the right to visit with the child as well as to make inquiries and to be given information regarding the child's health, education, and welfare.

Both statutes allow any person to apply for custody or access of a child, although under the *Divorce Act*, a non-parent requires the permission of the court. The *Children's Law Reform Act* contains provisions expanding the definition of "parent" to address developments in reproductive technology. Under either statute, a court may grant custody or access to any one or more persons. The court may impose such terms, conditions, or restrictions as it considers appropriate under the circumstances.

Custody is always determined on the basis of the "best interests of the child." The most important factor in any custody dispute is maintaining the status quo, so the parent who is awarded interim custody will generally win permanent custody at the trial. The *Children's Law Reform Act* directs the court to consider "all the needs and circumstances of the child" when granting custody or access, and lists specific factors. Under this Act, the court can appoint someone to assess the needs of the child and the "ability and willingness" of the parties to satisfy those needs.

The spouses' lawyers must advise mediation under the *Divorce Act*. The court may appoint a mediator at the request of the parties under the *Children's Law Reform Act*.

A court's orders under the *Children's Law Reform Act* may include supervised custody or access, restraining orders, and prevention of a party from unlawfully removing a child from Ontario. Under the *Divorce Act*, custody or access orders have legal effect throughout Canada. A custody or access order is never final and is always subject to variation if circumstances change.

KEY TERMS

access, 58
custody, 58
de facto custody, 59

joint custody, 58
jurisdiction shopping, 57
sole custody, 58

REVIEW QUESTIONS

1. When do the Ontario courts have jurisdiction over custody under the *Divorce Act*?

2. When do the Ontario courts have jurisdiction over custody under the *Children's Law Reform Act*?

3. What is meant by "custody"?

4. What is meant by "access"?

5. What is the primary factor in determining custody?

6. Why do courts make interim or temporary custody awards?

7. What is the definition of "child of the marriage" under the *Divorce Act*?

8. Does a court have jurisdiction to make a custody order with respect to a disabled child over the age of 18 under the *Divorce Act*?

9. Who may apply for custody under the *Divorce Act*?

10. What is the definition of a "child" under the *Children's Law Reform Act*?

11. Does a court have jurisdiction to make a custody order with respect to a disabled child over the age of 18 under the *Children's Law Reform Act*?

12. Who may apply for custody under the *Children's Law Reform Act*?

13. When and how can a party obtain an order for a custody assessment under the *Children's Law Reform Act*?

14. What is mediation?

15. What provisions of the *Divorce Act* address mediation? What provisions of the *Children's Law Reform Act* address mediation?

16. Summarize the provisions of the *Children's Law Reform Act* that deal with enforcement of custody and access orders.

17. What factors must a court consider in varying a custody order under the *Divorce Act*?

18. What factors must a court consider in varying a custody order under the *Children's Law Reform Act*?

19. Summarize the changes to the custody provisions of the *Divorce Act* that were proposed in 2002.

DISCUSSION QUESTIONS

1. Hugh and Elizabeth were married in England and lived there after the marriage. They had one child and subsequently separated. In England, Elizabeth won custody of the child and Hugh was granted access. Hugh then moved to Ontario. While exercising access on a visit to England, Hugh decided that he should have custody of the child. He did not return the child to Elizabeth at the end of his access period, but instead took the child with him back to Ontario. On the day after he returned, Hugh commenced a custody proceeding under the *Children's Law Reform Act*. Should the Ontario courts assume jurisdiction in this matter? Discuss.

2. What is the concern of the courts in determining custody? What are some of the factors that a court might consider under the *Children's Law Reform Act*? What factors are the court directed to ignore under that Act? How can a court obtain objective information to help it determine the issue of custody?

3. Jodie and Alexandra are a married, same-sex couple, as are George and Brad. They are very good friends and want to have a child together. They arrange for Jodie to become pregnant through insemination by sperm donated by George. Jodie gives birth to a son named Charles. In the absence of any form of agreement, who will be recognized as the parents of Charles? Is there any sort of agreement that can change that situation?

4. Calista and Harrison divorced several years ago. They have always lived in Ontario. The divorce judgment gave Calista custody of the children, and access to Harrison. It contained no other provisions about custody. Calista is getting married again, and she and her new husband want to move to Hollywood, California. What right does Calista have to move with the children? Can Harrison do anything to stop her? Discuss.

Spousal Support

7

LEARNING OUTCOMES

After completing this chapter, you should be able to:

- State which legislation applies to a particular support situation.

- Explain the role of the *Spousal Support Advisory Guidelines* in determining spousal support.

- Calculate the amount and duration of spousal support payments using the "Without Child Support Formula" under the *Spousal Support Advisory Guidelines*.

- Explain the "With Child Support Formula" under the *Spousal Support Advisory Guidelines*.

- Describe the steps to be taken under the *Spousal Support Advisory Guidelines* after the formulas have been applied.

- Explain the tax treatment of spousal support orders.

And, with regard to the *Divorce Act* and the *Family Law Act*, you should be able to:

- Explain when a party is entitled to claim spousal support.

- Explain the factors that determine when a party is entitled to receive support.

- Explain the factors that determine the amount and duration of support payments.

- Describe the different types of support orders.

- State the statutory basis for variation of spousal support orders.

Introduction

In Ontario, every spouse has an obligation to be self-supporting to the extent that he or she is able. Once a spouse satisfies that obligation, he or she has an obligation, to the extent that he or she is able, to support the other spouse in accordance with that person's need. The obligation to support one's spouse continues after the parties separate, and a court may order one spouse to pay support to the other.

Spousal support is dealt with under both the *Family Law Act*[1] and the *Divorce Act*.[2] Support is decided on the basis of the need of the spouse applying for support, and the ability of the other spouse to pay.

In this chapter we will be looking at the law of spousal support, including:

- the parties entitled to claim support,
- the applicable legislation,
- the factors that determine support entitlement,
- the types of support orders,
- the amount and duration of support payments,
- the *Spousal Support Advisory Guidelines*,[3]
- the tax treatment of support orders, and
- the variation of support orders.

Parties Entitled to Claim Support

The parties entitled to assert a claim for support differ under the *Divorce Act* and the *Family Law Act*.

Under the Divorce Act

limitation period
a certain time allowed by a statute for the commencement of a court proceeding

Under section 2 of the *Divorce Act*, "spouse" is defined as "either of two persons who are married to each other" and includes a former spouse. Accordingly, only spouses who are or were validly married to each other have the right to make a claim for spousal support. To make a claim for support, one of the parties must have started a divorce action. The right to assert a claim for support continues indefinitely, even after the parties divorce. There is no **limitation period** set out in the Act.

---

1   RSO 1990, c F.3.

2   RSC 1985, c 3 (2d Supp).

3   Canada, Department of Justice, *Spousal Support Advisory Guidelines*, by Carol Rogerson and Rollie Thompson (Ottawa: Department of Justice, July 2008) online: <http://www.canada.justice.gc.ca/eng/rp-pr/fl-lf/spousal-epoux/spag/pdf/SSAG_eng.pdf>.

Under the Family Law Act

The definition of a "spouse" is much broader under the support provisions of the *Family Law Act*. "Spouse" is defined in section 29 to mean either of two persons

- who are married to each other, or
- who have entered into a void or voidable marriage in good faith on the part of the person asserting the claim for support, or
- who are not married to each other and have cohabited
  - continuously for a period of not less than three years, or
  - in a relationship of some permanence, if they are the parents of a child.

To "**cohabit**" means to live together in a conjugal relationship, whether within or outside of marriage.

The right to support arises as soon as one satisfies the definition of a "spouse." The right can be asserted before or after separation, and continues indefinitely. There is no limitation period set out in the Act.

cohabit
to live together in a conjugal relationship within or outside of marriage

Applicable Legislation

Courts apply the same principles in deciding the amount and duration of spousal support under both the *Divorce Act* and the *Family Law Act*. The circumstances of the parties determine which statute applies.

The *Divorce Act* applies only to validly married spouses. Spouses who are not validly married must apply for spousal support under the *Family Law Act*.

For the *Divorce Act* to apply, one of the spouses must start a divorce proceeding. To be able to do so, he or she must have been resident in the province in which the proceeding is started for at least one year immediately before the commencement of the proceeding. If neither spouse can satisfy the residence requirements of the *Divorce Act*, any application for spousal support must be made under the *Family Law Act*.

If the parties have already divorced, and no support claim was made at the time, subsequent claims for support must be made in corollary relief proceedings under the *Divorce Act*.

Section 36(1) of the *Family Law Act* sets out what happens when a support application is started under the *Family Law Act* before a divorce proceeding in which one of the spouses seeks support is commenced.

- Any support application under the *Family Law Act* that has not been adjudicated is stayed unless the court gives permission for it to continue.
- Any interim order made under the *Family Law Act* continues in force unless and until it is superseded by an order under the *Divorce Act*. Neither party can apply to vary the *Family Law Act* order, nor can either party apply for a final order under the *Family Law Act*.

- Any final support order obtained under the *Family Law Act* before the divorce proceeding was commenced continues in force unless and until it is superseded by an order under the *Divorce Act*. If neither party seeks a support order under the *Divorce Act*, the *Family Law Act* order continues in effect. If one of the parties seeks a support order under the *Divorce Act*, the *Family Law Act* order can be incorporated into the divorce judgment or replaced with a new and different order.

Factors That Determine Support Entitlement

Both the *Divorce Act* and the *Family Law Act* set out factors to be taken into account in determining whether a party is entitled to a support order.

Language of the Divorce Act

A claim for spousal support under the *Divorce Act* is made under section 15.2. Section 15.2(1) gives the court the power to make an order requiring a spouse to pay an amount that the court thinks reasonable for the support of the other spouse.

In making an order for spousal support, the court is directed by section 15.2(4) to take into consideration "the condition, means, needs and other circumstances of each spouse," including

- the length of time the spouses cohabited,
- the role played by each spouse during the marriage, and
- any orders or agreements with respect to support that may exist between the parties.

Section 15.2(6) sets out the objectives of a spousal support order as follows:

- to recognize any economic advantages or disadvantages to the spouses arising from the marriage or its breakdown,
- to apportion between the spouses any financial consequences arising from child care,
- to relieve economic hardship arising from the marriage breakdown, and
- to promote the economic self-sufficiency of the spouses as far as is practicable within a reasonable period of time.

Section 15.2(5) makes it clear that misconduct of a spouse is not a factor in determining spousal support.

Language of the Family Law Act

Under section 30 of the *Family Law Act*, every spouse has an obligation to provide support for himself or herself and for the other spouse, in accordance with need, to the extent that he or she is capable of doing so. In other words, an award of support is based on the dependent spouse's need and the other spouse's ability to pay, while still meeting his or her own needs.

A claim for support under the *Family Law Act* is made under section 33, which gives the court the power to order a person to provide support for his or her dependants.

Section 33(8) sets out the purposes of a support order, which are

- to recognize the spouse's contribution to the relationship and the economic consequences to the spouse of the relationship,
- to share the economic burden of child support equitably,
- to assist the spouse to become able to contribute to his or her own support, and
- to relieve financial hardship (if this has not been done by orders dividing the property of the spouses).

Under section 33(10), the obligation to provide support for a spouse exists without regard to the conduct of either spouse.

How the Courts Decide

The factors in the *Divorce Act* and the *Family Law Act* are similar, and a court considering a support claim would make the same decision under both statutes.

Although both statutes base entitlement to support on need, for some time, starting with the Supreme Court of Canada's decision in *Moge v Moge*,[4] the need of a spouse alone was not enough to warrant a support order. The courts looked for a causal connection between a spouse's need for support and the spousal relationship. Support orders were seen as a way to compensate a spouse for economic disadvantages, such as an abandoned career and/or missed opportunities, that arose as a result of the marriage or its breakdown. However, in *Bracklow v Bracklow*,[5] the Supreme Court of Canada made it clear that a spouse who needs support, but who has not been handicapped by the marriage, may still be entitled to support if the other spouse has the ability to pay. As a result, entitlement to spousal support falls into one or both of two categories:

- **Compensatory claims** based on (a) the recipient spouse's economic loss or disadvantage because of the marriage, usually a reduction in the ability to earn income because of the roles assumed by the spouses during the marriage, or (b) the recipient spouse's conferral of an economic benefit on the other spouse, such as supporting that spouse through professional training.
- **Non-compensatory claims** based on need, which can mean an inability to meet basic needs or a significant reduction in the recipient spouse's standard of living compared with that of the marriage.

compensatory claim
a claim for spousal support based on the recipient spouse's economic loss or disadvantage because of the marriage

non-compensatory claim
a claim for spousal support based on need

---

4   [1992] 3 SCR 813.

5   [1999] 1 SCR 420.

Rob and Laura were married when they were in their mid-20s. Laura was working as a keypunch operator (entering data on computer cards), and Rob was working as a television comedy writer. Rob and Laura had their first child three years later. The couple agreed that Laura should stop working to care for the child. Over the next nine years, Rob and Laura had three more children. Laura continued to stay home as a full-time mother. Rob continued to work in television and was very successful. Over time, Rob became the producer of a number of successful television shows and movies. Now Rob and Laura have recently separated after more than 25 years of marriage. The only child still at home is the youngest, aged 16. The oldest child is living on his own, and the other two children are in university. Laura would like spousal support from Rob.

The court should have no difficulty in finding Laura entitled to spousal support. While Laura no longer needs to stay at home to care for the children, she will find it very difficult to be self-supporting. She has not worked for 25 years because of the role that she and Rob agreed she should play in the family, and her only previous work experience is in a job that is now obsolete.

Amount and Duration of Support

Once it is established that a spouse is entitled to support, a court must decide the **quantum** of support (how much support should be paid) and the duration of the support payments (how long support should be paid).

quantum
amount

When a support order is made under the *Family Law Act*, the court is directed to consider the factors set out in section 33(9) of the Act, which include:

- the parties' current assets and means,
- the respondent's ability to pay,
- the dependant's needs with reference to the parties' accustomed standard of living,
- the dependant's ability to contribute to his or her own support,
- the measures available for the dependant to become self-supporting,
- the dependant's age and health, and
- contribution by the dependant to the realization of the respondent's career potential.

While the conduct of the couple is not a factor in determining entitlement to support, the court may, under section 33(10), "have regard to a course of conduct that is so unconscionable as to constitute an obvious and gross repudiation of the relationship." Under this section, such conduct of the dependent spouse could serve to reduce the support that might otherwise be paid. Poor conduct on the part of the respondent spouse does not increase the amount of support. The kind of conduct required to reduce support is such that could reasonably be expected to destroy the relationship.

When a support order is made under the *Divorce Act*, the quantum and duration of the support is determined in accordance with the factors set out in section 15.2(4) and the objectives set out in section 15.2(6). Under section 15.2(5), conduct is not a factor in determining the quantum and duration of support.

Although both the *Divorce Act* and the *Family Law Act* speak of an obligation to be self-supporting, in deciding on the quantum and duration of support payments, the courts have recognized that a person who has been out of the workforce for a number of years may never be able to be completely self-supporting.

The court requires information about the assets and debts and the income and expenses of both parties in order to determine the amount of support. The rules of procedure of the Ontario courts require the parties to make full and complete financial disclosure to each other and to the court so that this information is available. See Chapter 11 for a discussion of financial disclosure in connection with support applications.

Spousal Support Advisory Guidelines

In 2001, the federal government launched a Spousal Support Project to explore the possibility of developing advisory spousal support guidelines to bring more certainty and predictability to the determination of spousal support under the *Divorce Act*. In January 2005, the project released a report entitled *Spousal Support Advisory Guidelines: A Draft Proposal*.[6] Over the next few years, the draft advisory guidelines were used in thousands of support cases across Canada and were considered in over 350 reported court decisions. After obtaining feedback, submissions, comments, and suggestions from members of the public, lawyers, and mediators, the Spousal Support Project released a final revised version of the *Spousal Support Advisory Guidelines* in July 2008.

Unlike the *Federal Child Support Guidelines*,[7] the *Spousal Support Advisory Guidelines* have not been legislated. They are intended as informal guidelines, which operate on an advisory basis only, to help parties, lawyers, mediators, and judges determine the amount and duration of spousal support. The advisory guidelines do *not* deal with entitlement to support, but only the amount and duration of support once entitlement has been established.[8] They were developed specifically for use under the federal *Divorce Act*. However, because the applicable principles are the same as those under the *Family Law Act*, the guidelines may be used under that legislation as well.

The guidelines contain two basic formulas for calculating spousal support: the *without child support* formula and the *with child support* formula. The *without child*

---

6 Canada, Department of Justice, *Spousal Support Advisory Guidelines: A Draft Proposal*, by Carol Rogerson and Rollie Thompson (Ottawa: Department of Justice, January 2005) online: <https://www.law.utoronto.ca/documents/rogerson/spousal_draftreport_en.pdf>.

7 SOR/97-175.

8 According to the language of the guidelines, "Entitlement is a threshold issue before the Advisory Guidelines apply."

support formula is used if there are no dependent children and, therefore, no child support obligations. The *with child support* formula is used if there are dependent children for whom child support must be paid (by either spouse). As set out in the executive summary of the guidelines:

> Both formulas use *income sharing* as the method for determining the amount of spousal support, not budgets. The formulas produce *ranges* for the amount and duration of support, not just a single number. The precise number chosen within that range is a matter for negotiation or adjudication, depending upon the facts of a particular case.
>
> The starting point under both formulas is the definition of *income* used in the *Federal Child Support Guidelines*, subject to some minor adjustments. ...

The Without Child Support Formula

without child support formula
the formula used to calculate spousal support under the *Spousal Support Advisory Guidelines* if there are no dependent children and, therefore, no child support obligations

The **without child support formula** calculates the amount and duration of support by looking at the difference between the spouses' gross incomes (the *gross income difference*) and the length of the relationship (including periods of pre-marital cohabitation), as follows:

- *Amount of support* will be between 1.5 and 2 percent of the *gross income difference* for each year of cohabitation (during marriage and before) up to a maximum range of between 37.5 and 50 percent of the gross income difference for marriages of 25 years or more. (The upper end of this maximum range is capped at the amount that would result in equalization of the spouses' net incomes—the *net income cap*.)
- *Duration of support* is 0.5 to 1 year of support for each year of cohabitation, with duration becoming indefinite after 20 years or, if the marriage has lasted 5 years or longer, when the years of marriage and age of the support recipient at separation added together total 65 or more (the "rule of 65").

The formula produces a range both for amount and duration of support. The basis of entitlement to support—compensatory or non-compensatory—determines the location within the range. A compensatory claim for support would likely result in a support award at the higher end of the ranges for both amount and duration than would a non-compensatory claim. However, if the recipient has limited income and/or capacity to earn income, because of age or other circumstances, his or her needs may also result in an award at the higher end of the ranges for amount and duration.

The *without child support* formula calculations can be done manually, as can be seen in the examples reproduced below from the *Spousal Support Advisory Guidelines*.

The first example deals with a short marriage, one of under five years' duration. The basic formula applies in this situation, without modification, as to both amount and duration.

Example 1: A Short Marriage

Karl and Beth were married for only four years. They had no children. Beth was 25 when they met and Karl was 30. When they married, Beth was a struggling artist. Karl is a music teacher with a gross annual income of $60,000. Beth now earns $20,000 per year, selling her work and giving art lessons to children. Entitlement is a threshold issue before the Advisory Guidelines apply. On these facts, given the disparity in income and Beth's limited income at the point of the marriage breakdown, entitlement is likely to be found.

To determine the amount of support under the formula:

- Determine the **gross income difference** between the two parties.

    $60,000 − $20,000 = $40,000

- Determine the **applicable percentage** by multiplying the length of the marriage by 1.5 to 2 percent per year.

    1.5 × 4 years = **6 percent**

    to

    2 × 4 years = **8 percent**

- Apply the applicable percentage to the income difference.

    6 percent × $40,000 = $2,400/year (**$200 per month**)

    to

    8 percent × $40,000 = $3,200/year (**$267 per month**)

Duration of spousal support = (0.5 to 1) × 4 years of marriage = 2 to 4 years
The result under the formula is support in the range of $200 to $267 per month for a duration of 2 to 4 years.

The second example deals with a medium-length marriage, one of between five and 19 years' duration. The basic formula applies to a medium-length marriage in most situations. However, in this situation the rule of 65 applies because the marriage is over five years in duration *and* the wife's age at separation plus the length of the marriage is 65 or over. The rule of 65 affects the duration of support only. The basic rule still applies to the calculation of the amount of support.

Example 2: A Medium-Length Marriage Where the "Rule of 65" Applies

David and Jennifer were married for 12 years. It was a second marriage for both. David was 50 when they met. He is a businessman whose gross annual income is now $100,000 per year. Now 62, he is in good health, loves his work, and has no immediate plans to retire. Jennifer was 45 when they met, while Jennifer was working in his office. She had been a homemaker for 20 years during her first marriage and had received time-limited support. When they met, she was working in a low-level clerical position earning $20,000 gross per year. Jennifer, now 57, did not work outside the home during the marriage.

Entitlement is a threshold issue before the Advisory Guidelines are applicable. Given the length of the marriage and Jennifer's lack of income, entitlement to support on non-compensatory grounds would be relatively uncontentious.

The **amount** of support on an income difference of $100,000 and a 12-year marriage would be calculated as follows:

18 percent × $100,000 = $18,000/year (**$1,500/month**)

to

24 percent × $100,000 = $24,000/year (**$2,000/month**)

This is a case where the rule of 65 governs duration. Because Jennifer's age at separation plus years of marriage is 65 or over (57 + 12 = 69), the formula provides for indefinite support, rather than the durational range of 6 to 12 years based on length of marriage alone. A variation in amount would, however, be likely when David retires.

The result under the formula is support in the range of $1,500 to $2,000 a month on an indefinite basis, subject to variation.

The last example deals with a long marriage, one of twenty years or longer in duration. The basic formula continues to apply to the calculation of the amount of support in a long marriage unless the marriage has lasted more than 25 years. At that point, no matter how long the marriage, the percentages applied to the gross income difference (usually 1.5 to 2 percent for each year of marriage) are capped at 37.5 to 50 percent (equivalent to 1.5 to 2 percent for each of 25 years). The basic formula does not apply to the calculation of duration in a long marriage; support is always paid for an indefinite period. This example also illustrates the application of the "net income cap" under which the maximum amount of the support range is capped at the amount that would result in equalization of the spouses' net incomes.

Example 3: A Long Marriage

John and Mary were married for 28 years. Theirs was a traditional marriage in which John worked his way up the career ladder and now earns $100,000 gross per year, while Mary stayed home and raised their two children, both of whom are now grown and on their own. Mary is 50 years of age and has no income. John is 55.

Entitlement to spousal support is clear on these facts and thus the Advisory Guidelines are applicable. Because the length of the marriage is over 25 years, the maximum range for the amount applies—37.5 to 50 percent of the gross income difference (capped at equalization of net incomes).

> The range for amounts on an income difference of $100,000 after a 28-year marriage would be
>
> 37.5 percent × $100,000 = $37,500/year (**$3,125/month**)
>
> to
>
> 50 percent × $100,000 = $50,000/year (**$4,167/month, capped at $4,048**)
>
> **Duration** is indefinite because the marriage is 20 years or over in length.
>
> **The formula results in a range for support of $3,125 to $4,048 per month for an indefinite duration, subject to variation.**

The With Child Support Formula

The *with child support* formula is, in fact, a group of formulas depending on the custody and child support arrangements for the children:

- the *basic* formula—used where the recipient spouse has primary care of the children and is receiving both child and spousal support;
- the *shared custody* formula—used where the spouses share custody of the children;
- the *split custody* formula—used where spouses have more than one child, and each spouse has custody of one or more children;
- the *custodial payor* formula—used where the paying spouse has custody of the children; and
- the *adult child* formula—used where the only child support obligation exists with respect to children who are over the age of majority.

The *without child support* formula is different from the *with child support* formula in several ways. While the *without child support* formula uses the gross income of the spouses, the *with child support* formula uses the net income of the parties. In addition, the formula divides the *combined net incomes* of the spouses, not just the difference between their incomes. Finally, the percentages for the division of income do not change with the length of the marriage.

Under the basic formula, the amount of spousal support is calculated as follows:

1. Determine the *individual net disposable income* (INDI) of each spouse.
   a. Guidelines Income – Child Support – Taxes and Deductions = Payor's INDI
   b. Guidelines Income – Notional Child Support – Taxes and Deductions + Government Benefits and Credits = Recipient's INDI
2. Add together the INDIs. By iteration, determine the range of spousal support amounts that would be required to leave the lower income recipient spouse with between 40 and 46 percent of the combined INDI.

Each part of the formula is explained more fully under the headings below.

Calculating INDI

The starting point in this calculation is the Guidelines income of each spouse—in other words, the income of each spouse as defined in the *Federal Child Support Guidelines*.

From that amount, deduct the spouse's contribution to child support. For the payor spouse, that amount will be the amount of support determined under the *Federal Child Support Guidelines*, which is usually the table amount plus any contributions to special or extraordinary expenses. For the recipient spouse, a notional table amount is deducted along with any contributions by that spouse to special or extraordinary expenses.

Next, deduct income taxes and other deductions such as employment insurance premiums, Canada Pension Plan contributions, union dues and professional fees, and group insurance premiums.

Finally, add to the recipient spouse's income any government benefits and credits: the Child Tax Benefit, the National Child Benefit Supplement, the GST credit, the refundable medical credit, the Child Disability Benefit, various provincial benefit and credit schemes, and the Universal Child Care Benefit.

Dividing INDI

Add the INDIs of the two spouses together. Then, by iteration, determine the amount of spousal support that will leave the recipient spouse with between 40 and 46 percent of the combined INDIs of the spouses. Iteration involves calculating the after-tax positions of each spouse at a variety of hypothetical spousal support levels. These calculations require specialized computer software.

Most spousal support orders, where there are dependent children, are indefinite in duration. However, the guidelines set out ranges for duration based on a combination of the length of the relationship and the length of the remaining child-rearing period, in the form of two tests: the *length-of-marriage* test and the *age-of-children* test. The test that provides the longer duration is used at each end of the range. In general, the length-of-marriage test applies for marriages of 10 years or more, while the age-of-children test applies for shorter marriages.

Under the basic formula, the range for duration is calculated as follows:

Initial orders indefinite (duration not specified) subject to cumulative durational limits implemented by review or variation:

Upper End of the Range
The longer of
- the length of the marriage, and
- the date the last or youngest child finishes high school.

Lower End of the Range
The longer of
- one-half the length of the marriage, and
- the date the youngest child starts full-time school.

The following example reproduced from the *Spousal Support Advisory Guidelines* illustrates the calculation of both amount and duration under the basic *with child support* formula.

Bob and Carol have separated after eight years of marriage and two children, now aged 4 and 6, who are both living with Carol. Bob earns $40,000 gross annually at a local building supply company, while Carol has found part-time work, earning $10,000 per year. Carol's mother lives with Carol and provides care for the children when needed. Bob pays the table amount of $601 per month for the children. Carol's notional table amount of child support would be $61 per month. There are no special or extraordinary expenses.

Under the formula, Bob would pay spousal support in the range of zero to $34 per month.[9]

With respect to duration, the *length-of-marriage* test suggests a durational range of 4 to 8 years, while the *age-of-children* test suggests a range of 2 to 14 years. The result for Bob and Carol would be a durational range where the lower end of the range is 4 years (from the *length-of-marriage* test) and the upper end of the range is 14 years (from the *age-of-children* test).

The *shared custody*, *split custody*, *custodial payor*, and *adult child* formulas differ slightly from the basic formula.

After the Formulas Have Been Applied

After the formulas have been applied, there are three more steps:

1. *Use the ranges.* Determine the appropriate amount and duration within the ranges by considering the particular circumstances of the case, such as:
   - the strength of any compensatory claim;
   - the recipient's needs;
   - the age, number, needs, and standard of living of any children; and
   - the needs of the payor and his or her ability to pay.
2. *Consider restructuring.* The figures for amount and duration can be restructured by trading off *amount* against *duration* to yield an award of similar value. Restructuring can be used in three ways:
   - to *front-end load* awards by increasing the amount of support beyond the upper range of the formula while shortening the duration of the award;
   - to *extend duration* beyond the upper range of the formula while lowering the amount of support; or
   - to arrive at a *lump-sum* payment.
3. *Consider whether any exceptions apply.* The advisory guidelines set out exceptions in which the formulas, even after restructuring, may not generate an appropriate support award, including:
   - compelling financial circumstances in the interim period;
   - debt payments;
   - prior support obligations;
   - illness or disability of a recipient spouse;

---

9   The actual calculations are not set out because this amount is calculated by iteration, using computer software.

- a compensatory exception for shorter marriages under the *with child support* formula;
- basic needs/hardship under the *without child support* and *custodial payor* formulas;
- non-taxable payor income;
- non-primary parent to fulfill a parenting role under the *custodial payor* formula; and
- the special needs of a child.

Types of Support Orders

The courts are empowered to make a variety of support orders under both the *Divorce Act* and the *Family Law Act*.

Periodic Support Payments

Most support orders are for periodic support payments. In these orders, the paying spouse is ordered to make payments of a fixed amount of support at regular intervals, usually monthly.

The court's authority to order periodic support under the *Divorce Act* is found in section 15.2(1), and under the *Family Law Act* is found in section 34(1)(a).

Time-Limited Support

Under section 15.2(3) of the *Divorce Act* and section 34(1)(a) of the *Family Law Act*, the court may order that periodic support be paid either for an indefinite period of time or for a definite or time-limited period.

Time-limited support orders are generally made in the context of short relationships without children to force dependent spouses to gain economic self-sufficiency. Time-limited support is generally not ordered for women who have been out of the workforce for a long time.

Lump-Sum Support

Section 15.2(1) of the *Divorce Act* and section 34(1)(b) of the *Family Law Act* give the court the power to order payment of support by way of a lump sum. Generally, lump-sum payments are ordered only where the parties' relationship has been short (to encourage a clean break between the parties) or where there are serious concerns that the paying spouse will not make periodic payments.

Indexing Orders

Section 34(5) of the *Family Law Act* gives the court the power to order that periodic support payments be indexed to the cost of living. While the *Divorce Act* does not contain a provision specifically authorizing indexing, the Supreme Court of Canada in *Richardson v Richardson*[10] held that the court has the power to order indexing under the *Divorce Act*.

---

10   [1987] 1 SCR 857.

When a periodic support payment is indexed to the cost of living, the amount of support is increased automatically on its anniversary date in an amount proportionate to the annual increase in the cost of living. See Chapter 16 for an explanation of how the increase in support payments is calculated.

Securing Support

Under section 15.2(1) of the *Divorce Act*, the court has the power to make an order "to secure or pay, or to secure and pay," support. Accordingly, the court may order a spouse to make periodic payments of support and to post security that can be looked to if he or she defaults in making the periodic payments. Similar power is given to the court under section 34(1)(k) of the *Family Law Act*.

Interim Support

A final determination of support is not made until trial, yet the need for support may arise as soon as the parties separate. In that case, the dependent party may apply for interim support until the trial. The court has power to make interim support orders under both section 15.2(2) of the *Divorce Act* and section 34(1) of the *Family Law Act*.

Tax Treatment of Support Orders

Under the *Income Tax Act*,[11] periodic support payments paid pursuant to a court order or separation agreement for a spouse or common law partner are taxable as income in the hands of the receiving person and are deductible from the paying person's income. The tax implications of support payments are considered by the court when it determines the amount of these payments. The dependent party will need enough support to cover the additional income tax he or she must pay as a result of receiving that additional income. The payer's ability to pay support is increased by the fact that his or her income tax payments will be reduced because of the deductibility of the support payments.

Variation of Support Orders

Support orders under both the *Divorce Act* and the *Family Law Act* may be varied by the court if there has been a change in circumstances of either or both of the parties.

Under section 17 of the *Divorce Act*, a court must be satisfied that there has been "a change in the condition, means, needs or other circumstances" of either person since the making of the support order. Under section 37 of the *Family Law Act*, a court must be satisfied that there has been "a material change in the dependant's or respondent's circumstances or that evidence not available on the previous hearing has become available."

See Chapter 16 for a more complete discussion of variation applications.

---

11 RSC 1985, c 1 (5th Supp).

CHAPTER SUMMARY

In Ontario, spouses have an obligation to be self-supporting and to support each other to the extent that they are able. These obligations continue after separation. Both the *Family Law Act* and the *Divorce Act* deal with spousal support.

Under the *Divorce Act*, only spouses who are or were validly married can make a claim for support. Under the *Family Law Act*, the right to support arises as soon as one satisfies a broader definition of "spouse." For the *Divorce Act* to apply, one of the spouses must start a divorce proceeding. If neither spouse can or wishes to start a divorce proceeding, an application for support must be made under the *Family Law Act*.

Both statutes base entitlement to support on need. Entitlement falls into one or both of two categories: compensatory claims and non-compensatory claims. The conduct of a spouse never affects entitlement to support, but may, in rare cases, affect the quantum. The *Spousal Support Advisory Guidelines* are informal guidelines that help determine the amount and duration of spousal support. They contain two basic formulas for calculating spousal support: the "without child support" formula and the "with child support" formula.

Periodic support payments, which may be ordered either for an indefinite period of time or for a time-limited period, are most common, but the court can also order payment by way of a lump sum. The court may order a spouse to post security that can be looked to if he or she defaults on periodic payments. Periodic support payments maybe indexed to the cost of living under the *Family Law Act*.

Under the *Income Tax Act*, periodic spousal support payments are taxable as income in the hands of the receiving person and are deductible from the paying person's income. The tax implications of support payments are considered when the amount of these payments is determined.

Support orders under both statutes may be varied if the circumstances of the parties change.

KEY TERMS

cohabit, 75
compensatory claim, 77
limitation period, 74

non-compensatory claim, 77
quantum, 78
without child support formula, 80

REVIEW QUESTIONS

1. What is the definition of "spouse" under the *Divorce Act*?

2. What is the definition of "spouse" under the support provisions of the *Family Law Act*?

3. When must a spousal support application be dealt with under the *Divorce Act*?

4. When must a spousal support application be dealt with under the *Family Law Act*?

5. What factors is the court directed to take into consideration when making an order for spousal support under the *Divorce Act*?

6. What are the purposes of an order for spousal support under the *Family Law Act*?

7. What factors must a court consider when making an order for spousal support under the *Family Law Act*?

8. What is periodic support?

9. What is time-limited support, and when is it likely to be ordered?

10. What is lump-sum support, and when is it likely to be ordered?

11. What authority does the court have to order spousal support payments under the *Family Law Act*?

12. What authority does the court have to order spousal support payments under the *Divorce Act*?

13. What is the tax treatment of spousal support payments?

DISCUSSION QUESTION

1. Igor and Elena have been married for 35 years and have three children, now fully grown. They have just separated. Igor is a dentist. Elena worked as a law clerk in the early years of the marriage, and supported the two of them while Igor attended dental school full-time. Once the children were born she stayed home with them full time, and has not worked outside the home for 30 years. Elena does not want to start divorce proceedings but requires spousal support. Is she entitled to support from Igor? Explain your answer, referring to the appropriate legislation.

EXERCISES

1. Will and Amy were married for 12 years. They have no children. Will (aged 40) is a musician earning $40,000 per year. Amy (aged 35) is a lawyer earning $175,000 per year. Assuming that the court finds that Will is entitled to spousal support, use the "without child support" formula under the *Spousal Support Advisory Guidelines* to calculate the amount and duration of Will's support.

2. Ricky and Jwan were married for eight years. They have no children. Ricky (aged 55) is a high school teacher earning $80,000. Jwan (aged 61) is a dance instructor earning $30,000 per year. Assuming that the court finds that Jwan is entitled to spousal support, use the "without child support" formula under the *Spousal Support Advisory Guidelines* to calculate the amount and duration of Jwan's support.

Child Support

8

LEARNING OUTCOMES

After completing this chapter, you should be able to:

- State which legislation applies to a particular child support situation.

- Explain when a parent is obligated to provide child support under both the *Divorce Act* and the *Family Law Act*.

- Describe the different types of support orders under both the *Divorce Act* and the *Family Law Act*.

- Explain the function of the *Child Support Guidelines*.

- Calculate child support using the child support tables.

- Explain the circumstances in which the court is given discretion not to use the child support tables.

- Use the comparison of household standards of living test in Schedule II of the *Child Support Guidelines*.

- Explain the tax treatment of child support orders.

Introduction

Parents have an obligation to provide support for their children. A parent's obligation to support his or her children continues after a separation, even if the parent does not get custody of the children. After separation, the obligation to provide support is satisfied by the payment of child support to the party who has custody.

Child support is dealt with under both the *Family Law Act*[1] and the *Divorce Act*.[2] Unlike spousal support, which is calculated by taking into account the assets and debts and the income and expenses of both the dependent spouse and the paying spouse, child support is determined in accordance with *Child Support Guidelines*. These Guidelines calculate support in accordance with tables that set out amounts of support based on the income of the paying party and the number of children for whom support is being paid. The income of the recipient party is, generally speaking, irrelevant.

In this chapter, we will be looking at the law of child support, including:

- the obligation to provide child support,
- the applicable legislation,
- the types of support orders,
- the federal and provincial *Child Support Guidelines*,
- the tax treatment of child support orders, and
- the variation of child support orders.

Obligation to Provide Child Support

The *Family Law Act* and the *Divorce Act* each require parents to provide support for their children, but the obligation is defined somewhat differently under each Act.

Under the Divorce Act

Under the *Divorce Act*, a spouse has the obligation to provide support for any "child of the marriage."

A "child of the marriage" is defined in section 2(1) to be a child of two spouses or former spouses who

- is under the age of majority (18 years in Ontario) and who has not withdrawn from their charge, or
- is the age of majority or over and under their charge but unable, by reason of illness, disability, or other cause, to withdraw from their charge or to obtain the necessaries of life.

Accordingly, the obligation to provide support continues past the age of 18 if the child is unable to support himself or herself for any reason—for example, if the child is ill, disabled, or a full-time student.

---

1 RSO 1990, c F.3.

2 RSC 1985, c 3 (2d Supp).

Under section 2(2), a child of the marriage includes

- any child for whom both spouses or former spouses stand in the place of parents, and
- any child of whom one spouse or former spouse is the parent and for whom the other stands in the place of a parent.

In other words, a spouse or former spouse who has acted as a parent to his or her spouse's or former spouse's child may have an ongoing obligation to provide support for that child, even if he or she did not formally adopt the child.

Under the Family Law Act

Under section 31 of the *Family Law Act*, every parent[3] has an obligation to provide support for his or her unmarried child who is a minor or is enrolled in a full-time program of education, to the extent that the parent is capable of doing so. Accordingly, unlike under the *Divorce Act*, the obligation to provide support for a child over the age of 18 does not extend to a disabled child unless the child is in full-time attendance at school.[4] The obligation does not extend to a child 16 years of age or older who has withdrawn from parental control.

Like the *Divorce Act*, the *Family Law Act* uses an extended definition of "child." Under section 1(1), a child is defined to include a person whom a parent has demonstrated a settled intention to treat as a child of his or her family.

Applicable Legislation

As stated above, child support is dealt with by both the *Divorce Act* and the *Family Law Act*, and the courts apply the same principles in deciding the quantum of child support under both statutes. As with spousal support, the circumstances of the parties determine which statute applies.

Because the *Divorce Act* applies only to validly married spouses, all other parties must apply for child support under the *Family Law Act*.

There is no obligation for a parent to support a disabled adult child under the *Family Law Act*. Accordingly, a parent seeking support for such a child would have to do so under the *Divorce Act*.

For the *Divorce Act* to apply, one of the spouses must start a divorce proceeding and meet the residence requirements of the Act—that is, one of them must have been resident in the province in which the proceeding is started for at least one year

---

3   See the discussion in Chapter 6 of the expanded definition of "parent" in the *Children's Law Reform Act*. In accordance with section 4(4) that definition "applies for all purposes of the law of Ontario."

4   In the case of *Coates v Watson*, 2017 ONCJ 454, the single mother of an adult disabled child launched a constitutional challenge to this difference in language claiming that it discriminates against disabled children of unmarried parents. Following that challenge, NDP MPP Peggy Sattler introduced a private bill to amend section 31 to extend the parental support obligation to an "unmarried child who is unable, by reason of illness, disability or other cause, to obtain the necessaries of life." As of the date of publication, that bill has received first reading.

immediately before the commencement of the proceeding. If neither spouse can satisfy the residence requirements of the *Divorce Act*, an application for child support must be made under the *Family Law Act*.

If the parties have already divorced, and no support claim was made at the time, any subsequent claim for support must be made as a corollary relief proceeding under the *Divorce Act*.

Section 36(1) of the *Family Law Act* sets out what happens when a support application is started under the *Family Law Act* before the commencement of a divorce proceeding in which one of the spouses seeks child support.

stayed
temporarily stopped
or suspended

- Any support application under the *Family Law Act* that has not been adjudicated is **stayed** unless the court gives permission for it to continue.

- An interim order made under the *Family Law Act* continues in force unless and until it is superseded by an order under the *Divorce Act*. Neither party can apply to vary the *Family Law Act* order, nor can either party apply for a final order under the *Family Law Act*.

- Any final support order obtained under the *Family Law Act* before the divorce proceeding was commenced continues in force unless and until it is superseded by an order under the *Divorce Act*. If neither party seeks a support order under the *Divorce Act*, the *Family Law Act* order continues in effect. If one of the parties seeks a support order under the *Divorce Act*, the *Family Law Act* order can be incorporated into the divorce judgment or replaced with a new and different order.

Support Orders

The court's power to make a child support order is found in section 15.1(1) of the *Divorce Act* and in section 33(1) of the *Family Law Act*. Under both Acts, the courts are empowered to make a variety of support orders.

Periodic Support Payments

Most support orders are for periodic support payments. In these orders the paying party is ordered to make payments of a fixed amount of support at regular intervals, usually monthly.

The court's authority to order periodic support under the *Divorce Act* is found in section 15.1(1), and under the *Family Law Act* in section 34(1)(a).

Time-Limited Support

Under section 15.1(4) of the *Divorce Act* and section 34(1)(a) of the *Family Law Act*, the court may order that periodic support be paid either for an indefinite period of time or for a definite or time-limited period.

Lump-Sum Support

Section 11 of the *Federal Child Support Guidelines*,[5] which are made under the *Divorce Act*, and section 34(1)(b) of the *Family Law Act* give the court the power to

---

5 SOR/97-175.

order payment of support by way of a lump sum. Generally, a lump-sum child support payment is ordered only if there are serious concerns that the paying party will fail to make periodic payments.

Securing Support

Under section 12 of the *Federal Child Support Guidelines*, the court has the power to order that the amount payable "be paid or secured, or paid and secured, in the manner specified in the order." Accordingly, the court may order a party to make periodic payments of support and to post security that can be looked to if he or she defaults in making the periodic payments. Similar power is given to the court under section 34(1)(k) of the *Family Law Act* to require that payment be secured "by a charge on property or otherwise."

Indexing Orders

There is no provision for the indexing of child support orders under either statute. Under both the federal and provincial *Child Support Guidelines*, the amount of child support payments is tied solely to the income of the paying party. If the income of the paying party goes up, the receiving party may apply to have the amount of child support increased.

Under section 39.1 of the *Family Law Act* (passed in 2009, but at the time of writing not yet proclaimed in force) there is provision for the automatic recalculation of the amount of a child support order by "the child support service established by the regulations" in order to reflect updated income information.

Interim Support

A final determination of child support is not made until trial, yet the need for support may arise as soon as the parties separate. In that case, the party in need may apply for interim support until the trial. The court has power to make interim support orders under section 15.1(2) of the *Divorce Act* and section 34(1) of the *Family Law Act*.

The Child Support Guidelines

Under both section 15.1(3) of the *Divorce Act* and section 33(11) of the *Family Law Act*, child support orders are determined in accordance with child support guidelines. The *Federal Child Support Guidelines* are a regulation made pursuant to the *Divorce Act*, and the Ontario *Child Support Guidelines*[6] are a regulation made pursuant to the *Family Law Act*. The *Child Support Guidelines* under both statutes are essentially the same.

The *Child Support Guidelines* contain provisions that address

- the calculation of child support in a variety of situations,
- the elements of a child support order,

---

6 O Reg 391/97.

- the variation of child support orders,
- the determination of income for the purposes of calculating child support orders, and
- child support tables.

Child Support Tables

The child support tables, which are a schedule to the Guidelines, set out the amount of monthly child support payments calculated on the basis of the annual income of the paying party and the number of children for whom support is being paid. There is a separate table for each province and territory, and the amounts vary from one province to another because of differences in provincial income tax rates. While the schedule to the *Federal Child Support Guidelines* includes the tables for each province and territory, the schedule to the Ontario *Child Support Guidelines* includes only the Ontario table. However, the definition of "table" in the Ontario Guidelines includes a reference to *Federal Child Support Guidelines* tables for the other provinces and territories.

In calculating child support, the courts use the table for the province in which the paying party ordinarily resides at the time the application is made. If the paying party resides outside Canada, the courts use the table for the province in which the applicant ordinarily resides at the time of the application.

The amounts in the tables are based on economic studies of the average spending on children in families at different income levels in Canada. They are calculated using a formula that reflects the average expenses of a parent with a particular number of children and a particular level of income.

The Ontario child support tables can be found in Volume II. Note that the tables give the monthly child support amounts in $1,000 increments of income and a percentage to calculate child support amounts between the increments to be added to the base amounts.

Consider two examples of how child support is calculated using the tables. Notice that the amount of support payable for two children is not double the amount of support payable for one child.

David and Lisa both live in Ontario, and Lisa has custody of their one child. David earns $72,500.

The basic amount of support paid by a parent earning $72,000 is $673 per month.

The percentage for amounts in excess of $72,000 is 0.78.

David's monthly child support obligation is calculated as follows:

$673.00 + [0.78% × (72,500 − 72,000)]
$673.00 + [0.78% × 500]
$673.00 + 3.90
$676.90

Assume now that David and Lisa have two children.

The basic amount of support paid by a parent earning $72,000 is $1,066 per month.

The percentage for amounts in excess of $72,000 is 1.14.

David's monthly child support obligation is calculated as follows:

$1,097.00 + [1.14% × (72,500 − 72,000)]
$1,097.00 + [1.14% × 500]
$1,097.00 + 5.70
$1,103.00

The federal government created simplified tables in 2006. These tables are based on the regulation tables, but set out child support amounts for various income levels calculated in increments of $100, and provide an easier method to determine child support by simply rounding the support amount to the nearest hundred dollar amount. The simplified tables are now more commonly used by the courts than the regulation tables.

The simplified tables for Ontario child support for between one and four children can be found in Volume II.

Consider again the two examples involving David and Lisa, this time calculating support using the simplified tables.

David and Lisa both live in Ontario, and Lisa has custody of their one child. David earns $72,500.

The amount of support paid by a parent earning $72,500 for one child is $677 per month.

Assume now that David and Lisa have two children.

The amount of support paid by a parent earning $72,500 for two children is $1,103 per month.

Application of Child Support Tables

Generally, child support is calculated by using the amount set out in the appropriate child support table. The court may also order an additional amount to cover special or extraordinary expenses for the child. There are, however, circumstances where the table amounts may not be applicable.

The court is given discretion not to apply the table amounts in the following situations:

- the child is over the age of majority,
- the income of the paying party is over $150,000,
- the paying party is not the natural parent of the child,
- the parties split or share custody of the children,

- the application of the guideline amounts would result in undue hardship,
- a court order or agreement exists with respect to support, or
- the parties consent to an order in a different amount.

Special or Extraordinary Expenses

Section 7 of the Guidelines provide that the court may order the payment of an amount in addition to the table amount to cover all or a portion of the following expenses:

- child care expenses if incurred as a result of the custodial parent's employment, illness, disability, or education or training for employment;
- the portion of medical and dental insurance premiums attributable to the child;
- health-related expenses that exceed insurance reimbursement by at least $100 annually—for example, orthodontic treatment, professional counselling, physiotherapy, occupational therapy, speech therapy, prescription drugs, hearing aids, prescription glasses, and contact lenses;
- *extraordinary expenses* for primary or secondary school education or for any other education programs that meet the child's particular needs—for example, private school or religious school tuition fees and tutoring costs;
- expenses for post-secondary education (unlike primary or secondary school expenses, these do not need to be "extraordinary"); and
- *extraordinary expenses* for extracurricular activities.

The term "extraordinary expenses" is defined in section 7(1.1) as follows:

(a) expenses that exceed those that the parent or spouse requesting an amount for the extraordinary expenses can reasonably cover, taking into account that parent's or spouse's income and the amount that the parent or spouse would receive under the applicable table or, where the court has determined that the table amount is inappropriate, the amount that the court has otherwise determined is appropriate, or

(b) where clause (a) is not applicable, expenses that the court considers are extraordinary taking into account,

(i) the amount of the expense in relation to the income of the parent or spouse requesting the amount, including the amount that the parent or spouse would receive under the applicable table or, where the court has determined that the table amount is inappropriate, the amount that the court has otherwise determined is appropriate,

(ii) the nature and number of the educational programs and extracurricular activities,

(iii) any special needs and talents of the child,

(iv) the overall cost of the programs and activities, and

(v) any other similar factors that the court considers relevant.

In making an order to cover these expenses, section 7 of the Guidelines requires the court to take into account the necessity of the expense in relation to the child's best interests. The court must also take into account the reasonableness of the expense in relation to the means of the parents or spouses and those of the child and in relation to to the spending pattern of the parents or spouses in respect of the child during cohabitation. In other words, the court looks at the family's historical spending patterns.

If the court decides that an expense falls within this section, the guiding principle is that the expense is shared by each parent or spouse in proportion to his or her income after deducting any contribution from the child.

Consider the following example of how special or extraordinary expenses would be shared between the spouses.

Esther and William are separated. Esther has custody of their one daughter, who is a gifted athlete and is enrolled in an elite gymnastics program costing $900 per month. Esther earns $50,000 per year and William earns $100,000 per year. Assume that the cost of that program constitutes an extraordinary expense for extracurricular activities, and that William must pay an amount in addition to his table amount of support. That extra amount is calculated as follows:

$$\frac{\text{Income of the paying spouse (William)}}{\text{Combined income of both spouses}} \times \text{expense amount} = \text{additional support}$$

$$\frac{\$100,000}{\$150,000} \times \$900 = \$600$$

In this example, William contributes $600 per month to the $900 monthly expense, leaving Esther to pay the remaining $300 per month. William, who earns twice as much as Esther, contributes twice as much as Esther to the monthly expense.

Child Over the Age of Majority

Under section 3(2) of the Guidelines, if the child is over 18, the amount of support is to be determined in accordance with the tables (plus any amount for special or extraordinary expenses) unless the court considers that approach to be inappropriate. In such a case, the court may order the amount that it considers appropriate, having regard to the condition, means, needs, and other circumstances of the child and the financial ability of each parent or spouse to contribute to the support of the child.

Incomes Over $150,000

It is possible to calculate child support using the tables even if the income of the paying party is over $150,000. The child support tables set out incremental support payment amounts for paying parents whose incomes range from $6,730 up to $150,000. For incomes over $150,000, the tables set out a basic monthly amount for the first $150,000 and a percentage applicable to the portion of income that is greater than $150,000.

Under section 4 of the Guidelines, a court may order support in that amount (plus any amount for special or extraordinary expenses). However, if a court considers that amount to be inappropriate, it may order:

- the table amount in respect of the first $150,000 of the paying parent's income;
- the amount the court considers appropriate, having regard to the condition, means, needs, and other circumstances of the child and the financial ability of each parent or spouse to contribute to the support of the child in respect of the balance of the parent's income; and
- any amount for special or extraordinary expenses.

Paying Party Is Not the Natural Parent of the Child

If a paying party is not the natural parent of the child, but stands in the place of a parent of the child, the amount of support is not automatically determined in accordance with the tables. Under section 5 of the Guidelines, the court is to order the amount the court considers appropriate, having regard to the Guidelines and any other parent's legal duty to support the child. In these cases, the courts consider the financial circumstances and roles of the step-parent and the natural parent in the child's life.

Split or Shared Custody

The term "split custody" refers to the situation where the parties have more than one child, and each party has custody of one or more children. In this case, section 8 of the Guidelines provides that the amount of child support is the difference between the amount that each parent would otherwise pay if a child support order were sought against each of the parents. For example, a court would calculate the support that Parent 1 would be entitled to from Parent 2 based on the number of children in her custody and the income of Parent 2. The court would then calculate the support that Parent 2 would be entitled to from Parent 1 based on the number of children in his custody and the income of Parent 1. The parent with the obligation to pay the higher amount would pay the difference between the two amounts to the parent with the obligation to pay the lower amount.

Consider the following example of how support would be calculated in a split custody situation:

> Adam and Behati are separated. They agree that Adam is to have custody of two of their children and Behati is to have custody of the third. Adam earns $75,000 per year and Behati earns $90,000 per year.
>
> First, calculate how much support Adam would have to pay Behati for the one child in her custody. Based on his income of $75,000 per year, the table amount of support for one child is $700 per month.

> Next calculate how much support Behati would have to pay Adam for the two children in his custody. Based on her income of $90,000 per year, the table amount of support for two children is $1,351 month.
> $1,351 − $700 = $651
> Behati will have to pay Adam $611 per month.

"Shared custody" refers to a situation where a parent exercises access to or has physical custody of a child for not less than 40 percent of the time over the course of a year. In that case, section 9 of the Guidelines directs the court to set the amount of support by taking into account

- the amounts set out in the applicable tables for each parent;
- the increased costs of shared custody arrangements; and
- the "condition, means, needs and other circumstances" of each parent and of the child.

Undue Hardship

Under section 10 of the Guidelines, on the application of either parent, the court may award an amount of child support that is different from the amount under the Guidelines if the court finds that either the party making the request or the child would otherwise suffer undue hardship.

The section states that the following circumstances may cause undue hardship:

- an unusually high level of debt reasonably incurred to earn a living or support the parents or spouses and their children before the separation;
- unusually high expenses in relation to exercising access to a child;
- a legal duty under a judgment, order, or separation agreement to support someone;
- a legal duty to support a child, other than a child of the marriage; or
- a legal duty to support someone who is ill or disabled.

If a court is satisfied that there is undue hardship, it must then compare the standards of living of the households of the two parents. If the household of the party who claims undue hardship would, after setting support in accordance with the guidelines, have a higher standard of living than the household of the other party, the application to award a different amount of support must be denied. In other words, to succeed in an application under this section, the applicant must not only establish undue hardship; he or she must also establish that the standard of living of his or her household is lower than that of the respondent's household.

In comparing standards of living for the purpose of this section, the court may use the comparison of household standards of living test in schedule II of the Guidelines. Using this test, a court examines the income of every person in the household, including domestic partners and children.

The test sets out the following series of steps:

Step 1: Establish the annual income of each person in each household. This involves determining the income in accordance with sections 15 to 20 of the Guidelines, and then deducting federal and provincial income taxes, employment insurance premiums, and Canada Pension Plan or Quebec Pension Plan contributions.

Step 2: Adjust the annual income of each party by

  a. deducting
    - any amount relied on by the court as a factor that resulted in the determination of undue hardship,
    - the amount that would be payable by the person for child support if no finding of undue hardship were made, and
    - any amount of support that is paid by the person under a judgment, order, or written separation agreement that is not already included as a hardship amount above, and by

  b. adding
    - the amount of child support that would be received by the person if no finding of undue hardship were made, and
    - any amount of child support that the person receives under a judgment, order, or written separation agreement.

Step 3: Add all adjusted incomes in the household.

Step 4: Determine the applicable "low-income measures amount" for each household as set out in the schedule.

Step 5: Divide the household income amount (from Step 3) by the low-income measures amount (from Step 4).

Step 6: Compare the household income ratios. The household that has the higher ratio has the higher standard of living.

Fred and Wilma are divorced. Wilma has custody of their two children. Wilma now lives with Barney and the two children. Wilma and Barney have moved to another city, and a result of this is that Fred incurs travel costs of $2,000 per year to exercise access to his children with Wilma. Fred is claiming undue hardship as a result of those expenses. Fred earns $40,000, on which he pays income tax, employment insurance premiums, and Canada Pension Plan contributions of $15,000. He is remarried to Betty, who does not earn a salary. They have one child. Wilma earns $30,000, on which she pays income tax, employment insurance premiums, and Canada Pension Plan contributions of $10,000. Barney earns $40,000, on which he pays income tax, Employment Insurance premiums, and Canada Pension Plan contributions of $15,000. In the absence of a finding of undue hardship, Fred would be required to pay child support in the table amount of $597 per month or $7,164 per year.

Fred's Household

Step 1	Fred's income		$40,000
	Subtract taxes, EI, and CPP		(15,000)
	Fred's after-tax income		$25,000
Step 2	Subtract hardship amounts		$(2,000)
	Subtract child support		(7,164)
			$15,836
Step 3	Add income of other household members		0
			$15,836

Step 4 Low-income measures amount
(for two adults and one child) = $17,649

Step 5 $\dfrac{\$15,836}{\$17,649} = 0.90$

Wilma's Household

Step 1	Wilma's income		$30,000
	Subtract income tax, EI, and CPP		(10,000)
	Wilma's after-tax income		$20,000
Step 2	Add child support to Wilma's after-tax income		$7,164
			$27,164
Step 3	Add income of other household members		
	Barney's income		$40,000
	Subtract income tax, EI, and CPP		(15,000)
	Barney's after-tax income		$25,000
	Wilma's total household income (with Barney's income)		$52,164

Step 4 Low-income measures amount
(for two adults and two children) = $20,764

Step 5 $\dfrac{\$52,164}{\$20,764} = 2.51$

Wilma's household has a higher standard of living than Fred's household.

Existing Court Order or Agreement with Respect to Support

Under both section 15.1(5) of the *Divorce Act* and section 33(12) of the *Family Law Act*, a court may order an amount of child support that is different from the amount that would be determined under the Guidelines if the court is satisfied that special provisions in an order or a written agreement with respect to the financial obligations of the parents, or the division or transfer of their property, directly or indirectly benefit a child, or that special provisions have otherwise been made for the benefit of a child, and that the application of the *Child Support Guidelines* would result in an amount of child support that is inequitable given those special provisions.

Consent of the Parties

Under section 15.1(7) of the *Divorce Act* and section 33(14) of the *Family Law Act*, the court may award an amount different from the amount that would be determined under the Guidelines on the consent of both parents if the court is satisfied that reasonable arrangements have been made for the support of the child. Under section 15.1(8) of the *Divorce Act* and section 33(15) of the *Family Law Act*, the court is to have regard to the applicable Guidelines in determining whether reasonable arrangements have been made. However, the court may not consider the arrangements to be unreasonable only because the amount of support agreed to is not the same as the guideline amount.

Income Information

Under section 21 of the Guidelines, a person against whom an application for child support is made has an obligation to provide information about his or her income so that a determination of the appropriate level of support may be made.

The applicant, on the other hand, is required to provide income information only in those circumstances in which the Guidelines require the court to consider the income of the applicant:

- if the applicant is seeking an additional amount for special or extraordinary expenses;
- if the child is over the age of majority and it is determined that the table amount of support is inappropriate;
- if the income of the paying party is over $150,000 and the court considers the table amount of support to be inappropriate;
- if there is split or shared custody; or
- if there is a claim of undue hardship (in which case income information from any domestic partners would also be required).

There are also ongoing obligations to provide updated income information:

- Under section 24.1, every person whose income or other financial information is used to determine the amount of an order for the support of a child shall, no later than 30 days after the anniversary of the date on which the order was made, provide updated financial information to every party to the order.

- Under section 25.1, every person whose income or other financial information is used to determine the amount of a child support obligation under a domestic contract or other written agreement shall, no later than 30 days after the anniversary of the date on which the agreement was entered into, provide updated financial information to every party to the contract or agreement.

- Under section 25, a spouse against whom a child support order has been made must, on the written request of the other spouse, provide updated financial information not more than once per year.

Administrative Calculation and Recalculation of Child Support

An online Child Support Calculation Service became available on April 4, 2016, when sections 39 and 39.1 of the *Family Law Act* and O.Reg 190/15 (Administrative Calculation and Recalculation of Child Support) came into effect. The service allows separated parents to establish support payments in the first instance (referred to in the Act as "calculation"), or to vary existing support payments (referred to in the Act as "recalculation"), under both the *Family Law Act* and the *Divorce Act*,[7] using an online portal rather than going to court. The online portal is found on the government of Ontario website at <https://www.ontario.ca/page/set-up-or-update-child-support-online>.

Eligibility Considerations

The service cannot be used for either a calculation or a recalculation of child support if

- either parent or any of the children live outside Ontario;
- any children are over 17.5 years old or married;
- there is split or shared custody of the children; or
- the party paying support:
  - earns more than $150,000 or less than $10,821 per year,
  - earns income in cash,
  - earns more than 20 percent of his or her annual income from self-employment,
  - earns more than 20 percent of his or her income as a landlord,
  - earns more than 20 percent of his or her income as a seasonal worker,[8] or
  - earns any income from a partnership in which he or she is a partner or a corporation of which he or she is a director, officer, or majority shareholder.

---

7 See section 25.1 of the *Divorce Act*.

8 If the payor has not filed an income tax return for the most recent taxation year, or his or her most recent income tax return shows an income that is significantly different from his or her current income.

The service cannot be used for a recalculation of child support if, in addition to the above conditions,

- fewer than six months have passed since the existing child support amount was established or changed;
- the existing child support amount was not calculated in accordance with the child support tables (plus any amount for special or extraordinary expenses under section 7 of the *Child Support Guidelines*);
- the existing child support amount was calculated on the basis of imputed income;
- the existing child support amount contains an amount for post-secondary education expenses; or
- the existing child support order was made in a jurisdiction other than Ontario.

Special or Extraordinary Expenses under Section 7 of the Child Support Guidelines

On a calculation of support, the service may calculate amounts to cover expenses under section 7 of the *Child Support Guidelines*, other than post-secondary expenses, extraordinary expenses for primary or secondary school education, or extraordinary expenses for extracurricular activities.

On a recalculation of support, the service may recalculate any amounts for special or extraordinary expenses, other than post-secondary expenses, that are included in the original order. The service may also add new amounts to cover expenses under section 7 of the Guidelines, other than post-secondary expenses, extraordinary expenses for primary or secondary school education, or extraordinary expenses for extracurricular activities. Both parties must consent to proceed if a change to special expenses is requested.

How the Service Works

Either parent (either the payor or the recipient) may apply online for a calculation or recalculation of child support. The applicant completes an online application and pays an $80 fee. The service notifies the other parent by mail, inviting him or her to visit the online portal within 25 days. The consent of the responding parent is required for a calculation. If the responding parent agrees to proceed with calculation or recalculation, he or she also pays the $80 fee. The service can proceed on a recalculation without the consent of the other parent, as long as the applicant is not seeking a change to any special expenses included in the original order.

Both parents are required to provide income information to the service.

Once the service makes a decision, it mails a notice of calculation or recalculation to each parent setting out the new child support arrangement. It is enforceable like a court order.

Tax Treatment of Child Support Orders

Unlike spousal support payments, child support payments are neither taxable in the hands of the receiving party nor deductible by the paying party for income tax purposes.

Variation of Child Support Orders

Both section 17.1 of the *Divorce Act* and section 37 of the *Family Law Act* provide for variation of child support orders in the event of a change of circumstances as provided for in the *Child Support Guidelines*.

Section 14 of the Guidelines sets out the changes in circumstances that justify a variation:

- if child support was previously determined in accordance with the tables, any change in circumstances that would result in a different child support order; or
- if child support was previously determined without reference to the tables, any change in the condition, means, needs, or other circumstances of either parent or of any child who is entitled to support.

See Chapter 16 for a more complete discussion of variation applications.

CHAPTER SUMMARY

Child support is dealt with under both the *Family Law Act* and the *Divorce Act*, although the latter applies only to validly married spouses. Unmarried parties must apply for child support under the *Family Law Act*. Both parents, regardless of marital status and custody, have an obligation to support their children.

Support orders obtained before divorce proceedings commence under the *Family Law Act* continue until superseded by an order under the *Divorce Act*. A *Family Law Act* order can be incorporated into a *Divorce Act* order or replaced with a new and different order.

Most support orders are for periodic support payments. In these orders, the paying party is ordered to make payments of a fixed amount of support at regular intervals, usually monthly, either indefinitely or for a time-limited period. Instead of periodic payments, the court may order support to be paid in a lump sum. A party may be ordered to post security in case he or she defaults in making periodic payments. There is no indexing of child support orders.

The court may award an amount of child support that is different from the amount under the Guidelines if the court finds that the party making the request or the child would otherwise suffer undue hardship.

Unlike spousal support payments, child support payments are neither taxable in the hands of the receiving party nor deductible by the paying party for income tax purposes.

KEY TERM

stayed, 94

REVIEW QUESTIONS

1. In what circumstances can a parent be required to support a child over the age of 18 under the *Divorce Act*?

2. In what circumstances can a parent be required to support a child over the age of 18 under the *Family Law Act*?

3. When must a child support application be dealt with under the *Divorce Act*?

4. When must a child support application be dealt with under the *Family Law Act*?

5. Why is there no provision for the indexing of child support orders under either the *Divorce Act* or the *Family Law Act*?

6. What are the *Federal Child Support Guidelines* and the Ontario *Child Support Guidelines*?

7. What do the *Child Support Guidelines* contain?

8. What are the child support tables?

9. Under what circumstances is the court given discretion not to apply the table amounts in determining child support?

10. Under what circumstances may the court order the payment of an additional amount over and above the table amount?

11. Give examples of "extraordinary expenses."

12. How is child support calculated if the child is over the age of majority?

13. How is child support calculated if the income of a paying parent is over $150,000?

14. How is child support calculated if a paying party is not the natural parent of the child?

15. What is "split custody"? How is child support calculated in the case of split custody?

16. What is "shared custody"? How is child support calculated in the case of shared custody?

17. What may the court do in the case of undue hardship?

18. What is the effect of an existing court order or agreement on the making of a child support order?

19. When must a person against whom an application for child support is made provide income information?

20. When must the applicant provide income information?

21. What is the tax treatment of child support?

DISCUSSION QUESTION

1. Tristan and Isolde were married and have one child, who is 19 years old and mentally disabled. Tristan and Isolde have separated, and the child lives with Tristan. Tristan wants child support from Isolde. Can Tristan obtain child support? Under what statute? Explain.

EXERCISES

1. Will and Grace both live in Ontario and Will has custody of their one child. Grace earns $97,500. Based on the child support tables, how much support will Grace be required to pay?

2. Harvey and Wendy were married with three children, Steve (aged 16), Sally (aged 14), and Lola (aged 6). They have now separated, and Steve is living with his father, while the girls have stayed with their mother. Harvey earns $100,000 per year, and Wendy makes $85,000 per year. Calculate the amount of support that should be paid under the tables.

3. Sheldon and Amy were married with three children, Harry (now aged 16), Sam (now aged 14), and Lance (now aged 6). Three years ago, they divorced, and the three children stayed with their mother. He has been paying child support of $1,583 per month. Last year, Sheldon remarried and his new wife Penny recently gave birth to twins. Sheldon would like to reduce his support payments to Amy, based on undue hardship because he is still paying off debts he incurred while he was married to Amy. Those debt payments are $3,600 per year.

Additional facts:

- Sheldon makes $80,000 per year from which $30,000 is deducted for income tax, CPP, and EI.

- Sheldon's new wife is presently on maternity leave, and is collecting $800 per month in EI payments.

- Amy makes $70,000 per year, and $25,000 is deducted for income tax, CPP, and EI.

- Harry and Sam both have part-time jobs. Harry makes $400 per month (no deductions), and Sam makes $350 per month (no deductions).

Assuming that the court agrees that a situation of undue hardship exists, do a comparison of household standards of living test, and determine whether or not Sheldon's claim for undue hardship will be successful.

Property Rights

9

LEARNING OUTCOMES

After completing this chapter, you should be able to:

- Calculate the net family property of a spouse.

- Calculate the equalization payment owed by one spouse to another.

- Define "matrimonial home."

- Describe the rights given to a spouse under Part II of the *Family Law Act* with respect to the matrimonial home.

- Explain the equitable principles that apply to property owned by spouses.

- Describe briefly the property rights of unmarried couples.

- Explain briefly the tax consequences of property transfers between spouses.

Introduction

When spouses separate, they have the right to seek a division of their property. If the parties are married, the property division takes place in accordance with a formula set out in the *Family Law Act*. If the parties are not married, their property is divided on the basis of common law principles of property ownership and equitable principles of trust.

In this chapter, we will be looking at the law of property rights, including:

- an overview of property rights under the *Family Law Act*,
- the equalization of net family properties on marriage breakdown,
- equitable property rights,
- the matrimonial home,
- the rights of unmarried couples, and
- the tax consequences of property transfers.

Overview of Property Rights Under the Family Law Act

Family property is dealt with in part I of the *Family Law Act*.[1] Section 5(7) states that the purpose of the property provisions of the Act is

> to recognize that child care, household management and financial provision are the joint responsibilities of the spouses and that inherent in the marital relationship there is equal contribution, whether financial or otherwise, by the spouses to the assumption of these responsibilities . . . .

The property provisions of the *Family Law Act* allow spouses to share equally in the value of most property acquired during the marriage, and in the increase in value during the marriage of previously owned property. With the exception of the matrimonial home (discussed below), the spouses do not share the value of property that they bring into the marriage; they share only in the increase in value during the marriage of that property. Here's an example.

George and Elaine were married. During the marriage, George bought a painting for $10,000. George and Elaine later separate, at which time the painting is worth $100,000. The entire $100,000 value of the painting is divided between George and Elaine because the painting was acquired during the marriage. If George had bought the painting before the marriage, the result would be different. George would have to share with Elaine only the amount by which the painting had increased in value during the marriage. So, if he paid $10,000 for the painting, and it

---

1 RSO 1990, c F.3.

was worth $50,000 at the time of the marriage and $100,000 at the time of separation, Elaine would be entitled to share only in the increase in value of the painting during the marriage, or $50,000, which would then be divided between George and Elaine.

Certain property, such as gifts or inheritances from third parties, even though acquired during marriage, is not shared. One category of property, the matrimonial home, is shared fully even if it was acquired before the marriage.

The division of property under the Act is achieved through a series of calculations. The purpose of these calculations is (subject to certain excluded property) to arrive at the dollar amount of

- the value of the property acquired by each spouse during the marriage, and
- the increase in value during the marriage of property owned by each spouse at the time of the marriage,

and then to divide that dollar amount equally between the spouses.

This dollar value is arrived at by calculating the net worth (subject to exclusions under the Act) of each spouse, both at the time of separation and at the time of marriage. The difference between a spouse's net worth at separation and his or her net worth at marriage is the amount by which the spouse's net worth has gone up in value over the course of the marriage, either because of property acquired by the spouse during the marriage or because of the increase in value of property owned by the spouse during the marriage.

This process of calculation and division is called "equalization of net family properties."

Equalization of Net Family Properties

Who May Apply for an Equalization and When

The property provisions of the *Family Law Act* apply only to spouses as defined under section 1(1). Under that section, a spouse means either of two persons who are married to each other, or who have gone through a marriage that is voidable or void, in good faith on the part of the person asserting a right to property. In other words, the provisions of the Act do not apply to parties who are simply cohabiting, regardless of the length of their relationship.

Section 5 of the Act sets out the five triggering events that give rise to a spouse's right to seek an equalization of net family properties (NFP):

- a divorce is granted,
- a marriage is declared a nullity,
- the spouses are separated and there is no reasonable prospect that they will resume cohabitation,

- one of the spouses dies, or
- a "serious danger" arises, during cohabitation, that one spouse may "improvidently deplete" his or her net family property.

This chapter discusses only the triggering events that arise from the breakdown of a marriage.

Section 7 sets out the right of a spouse, a former spouse, or a deceased spouse's personal representative to apply to court for an equalization of NFP. Pursuant to section 7(3), an application cannot be brought after the earliest of

- two years after the date the marriage is terminated,
- six years after the day the spouses separate and there is no reasonable prospect of their resuming cohabitation, and
- six months after the death of the first spouse.

There is no limitation period for an application based on an improvident depletion of assets.

There have, however, been many successful applications to extend the time limit for bringing an application for equalization.

Powers of the Court on an Equalization Application

The powers of the court on an equalization application are set out in section 9 of the Act. The court's primary power is to order the spouse with the higher NFP to pay the equalization amount to the spouse with the lower NFP. The court does not have the power to order the transfer of specific assets except as a means of satisfying the obligation to make the equalization payment. Accordingly, a spouse in an equalization application seeks an order that the other spouse make an equalization payment; a spouse does not claim a share in any particular asset or assets.

Net Family Properties Definitions

Section 4 of the Act contains a number of definitions that give us the formula for calculating the net family properties of the spouses. Each spouse has his or her own net family property. The calculation of net family property is done with respect to each spouse. The equalization takes place when comparing the net family properties of the two spouses.

It is necessary to be familiar with the definitions of terms under the Act before using the formula for NFP calculation.

"Net family property" is defined in section 4(1) to mean the value of all property, except property excluded by section 4(2), that a spouse owns on the valuation date (see below), after deducting

- the spouse's debts and other liabilities, including, for greater certainty, any contingent tax liabilities in respect of the property, and
- the value of property, other than a matrimonial home, that the spouse owned on the date of the marriage, after deducting the spouse's debts and other

liabilities, other than debts or liabilities related directly to the acquisition or significant improvement of a matrimonial home, calculated as of the date of the marriage.

"Property" is defined in section 4(1) to mean "any interest, present or future, vested or contingent, in real or personal property." The definition is broad and is meant to include real estate, vehicles, cash, bank accounts, RRSPs, stocks, bonds, pensions,[2] annuities, businesses, and equipment. Cases have held that the definition also includes:

- a right to receive income from a trust,
- accounts receivable, and
- an interest in a professional practice.

It does not include a professional degree or a licence to practise.

"Valuation date" is defined in section 4(1) to mean the earliest of the following dates:

- the date the spouses separate and there is no reasonable prospect of their resuming cohabitation,
- the date their divorce is granted,
- the date the marriage is declared a nullity,
- the date one of the spouses commences an application based on improvident depletion of assets, and
- the date before the date on which the first spouse dies.

In other words, the valuation date (V-day) is the date of the triggering event that gives rise to the application. In the case of a marriage breakdown, that date is usually the date of separation.

Undefined Terms

Although the definition of net family property refers to the value of property, section 4 does not define the term "value," which can have the following different meanings:

- replacement value—what it would cost to replace the piece of property;
- book value—the value of a piece of property as shown in the financial statements of the business that owns the property (usually this is the purchase price, less depreciation);
- fair market value—the price for which the property could be sold on the open market; and

---

2 Under recent amendments to the Act, the term "property" is stated to include, "in the case of a spouse's rights under a pension plan, the imputed value, for family law purposes, of the spouse's interest in the plan, as determined in accordance with section 10.1."

- fair value—the value that is just and equitable in the circumstances, which might mean intrinsic value, value to the owner, fair market value, or some other amount.

The value of particular pieces of property is often arrived at with the help of professional valuations and appraisals. A law clerk will not generally be required to assign a value to a piece of property, but will be asked to calculate net family property based on values provided by the supervising lawyer.

The definition of net family property talks about property that was owned as of the relevant dates, but does not define what is meant by "owned." Ownership can mean *legal ownership*, in which case the owner of property is the person who is the registered owner, or it can mean *equitable ownership*, in which case ownership is decided on the basis of equitable principles of trust law. (These principles are discussed later in this chapter under the heading "Equitable Property Rights.") It is necessary to decide who owns or owned the various pieces of property before an NFP calculation can be done. However, a law clerk will not be required to make a determination of ownership. Rather, the clerk will be asked to calculate the NFP on the basis of decisions about ownership made by the supervising lawyer.

Excluded Property

Under section 4(2), the value of the following property that a spouse owns on V-day does not form part of the spouse's NFP:

- Property, other than a matrimonial home,[3] that was acquired by gift or inheritance from a third party after the date of the marriage—for example, a gift of a car to the wife from her parents, or a rental property left to the husband by his mother during the marriage.

donor
one who makes a gift

testator
one who makes a will;
one who leaves property
to another by will

- Income from property acquired by gift or inheritance (as described above) if the **donor** or **testator** has expressly stated that it is to be excluded from the spouse's net family property—for example, the rental income from the inherited rental property, if the husband's mother's will specifically stated that the income was to be excluded from the husband's net family property.

- Damages received for personal injuries, nervous shock, mental distress, or loss of guidance, care, and companionship, or the part of a settlement that represents those damages—for example, damages awarded to the husband for injuries suffered as a result of medical malpractice.

- Proceeds of a life insurance policy that are payable on the death of the life insured—for example, life insurance proceeds payable to the wife on the death of her father.

- Property, other than a matrimonial home, into which any of the property referred to above can be traced—for example, corporate shares bought

---

3 "Matrimonial home" is defined in section 18 of the Act to be a property in which one or both of the spouses has an interest and that is or, if the parties have separated, was at the time of the separation ordinarily occupied by the spouses as their family residence.

by the wife using the life insurance proceeds she received on the death of her father.

- Property that the spouses have agreed by way of domestic contract to exclude from a spouse's NFP.
- Unadjusted pensionable earnings under the Canada Pension Plan.

Financial Disclosure

Section 8 of the Act requires each party to a section 7 application to make full and complete financial disclosure to the other side of the matters necessary to calculate that party's NFP.

Each party is required to serve on the other and file with the court a statement verified by oath or statutory declaration disclosing particulars of the following:

- the party's property, debts, and other liabilities
  - as of the date of the marriage,
  - as of V-day, and
  - as of the date of the statement;
- the deductions claimed by the party under the definition of net family property;
- the exclusions claimed by the party under section 4(2); and
- all property that the party disposed of during the two years immediately preceding the making of the statement, or during the marriage, whichever period is shorter.

See Chapter 11 for a more complete discussion of the financial statements required in an NFP application.

Calculating NFP

The actual calculation of NFP involves listing the various categories of property and their values. Working with the wording of section 4, these are the steps to calculate the NFP of a spouse.

Step 1: List and value in V-day amounts all property owned by the spouse at V-day.

Step 2: List and value in V-day amounts all excluded property, and deduct the value of property excluded under section 4(2) from the Step 1 total. Because of the disclosure requirements of section 8, it is necessary to list all property owned on V-day in Step 1 (even though it is excluded property), and then to list and deduct the value of the excluded property in Step 2.

Step 3: List and value in V-day amounts all debts owed by the spouse at V-day, and deduct the total of those debts.

If the value of the debts owed at separation is greater than the value of the property owned at separation, this total will be a negative number.

Step 4: Arrive at a value of assets owned less debts owed by the spouse at the date of marriage:

    a. List and value in marriage-date amounts all property other than a matrimonial home owned by the spouse at the date of marriage.

    b. List and value in marriage-date amounts all debts owed by the spouse other than debts related directly to the acquisition or improvement of a matrimonial home at the date of marriage.

    c. Deduct the total value of the debts from the total value of the assets.

If the value of the debts owed at marriage is greater than the value of the property owned at marriage, this total will be a negative number.

Step 5: Deduct the Step 4 total from the Step 3 total. The total you arrive at is the spouse's NFP. Pursuant to section 4(5), this figure cannot be less than zero. If the calculation produces a result that is less than zero, the spouse's NFP is deemed to be zero.

Repeat Steps 1 through 5 for the other spouse.

Sample Net Family Property Calculation

The best way to gain an understanding of NFP calculations is to do one, so here's a fact situation:

Husband's Financial Situation

At the date of the marriage

- Owned a home worth $400,000 subject to a $75,000 mortgage
- Had a savings account with a balance of $5,000
- Had a student loan with a balance of $10,000

During the marriage

- Sold the home owned at the date of marriage for $475,000
- Purchased a new home jointly with wife for $500,000

At the date of the separation

- Owned a home jointly with wife, now worth $750,000
- Had a savings account with a balance of $10,000
- Had a joint savings account with wife with a balance of $10,000
- Had a credit card balance owing of $10,000

Wife's Financial Situation

At the date of the marriage

- Had shares left to her by her mother worth $20,000
- Had a student loan with a balance of $3,000

During the marriage

- Inherited shares from her father worth $75,000 (father's will was silent on the issue of income from the shares)
- Purchased a home jointly with husband for $500,000

At the date of the separation

- Owned a home jointly with husband, now worth $750,000
- Had a joint savings account with husband with a balance of $10,000
- Owned the shares inherited from her mother before the marriage, now worth $50,000
- Owned the shares inherited from her father during the marriage, now worth $100,000
- Had $15,000 in dividends earned on her father's shares
- Had a credit card balance owing of $3,000

Here's how to do the NFP calculation using the formula as set out in the Act:

Calculation of Husband's NFP

Step 1:   List and value in V-day amounts all property owned by the husband at V-day:

Matrimonial home (1/2 interest)	$375,000
Joint savings account (1/2)	5,000
Savings account	10,000
	$390,000

Step 2:   List and value in V-day amounts all excluded property, and deduct the value of property excluded under section 4(2) from the Step 1 total:

Value of excluded property	$0
	$390,000

Step 3:   List and value in V-day amounts all debts owed by the husband at V-day and deduct the total of those debts:

Credit card balance	$(10,000)
	$380,000

Step 4:   Arrive at a value of assets owned less debts owed by the spouse at the date of marriage:

a. List and value in marriage-day amounts all property other than a matrimonial home owned by the spouse at the date of marriage:

Home	$400,000
Savings	5,000
	$405,000

b. List and value in marriage-date amounts all debts other than debts related directly to the acquisition or improvement of a matrimonial home owed by the husband at the date of marriage:

Student loan	$10,000
Mortgage	75,000
	$85,000

c. Deduct the total value of the debts from the total value of the assets:

	$405,000
	(85,000)
	$320,000

Step 5: Deduct the Step 4 total from the Step 3 total.

	$380,000
	(320,000)
Husband's NFP	$ 60,000

Calculation of Wife's NFP

Step 1: List and value in V-day amounts all property owned by the wife at V-day:

Matrimonial home (1/2 interest)	$375,000
Joint account (1/2)	5,000
Shares from mother	50,000
Shares from father	100,000
Dividends	15,000
	$545,000

Step 2: List and value in V-day amounts all excluded property, and deduct the value of property excluded under section 4(2) from the Step 1 total:

Shares from father	$(100,000)
	$445,000

Step 3: List and value in V-day amounts all debts owed by the wife at V-day and deduct the total of those debts:

Credit card balance	$(3,000)
	$442,000

Step 4: Arrive at a value of assets owned less debts owed by the wife at the date of marriage:

a. List and value in marriage-day amounts all property other than a matrimonial home owned by the spouse at the date of marriage:

Shares from mother	$20,000

b. List and value in marriage-date amounts all debts owed other than debts related directly to the acquisition or improvement of a matrimonial home by the wife at the date of marriage:

Student loan	$3,000

c. Deduct the total value of the debts from the total value of the assets:

	$20,000
	(3,000)
	$17,000

Step 5:   Deduct the Step 4 total from the Step 3 total.

	$442,000
	(17,000)
Wife's NFP	$425,000

The calculation of the equalization payment is as follows:

Wife's NFP	$425,000
Husband's NFP	(60,000)
	$365,000

$$\frac{\$365,000}{2} = \$182,500$$

The wife must pay the husband an equalization payment of $182,500.

Some Key Points

It's important to understand the following issues that arise in connection with the calculation of net family property:

- the determination of excluded property,
- the impact of ownership on NFP calculations, and
- the special treatment given to the matrimonial home.

Determination of Excluded Property

Property is excluded under section 4(2) only if it was acquired by a spouse during the marriage. Property of the same type is treated differently if it was acquired before the marriage. The following example illustrates the difference between property inherited before the marriage and property inherited during the marriage.

During Harry and Sally's marriage, Sally's father died, leaving Sally some Microsoft shares worth $20,000. When Harry and Sally separated, the shares were worth $50,000. Because these shares were inherited during the marriage, they are excluded from Sally's NFP, and Harry does not get to share in their value. If Sally's father had died before her marriage to Harry, the result would be different. Sally would have to share with Harry the increase in value of the shares because the shares would not be excluded from Sally's NFP. Sally would be allowed to deduct only the value of the shares as of the time of the marriage. If the shares were worth $20,000 when she inherited them, $30,000 when she married Harry, and $50,000 when she and Harry separated, the shares would be included in Sally's NFP at the V-day value of $50,000, and she would be able to deduct their marriage-day value of $30,000. Harry would be entitled to a share of the $20,000 increase in value during the marriage.

Impact of Ownership on NFP Calculations

When spouses acquire property during the marriage, title may be put into the name of one or both spouses for a variety of reasons, such as tax considerations, business considerations, or convenience. For example, income-producing property may be put into the name of the spouse with the lower taxable income so that the income from the property will be taxed at a lower tax bracket. Real estate may be put in the name of one spouse because the other spouse is starting a new business, and the spouses don't want to risk losing the property if the business should fail.

Spouses generally do not intend their property to be treated differently on a marriage breakdown because of these decisions. However, the following example shows that the way in which title is held can have a major impact on the NFP of each spouse.

Peter and Wendy were married. At the time of the marriage Peter had $100,000 in cash and Wendy had nothing. At the time of their separation their only asset was their matrimonial home worth $150,000.

(1) If the home is in Peter's name only:

Peter's NFP	
Value of property at separation	$150,000
Less value of property at marriage	(100,000)
	$50,000

Peter's NFP is $50,000

Wendy's NFP is 0

Peter has to pay Wendy an equalization payment of $25,000.

Peter ends up with the following assets:

The house	$150,000
Less a loan to cover the NFP payment to Wendy	(25,000)
	$125,000

Wendy ends up with $25,000

(2) If the home is in Wendy's name only:

Peter's NFP	
Value of property at separation	$0
Less value of property at marriage	(100,000)
	($100,000)

Peter's NFP is 0 (NFP can't be less than 0)

Wendy's NFP	
Value of property at separation	$150,000
Less value of property at marriage	0
	$150,000

Wendy's NFP is $150,000

Wendy has to pay Peter an equalization payment of $75,000.

Peter ends up with the following assets:

Cash	$75,000

Wendy ends up with the following assets:

The house	$150,000
Less a loan to cover the NFP payment to Peter	(75,000)
	$75,000

(3) If the home is in the name of Peter and Wendy jointly:

Peter's NFP	
Value of property at separation	$75,000
Less value of property at marriage	(100,000)
	$(25,000)

Peter's NFP is 0

Wendy's NFP	
Value of property at separation	$75,000
Less value of property at marriage	0
	$75,000

Wendy's NFP is $75,000

Wendy has to pay Peter an equalization payment of $37,500.
Assuming they sell the matrimonial home,

Peter ends up with:

Cash from half-interest in matrimonial home	$75,000
Cash from equalization payment	37,500
	$112,500

Wendy ends up with:

Cash from half-interest in matrimonial home	$75,000
Less payment to Peter	(37,500)
	$37,500

Special Treatment of the Matrimonial Home

The matrimonial home is defined in section 18 of the Act to be a property in which one or both of the spouses has an interest and that is or, if the parties have separated, was at the time of the separation ordinarily occupied by the spouses as their family residence.

The matrimonial home of the spouses is given special treatment in the calculation of NFP:

- If property that is the matrimonial home of the parties was owned by a spouse before the marriage, the spouse cannot deduct its marriage-date value from his or her NFP.

- Property that is the matrimonial home of the parties is not excluded from equalization even though it may have been acquired during marriage by gift or inheritance from a third party, or though it may have been purchased with the proceeds of property excluded under section 4(2).

Here's an example to illustrate the difference in treatment of a matrimonial home acquired by a spouse during the marriage and a matrimonial home acquired by a spouse before the marriage.

At the time of her marriage to Louis, Thelma had $100,000 in cash. Louis had nothing. The day after the wedding, Thelma bought a home which she put in her name alone. The house became the couple's matrimonial home. The home is worth $150,000 at the time of their separation. Louis still has nothing.

Thelma's NFP	
Value of the house at separation	$150,000
Less assets other than matrimonial home owned at time of marriage	(100,000)
Thelma's NFP is	$50,000

Louis's NFP is 0

Thelma must pay Louis an equalization payment of $25,000

Thelma ends up with the following assets:

The house	$150,000
Less loan to pay NFP	(25,000)
	$125,000

Louis ends up with the following assets:

NFP payment of $25,000

If Thelma had bought the house before the marriage:

Thelma's NFP	
Value of the house at separation	$150,000
Less assets other than matrimonial home owned at time of marriage	0
	$150,000

> Louis's NFP is still 0
>
> Thelma must pay Louis an equalization payment of $75,000. Louis ends up with $75,000 and Thelma also ends up with $75,000 (the house, less the $75,000 payment).

Here's an example of the treatment of a matrimonial home purchased with the proceeds of property excluded under section 4(2).

> Neither Homer nor Marge had any assets at the time of their marriage. During their marriage, Homer inherited $100,000. He used the money to purchase a house in his name alone, which became the couple's matrimonial home. The matrimonial home is worth $150,000 at the time of the separation.
>
> Homer cannot exclude the $100,000 inheritance from his NFP because it no longer exists, nor can he exclude the asset into which the inheritance is traceable, because that asset is the matrimonial home. Accordingly, Homer's NFP is $150,000 (the value of the matrimonial home) and Marge's NFP is 0. Homer will be able to keep the house, but will have to pay Marge an equalization payment of $75,000.
>
> If Homer had used the same $100,000 to purchase shares, the result would be different. If the shares are worth $150,000 at the time of the separation, Homer would be able to exclude the full value of the shares from his NFP because the shares are property other than a matrimonial home into which Homer's inheritance can be traced. In this case, Homer's NFP would be 0. He would not have to make an equalization payment to Marge and would get to keep the shares.

If the parties have separated, this special treatment extends only to property that was the matrimonial home of the parties at the time of separation. If property was occupied as a matrimonial home during the marriage, but was no longer being used as a family residence at the time of separation, the property will not be considered a matrimonial home.

Orders the Court May Make

Section 9 of the Act sets out the orders the court may make on an application for an equalization of NFP. A court's primary power is to order one spouse to pay money to the other spouse. In addition, the court may order that

- security be given for the performance of any obligation imposed by the order;
- if it is necessary to avoid hardship, an amount payable be paid in installments during a period not exceeding ten years, or that payment of all or part of the amount be delayed for a period not exceeding ten years; and
- if it is needed to satisfy an obligation imposed by the order,
  - property be transferred to or in trust for or vested in a spouse, or
  - property be **partitioned** or sold.

partition
divide

Section 10.1 of the Act sets out the orders the court may make with respect to a spouse's interest in a pension plan.

Power of Court Not to Equalize

The court has the power under section 5(6) not to order a strict equalization if it is of the opinion that equalizing the net family properties would be *unconscionable* having regard to any of the following circumstances:

- a spouse's failure to disclose debts or other liabilities existing at the date of marriage,
- the fact that debts or other liabilities used to reduce a spouse's net family property were incurred recklessly or in bad faith,
- the extent to which a spouse's net family property consists of gifts from the other spouse,
- a spouse's intentional or reckless depletion of his or her net family property,
- the fact that the amount a spouse would receive on an equalization is disproportionately large in relation to a period of cohabitation that is less than five years,
- a written agreement between the spouses that is not a domestic contract, or
- any other circumstance relating to the acquisition, disposition, preservation, maintenance, or improvement of property.[4]

It is not enough that a strict equalization would be unfair. It must be grossly unfair, to the point that it shocks the conscience.

The Matrimonial Home

In addition to the right to seek an equalization of NFP, married spouses are given special rights under part II of the *Family Law Act* with respect to the matrimonial home.

Definition of Matrimonial Home

The matrimonial home is defined in section 18 of the Act to be "[e]very property in which a person has an interest and that is or, if the spouses have separated, was at the time of separation ordinarily occupied by the person and his or her spouse as their family residence." Subject to the effects of a designation of a matrimonial home (discussed below), it is possible for spouses to have any number of matrimonial homes.

---

4 The Ontario Court of Appeal has held that a significant post-separation market-driven decrease in value of a spouse's assets may render a strict equalization unconscionable.

Right to Possession of the Matrimonial Home

Under section 19, both spouses have an equal right to possession of a matrimonial home. This right exists even if title to the matrimonial home is registered in the name of only one of the spouses, although in that case the right of the other spouse to possession is personal as against the titled spouse—that is, the right can be asserted only against the spouse who holds title to the property—and ends when the couple ceases to be spouses, unless a separation agreement or court order provides otherwise.

Under section 24, regardless of ownership of the matrimonial home, and despite section 19, a court may make an order granting one spouse **exclusive possession** of the matrimonial home or part of it for a period stipulated by the court. Without this order, one spouse, even if he or she is the sole registered owner of the property, does not have the right to force the other spouse to leave the matrimonial home on a marriage breakdown.

exclusive possession
the sole right to reside in the home to the exclusion of the other spouse

In determining whether to make an order for exclusive possession, the court is required to consider the following:

- the best interests of the children who are affected,
- the existence of any property and support orders,
- the financial positions of both spouses,
- any written agreement between the spouses,
- the availability of other affordable and suitable accommodation, and
- any violence committed by one spouse against the other spouse or against the children.

In determining the best interests of a child, the court is required to consider the following:

- the possible disruptive effects on the child of a move to other accommodation, and
- the views and preferences of the child, if they can be reasonably ascertained.

Orders for exclusive possession are generally made only if it can be shown that there is domestic violence or that the order is required in the best interests of a child.

Disposition and Encumbrance of the Matrimonial Home

Whichever spouse is the registered owner of the matrimonial home, section 21 forbids the spouses from disposing of or encumbering an interest in the home unless:

- the other spouse consents to the transaction,
- the other spouse has released all rights under part II of the Act by way of a separation agreement,
- a court order authorizes the transaction or releases the property from the application of part II of the Act, or
- another property has been designated by both spouses to be their matrimonial home.

If a spouse tries to transfer title or mortgage a matrimonial home without complying with section 21, the court may hold that the mortgage or transfer is not valid if the transferee or mortgagee was aware of the fact that the property was a matrimonial home or was acting in concert with the spouse. If, however, the transferee or mortgagee actually paid for the property or advanced money under a mortgage, was not acting in concert with the spouse, and had no knowledge that the property was a matrimonial home, the transaction will not be considered invalid.

Joint Tenancy in the Matrimonial Home

joint tenancy
property is owned by two or more people and, on the death of one owner, the property passes to the other(s) automatically and not to the estate of the owner who died

Ordinarily, if title to property is held in **joint tenancy** and one of the joint tenants dies, the other joint tenant receives full title to the property by right of survivorship. Under section 26 of the Act, however, the right of survivorship does not apply if a spouse dies while owning an interest in a matrimonial home as a joint tenant with a third person and not with the surviving spouse. In this case, the joint tenancy is considered to have been severed immediately before the spouse's death.

Designation of the Matrimonial Home

Under section 20, one or both spouses may designate a property owned by one or both of them as a matrimonial home by registering the prescribed designation form on the title to the property.

On registration of a designation made by both spouses, the property becomes the matrimonial home of the spouses, and any other property that otherwise satisfies the definition of matrimonial home, but is not also designated by both spouses, ceases to be a matrimonial home. If the parties subsequently cancel the designation, all properties that satisfy the definition of matrimonial home again become the matrimonial homes of the spouses.

If only one spouse registers a designation, it does not affect the status of other potential matrimonial homes. Why would one spouse designate a property as a matrimonial home? To alert prospective purchasers or mortgagees that the property is a matrimonial home and subject to the rights of the spouse.

presumption of resulting trust
an equitable principle under which it is presumed that a person who places property in the name of another person intends that person to hold the property in trust for the donor

Equitable Property Rights

Historically, if one person pays for property but places title to the property in the name of another person, there is a presumption that the second person holds title in trust for the person who paid for the property. This is called the **presumption of a resulting trust**, and it is an attempt to give effect to the intention of both parties. Under section 14 of the *Family Law Act*, the presumption of a resulting trust applies in questions of property ownership between husband and wife, as if they were not married.

constructive trust
a trust imposed on the legal owner of property in favour of another person who has contributed work, money, or money's worth to the acquisition, preservation, or maintenance of the property

More recently, equitable principles have been applied to impose on the legal owner of property a **constructive trust** in favour of another person who has contributed work, money, or money's worth to the acquisition, preservation, or maintenance of a piece of property. The remedy of constructive trust is available to married spouses in determining questions of ownership of property under the *Family Law Act*.

Here's an example.

Lucy and Ricky were married. Ricky bought and paid for a small apartment building that he registered in his name alone. Lucy did not contribute any money to the purchase of the building; however, she managed the building throughout the marriage—finding tenants, collecting rents, evicting troublesome tenants, maintaining the building, and making repairs. On separation, Lucy may make a claim that she has an ownership interest in the building because of her contribution of work and money's worth to the preservation and maintenance of the property. A court would determine a value for her contribution and decide that Ricky holds that portion of the value of the property in trust for Lucy. That portion of the property would form part of Lucy's NFP.

Rights of Unmarried Couples

As stated earlier, only married spouses are entitled to seek an equalization of their net family properties under the *Family Law Act*. The property provisions of the Act do not apply to parties who are simply cohabiting, regardless of the length of their relationship.

The division of property between unmarried spouses is determined purely on the basis of ownership, using legal and equitable principles. Generally speaking, each unmarried spouse is entitled to the property registered in his or her name, unless the non-titled spouse can prove that the property is being held in trust for him or her under either a resulting trust (because the non-titled spouse in fact paid for the property) or a constructive trust (because the non-titled spouse contributed work, money, or money's worth to the acquisition, preservation, or maintenance of the property).

In addition, the definition of matrimonial home does not apply to non-married spouses, so they have no special rights with respect to their family residence.

Tax Consequences of Property Transfers

Although the *Family Law Act* provides for the making of an equalization payment rather than the transfer of property between spouses, most separating spouses settle the equalization issue by transferring various properties between them. There are income tax implications to these transfers.[5]

Spousal Rollovers

In ordinary circumstances, when a person transfers a piece of property (whether by way of a sale or a gift) that has increased in value since it was acquired, a **capital gain** results. The capital gain is the difference between the cost at which the property was acquired (the **adjusted cost base**) and the value at which it is transferred (the **adjusted sale price**). One-half of any capital gain is added to the person's income and taxed.

capital gain
the profit made on the sale or other disposition of capital property

adjusted cost base
the cost at which capital property was acquired

adjusted sale price
the value at which capital property is transferred

---

5 These provisions also apply to a "common law partner"—a person of the same or opposite sex with whom the taxpayer has a relationship and with whom the taxpayer has been living for 12 continuous months.

There is no capital gain, however, when a person transfers property to his or her spouse. Instead, the government treats the property as if it had been originally acquired by the transferee spouse at the same time and at the same cost as it was actually acquired by the transferor spouse. When the transferee spouse ultimately disposes of the property, he or she bears the full tax liability for any capital gain calculated from the original acquisition cost. This is called a "spousal rollover." There is an automatic spousal rollover for all transfers of property between spouses during marriage or as part of a family law settlement.

The spouses may choose to opt out of the automatic rollover provisions of the *Income Tax Act*.[6] In that case, the transfer is treated as a transfer between non-spouses. The transferring spouse will be liable for tax on any capital gain based on the increase in value between the date the property was acquired and the date it is transferred to his or her spouse. When the spouse to whom the property is transferred in turn disposes of the property, he or she is liable for tax on any capital gain based on the increase in value between the date the property was transferred to him or her and the date he or she disposes of the property. If the spouses do not want the automatic rollover provisions to apply, one of them must file an election to that effect with his or her tax return for the year.

Attribution of Capital Gains

attribution of capital gains
the decision by the Canada Revenue Agency to treat the capital gain of one spouse as the capital gain of the other spouse

If there is a spousal rollover, and the transferee spouse disposes of the property before the end of the year in which the original transfer took place, the tax department can choose not to tax the capital gain in the hands of the transferee spouse, but rather to **attribute the capital gain** to the transferor spouse—in other words, to treat the capital gain as if it were that of the transferor spouse. The tax department will do this if the transferor's income is higher than the transferee's because the capital gain will then be taxed at the transferor's higher tax rate. When the transfer of property comes about as a result of a separation, the parties can avoid this risk of attribution of capital gains by filing a joint election with their income tax returns for the year.

Principal Residence Exemption

principal residence
under the *Income Tax Act*, a residential property in which the taxpayer or other family member has resided during the taxation year

There is no capital gain when a taxpayer disposes of his or her **principal residence**. A property qualifies as a principal residence if a taxpayer or other family member has resided in the property during the taxation year. A taxpayer may have only one principal residence for any given period. Spouses are allowed only one principal residence between them until the year after they separate.

If the spouses own more than one property that could qualify as a principal residence, they should agree which property should be designated as the principal residence for each of the relevant years.

Registered Retirement Savings Plans

Ordinarily, a person who wishes to transfer his or her RRSP to another person must "collapse" the plan by withdrawing all of the money in the plan. When a person withdraws money from his or her RRSP, the amount is taxed as income. However, when an RRSP is transferred as a result of a marriage breakdown under a separation agreement or court order, there is no tax payable.

---

6 RSC 1985, c 1 (5th Supp), as amended.

CHAPTER SUMMARY

When spouses separate, they have the right to seek a division of their property. The way property is divided depends on whether or not the couple is married.

If the parties are married, the property division is achieved through a process called equalization of net family properties in accordance with a formula set out in the *Family Law Act*. The equalization process allows spouses to share equally in the value of most property acquired during the marriage and in the increase in value during the marriage of property owned at the time of marriage. Only married spouses are entitled to seek an equalization of their net family properties under the *Family Law Act*. The division of property between unmarried spouses is based purely on ownership, using legal and equitable principles.

Married spouses also have an equal right to possession of a matrimonial home owned by either or both of them.

Unmarried spouses have no special rights with respect to their family residence.

Both married and unmarried spouses may claim an interest in property owned by their spouses based on equitable principles. Under the "presumption of resulting trust," if one spouse pays for property but places title to the property in the name of the other spouse, it is presumed that the second spouse holds title in trust for the first. Under the principle of "constructive trust," a person, other than the legal owner of a property, who has contributed work, money, or money's worth to the acquisition, preservation, or maintenance of a piece of property may be entitled to an interest in the property.

Most separating spouses settle the equalization issue by transferring various properties between them, but there are income tax implications to these transfers.

KEY TERMS

adjusted cost base, 129
adjusted sale price, 129
attribution of capital gains, 130
capital gain, 129
constructive trust, 128
donor, 116

exclusive possession, 127
joint tenancy, 128
partition, 125
presumption of resulting trust, 128
principal residence, 130
testator, 116

REVIEW QUESTIONS

1. Who may apply for an equalization of NFP? Who may not apply? Why not?

2. What triggering events give rise to the right to seek an equalization of NFP?

3. What is the definition of "net family property" in the *Family Law Act*?

4. What is the definition of "property" in the *Family Law Act*?

5. What is the definition of "valuation date" in the *Family Law Act*?

6. How may the term "value" be defined? Is a definition provided in the *Family Law Act*?

7. How may the term "ownership" be defined? Is a definition of "ownership" provided in the *Family Law Act*?

8. What property is excluded from a spouse's NFP?

9. What financial disclosure are the spouses required to make on an NFP application?

10. How is "matrimonial home" defined in the *Family Law Act*?

11. What special treatment is the matrimonial home given in the equalization of NFP?

12. What orders may a court make on an equalization application?

13. What is "the presumption of resulting trust"?

14. What is a "constructive trust"?

15. How many matrimonial homes may spouses have?

16. How do spouses designate property as a matrimonial home? What is the effect of such a designation?

17. What rights of possession does a spouse have to a matrimonial home?

18. What rights does a spouse have with respect to the disposal or encumbrance of a matrimonial home?

19. What is a "capital gain"?

20. What is the "adjusted cost base" of a property?

21. What is the "adjusted sale price" of a property?

22. What is a "spousal rollover"?

23. What is meant by "attribution of capital gains"?

24. What is the "principal residence exemption"?

EXERCISES

1. Using the following facts, calculate the NFPs of the spouses and the equalization of their NFPs.

Husband's Financial Situation

At the date of the marriage
- Owned a home worth $400,000 subject to a $75,000 mortgage.
- Had a stock account at Merrill Lynch worth $400,000.
- Had shares (private corporation) in a sales business worth $500,000.
- Had a savings account with a balance of $80,000.

During the marriage
- Took $300,000 from his Merrill Lynch account and purchased a condominium in Florida, taking title jointly with the wife.
- Took the remaining $100,000 in the Merrill Lynch account and placed it in the joint names of the husband and wife.

- Received a settlement for a personal injury claim in the amount of $60,000.
- Lost his business, which went bankrupt.

At the date of separation
- Continues to own the same home he owned at marriage. (The parties reside there most of the year.) Home is now worth $600,000 and is subject to a mortgage of $50,000.
- Has the condominium in Florida (jointly owned with the wife) worth $400,000. The parties reside there during the winter months.
- Has the joint stock account (with the wife) at Merrill Lynch, now worth $200,000.
- Has the personal injury settlement of $60,000.
- Has a savings account with a balance of $10,000.

Wife's Financial Situation

At the date of the marriage
- Had no assets and no debts.

During the marriage
- The husband purchased a condominium in Florida for $300,000 and took title jointly with her.
- The husband placed $100,000 into a Merrill Lynch account in joint names with her.

At the date of separation
- Has the condominium in Florida (jointly owned with the husband) worth $400,000. The parties reside there during the winter months.
- Has the joint stock account (with the husband) at Merrill Lynch, now worth $200,000.
- Has a savings account with a balance of $10,000.

2. Using the following facts, calculate the NFPs of the spouses and the equalization of their NFPs.

Wife's Financial Situation

At the date of the marriage
- Owned a condominium townhouse then worth $100,000 which she and her husband lived in during the marriage until separation.
- Had a fur coat valued at $2,000.
- Had a car worth $8,000.
- Had a sculpture, which she had inherited from her father, worth $5,000.
- Had a bank account containing $1,000.
- Had credit card debts of $1,000.

During the marriage
- The wife received $40,000 as damages from a car accident in which she was injured. She invested the $40,000 in Cineplex shares.

Husband's Financial Situation

At the date of marriage
- Had a Jeep worth $5,000.
- Owned a small courier company valued at $15,000.
- Had a bank account containing $5,000.
- Had no debts.

During the marriage
- The husband inherited some Bell Canada shares from his father, then worth $20,000.

At the date of separation
- Has the same condominium she owned at marriage, in which she and the husband lived until separation, now worth $350,000.
- Has the fur coat which she owned at marriage, now worth only $1,000.
- Has a new car worth $30,000 (the old one was sold).
- Has the sculpture which she owned at marriage, now worth $10,000.
- Has the Cineplex shares purchased with her settlement proceeds, now worth $50,000.
- Has a joint savings account with the husband with a total balance of $20,000.
- Has no debts.

At the date of separation
- Has a Cadillac worth $50,000 (the Jeep was sold).
- Still owns the courier company, now worth $250,000.
- Has the joint account with the wife with a total balance of $20,000.
- Still has the inherited Bell Canada shares, now worth $25,000.
- Has a car loan with an outstanding balance of $5,000.

PART III

Procedure in Family Law Matters

The Family Law Rules

10

LEARNING OUTCOMES

After completing this chapter, you should be able to:

■ Explain the organization of the *Family Law Rules*.

■ Identify the steps in a family law case.

■ Identify and apply the relevant rules to various procedural issues.

Introduction

The procedure in family law matters in all courts is governed by the *Family Law Rules*.[1] The *Family Law Rules* is a regulation made pursuant to the *Courts of Justice Act*.[2]

Overview of the Family Law Rules

The *Family Law Rules* are written in plain language, and the forms under the rules are designed to be comprehensive and easy to use.

The Primary Objective

Rule 2(2) states that the "primary objective" of the *Family Law Rules* is to enable the court to deal with cases justly. This means

- ensuring that the procedure is fair to all parties,
- saving expense and time,
- dealing with the case in ways that are appropriate to its importance and complexity, and
- giving appropriate court resources to the case while taking account of the need to give resources to other cases.

For the purposes of promoting the primary objective, the court is given the power, under Rule 1(7.2), to make various procedural orders at any point in a case. Under Rule 1(8) if a person fails to obey an order, the court may

- make an order for costs,
- dismiss a claim,
- strike out any document filed by a party,
- order that all or part of a document that was required to be provided but was not, may not be used in the case,
- order that a party is not entitled to any further order from the court unless the court orders otherwise,
- postpone the trial or any other step in the case, or
- make a contempt order.

The same orders, other than a contempt order, may be made if a person fails to follow the rules.

In addition, under Rule 1(8.2), the court may strike out all or part of any document that may delay or make it difficult to have a fair trial or that is inflammatory, a waste of time, a nuisance, or an abuse of the court process. Under Rule 1(8.4), if an order is made striking out a party's application, answer, motion to change or

---

1   O Reg 114/99.

2   RSO 1990, c C.43.

response to motion to change in a case, the party is not entitled to any further notice of steps in the case and is not entitled to participate in the case in any way.

Case Management

Case management is one of the key features of the *Family Law Rules*. All cases under the *Family Law Rules* are case managed. Rule 2(5) requires the court to promote the primary objective, of dealing with cases justly, by active management of cases, which includes the following:

- at an early stage, identifying the issues, and separating and disposing of those issues that do not need full investigation and trial;
- encouraging and facilitating use of alternatives to the court process;
- helping the parties to settle all or part of the case;
- setting timetables or otherwise controlling the progress of the case;
- considering whether the likely benefits of taking a step justify the cost;
- dealing with as many aspects of the case as possible on the same occasion; and
- if appropriate, dealing with the case without parties and their lawyers needing to come to court, on the basis of written documents or by holding a telephone or video conference.

A case management judge is assigned to each case. The role of the case management judge is to

- generally supervise the progress of the case,
- conduct case and settlement conferences,
- schedule a case or settlement conference if appropriate, and
- hear motions in the case.

Rule 17 provides for three types of case management conferences: a case conference, a settlement conference, and a trial management conference.

The purpose of these conferences is to define, narrow, or even settle the issues in dispute. The various types of conferences may be combined in appropriate circumstances. Under Rule 14, except in cases of urgency or hardship, no motion may be brought before a case conference is held.

Under Rule 39 (which applies to cases in the Family Court of the Superior Court of Justice),[3] all cases are placed on either a standard track or a fast track. Cases that involve divorce or property claims are standard track cases. All other cases are fast track cases.

Fast track cases are assigned a first court date at the time the proceeding is commenced. On or before the first court date, the court clerk will review the file to make

---

3 Case management in the Ontario Court of Justice is governed by Rule 40, and case management in the Superior Court of Justice (other than the Family Court of the Superior Court of Justice) is governed by Rule 41.

sure that the case is ready to proceed before a judge. A case management judge is assigned to the case before the first time the case comes to court.

Cases on the standard track are not assigned a court date at the time the proceeding is commenced. These cases do not come before a judge until a party requests a case conference or brings an urgent motion. A case management judge is assigned to the case at that time.

Rule 39 also sets timelines for the trial of family law cases. In both fast track and standard track cases, if a case has not been scheduled for trial within 365 days from the start of the case, the court sends a notice to the parties advising them that the case will be dismissed in 60 days if no steps are taken.

Steps in a Case

A case goes through the following steps:

1. *Application*—The case is started by the filing of an application. The party who files the application is the applicant. The other party is the respondent. The application sets out the issues that the court is being asked to resolve. If the application includes a claim for support and/or an equalization of net family property, the applicant must also file a financial statement. The application and any financial statement must be served on the respondent.

2. *Answer*—If the respondent wishes to defend the application, he or she must serve the applicant with an answer and file it with the court. If financial support or an equalization of net family property is claimed in the application, or if the respondent wishes to make such a claim, he or she must also serve and file a financial statement.

3. *Mandatory Information Program*—In most contested cases the parties must attend a Mandatory Information Program, which provides information about separation and the legal process.

4. *First court date*—Fast track cases are given a first court date at the time the application is filed. If an answer has not been filed and the respondent does not appear at the first court date, the matter will proceed as an uncontested trial. If the respondent files an answer and/or appears at the first court date, the next step is a case conference.

5. *Case conference*—A case conference takes place after the first court date in fast track cases, and when either party requests one in standard track cases. The case conference is the first opportunity for the parties to discuss the case with a judge.

6. *Settlement conference*—A judge may schedule a settlement conference if he or she thinks it is necessary. The primary purpose of a settlement conference is to try to settle or narrow the issues in dispute.

7. *Trial management conference*—If the case does not settle, a judge may schedule a trial management conference if he or she thinks it is necessary. The purpose of a trial management conference is to continue to explore settlement possibilities, and, failing settlement, to make decisions affecting how the trial will proceed.

8. *Trial*—The trial judge will hear the evidence of the parties and their submissions as to the relevant law and then make final orders on any unresolved issues.

While the case is ongoing, either party may bring a motion to ask the court to make temporary orders to resolve certain issues before trial—for example, orders for interim custody and support. Only emergency or procedural motions may be brought before the case conference. Other motions may be brought after the case conference.

Table 10.1 lists the principal rules that govern each of these steps.

TABLE 10.1   Steps in a Case

Step	Rule	Description
1.	Rule 8	Application
2.	Rule 10	Answer
3.	Rule 8.1	Mandatory Information Program
4.	Rule 39(5)	First court date for fast track cases
5.	Rule 17(4)	Case conference
6.	Rule 17(5)	Settlement conference
7.	Rule 17(6)	Trial management conference
8.	Rule 23	Trial

The Family Law Rules: A More Detailed Look

There are 48 rules. For the most part, they are sequenced in the same order as the steps in a case. The forms required by the Rules are numbered to correspond to the rule that governs the particular form. Some of the more important rules are discussed below.

Rule 3: Time

Rule 3 states how the number of days between two events is counted:

- The first day counted is the day after the first event, and the last day counted is the day of the second event.
- For example, motion documents must be served at least four days before the motion date. The date of service is considered to be the first event and the date of the motion is considered to be the second event. If a motion is scheduled for Friday, November 7 and the motion documents are served on Monday, November 3, Tuesday is the first day counted, Wednesday is the second day, Thursday is the third day, and Friday is the fourth day. Therefore, service on Monday is four days before the motion on Friday.

- If a rule or order gives less than seven days for something to be done, Saturdays, Sundays, and other days when court offices are closed do not count as days of the period.
- If the last day of a period of time under a rule or order falls on a day when court offices are closed, the period ends on the next day that they are open.

The rule also states that late filing of documents is not permitted without a court order or the written consent of the other party.

Rule 5: Where a Case Starts and Is to Be Heard

There are strict rules governing the place where a case can be started. A case must be started

- in the municipality where a party resides;
- if the case deals with custody or access, in the municipality where the child ordinarily resides; or
- in a municipality chosen by all parties, but only with the court's permission.

All steps in a case, other than enforcement of an order, are to take place where the case is started.

Rule 6: Service of Documents

Most court documents must be served on the other party. There are two levels of service under the *Family Law Rules*—special service and regular service.

Special service, which is dealt with in Rule 6(3), is required for an application, a summons to witness, a notice of contempt motion, and any other document that can lead to imprisonment. Special service of a document is carried out by

- leaving a copy with the person to be served or, if the person is a corporation, by leaving a copy with an officer, director, or agent of the corporation, or with a person who appears to be managing a place of business of the corporation (if the person to be served is mentally incapable, a copy must also be left with the person's guardian; if the person is a child, a copy must also be left with the child's lawyer, if there is one); (service is effective on the day the copy of the document was left or on the following day if the document was left after 4 p.m.);
- leaving a copy with the person's lawyer of record in the case, or with a lawyer who accepts service in writing on a copy of the document (service is effective on the day the copy of the document was left or on the following day if the document was left after 4 p.m.);
- mailing a copy to the person, together with an acknowledgment of service postcard, in which case service is not valid unless the return postcard, signed by the person, is filed with the court; or

- leaving a copy at the person's place of residence with anyone who appears to be an adult person resident at the same address and, on the same day or on the next day, mailing another copy to the person at that address (service is effective on the fifth day after the document was mailed).

Regular service, which is dealt with in Rule 6(2), applies to all other documents. Methods of regular service include

- mailing a copy to the person's lawyer or, if none, to the person (service is effective on the fifth day after mailing);
- sending a copy by courier to the person's lawyer or, if none, to the person (service is effective on the day after the day the courier picks up the document);
- depositing a copy at a **document exchange** to which the person's lawyer, or if none, the person belongs (service is effective on the day after the date-stamp given by the document exchange);
- if the person consents or the court orders, using an electronic document exchange (service is effective on the date shown on the record of service provided by the electronic document exchange, or if served after 4 p.m., the following day);
- faxing a copy to the person's lawyer or, if none, to the person (service is effective on the date shown on the first page of the fax, or if served after 4 p.m., the following day); or
- if the person consents or the court orders, emailing a copy to the person's lawyer or, if none, to the person (service is effective on the date shown in the email message, or if served after 4 p.m., the following day).

In all cases, if the effective date of service would be a day on which court offices are closed, service is instead effective on the next day the court offices are open.

Under Rule 6(15), the court may order **substituted service**, using a method chosen by the court, if the party making the motion provides detailed evidence showing what steps have been taken to locate the person to be served and, if located, what steps have been taken to serve the person. The party making the motion must also show that the method of substituted service is likely to bring the document to the person's attention.

Under Rule 6(16), the court may dispense with service if reasonable efforts to locate the person to be served have not been or would not be successful, and there is no method of substituted service that could reasonably be expected to bring the document to the person's attention.

Pursuant to Rule 6(19), service of a document may be proved by

- an acceptance or admission of service, written by the person to be served or his or her lawyer,
- an affidavit of service (Form 6B),
- a return postcard of the kind mentioned in Rule 6(3)(c),

document exchange
a subscription service in which law firms have access to a central facility to deliver and pick up documents

substituted service
service using a method ordered by the court in circumstances when the usual methods of service provided by the court rules are not effective

- the date stamp on a copy of the document served by deposit at a document exchange, or
- a record of service provided by an electronic document exchange.

Rule 7: Parties

The parties in a case are the applicant—the person who makes a claim—and the respondent—the person against whom a claim is made. All cases have a permanent case name and court file number. The person named as the applicant remains the applicant, even if the respondent later moves to vary a final order.

Rule 8: Starting a Case

All cases are started by filing an application. In fast track applications, the court clerk assigns a court date. The applicant is required to serve the application immediately on every other party, using special service.

Rule 8.1: Mandatory Information Program

This rule applies to cases that deal with property, support and custody, a restraining order, or a motion to change a final order or agreement. All parties are required, within 45 days after the case is started, to attend a mandatory information program that provides information about separation and the legal process. The applicant must arrange his or her own appointment and then obtain an appointment for the respondent, and serve notice of the appointment on the respondent with the application. Each party must file a certificate of attendance with the court not later than 2 p.m. two days before the case conference in the case.

A party is not permitted to take any step in a case before filing his or her certificate of attendance, except that the respondent may file an answer and either party may make an appointment for a case conference. The court may order that the provisions of the rule not apply because of urgency or hardship, or for some other reason in the interest of justice.

Rule 9: Continuing Record

A person starting a case is required to prepare a continuing record of the case, which will be the court's permanent record of the case. The general rule is that any document that is served and filed must be inserted into the continuing record. The party must serve the continuing record on all other parties and file it with the court, along with the affidavits of service or other documents proving that the continuing record was served.

Once the continuing record is filed, the parties, under the supervision of the court clerk, are responsible for maintaining the continuing record. In a number of circumstances, instead of a single continuing record, the continuing record may be separated into separate records for the applicant and the respondent.

Under Rule 9(6), in preparing and maintaining the continuing record, the parties must meet the requirements set out in a document entitled "Formal Requirements of the Continuing Record Under the *Family Law Rules*," which is published by the Family Rules Committee and available online at <http://www.ontariocourtforms .on.ca>. There is a more detailed discussion of the continuing record later in this chapter.

Rule 10: Answering a Case

A respondent who wants to defend a case must serve and file an answer within 30 days (60 days if the respondent was served outside Canada or the United States). A respondent may include a claim against the applicant or any other person in his or her answer.

If a respondent does not serve and file an answer, or if an answer is struck out, the respondent is not entitled to notice of any step in the case, or to participate in the case in any way.

A party may, within 10 days after being served with an answer, serve and file a reply in response to a claim made in the answer.

Rule 11: Amending an Application, Answer, or Reply

An applicant may amend the application without the court's permission if no answer has been filed or, if an answer has been filed, with the consent of all parties. A respondent may amend the answer without the court's permission within 14 days after being served with an amended application or, otherwise, with the consent of all parties. If court permission is required, under Rule 11(3) the court shall give permission unless the amendment would disadvantage another party in a way for which costs or an adjournment could not compensate.

In accordance with Rule 11(4), an amendment shall be clearly shown by underlining all changes; the rule or order permitting the amendment and the date of the amendment shall be noted in the margin of each amended page.

Rule 13: Financial Disclosure

Under Rule 13(1), parties are required to serve and file the appropriate financial statement (Form 13 or Form 13.1) if an application, answer, reply, or motion contains a claim for support, property, or exclusive possession, whether or not the matter is defended. The applicant must serve and file the financial statement with his or her application, and the respondent must serve and file his or her financial statement within the time for serving and filing his or her reply.[4]

---

4 If the only claim is for child support in the table amount under the *Child Support Guidelines*, (SOR/97-175) or O Reg 391/97, no financial statement is required by the applicant. However, the respondent must file a statement. In addition, parties to a claim for spousal support under the *Divorce Act* (RSC 1985, c 3 (2d Supp)) do not need to serve and file financial statements if they file a consent agreeing not to serve and file financial statements or agreeing to a specified amount of support.

According to Rules 13(3.1) and (3.2), a party required to serve a financial statement (Form 13) in a support claim is required to serve at the same time a certificate of financial disclosure (Form 13A) along with the following documents:

- the income and financial information referred to in subsection 21(1) of the *Child Support Guidelines*;
- if the party became unemployed within the last three years, a complete copy of the party's Record of Employment, or other evidence of termination, and a statement of any benefits or income that the party is still entitled to receive from his or her former employer despite or as a result of the termination;
- in the case of a claim for the support of a child, proof of the amount of any special or extraordinary expenses, within the meaning of section 7 of the *Child Support Guidelines*.

According to Rules 13(3.3) and (3.4), a party required to serve a financial statement (Form 13.1) in a property claim is required to serve a certificate of financial disclosure (Form 13A) along with supporting documents, as specified in the rule, no later than 30 days after the financial statement was due. See Chapter 11 for a list of the required documents.

The certificate of disclosure must be filed by the applicant no later than seven days before a case conference, and by the respondent no later than four days before the case conference.

Under Rule 13(7), in a claim for support, the court will not accept a financial statement for filing unless it includes copies of the party's income tax returns and notices of assessment for the three previous taxation years. If those documents are unavailable for any of those three years, an Income and Deductions printout from the Canada Revenue Agency, or a sworn statement that the party is not required to file an income tax return because of the *Indian Act*[5] must be included.

Under Rule 13(10), if the Rules require the delivery of a financial statement, the court will not accept an application, answer, reply, notice of motion, or affidavit for filing without the financial statement.

A party who believes that the other party's financial statement does not contain enough information for a full understanding of that party's financial circumstances may ask for additional information. If the other party does not comply within seven days, the dissatisfied party may apply to the court for an order that the other party give the information under Rule 13(11). According to Rule 13(13), a party may question the other party on his or her financial statement under Rule 20, but only after a request for additional information has been made.

The parties are required to update their financial statements as the case progresses. Under Rules 13(12), (12.1), (12.2), and (13.1), the parties must serve and file a new financial statement and certificate of disclosure, or an affidavit that the information in the financial statement has not changed, before any case conference, motion, settlement conference, or trial. Rule 13(15) also requires the parties to

---

5   RSC 1985, c I-5.

immediately correct any information that has materially changed or that is discovered to be incorrect or incomplete.

The parties to a property claim under part I of the *Family Law Act* must also serve and file a net family property statement (Form 13B) before a settlement conference or trial, under Rule 13(14), and a comparison of net family properties (Form 13C) before a settlement conference, under Rule 13(14.2).

Rule 13 is discussed in greater detail in Chapter 11.

Rule 14: Motions for Temporary Orders

A person may make a motion to the court for any of the following:

- a temporary order for a claim made in an application,
- directions on how to carry on the case, and
- a change in a temporary order.

Except in cases of urgency or hardship, motions are not permitted before a conference that deals with the substantive issues in the case has been held.

Rules 14(9) and (10) set out the documents required on a motion. Most motions require a notice of motion (Form 14) and affidavit (Form 14A). However, if the motion is limited to procedural, uncomplicated, or unopposed matters, the party making the motion may use a motion form (Form 14B) instead of a notice of motion and affidavit.

Most motions are made on notice to the other party. Pursuant to Rule 14(11), the motion documents must be served on the other parties no later than four days before the motion date, and filed with the court no later than two days before the motion date. The party making the motion must also file a confirmation (Form 14C) with the court no later than 2 p.m. two days before the motion date. Under Rule 14(11.1), no documents for use on the motion may be filed after that time.

Under Rule 14(12), a motion may be made without notice if

- the nature or circumstances of the motion make notice unnecessary or not reasonably possible;
- there is an immediate danger of a child's removal from Ontario, and the delay involved in serving a notice of motion would probably have serious consequences;
- there is an immediate danger to the health or safety of a child or of the party making the motion, and the delay involved in serving a notice of motion would probably have serious consequences; or
- service of a notice of motion would probably have serious consequences.

Under Rule 14(14), any order made on a motion without notice must require the matter to come back before the court, and before the same judge if possible, within 14 days. It is to be served immediately on the other parties (Rule 14(15)).

Pursuant to Rule 14(21), if a party tries to delay the case, add to its costs, or in any other way tries to abuse the court's process by making numerous motions without merit, the court may order the party not to make any other motions in the case without the court's permission.

Rule 15: Motions to Change a Final Order or Agreement

Rule 15 sets out the procedure to vary an agreement for support filed under section 35 of the *Family Law Act* or a final order, such as a final custody or support order.

Rule 5 (where a case starts) applies to a motion to change a final order or agreement as if the motion were a new case. The party making the motion must serve and file a motion to change form and a change information form, with all required attachments. The documents must be served by special service, not regular service, and 30 days' notice (60 days' notice if the other party to be served resides outside Canada or the United States) is required.

Rule 16: Summary Judgment

motion for summary judgment
a motion for a final order without a trial

In any case other than a divorce,[6] either party may make a **motion for summary judgment** for a final order without a trial, after the respondent has served an answer or after the time for serving an answer has expired.

Under Rule 16(4), a motion for summary judgment is to be supported by an affidavit or other evidence demonstrating that there is no genuine issue requiring a trial.

Rule 17: Conferences

Rule 17 deals with the conferences that are at the heart of the case management system. Each contested case must have at least one conference.

The purposes of a case conference, which are set out in Rule 17(4), include

- exploring the chances of settling the case;
- identifying the issues that are in dispute and those that are not in dispute;
- exploring ways to resolve the issues in dispute;
- ensuring disclosure of the relevant evidence;
- noting admissions that may simplify the case;
- setting the date for the next step in the case;
- if possible, having the parties agree to a specific timetable for the case;
- organizing a settlement conference, or holding one if that is appropriate; and
- giving directions with respect to any intended motion.

In a fast track case, the parties may be given a date for the case conference when they go to court for the first court date,[7] or a party may ask that the case conference be held at the same time as the first court date. In a standard track case, a case conference will be scheduled when either party requests one. Under Rule 17(4.1),

---

6   In a divorce case, Rules 36(5) to 36(7) set out the procedure to be followed if a divorce is undefended.

7   In fast track cases, the first court date is set by the court clerk when the application is filed.

a party who asks for a case conference must serve and file a case conference notice (Form 17).

The purposes of a settlement conference, which are set out in Rule 17(5), include

- exploring the chances of settling the case;
- settling or narrowing the issues in dispute;
- ensuring disclosure of the relevant evidence;
- noting admissions that may simplify the case;
- if possible, obtaining a view of how the court might decide the case;
- considering any other matter that may help bring a quick and just conclusion to the case;
- if the case is not settled, identifying the witnesses and other evidence to be presented at trial, estimating the time needed for trial, and scheduling the case for trial; and
- organizing a trial management conference, or holding one if that is appropriate.

Under Rule 17(10), a case cannot be scheduled for trial unless a judge has conducted a settlement conference or has ordered that the case be scheduled for trial without a settlement conference. A judge who conducts a settlement conference on an issue will not be the judge who hears the issue at trial (see Rule 17(24)).

The purposes of a trial management conference, which are set out in Rule 17(6), include

- exploring the chances of settling the case;
- arranging to receive an agreed statement of fact or evidence in written form, if appropriate;
- deciding how the trial will proceed;
- ensuring that the parties know what witnesses will testify and what other evidence will be presented at trial;
- estimating the time needed for a trial; and
- setting the trial date, if this has not already been done.

The various conferences may be combined on the direction of the judge. Rule 17(8) allows the judge to make various orders at a conference, if notice has been served.

Under Rule 17(13.1), the party requesting the conference is required to serve and file the appropriate **conference brief** no later than seven days before the date scheduled for the conference, and the other party is obliged to do so no later than four days before that date. The conference briefs are

- case conference brief (Form 17A or Form 17B),
- settlement conference brief (Form 17C or Form 17D), and
- trial management conference brief (Form 17E).

conference brief
a case conference brief (Form 17A or Form 17B), a settlement conference brief (Form 17C or Form 17D), or a trial management conference brief (Form 17E)

Under Rule 17(14), each party must also file a confirmation (Form 14C) no later than 2 p.m. two days before the date scheduled for the conference. No documents for use at the conference may be served or filed after this time.

Under Rule 17(21), trial management conference briefs form part of the continuing record. Under Rule 17(22), case conference briefs do not form part of the continuing record unless the court orders otherwise and, in that case, under Rule 17(22.1), any portion of the brief that deals with settlement of the case is to be deleted. Under Rule 17(22.2), settlement conference briefs do not form part of the continuing record.

Pursuant to Rule 17(15), the parties and their lawyers must attend each conference. If a conference is adjourned because a party is not prepared, has not served the required brief, has not made the required disclosure, or has otherwise not followed the rules under Rule 17(18), that party will be ordered to pay costs.

Rule 18: Offers to Settle

A party may serve an offer to settle on any other party. Under Rule 18(4), the offer is to be signed personally by the party making it, and also by that party's lawyer, if there is one. Once an offer is made, under Rule 18(5) it may be withdrawn by serving a notice of withdrawal at any time before the offer is accepted. An offer may also be time-limited. An offer that is not accepted within the time set out in the offer is considered to have been withdrawn under Rule 18(6). An offer that has not expired or been withdrawn may be accepted by a party, even if the party has previously rejected the offer or made a counteroffer (see Rule 18(10)). An offer expires and may not be accepted after the court begins to give a decision that disposes of a claim dealt with in the offer (Rule 18(7)).

The terms of an offer are confidential; under Rule 18(8), they may not be mentioned in any document filed in the continuing record and may not be mentioned to the judge hearing the claim dealt with in the offer.

Under Rule 18(14), a party who makes an offer that is not accepted and who obtains an order that is as favourable as or more favourable than the offer is entitled to partial costs to the date the offer was made, and full recovery of costs from the date it was made, as long as an offer relating to a motion was made at least one day before the motion date and an offer relating to a trial was made at least seven days before the trial.

Rule 19: Document Disclosure

If requested by the other party, a party must, within 10 days, give an affidavit listing every document that is relevant to any issue in the case and in the party's control, or available to the party on request.

Rule 20: Questioning a Witness and Disclosure

as of right
without needing the consent of the other party or an order of the court

Under Rule 20(3), in a child protection case, a party is entitled, **as of right**, to obtain information from another party about any issue in the case. In all other cases, a party is entitled to obtain information only with the consent of the party or an order of the court (Rule 20(4)).

Under Rule 20(5), the court may make an order that a person be questioned under oath or disclose information by affidavit if

- it would be unfair to the party who wants the questioning or disclosure to carry on with the case without it,
- the information is not easily available by another method, and
- the questioning or disclosure will not cause unacceptable delay or undue expense.

The court may make an order that a person be questioned or disclose details about information in an affidavit or net family property statement.

Rule 22: Admission of Facts

A party may, at any time, serve a request to admit (Form 22) on another party, asking the party to admit, for the purposes of the case only, that a fact is true or that a document is genuine. The other party served is deemed to admit that the fact is true or the document is genuine, unless he or she serves a response (Form 22A) within 20 days.

Rule 23: Evidence and Trial

Under Rule 23(1), the applicant must serve and file a **trial record** at least 30 days before the start of the trial. A trial record must contain a table of contents and the following documents:

- the application, answer, and reply, if any;
- any agreed statement of facts;
- financial statements and net family property statements, if applicable, completed not more than 30 days before the record is served;
- if the trial involves a claim for custody of or access to a child, the applicable documents referred to in Rule 35.1;
- any assessment report ordered by the court or obtained by consent of the parties;
- any temporary order relating to a matter still in dispute;
- any order relating to the trial; and
- the relevant parts of any transcript on which the party intends to rely at trial.

Under Rule 23(2), no later than seven days before the start of the trial, the respondent may serve, file, and add to the trial record any document not already in the record.

Under Rule 23(3), a party who wants a witness to give evidence in court must serve a summons to witness (Form 23), together with a witness fee of $50.

trial record
a document that assembles and organizes documents relevant to the trial to be used by the trial judge

Pursuant to Rule 23(23), a party who wants to call an expert witness at trial must serve and file the expert's report at least 90 days before the start of the trial.

Rule 24: Costs

There is a presumption that a successful party is entitled to costs at each step in the case. However, under Rule 24(4), a successful party who has behaved unreasonably during a case may be deprived of all or part of the party's own costs or ordered to pay all or part of the unsuccessful party's costs. Under Rule 24(10), the judge must decide who is entitled to costs and shall set the amount of the costs promptly after each step.

Rule 25: Orders

Under Rule 25(2), the party in whose favour an order is made is required to prepare a draft of the order (Form 25, 25A, 25B, 25C, or 25D). If that party does not have a lawyer or does not prepare the draft order within 10 days after the order is made, any other party may do so unless the court orders otherwise (Rule 25(3)). If neither party has a lawyer, the clerk will prepare the order.

Pursuant to Rule 25(4), the party who prepares an order is required to serve a draft, for approval of its form and content, on every other party who was in court or was represented when the order was made (including a child who has a lawyer). The order will then be signed by the judge who made it or by the clerk.[8] In accordance with Rule 25(13), once the order is signed, the person who prepared the order is required to serve it on every other party, including a respondent who did not attend.

Rule 35.1: Custody and Access

Rule 35.1 sets out the procedure to be followed in a case that involves custody and/or access. The rule and the procedure under it are discussed in Chapter 13.

Rule 36: Divorce

Rule 36 sets out the procedure to be followed in a divorce case. The rule and the procedure under it are discussed in Chapter 12.

Rule 39: Case Management in Family Court of the Superior Court of Justice

Rule 39 applies only to cases in the Family Court of the Superior Court of Justice. All cases are placed on either a standard track or a fast track. Cases involving claims for divorce or property claims are standard track cases. All other cases are fast track cases.

In fast track cases, a case management judge is assigned to the case before the case comes to court. In standard track cases, a case management judge is assigned to the case when a party requests a case conference or brings an urgent motion.

---

8   Rules 25(5) to 25(7) set out the procedure for settling the contents of a disputed order.

Rule 39(9) sets out the functions of a case management judge. The case management judge assigned to a case

- generally supervises its progress,
- conducts the case conference and the settlement conference,
- on his or her own initiative, schedules a case conference or settlement conference at any time, and
- hears motions in the case, when available to hear motions.

Rule 39 also sets timelines for the trial of family law cases. In both fast track and standard track cases, if a case has not been settled, withdrawn, or scheduled or adjourned for trial within 365 days from the start of the case, the court sends a notice to the parties advising them that the case will be dismissed in 60 days if no steps are taken.

Rule 40: Case Management in Ontario Court of Justice

Because the Ontario Court of Justice does not have jurisdiction over property or divorce cases, all cases before this court are fast track cases. Rule 40[9] contains the same provisions as Rule 39 as they relate to fast track cases.

Rule 41: Case Management in the Superior Court of Justice (Other Than the Family Court of the Superior Court of Justice)

Under Rule 41, all cases before the Superior Court of Justice are treated like standard track cases, and Rule 40 contains the same provisions as Rule 39 as they relate to standard track cases.

The Continuing Record

Under the *Family Law Rules*, a **continuing record** is required for most cases. The continuing record is the court's record of all the documents in a case. The general rule is that any document that is served and filed must be inserted into the continuing record.

The continuing record is governed by Rule 9. In addition, a document entitled "Formal Requirements of the Continuing Record Under the *Family Law Rules*" (published by the Family Rules Committee and available online at <http://www .ontariocourtforms.on.ca>) sets out the requirements for preparing and maintaining the continuing record.

continuing record
the court's records of all the documents in a case

---

9 In those areas where the Family Court of the Superior Court of Justice does not operate, including the City of Toronto and the Regional Municipality of Peel, jurisdiction over family law matters continues to be divided between the Superior Court of Justice and the Ontario Court of Justice. In those locations, cases that include divorce or property claims must be brought before the Superior Court of Justice, while cases that involve only custody and/or support claims may be brought before either the Superior Court of Justice or the Ontario Court of Justice.

Creation of the Continuing Record

According to Rule 9(1), a person starting a case must prepare a single continuing record of the case, serve it on all other parties, and file it, along with the affidavits of service or other documents proving that the continuing record was served.

Pursuant to Rules 9(3) and 9(4), there are, in addition, two specialized continuing records:

- a *support enforcement continuing record*, which is used if a support order is filed with the director of the Family Responsibility Office, and is to be filed by the person bringing the case before the court; and
- a *child protection continuing record*, which is used in an application for a child protection order.

Formal Requirements of the Continuing Record

Rule 9(6) states that, in preparing and maintaining the continuing record, the parties must meet the requirements set out in a document entitled "Formal Requirements of the Continuing Record Under the *Family Law Rules*" published by the Family Rules Committee and available online at <http://www.ontariocourtforms.on.ca/>. See below for a detailed discussion of that document.

Separate or Combined Continuing Record

Pursuant to Rule 9(7), in any case other than a child protection case, instead of a single continuing record, the continuing record may be separated into separate records for the applicant and the respondent. The court may order separate records on its own initiative or at the request of either party at a case conference, settlement conference, or trial management conference. If the continuing record is separated, the separate records are called the applicant's record and the respondent's record.

Under Rule 9(8), the court may order that separated continuing records be combined into a single record on its own initiative or at the request of either party at a case conference, settlement conference, or trial management conference. Under Rule 9(9), the parties may, on agreement, combine the separate records into a single continuing record, in which case the parties must arrange together for the combining of the records.

If the court orders on its own initiative that the continuing record is to be separated or combined, the court must give directions as to which party should separate or combine the record as required. If the court makes the order at the request of a party, the party that makes the request must separate or combine the record, as required, unless the court orders otherwise.

Maintaining the Continuing Record

According to Rule 9(11), in a case with a single continuing record, the parties are responsible, under the clerk's supervision, for adding all documents filed to the continuing record. In a case with separate records, each party is responsible, under the clerk's supervision, for adding the documents the party files to the party's own record.

Under Rule 9(12) if there is a single record, a party serving documents must serve and file any documents that are not already in the continuing record, and serve with the documents an updated cumulative table of contents listing the documents being filed. If the continuing record has been separated, a party serving documents must serve and file any documents that are not already in that party's separate record, and serve with the documents an updated cumulative table of contents listing the documents being filed in that party's separate record. According to Rule 9(13), a party is not to serve and file any document that is already in the record. Under Rule 9(15) a party who is relying on a document in the record shall refer to it by its tab in the record. Once a document is placed in the continuing record, under Rule 9(16), it is not to be removed except by order.

If a court gives written reasons for making an order, according to Rule 9(17), it may be written by hand on an endorsement sheet in the continuing record, or the endorsement on the endorsement sheet may be a short note that written reasons are being given separately. The clerk of the court is required to add a copy of the reasons to the endorsement section of the record.

Continuing Record on Appeal

If a final order is appealed, under Rule 9(19) only the notice of appeal and any order of the appeal court are to be added to the continuing record.

Overview of "Formal Requirements of the Continuing Record Under the Family Law Rules"

Rule 9(6) states that, in preparing and maintaining the continuing record, the parties must meet the requirements set out in a document entitled "Formal Requirements of the Continuing Record Under the *Family Law Rules*" published by the Family Rules Committee and available online at <http://www.ontariocourtforms.on.ca/>.

Contents of the Record

Generally, the continuing record consists of two volumes: an endorsements volume and a documents volume. The applicant is required to file both volumes at the same time. No separate endorsements volume is required in

- joint applications for divorce;
- uncontested divorces in which the only claim is for divorce, when the respondent does not file an answer;
- consent orders to change child support when the applicant files a change information form and the respondent does not file an affidavit; or
- a consent motion for a final order.

In these situations, the continuing record must include a separate section for endorsements and one blank sheet on which the judge dealing with the case will note the disposition and the date.

A new continuing record is required for all applications, motions to change, and enforcement proceedings filed in the same court file, but the same endorsement volume may be used.

Record Cover

The endorsements volume will have a yellow cover, which will include the court file number and names of the parties to the case. The documents volume will have a red cover. It must conform with the sample cover in Appendix B to the "Formal Requirements of the Continuing Record Under the *Family Law Rules*," a copy of which is reproduced as Figure 10.1 at the end of this chapter.

All elements of the sample cover must appear on a party's record cover. The title of the record must appear in bold, font size 20, below the names of the parties to the case. The cover must identify the volume number of the record.

Filing Documents

Documents must be filed in chronological order, with the most recently filed document at the back. All documents filed in the record must be three-hole punched. A numbered tab must identify each document filed. Tabs must be in sequential order. A new volume must start with a new tab sequence starting with tab 1. Pages between numbered tabs must be numbered consecutively. Page numbers are not required to appear in the table of contents.

Table of Contents

The one cumulative table of contents for the continuing record is located in the endorsements volume. The table of contents must list the documents in the order in which they are filed and indicate the volume in which the document is located, the tab number that locates the document, the kind of document, which party filed it, the date of the document, and the date it was filed. For an affidavit or transcript of evidence, the name of the person who gave the affidavit or the evidence must also be shown. Affidavits of service must be listed in the table of contents, including a notation as to the document(s) served and the party who was served. The table of contents must be updated every time a document is filed. A sample table of contents is attached to the "Formal Requirements of the Continuing Record Under the *Family Law Rules*" at Appendix C, and is reproduced in Figure 10.2 at the end of this chapter.

Endorsements

The endorsements section of the endorsements volume must be identified by a tab or divider, and must contain three blank sheets (or more if necessary) on which the judge dealing with any step in the case will note the disposition of that step and the date. Any written reasons for judgment and minutes of settlement that form the basis of an order must be put in the endorsements section.

Orders

The orders section of the endorsements volume must be identified by a tab or divider. The court's file copy of each order made in the case must be put in the orders section.

Documents Volume

The documents volume contains the documents filed in the case, each under its own numbered tab, including

- applications,
- answers,
- replies,
- financial statements (income tax returns need not be attached unless the court orders),
- motions,
- affidavits, and
- trial management conference briefs.

Affidavits of Service

Affidavits of service must be filed within the tab of the document to which the affidavit of service relates, behind the document. If the affidavit of service relates to more than one document, it must be filed within the tab of the first document to which it relates.

Separating or Combining Records

If the court orders that the continuing record is to be separated or that separate continuing records are to be combined, the court staff must supervise the separation or combination.

- If the continuing record is separated, unless otherwise ordered by the court, the party requesting the separate records must prepare an updated cumulative table of contents reflecting the contents of both records.
- If separate continuing records are combined, the party directed to combine the record, or the party that requested the combination, must prepare an updated cumulative table of contents that reflects the contents of the combined record.

Summary

Attached to the "Formal Requirements of the Continuing Record Under the *Family Law Rules*" at Appendix A is a summary of the contents of the continuing record. This summary is reproduced in Figure 10.3 at the end of this chapter.

CHAPTER SUMMARY

The procedure in family law matters is governed by the *Family Law Rules*, a regulation made pursuant to the *Courts of Justice Act*. The rules are designed to ensure that the procedure is fair to all parties, saves expense and time, and allocates court resources appropriately. There are 48 Rules, which are generally sequenced in the same order as the steps in a case.

Case management is one of the key features of the *Family Law Rules*. There are three types of case management conferences—case conferences, settlement conferences, and trial management conferences—which define, narrow, or settle disputed issues. All cases are placed on either a standard track or a fast track.

A family law case follows a series of steps. First, the applicant files an application setting out the issues that require resolution. A respondent wishing to defend the application serves and files an answer. Parties in most cases must attend a Mandatory Information Program to get information about separation and the legal process. The first court date is then set. In every case in which an answer is filed there will be at least one case management conference. While the case is ongoing, either party may bring a motion to ask the court to make temporary orders. If the case is not settled, a trial will take place during which a judge hears the parties' evidence and submissions as to the relevant law before making final orders on any unresolved issues.

The continuing record is the court's record of all the served and filed documents in a case, and is required for all cases. A person starting a case must prepare a single continuing record of the case, serve it on all other parties, and file it with the court.

KEY TERMS

as of right, 150
conference brief, 149
continuing record, 153
document exchange, 143

motion for summary judgment, 148
substituted service, 143
trial record, 151

REVIEW QUESTIONS

1. What is the primary objective of the *Family Law Rules*?

2. How is the court required under Rule 2(5) to promote the primary objective?

3. What is the role of the case management judge?

4. What types of case management conferences are provided for under the *Family Law Rules*?

5. What types of cases are placed on the standard track? What types of cases are placed on the fast track?

6. What eight steps does a family court case go through?

7. In what municipality must a case be started?

8. When is special service of a document required? What are the methods of special service?

9. When is regular service of a document permitted? What are the methods of regular service?

10. How may service of a document be proved?

11. How are cases started under the *Family Law Rules*?

12. Who is responsible for maintaining the continuing record?

13. What must a respondent who wants to defend a case do?

14. Who may amend an application, answer, or reply?

15. When may a party make a motion? What documents are required on a motion?

16. What rule governs the procedure to vary an agreement or final order?

17. In what circumstances may a party apply for a summary judgment?

18. What cost consequences may flow from the making of an offer to settle?

19. Who is required to prepare a draft order?

20. When is a continuing record required?

21. When is a continuing record not required?

22. What are the two specialized continuing records?

23. What document sets out the formal requirements for the continuing record and where can the document be found?

24. When may the continuing record be separated into separate records for the applicant and the respondent?

25. When may separated continuing records be combined into a single record?

26. Who is responsible for maintaining the continuing record?

27. What must a party serving documents do?

28. Describe the contents of the continuing record.

29. How are documents to be filed in the continuing record?

FIGURE 10.1 Appendix B: Sample Cover

APPENDIX B – SAMPLE COVER

ONTARIO

Court File Number / *Numéro de dossier du greffe*

_____
(Name of court / *Nom du tribunal*)

at / *situé(e) au* _____
Court office address / *Adresse du greffe*

Volume / *Volume* : _____

Applicant(s) / *Requérant(e)(s)*

Full legal name & address for service — street & number, municipality, postal code, telephone & fax numbers and e-mail address (if any). *Nom et prénom officiels et adresse aux fins de signification — numéro et rue, municipalité, code postal, numéros de téléphone et de télécopieur et adresse électronique (le cas échéant).*	Lawyer's name & address — street & number, municipality, postal code, telephone & fax numbers and e-mail address (if any). *Nom et adresse de l'avocat(e) — numéro et rue, municipalité, code postal, numéros de téléphone et de télécopieur et adresse électronique (le cas échéant).*

Respondent(s) / *Intimé(e)(s)*

Full legal name & address for service — street & number, municipality, postal code, telephone & fax numbers and e-mail address (if any). *Nom et prénom officiels et adresse aux fins de signification — numéro et rue, municipalité, code postal, numéros de téléphone et de télécopieur et adresse électronique (le cas échéant).*	Lawyer's name & address — street & number, municipality, postal code, telephone & fax numbers and e-mail address (if any). *Nom et adresse de l'avocat(e) — numéro et rue, municipalité, code postal, numéros de téléphone et de télécopieur et adresse électronique (le cas échéant).*

Children's Lawyer / *Avocat des enfants*

Name & address of Children's Lawyer's agent for service (street & number, municipality, postal code, telephone & fax numbers and e-mail address (if any) and name of person represented. *Nom et adresse de la personne qui représente l'avocat(e) des enfants aux fins de signification (numéro et rue, municipalité, code postal, numéros de téléphone et de télécopieur et adresse électronique (le cas échéant) et nom de la personne représentée.*

Continuing Record

(Title of record in bold, font size 20 or equivalent / *Intitulé du dossier en caractères gras; police de taille 20 ou l'équivalent*)

FIGURE 10.2   Appendix C: Sample Table of Contents

APPENDIX C – SAMPLE TABLE OF CONTENTS

ONTARIO

	Court File Number

_____
(Name of court)

at _____
Court office address

**Cumulative Table of Contents
Continuing Record**

Applicant(s)

Full legal name & address for service — street & number, municipality, postal code, telephone & fax numbers and e-mail address (if any).	Lawyer's name & address — street & number, municipality, postal code, telephone & fax numbers and e-mail address (if any).

Respondent(s)

Full legal name & address for service — street & number, municipality, postal code, telephone & fax numbers and e-mail address (if any).	Lawyer's name & address — street & number, municipality, postal code, telephone & fax numbers and e-mail address (if any).

Document (For an affidavit or transcript of evidence, include the name of the person who gave the affidavit or the evidence.)	Filed by (A = applicant or R = respondent)	Date of Document (d, m, y)	Date of Filing (d, m, y)	Volume/Tab
Application	A	11/10/06	20/10/06	Volume 1, Tab 1 (page # in support enforcement continuing record)
Affidavit of Service of Application on Respondent	A	18/10/06	20/10/06	Volume 1, Tab 1
Financial Statement	A	11/10/06	20/10/06	Volume 1, Tab 2
Answer	R	6/12/06	6/12/06	Volume 1, Tab 3
Affidavit of Service of Answer on Applicant	R	6/12/06	6/12/06	Volume 1, Tab 3
Financial Statement	R	6/12/06	6/12/06	Volume 1, Tab 4
Notice of Motion	R	5/6/07	5/6/07	Volume 1, Tab 5
Affidavit of Service of Notice of Motion on Applicant	R	5/7/07	5/6/07	Volume 1, Tab 5
Affidavit (name of person)	R	5/6/07	5/6/07	Volume 1, Tab 6
Affidavit in Response (name of person)	A	4/7/07	4/7/07	Volume 2, Tab 1
Affidavit of Service of Affidavit in response on Respondent	A	4/7/07	4/7/07	Volume 2, Tab 1
Notice of Motion to change final order dated 1/08/07	R	1/02/09	10/02/09	Volume 3, Tab 1
Affidavit of Service of Notice of Motion on Applicant	R	5/02/09	10/02/09	Volume 3, Tab 1
Financial Statement	R	1/02/09	10/02/09	Volume 3, Tab 2

☐ *Continued on next sheet*
(Français au verso)

FIGURE 10.3   Appendix A: Summary of Contents

APPENDIX A – SUMMARY OF CONTENTS

CONTINUING RECORD		
SINGLE RECORD	**SEPARATE RECORDS IF ORDERED**	
	Applicant's Record	**Respondent's Record**
Endorsements Volume	**Endorsements Volume**	**Endorsements Volume**
Yellow cover	Yellow cover	
- Table of Contents - Endorsements, incl. Reasons for Judgment and Minutes of Settlement - Orders	- Table of Contents - Endorsements, incl. Reasons for Judgment and Minutes of Settlement - Orders	N/A
Documents	**Documents**	**Documents**
Red cover	Red cover	Blue cover
- All documents, including affidavits of service, in chronological order	- All applicant documents, including affidavits of service, in chronological order	- All respondent documents, including affidavits of service, in chronological order

Financial Disclosure

11

LEARNING OUTCOMES

After completing this chapter, you should be able to:

- Explain the history of financial disclosure in family cases.

- Explain the legislative requirements for financial disclosure.

- Complete financial statement Forms 13 and 13.1.

163

Introduction

Whenever the parties have claims against each other for support, exclusive posses-sion of the matrimonial home, and/or equalization of net family property, they must make full and complete financial disclosure of all of their assets and liabilities, and their incomes and expenses.

In this chapter we will look at

- the history of financial disclosure in family cases,
- the legislative requirements for financial disclosure,
- the specific financial statements required by the *Family Law Rules*,[1] and
- the completion of the financial statement forms.

History of Financial Disclosure

Financial disclosure in family law cases is now routine—it is the usual first step in the negotiation of a separation agreement, and an integral part of any litigation. However, this was not always the case.

Historically, it was up to the plaintiff to prove all elements of his or her claim. So, if a plaintiff asserted a claim to a share in the property of his or her spouse, it was up to the plaintiff to prove that the property existed, that the defendant owned the property, that the property had a certain value, and that part of this value was owing to the plaintiff. If the plaintiff claimed support for himself or herself or for a child, in addition to proving his or her need for support, the plaintiff had to prove that the defendant had the ability to pay support by establishing what the defendant earned.

This approach to family law litigation changed when the *Family Law Reform Act*[2] was passed in 1978, requiring parties to a family law matter to serve and file financial statements on each other. Early on, the courts made it clear that what was required under the Act was full, complete, and up-to-date disclosure, and that failure to make such disclosure could have unfavourable consequences.

In *Silverstein v Silverstein*,[3] Mr. Justice Galligan stated:

> [T]he legislature of Ontario ... intended to require that full, complete and up-to-date information be provided to the opposite party and to the court at the earliest possible opportunity. ... Such statements must not be perfunctory *pro forma* docu-ments, but they must be real, complete, up-to-date and meaningful. ... [A]ny party who does not comply with the letter and the spirit of [the legislation] must real-ize that a court might very well draw unfavourable inferences against that party if a statement under those sections is less than frank and complete. Any unneces-sary prolonging of proceedings because of the failure of such statements to be full,

---

1   O Reg 114/99.
2   RSPEI 1988, c F-3, repealed.
3   1978 CanLII 1605, 20 OR (2d) 185 (SC).

frank and complete ought to be at the cost of the person whose statement or statements are deficient.

Since 1978, the financial disclosure process has been an important part of all family law cases.

Legislative Requirements for Financial Disclosure

The current requirements for financial disclosure are found in the *Family Law Act*,[4] the *Child Support Guidelines*,[5] and the *Family Law Rules*.

The Family Law Act

Section 8 of the *Family Law Act* governs disclosure in net family property equalization applications. The parties are required to serve and file a statement under oath that discloses particulars of

- each party's property and debts and other liabilities:
  - as of the date of the marriage,
  - as of the valuation date (see Chapter 9), and
  - as of the statement date;
- the deductions that each party claims under the definition of "net family property";
- the exclusions claimed by each party under section 4(2); and
- all property disposed of during the previous two years or the period of the marriage (whichever is shorter).

Section 41 of the Act also requires disclosure in support applications, by requiring the parties to serve and file a financial statement under oath in the form required by the rules of the court.

There is no legislative requirement that the parties exchange financial statements if they decide to negotiate a separation agreement without starting court proceedings. However, under section 56(4) of the Act, a court may set aside a domestic contract if one party failed to disclose to the other party significant assets, or significant debts or other liabilities that existed when the domestic contract was made. As a result, most lawyers insist on full and complete financial disclosure before entering into negotiations—usually by the exchange of the sworn financial statements that would be filed in a court proceeding.

---

4   RSO 1990, c F.3.

5   SOR/97-175 and O Reg 391/97.

The Child Support Guidelines

Section 21 of the *Child Support Guidelines* requires the parent or spouse against whom a support claim is made to provide a copy of his or her personal income tax return and notice of assessment and reassessment for each of the three most recent taxation years. A self-employed parent or spouse is required to provide supporting financial statements for his or her business. The applicant parent or spouse must also provide this information if it is necessary to determine his or her income for the purpose of calculating the amount of support.

The Family Law Rules

Rule 13 of the *Family Law Rules* sets out the requirement for financial statements in all family law proceedings.

Form 13—Financial Statement (Support Claims)—must be served and filed if there is a claim for support, but no claim for property or exclusive possession of the matrimonial home. If the only claim is for child support in the table amount under the *Child Support Guidelines*, no financial statement is required by the applicant. However, the respondent must file a statement.

The longer Form 13.1—Financial Statement (Property and Support Claims)—must be filed where there is a claim for property and/or exclusive possession of the matrimonial home, whether or not support is also claimed. In addition, the parties to a net family property equalization case must file Form 13B—Net Family Property Statement.

Under Rule 13(1), both parties are required to serve and file the appropriate financial statement (Form 13 or Form 13.1) if an application, answer, reply, or notice of motion contains a claim for support, property, or exclusive possession, whether or not the matter is defended. The applicant must serve and file the financial statement with his or her application (unless the only claim is for child support in the table amount under the *Child Support Guidelines*), and the respondent must serve and file the financial statement within the time for serving and filing his or her answer.[6]

A party who serves and files a financial statement is also required to serve a certificate of financial disclosure (Form 13A) along with supporting documents, as specified in the rule. According to Rules 13(3.1) and 13(3.2) a party serving a financial statement (Form 13) in a support claim is required to serve the certificate of financial disclosure at the time the financial statement is served. According to Rules 13(3.3) and 13(3.4) a party required to serve a financial statement (Form 13.1) in a property claim is required to serve the certificate of financial disclosure no later than 30 days after the financial statement was due. The required supporting documents will be discussed later in this chapter under the heading "Form 13A: Certificate of Financial Disclosure."

The certificate of financial disclosure must be filed by the applicant no later than seven days before a case conference, and by the respondent no later than four days before the case conference.

In addition, according to Rule 13(14), each party to a property claim must also deliver a net family property statement (Form 13B) not less than seven days before

---

6 Under Rule 13(8), parties to a claim for spousal support under the *Divorce Act* do not need to serve and file financial statements if they file a consent agreeing not to serve and file financial statements or agreeing to a specified amount of support.

a settlement conference, and not more than 30 days and not less than seven days before a trial, and a comparison of net family properties (Form 13C) no later than seven days before a settlement conference, under Rule 13(14.2). Forms 13B and 13C are not required if the claim in the case arises out of a family arbitration claim.

Under Rule 13(7), the court will not accept a financial statement for filing in a support proceeding unless it includes copies of the party's income tax returns and notices of assessment for the three previous taxation years, or a copy of the party's Income and Deduction printout provided by the Canada Revenue Agency. Under Rule 13(10), if the Rules require the delivery of a financial statement, the court will not accept an application, answer, reply, notice of motion, or affidavit for filing without the financial statement.

A party who believes that the other party's financial statement does not contain enough information for a full understanding of the other party's financial circumstances may ask for additional information. If the other party does not comply within seven days, under Rule 13(11) the dissatisfied party may apply to the court for an order that the other party give the information. One party may question the other party on his or her financial statement under Rule 20, but only after a request for additional information has been made.

The parties are required to update their financial statements as the proceeding progresses. Under Rules 13(12), (12.1), (12.2), and (13.1), before any case conference, motion, settlement conference, or trial, the parties must serve and file new financial statements and certificates of disclosure, or affidavits that the information in their financial statements has not changed. Rule 13(15) also requires the parties to correct immediately any information that has materially changed or that is discovered to be incorrect or incomplete.

Collecting Information

The preparation of financial statements is time-consuming and must be done meticulously. Often the client has little knowledge of his or her financial affairs, or how to go about finding the information necessary to complete the statements. The task of completing the statement usually falls to the lawyer—who often delegates the task to an articling student, law clerk, or secretary.

The law firm prepares the financial statement using documents and information provided by the client. The client must be advised of the requirement to provide full, complete, and up-to-date financial information, and that failure to make proper disclosure can result in a judge making adverse findings of fact against the client and/or cost penalties. The client must also understand that he or she is likely to be cross-examined on the content of his or her statement. For all of these reasons, it is important for the client to provide as much information as possible and for that information to be accurate and current.

The client must collect all of the financial documents required to be provided with the certificate of financial disclosure. The required documents will be discussed later in this chapter under the heading "Form 13A: Certificate of Financial Disclosure."

These documents should be organized so that copies are available for delivery to the lawyer for the opposing party as attachments to the certificate of financial disclosure or otherwise as requested.

If the client is cross-examined on the financial statement, he or she is likely to be asked how various amounts in the financial statement were arrived at. As a result, it is important to make and keep notes on these calculations. See Figure 11.1 for an example of notes to a financial statement.

FIGURE 11.1   Notes to Financial Statement of Laura Petrie

Food (Weekly)

• One weekly trip to supermarket	$150.00
• Fresh fruits and vegetables	25.00
• Butcher	50.00
	$225.00

Gifts (Yearly)

• Children's birthdays (2 @ $75.00)	$150.00
• Children's Christmas (2 @ $100.00)	200.00
• Family birthdays (5 @ $40.00)	200.00
• Family Christmas (5 @ $75.00)	375.00
• Children's friends' birthdays (10 @ $25.00)	250.00
	$1,175.00

Form 13: Financial Statement (Support Claims)

This financial statement must be filed by

- a party who is making or responding to a claim for spousal support,
- a party who is responding to a claim for child support, or
- a party who is making a claim for child support in an amount different from the table amount specified under the *Child Support Guidelines.*

A copy of Form 13 can be found at the end of this chapter. Because the form is used for support claims only, it focuses primarily on the income and expenses of the parties.

The party must complete all parts of the form unless he or she is only responding to a claim for child support in the table amount specified under the *Child Support Guidelines* and agrees with the claim. In that case, the party must complete only Parts 1, 2, and 3 of the financial statement.

General Information: Form 13

The first page of the form sets out information about the proceeding and the parties. Complete page one as follows:

- Set out the name of the court and the court office address.
- Insert the court file number if the application has already been started and a court file number has been assigned.
- Set out the full legal name and complete address of each of the parties, along with telephone and fax numbers, and email address, if any.

- Set out the name, address, telephone and fax numbers, and email address of each party's lawyer.
- In paragraph 1, set out
  - the full legal name of the party completing the financial statement, and
  - the municipality and province where the party resides.

Part 1: Income

Paragraphs 2 to 5 of this part set out information about the party's source of income and proof of that income. Fill out these paragraphs by stating

- whether the party is employed, self-employed, or unemployed;
- what proof of current income is being provided—for example, the most current paycheque stub;
- the party's gross income for the previous year; and
- that supporting tax documentation is being provided: tax returns and assessments for three years or, if unavailable for any of those years, an Income and Deductions printout from the Canada Revenue Agency, or that the party is an Indian within the meaning of the *Indian Act*.[7]

The balance of this part details the party's income on a monthly basis. The party must use the most current information available. A party who is self-employed or receives an annual bonus may not know what his or her earnings will be in the next 12 months, and may have to estimate those amounts based on the previous year.

The party must set out his or her *monthly* income. It is important to accurately convert payments received at other intervals to monthly amounts. For example:

- If income is received annually, obtain the monthly income by dividing the yearly income by 12.
- If income is received weekly, multiply the weekly income by 4.33, *not* by 4—there are more than four weeks in each month.
- If income is received every two weeks, divide the biweekly amount by 2 and then multiply by 4.33.

The table on page 2 of the form requires the party to state all income that he or she is currently receiving, including

- Employment income (before deductions)—This information can be found by looking at the party's pay stubs. Usually, salary is paid weekly or biweekly. Set out the *gross* wages—the amount shown on the pay stub *before* deductions are taken for income tax, Canada Pension Plan, employment insurance, etc.
- Commissions, tips, and bonuses—If the party receives commissions, tips, or bonuses, determine the total amount of these items expected to be received over the next 12-month period, and divide by 12 to get a monthly figure. The party

---

7 RSC 1985, c I-5.

may estimate his or her income from these sources if the party's income fluctuates or cannot be ascertained. State on the form when a figure is an estimate.

- Self-employment income—If the party is self-employed, set out the monthly profits of the business (revenue less expenses). You must also set out the monthly amount received before expenses. The party may estimate his or her self-employment income if it fluctuates or cannot be ascertained. State on the form when a figure is an estimate.

- Employment insurance, workers' compensation, and social assistance—If the party receives any of these benefits, set out the monthly amount of the payments.

- Interest and investment income—If the party receives interest and/or other investment income, determine the total payments to be received during the next 12 months and divide by 12 to get a monthly figure. The party may estimate his or her income from these sources if the party's income fluctuates or cannot be ascertained. State on the form when a figure is an estimate.

- Pension income—If the party receives pension benefits, including Canada Pension Plan and Old Age Security, set out the monthly amount of the payments.

- Other sources of income—If the party has income from any sources not already listed, such as net partnership income, net rental income, dividends received from taxable Canadian corporations, net capital gains, and/or RRSP withdrawals, insert the monthly amount of the income from all of these sources, and complete Schedule A, which is discussed below.

Here's an example.

Facts

Laura Petrie is employed as a computer programmer with LRP Data Inc. According to her latest pay stub, her gross salary is $2,692.30 every second week. Her salary is reviewed annually, and she received her last raise on July 1 of this year. Laura usually receives a bonus every December. Her last bonus was $1,500, and she thinks it will be 5 percent higher this year. In addition to her salary, Laura owns shares in a corporation named CruiseCo Inc. on which she received dividends of $240 last year. She expects to be paid the same amount this year. Assume that Laura's financial statement is prepared on November 15, 2017.

Preparation

- Convert Laura's salary to a monthly figure:

  Biweekly salary of $2,692.30 ÷ 2 = weekly salary $1,346.15 × 4.33 = monthly salary of $5,828.83

- Estimate the amount of Laura's bonus for this year, and then convert it to a monthly figure:

  Last year's bonus $1,500.00 × 1.05 = expected bonus for this year of $1,575.00

  Expected bonus of $1,575.00 ÷ 12 = monthly bonus of $131.25

- Convert Laura's dividends to a monthly figure:

  Annual dividends of $240.00 ÷ 12 = monthly dividends of $20.00

Laura's financial statement

Assuming that the financial statement is prepared on November 15, 2017, the income table of Laura's financial statement would look like this:

(In this table you must show all of the income that you are currently receiving.)

	Income Source	Amount Received/Month
1.	Employment income (before deductions)	$ 5,828.83
2.	Commissions, tips and bonuses	$ 131.25 (est.)
3.	Self-employment income (Monthly amount before expenses: $)	$
4.	Employment Insurance benefits	$
5.	Workers' compensation benefits	$
6.	Social assistance income (including ODSP payments)	$
7.	Interest and investment income	$ 20.00
8.	Pension income (including CPP and OAS)	$
9.	Spousal support received from a former spouse/partner	$
10.	Child Tax Benefits or Tax Rebates (e.g. GST)	$
11.	Other sources of income (e.g. RRSP withdrawals, capital gains) *(*attach Schedule A and divide annual amount by 12)*	$
12.	**Total monthly income from all sources:**	$ 5,980.08
13.	**Total monthly income X 12 = Total annual income:**	$ 71,760.96

The table at the top of page 3 of the form requires the party to state the yearly market value of his or her non-cash benefits, such as the use of a company car, health benefits, a club membership, or room and board that the party's employer or someone else provides for the party or that are charged through or written off by the party's business.

This information can frequently be found on the party's T4 slip. If it is not there, contact the party's employee benefits or payroll officer for the information.

Here's an example that continues Laura Petrie's financial statement.

Facts

Assume that Laura's employer pays premiums for health and dental care insurance of $100 per month.

Preparation

- Convert the insurance premiums to an annual figure:

  Monthly premiums of $100.00 × 12 = $1,200.00

Laura's financial statement

The table on page 3 of Laura's financial statement will look like this:

14. Other Benefits

Provide details of any non-cash benefits that your employer provides to you or are paid for by your business such as medical insurance coverage, the use of a company car, or room and board.

Item	Details	Yearly Market Value
Insurance	Health and dental plan premiums	$ 1,200.00
		$
		$
		$

Part 2: Expenses

This part of Form 13 details the party's monthly living expenses in a table on pages 3 and 4 of the form.

The first part of the table details the amounts automatically deducted from the party's pay. Get information about these deductions from the party's pay stubs. Note that, depending on the income level of the party, deductions for Canada Pension Plan and employment insurance may be taken out of every paycheque for part of the year only—until the maximum amount is reached for the year. Accordingly, the pay stub figures for these deductions may not be accurate. You must find out the annual maximums for Canada Pension Plan and employment insurance deductions for the current year (this information is available from the Canada Revenue Agency). Then multiply the deduction amounts for each of these items (taken from the party's pay stub) by the number of pay periods in the year. If that amount is lower than the annual maximum amount, use the paystub amount to arrive at the monthly deduction. If the amount is greater than the annual maximum, use the annual maximum amount to determine the monthly deduction. Convert all amounts to monthly figures.

Here's an example that illustrates the Automatic Deductions portion of Laura Petrie's financial statement.

Fact situation

According to Laura's pay stub, the following amounts are deducted from the pay-cheque that she receives every second week:

- Income tax $604.55
- Canada Pension Plan   126.59
- Employment insurance   42.86
- Union dues   45.00

Preparation

Convert all amounts to monthly figures, keeping in mind that Laura is paid every second week:

- Biweekly income tax of $604.55 ÷ 2 = $302.28 × 4.33 = monthly tax of $1,308.87

- Canada Pension Plan annual maximum for 2017 is $2,564.10. Paystub deduction of $126.59 × 26 = $3,291.34 is higher than the annual maximum. Therefore, take current annual maximum $2,564.10 ÷ 12 = monthly CPP of $213.68

- Employment insurance annual maximum for 2017 is $836.10. Paystub deduction of $42.86 × 26 = $1,114.36 is higher than the annual maximum. Therefore, take current annual maximum $836.10 ÷ 12 = $69.68

- Biweekly union dues of $45.00 ÷ 2 = $22.50 × 4.33 = $97.43

Laura's financial statement

The Automatic Deductions portion of part 2 of Laura's financial statement will look like this:

Expense	Monthly Amount
Automatic Deductions	
CPP contributions	$ 213.68
EI premiums	$ 69.68
Income taxes	$ 1,308.87
Employee pension contributions	$
Union dues	$ 97.43
SUBTOTAL	$ 1,689.66

The rest of the table details the party's living expenses on a monthly basis.

The party should include all living expenses, including expenses of any children living with the party. Be careful when dealing with expenses of the children. For most of the categories of expenses, the amount used will be a total of the party's and the child(ren)'s expenses. In those cases, be sure to keep notes of how the total amount was calculated. For clothing expenses, however, there are separate categories for the party's clothing expense and the child(ren)'s clothing expense.

If the party is living with someone else, give the total household expense, not just the party's share. (Schedule B deals with the contribution of other income earners in the party's home.)

The party should use current expenses or, if the actual expenses cannot be ascertained, his or her best estimate. He or she should not simply guess at amounts, but should review past bills and chequing account records to get as much information as possible about the expenses. If the party has absolutely no idea of the amount of a particular expense, direct him or her to the proper place to find out the amount of a particular expense—for example, the cable company or telephone company for standard monthly rates—or make the inquiries yourself. In addition, Statistics Canada publishes material documenting standard expenses in various cities. Estimated amounts should be clearly indicated on the form.

It is very important that the expenses be as accurate as possible because, as stated earlier, the party will likely be cross-examined on his or her financial statement. For the same reason, it is a good idea to make and keep notes about expenses that are not based simply on regular monthly bills, such as food, clothing, gifts, and entertainment. That way, when the party is cross-examined, he or she will be able to remember and explain how a particular figure was arrived at. See Figure 11.1 for an example of these notes.

If the other party is paying some of the expenses directly—for example, mortgage, utilities, or taxes—the expenses should be included in the financial statement so that the court gets an idea of the actual lifestyle of the party. But mark these expenses with an asterisk and put a note at the bottom of the statement stating that the expenses are paid by the other party.

The party must set out his or her *monthly* expenses. It is important to accurately convert expenses paid at other intervals to monthly amounts:

- If an expense is paid annually, obtain the monthly expense by dividing the yearly expense by 12.
- If an expense is paid weekly, multiply the weekly expense by 4.33, *not* by 4.

There are eight major categories of expenses (in addition to automatic deductions from income) listed in the financial statement:

- Housing
- Utilities
- Household Expenses
- Childcare Costs
- Transportation
- Health
- Personal
- Other Expenses

Calculate a subtotal for each category, and add all subtotals to get the total amount of monthly expenses. Then multiply the monthly expenses by 12 to get the total amount of yearly expenses.

Housing and Utilities

The Housing category includes rent or mortgage, property taxes, condominium fees, home insurance and home repairs. The Utilities category includes water, heat, electricity, telephone, cell phone, cable and Internet.

Here's an example that illustrates the Housing and Utilities portions of Laura Petrie's financial statement.

Fact situation

Since the separation, Laura has remained in the matrimonial home and her Housing expenses are as follows:

- Her husband Rob has been making the monthly mortgage payments of $1,072.
- Rob has also been paying the property taxes, which will be $4,500 this year.
- Her municipal water bill comes twice a year. On the basis of last year's bills, she estimates this year's water bill will be $600.
- Her electric bill comes every two months and averages about $375.
- Her gas heating bill is $200 each month.
- Her basic telephone service is $50 per month and she averages about $35 per month in long-distance charges.
- Her home insurance costs $800 for the year.
- She and Rob have usually spent about $2,500 each year on home repairs and maintenance. In addition, she has a gardener who is paid $100 per month for the months of May through September.
- Her cell phone bill is $75 each month.
- Her cable and Internet bill combined is $100 each month.

Preparation

- Convert the property tax expense to a monthly figure:

  Yearly taxes of $4,500.00 ÷ 12 = $375.00

- Convert the water expense to a monthly figure:

  Yearly water bill of $600.00 ÷ 12 = $50.00

- Convert the electric expense to a monthly figure:

  Average bimonthly electric bill of $375.00 ÷ 2 = $187.50

- Convert the home insurance expense to a monthly figure:

  Yearly insurance expense of $800.00 ÷ 12 = $66.67

- Convert the repair, maintenance, and gardening expense to a monthly figure:

  Yearly maintenance and repairs of $2,500.00 ÷ 12 = $208.33

  Monthly gardening expense of $100.00 × 5 months = $500.00 per year ÷ 12 = $41.67

Laura's financial statement

Here's what the Housing and Utilities portions of Part 2 of Laura's financial statement will look like:

Housing		
Rent or mortgage	$	1,072.00*
Property taxes	$	375.00*
Property insurance	$	66.67
Condominium fees	$	
Repairs and maintenance	$	250.00
SUBTOTAL	$	1,763.67
Utilities		
Water	$	50.00 (est.)
Heat	$	200.00
Electricity	$	187.50
Telephone	$	85.00
Cell phone	$	75.00
Cable	$	100.00
Internet	$	
SUBTOTAL	$	697.50

* expenses paid by husband

Household Expenses

This category includes groceries, household supplies, meals outside the home, pet care, and laundry and dry cleaning. Sometimes an expense can be listed under more than one category—household cleaning supplies, for example, could be placed under groceries or under household supplies. It doesn't really matter which category is used, as long as the expense is claimed only once, and notes are kept so that the client knows how each category was calculated.

Here's an example that illustrates the Household Expenses portions of Laura Petrie's financial statement.

Fact situation

Laura's Household Expenses are as follows:

- She spends $225 each week on groceries, including household supplies
- She has dinner out once a week and spends on average $50.
- She spends on average $20 each month on dry cleaning.

Preparation

- Convert the grocery expense to a monthly figure:

  Weekly expense of $225.00 × 4.33 = $974.25 each month

- Convert the meals outside the home expense to a monthly figure:

  Weekly expense of $50.00 × 4.33 = 216.50

Laura's financial statement

Here's what the Household Expenses portion of Part 2 of Laura's financial statement will look like:

Expense	Monthly Amount
Household Expenses	
Groceries	$ 974.25
Household supplies	$
Meals outside the home	$ 216.50
Pet care	$
Laundry and Dry Cleaning	$ 20.00
SUBTOTAL	$ 1,210.75

Childcare Costs

This category includes daycare expenses and babysitting costs.

Laura's youngest child is 16 and he has no Childcare Costs, so this portion of Part 2 of Laura's financial statement is left blank, and looks like this:

Expense	Monthly Amount
Childcare Costs	
Daycare expense	$
Babysitting costs	$
SUBTOTAL	$

Transportation

This category includes public transit and taxis, gas and oil, car insurance and licence, repairs and maintenance, parking and car loan or lease payments.

Here's an example that illustrates the Transportation portion of Laura Petrie's financial statement.

Fact situation

Laura's Transportation expenses are as follows:
- She takes transit to work every day and spends $146.25 each month for a TTC Metropass
- She puts gas in her car every two weeks at a cost of $60.
- She pays $1,000 each year for car insurance.
- She pays $108 each year for license and registration.
- She spent $850 on car repairs last year and expects to spend the same this year.
- She has no ongoing parking expenses.
- Her car is fully paid for, so she has no loan or lease payments.

Preparation
- Convert the gas expense to a monthly figure:

  Biweekly expense of $60.00 ÷ 2 = $30.00 × 4.33 = $129.90 each month
- Determine combined monthly insurance and license expense:

  Convert insurance expense to a monthly figure:

  Annual expense of $1,000.00 ÷ 12 = $83.33 each month

Convert license expense to a monthly figure

Annual expense of $108.00 ÷ 12 = $9.00 each month

Combine the two monthly expenses

$83.33 + $9.00 = $92.33 each month

- Convert the repairs and maintenance expense to a monthly figure:

Yearly expense of $850.00 ÷ 12 = $70.83

Laura's financial statement

Here's what the Transportation expenses portion of Part 2 of Laura's financial statement will look like:

Expense	Monthly Amount
Transportation	
Public transit, taxis	$ 146.25
Gas and oil	$ 129.90
Car insurance and license	$ 92.33
Repairs and maintenance	$ 70.83
Parking	$
Car Loan or Lease Payments	$
SUBTOTAL	$ 439.31

Health

This category includes health insurance premiums, dental expenses, medicine and drugs, and eye care.

Here's an example that illustrates the Health portion of Laura Petrie's financial statement.

Fact situation

Laura's Health expenses are as follows:

- Her employer pays for her health and dental insurance, so she has no expense for premiums.

- Dental expenses for Laura and her son average $600 per year.

- Because of her health insurance, she does not have to pay for prescription drugs.
- Neither she nor her son wear glasses.

Preparation

- Convert the dental expense to a monthly figure:

   Annual expense of $600.00 ÷ 12 = $50.00 each month

Laura's financial statement

Here's what the Health expenses portion of Part 2 of Laura's financial statement will look like:

Expense	Monthly Amount
Health	
Health insurance premiums	$
Dental expenses	$ 50.00
Medicine and drugs	$
Eye care	$
SUBTOTAL	$ 50.00

Personal

This category includes clothing (for the party only; the children's clothing expense is entered separately under "Other expenses"), hair care and beauty, alcohol and tobacco, education, entertainment/recreation (including children's), and gifts.

Fact situation

Laura's Personal expenses are as follows:
- She spends $2,000 per year on clothing for herself.
- She has her hair cut every other month at a cost of $75 each time.
- She and her son have a family membership at the YMCA at a cost of $100 each month.
- She spends $1,175 each year on gifts.

Preparation

- Convert the clothing expense to a monthly figure:

  Annual expense of $2,000.00 ÷12 = $166.67

- Convert the hair care and beauty expense to a monthly figure:

  Bimonthly expense of $75.00 ÷ 2 = $37.50 × 4.33 = $162.38

- Convert the gift expense to a monthly figure:

  Annual expense of $1,175.00 ÷ 12 = $97.92

Laura's financial statement

Here's what the Personal expenses portion of Part 2 of Laura's financial statement will look like:

Expense	Monthly Amount
Personal	
Clothing	$ 166.67
Hair care and beauty	$ 162.38
Alcohol and tobacco	$
Education (*specify*)	$
Entertainment/recreation (including children's)	$ 100.00
Gifts	$ 97.92
SUBTOTAL	$ 526.97

Other Expenses

This category includes life insurance premiums, RRSP/RESP withdrawals, vacations, school fees and supplies, clothing for children, children's activities, summer camp expenses, debt payments, support paid for other children, and other expenses not shown elsewhere.

Fact situation

Laura's Other expenses are as follows:

- She spends $3,000 per year on vacations for herself and her son.
- She pays on average $500 per year on school supplies for her son.
- She spends $1,200 per year on clothing for her son.
- She pays $545 each year for her son to play in a hockey league.

Preparation

- Convert the vacation expense to a monthly figure:
  Annual expense of $3,000.00 ÷ 12 = $250.00
- Convert the school supply expense to a monthly figure:
  Annual expense of $500.00 ÷ 12 = $41.67
- Convert her son's clothing expense to a monthly figure:
  Annual expense of $1,200.00 ÷ 12 = $100.00
- Convert the hockey expense to a monthly figure:
  Annual expense of $545.00 ÷ 12 = $45.42

Laura's financial statement

Here's what the Other expenses portion of Part 2 of Laura's financial statement will look like:

Expense	Monthly Amount
Other expenses	
Life Insurance premiums	$
RRSP/RESP withdrawals	$
Vacations	$ 250.00
School fees and supplies	$ 41.67
Clothing for children	$ 100.00
Children's activities	$ 45.42
Summer camp expenses	$
Debt payments	$
Support paid for other children	$
Other expenses not shown above *(specify)*	$
SUBTOTAL	$ 437.09

Expense Totals

Add the subtotals for each category of expense to get the total amount of monthly expenses. Then multiply the monthly expenses by 12 to get the total amount of yearly expenses.

Laura's financial statement

Here's what the Totals portion of Part 2 of Laura's financial statement will look like:

Total Amount of Monthly Expenses	$	6,814.95
Total Amount of Yearly Expenses	$	81,779.40

Part 3: Assets

In this part, the party must give details and the estimated market value of all assets that he or she owns as of the date of the statement under the following categories:

- Real estate—set out the address of each property, the nature of ownership, the percentage of the party's interest and the estimated market value of that interest.
- Cars, boats, and vehicles—set out the year and make.
- Other possessions of value—this category includes property such as computers, jewellery, and collections; set out the address where the property is located.
- Investments—this category includes property such as bonds, shares, term deposits, and mutual funds; set out the type, issuer, due date, and number of shares.
- Bank accounts—set out the name and address of the institution and account number.
- Savings plans, RRSPs, pension plans, and RESPs—set out the type, issuer, and account number.
- Life insurance—set out the type, beneficiary, face amount, and cash surrender value.
- Interest in business—set out the name and address of each business, and attach a financial statement for each business.
- Money owed to you—this category includes assets such as court judgments in the party's favour, estate money, and income tax refunds.
- Other assets—include any other assets owned that do not fit into any of the previous categories.

Part 4: Debts

In this part, the party must give details and the current balance of any debts such as mortgages, lines of credit, other loans from a bank, trust or finance company, outstanding credit card balances, unpaid support amounts, and any other debts.

Part 5: Summary of Assets and Liabilities

This part calculates the party's net worth by deducting the total debts from the total assets.

Jurat

The financial statement must be sworn or affirmed under oath and must, therefore, be signed in the presence of a lawyer, justice of the peace, or commissioner for taking affidavits.

Schedule A—Additional Sources of Income

This schedule must be completed if the party has "other sources of income," shown on line 11 in Part 1, including net partnership income, net rental income, dividends received from taxable Canadian corporations, net capital gains, RRSP withdrawals, income from a Registered Retirement Income Fund or Annuity, and any other income.

Schedule B—Other Income Earners in the Home

This schedule is completed only if the party is making a claim for spousal support or is claiming undue hardship under the *Child Support Guidelines*. If this is the case, the party must state whether he or she lives alone or is married to or cohabiting with another person. If the party is married to or cohabiting with another person, he or she must state

- whether the person works outside the home,
- whether the person earns any money, and, if so, the amount, and
- whether the person contributes any money toward the household expenses, and, if so, the amount.

Schedule C—Special or Extraordinary Expenses for the Child(ren)

This schedule is to be completed if either party is seeking a contribution toward special or extraordinary expenses for the child(ren) under the *Child Support Guidelines*.

A copy of Form 13 can be found at the end of this chapter.

Form 13.1: Financial Statement (Property and Support Claims)

This financial statement must be filed by a party who is making or responding to a claim for property or exclusive possession of the matrimonial home and its contents, with or without a claim for other relief. A copy of Form 13.1 can be found at the end of this chapter.

Parts 1 and 2 (pages 1 to 4) and Schedule A (page 10) of the form deal with the income and expenses of the party and are identical to those parts of Form 13. Part 3 (page 4) of the form is identical to Schedule B of Form 13, and Schedule B (page 10) of the form is identical to Schedule C of Form 13. The balance of the form deals with the assets and debts of the party, and provides the information required for a net family property calculation. The asset and debt information set out in this form is more extensive than the asset and debt information in Form 13.

Part 4: Assets In and Out of Ontario

Part 4 details all property owned by the party, and starts with a statement of

- the date of marriage,
- the valuation date, and
- the date of commencement of cohabitation (if different from the date of marriage).

List all property the party owned either at the valuation date or at the date of the statement or both. (If the party owned property earlier in the marriage but disposed of it before the valuation date, do not include it.) If the party owns only a percentage of the property, state that fact clearly and show the value of the party's percentage only. Whenever the form asks for a value of property, give the *market* value of the property—the amount for which the property could be sold to an interested third party. Do not use the purchase price or the replacement value of the property.

Part 4(a): Land

Include any interest in land owned, including leasehold interests and mortgages,[8] by setting out:

- the nature and type of ownership and percentage interest where relevant—sole owner, joint tenant, tenant in common, etc.;
- the address of the property; and
- the estimated market value of the party's interest on the date of marriage, on the valuation date, and as of the date of the statement, as relevant—do not deduct **encumbrances** or **costs of disposition**.

encumbrances
mortgages or other liens registered against the property

costs of disposition
costs of disposing of the property, including real estate commission and legal fees

Here's an example.

> During their marriage, Laura and her husband Rob bought a home at 123 Maple Avenue, Toronto, as joint tenants for $300,000. At the time of the separation, the home was worth $800,000 and as of the date of the financial statement it is worth $850,000.

---

8   List only mortgages under which money is owing to the party as mortgagee.

Part 4(a) of Laura's financial statement will look like this:

Nature & Type of Ownership (Give your percentage interest where relevant.)	Address of Property	Estimated Market Value of YOUR Interest		
		on date of marriage	on valuation date	today
Joint tenancy (50%)	Matrimonial home at 123 Maple Avenue, Toronto	$	$ 400,000	$ 425,000
	15. TOTAL VALUE OF LAND	$	$ 400,000	$ 425,000

Part 4(b): General Household Items and Vehicles

List and give values for the following types of property:

- Household goods and furniture. It is sufficient to group all household contents together under the description "contents of matrimonial home" unless there are items of particular value. Items of particular value should be listed separately. Give the estimated market value at the relevant dates, keeping in mind that household contents are generally worth very little—half or less of the original purchase price. In most cases, household contents are owned equally by the spouses (in which case, show half the total value only), although some items may be owned by one spouse alone.

- Cars, boats, and vehicles. Include only cars, boats, or vehicles registered in the party's name. You can determine the value at the relevant dates by looking at newspaper ads or by calling a dealer.

- Jewellery, art, electronics, tools, and sports and hobby equipment. Obtain market values from appropriate dealers.

Here's an example.

Laura and her husband Rob bought most of their furniture and household contents together during their marriage. Laura estimates that their furniture, linens, kitchen supplies, and other household items have a market value of about $10,000. Laura also has a baby grand piano that she inherited from her grandmother during the marriage, with a market value of about $3,500. Laura and Rob each own a car. Laura's car is a five-year-old Dodge Caravan worth about $18,000. Laura has some jewellery, but nothing special or very valuable. She estimates the resale value of all of her jewellery to be no more than $500.

Part 4(b) of Laura's financial statement will look like this:

Item	Description	Indicate if NOT in your possession	Estimated Market Value of YOUR Interest		
			on date of marriage	on valuation date	today
Household goods & furniture	One-half contents of matrimonial home		$	$ 5,000	$ 5,000
Cars, boats, vehicles	2012 Dodge Caravan		$	$ 18,000	$ 18,000
Jewellery, art, electronics, tools, sports & hobby equipment			$	$ 500	$ 500
Other special items	Baby grand piano		$	$ 3,500	$ 3,500
16. TOTAL VALUE OF GENERAL HOUSEHOLD ITEMS AND VEHICLES			$	$ 27,000	$ 27,000

Part 4(c): Bank Accounts, Savings, Securities, and Pensions

Show these items by category; for example, cash, accounts in financial institutions, pensions, registered retirement or other savings plans, deposit receipts, any other savings bonds, warrants, options, notes, and other securities.

The party must disclose all bank accounts, even if they contain only a small amount of money. Look at the client's passbooks or get statements from the bank to determine the balances as of the appropriate dates. If an account is a joint account, show one-half of the balance as the value of the account.

If the party has a pension, it must be properly valued—the value is not simply the total of the employee and employer contributions. Under recent amendments to the Act, the term "property" is stated to include: "in the case of a spouse's right under a pension plan, the imputed value, for family law purposes, of the spouse's interest in the plan, as determined in accordance with section 10.1." Under section 10.1, the imputed value, for family law purposes, is to be calculated in accordance with the *Pension Benefits Act*.[9] Under that Act, pension members and, in some circumstances, their spouses may require the pension administrator to provide a statement of the imputed value for family law purposes. If no valuation is available at the time the statement is prepared, give details of the pension and under value state "to be valued."

Show the current market value of any securities.

---

9   RSO 1990, c P.8.

Here's an example.

Laura has a joint chequing account with Rob at Scotiabank, account number 12345. The account balance at separation was $1,200.00 and the current balance is $600.00. Laura also has had a small savings account at the Bank of Montreal, account number 2468 since before her marriage. At the date of marriage, the balance was $5,000, the balance at separation was $1,000, and the balance today is $1,200. In addition, she owns 500 shares in CruiseCo Inc. These shares were worth $5,000 at the time of separation and are worth $4,500 today.

Part 4(c) of Laura's financial statement will look like this:

Category	INSTITUTION *(including location)/* DESCRIPTION *(including issuer and date)*	Account number	Amount/Estimated Market Value		
			on date of marriage	on valuation date	today
Joint chequing account	ScotiaBank, 4000 Yonge Street, Toronto	12345	$	$ 600	$ 300
Savings account	Bank of Montreal, 4200 Yonge Street, Toronto	2468	5,000	1,000	1,200
Shares	CruiseCo Inc. -- 500 shares			5,000	4,500
17. TOTAL VALUE OF ACCOUNTS, SAVINGS, SECURITIES AND PENSIONS			$	$ 6,600	$ 6,600

Part 4(d): Life and Disability Insurance

List all life and disability insurance policies and give the cash surrender value as of the relevant dates.

Here's an example.

Laura owns a $50,000 whole-life insurance policy with Metropolitan Life, policy number 369. Rob is the beneficiary, and the policy has a cash surrender value of $20,000. She also owns a $100,000 term-life policy with Canada Life, policy number 5567. Rob is the beneficiary, and the policy has no cash surrender value.

Part 4(d) of Laura's financial statement will look like this:

Company, Type & Policy No.	Owner	Beneficiary	Face Amount	Cash Surrender Value		
				on date of marriage	on valuation date	today
Metropolitan Life - whole life - policy no. 369	Wife	Husband	50,000	$	$ 20,000	$ 20,000
Canada Life - term life - policy no. 5567	Wife	Husband	100,000			
18. TOTAL CASH SURRENDER VALUE OF INSURANCE POLICIES					$ 20,000	$ 20,000

Part 4(e): Business Interests

Show any interest in an unincorporated business. An interest in an incorporated business may be shown in this part or in Part 4(c). Give the market value of the party's interest in the business.

Here's an example.

In addition to her full-time job, Laura carries on a small business from her home as a computer programmer, called Petrie's Programming. The business owns some computer equipment, and has one or two clients. Laura estimates that the business is worth only $1,500.

Part 4(e) of her financial statement will look like this:

Name of Firm or Company	Interest	Estimated Market Value of YOUR Interest		
		on date of marriage	on valuation date	today
Petrie's Programming	Sole proprietor	$	$ 1,500	$ 1,500
19. TOTAL VALUE OF BUSINESS INTERESTS			$ 1,500	$ 1,500

Part 4(f): Money Owed to the Party

Give details of all money that other persons owe to the party, whether because of business or from personal dealings. The party must include any court judgments in his or her favour, any estate money, and any income tax refunds owed to him or her.
Here's an example.

Laura's business is owed $750 by a client named Jerry Mathers. In addition, Laura is expecting a tax refund of $375.
Part 4(f) of her financial statement will look like this:

Details	Amount Owed to You		
	on date of marriage	on valuation date	today
Owing to Petrie's Programming by Jerry Mathers	$	$ 750	$ 750
Expected income tax refund		375	375
20. TOTAL OF MONEY OWED TO YOU	$	1,125	$ 1,125

Part 4(g): Other Property

Show any other property here that has not already been listed.
Here's an example.

Laura has had a stamp collection since she was a child. At the date of the marriage, the collection was worth $150. At the time of separation and today, the collection is worth $1,000.
Part 4(g) of her financial statement will look like this:

Category	Details	Estimated Market Value of YOUR interest		
		on date of marriage	on valuation date	today
Stamp collection		$ 150	$ 1,000	$ 1,000
21. TOTAL VALUE OF OTHER PROPERTY		$	1,000	$ 1,000

Value of All Property Owned on the Valuation Date

After completing Parts 4(a) through 4(g), add items [15] to [21] to get the total value of all property owned on the valuation date.

Laura's total would be as follows:

22. VALUE OF ALL PROPERTY OWNED ON THE VALUATION DATE *(Add items [15] to [21].)*	$ 457,225	$ 481,625

Part 5: Debts and Other Liabilities

Set out the party's debts and other liabilities at the relevant dates, listing them by such categories as mortgages, charges, liens, notes, credit cards, and accounts payable. The party should include any money owed to the Canada Revenue Agency, any **contingent liabilities** such as guarantees or warranties (indicating that they are contingent), and any unpaid legal or professional bills as a result of the family law case. If a debt is jointly owed, show only one-half of the outstanding balance.

Here's an example.

contingent liability
a liability that is not fixed and absolute but will become fixed and absolute when a specified event occurs

Laura and Rob have a mortgage on the matrimonial home with CIBC on which $97,000 was owing at the date of separation. The balance owing today is $96,500. Laura also has an outstanding Visa balance of $1,000. At the time of separation her balance was $750.00.

Part 5 of her financial statement will look like this:

Category	Details	Amount Owing		
		on date of marriage	on valuation date	today
Mortgage	On matrimonial home with CIBC (50%)	$	$ 48,500	$ 48,250
Credit card	CIBC Visa		750	1,000
	23. TOTAL OF DEBTS AND OTHER LIABILITIES	$	49,250	$ 49,250

Part 6: Property, Debts, and Other Liabilities on Date of Marriage

This part details the party's assets and debts as of the date of marriage; this is information that is needed to calculate the party's net family property. The party must not include the value of a matrimonial home (or associated mortgage) that was owned on the date of marriage if this property is still a matrimonial home on the valuation date.

If the parties married young, they probably had very little in the way of assets or debts at the date of marriage.

Here's an example.

When Laura married Rob, her only assets were a savings account with a balance of $5,000 and a stamp collection worth $150. In addition, she had an outstanding student loan of $2,000, which she has since repaid.

Part 6 of her financial statement will look like this:

Category and details	Value on date of marriage	
	Assets	Liabilities
Land	$	$
General household items & vehicles	$	$
Bank accounts, savings, securities & pensions **Bank of Montreal account no. 2468**	$ 5,000	$
Life & disability insurance	$	$
Business interests	$	$
Money owed to you	$	$
Other property *(Specify.)* **Stamp collection**	$ 150	$
Debts and other liabilities *(Specify.)* **Student loan**	$	$ 2,000
TOTALS	$ 5,150	$ 2,000
24. NET VALUE OF PROPERTY OWNED ON DATE OF MARRIAGE *(From the total of the "Assets" column, subtract the total of the "Liabilities" column.)*	$ 3,150	$ 3,150

Value of All Deductions

In this part, the party adds together the total of the deductions he or she is entitled to claim in calculating his or her net family property—the debts and liabilities at the valuation date and the net value of property owned on the date of marriage.

Here's an example.

> Laura's total debts on valuation day were $49,250. The net value of her property on the date of marriage was $3,150. This part of her financial statement will look like this:

25. VALUE OF ALL DEDUCTIONS *(Add items* **[23]** *and* **[24]**.*)* $	52,400	$ 52,400

Part 7: Excluded Property

Show by category the value of property owned on the valuation date that is excluded from the definition of net family property. Excluded property is defined in section 4(2) of the *Family Law Act* to be

- property, other than a matrimonial home, that was acquired by gift or inheritance from a third person after the date of the marriage;
- income from such gifts or inheritances if the donor or testator has expressly stated that it is to be excluded from the spouse's net family property;
- damages or a right to damages for personal injuries, nervous shock, mental distress, or loss of guidance, care, and companionship;
- proceeds or a right to proceeds of a life insurance policy;
- property, other than a matrimonial home into which property referred to above can be traced;
- property that the spouses have agreed by a domestic contract is not to be included in the spouse's net family property; and
- unadjusted pensionable earnings under the Canada Pension Plan.

Here's an example.

> During the marriage, Laura inherited a baby grand piano from her grandmother. At the time of separation, the piano was worth $3,500.
>   Part 7 of her financial statement would look like this:

Category	Details	Value on valuation date
Inheritance	Baby grand piano inherited from grandmother during marriage	$ 3,500
	26. TOTAL VALUE OF EXCLUDED PROPERTY $	3,500

Part 8: Disposed-of Property

Show by category the value of all property the party disposed of during the two years immediately preceding the making of the statement, or during the marriage, whichever period is shorter.[10]

Part 9: Calculation of Net Family Property

This part calculates the party's net family property by starting with the total value of all property owned on the valuation date and deducting the value of all deductions and the value of excluded property calculated earlier in the financial statement.

Using the figures from Laura's financial statement, Part 9 would look like this:

	Deductions	BALANCE
Value of all property owned on valuation date *(from item* **[22]** *above)*		$ 457,225
Subtract value of all deductions *(from item* **[25]** *above)*	$ 52,400	$ 404,825
Subtract total value of excluded property *(from item* **[26]** *above)*	$ 3,500	$ 401,325
28. NET FAMILY PROPERTY		$ 401,325

Jurat

The financial statement must be sworn or affirmed under oath, and must, therefore, be signed in the presence of a lawyer, justice of the peace, notary public, or commissioner for taking affidavits.

A copy of Form 13.1 can be found at the end of this chapter.

Form 13A: Certificate of Financial Disclosure

According to Rules 13(3.1) and 13(3.2), a party required to serve a financial statement (Form 13) in a support claim is required to serve at the same time a certificate of financial disclosure (Form 13A) along with the following documents:

- the income and financial information referred to in subsection 21(1) of the child support guidelines;
- if the party became unemployed within the last three years, a complete copy of the party's Record of Employment, or other evidence of termination, and a statement of any benefits or income that the party is still entitled to receive from his or her former employer despite or as a result of the termination; and
- in the case of a claim for the support of a child, proof of the amount of any special or extraordinary expenses, within the meaning of section 7 of the child support guidelines.

---

10   The requirement to disclose this information is found in section 8(d) of the *Family Law Act*.

According to Rules 13(3.3) and 13(3.4), a party required to serve a financial statement (Form 13.1) in a property claim is required to serve a certificate of financial disclosure (Form 13A) along with the following documents, no later than 30 days after the financial statement was due:

- The statement issued closest to the valuation date for each bank account or other account in a financial institution, pension, registered retirement or other savings plan, and any other savings or investments in which the party had an interest on that date.

- A copy of an application or request made by the party to obtain a valuation of his or her own pension benefits, deferred pension or pension, as the case may be, if any, as of the valuation date.

- A copy of the Municipal Property Assessment Corporation's (MPAC's) assessment of any real property in Ontario in which the party had a right or interest on the valuation date, for the year in which that date occurred.

- If the party owned a life insurance policy on the valuation date, the statement issued closest to that date showing the face amount and cash surrender value, if any, of the policy, and the named beneficiary.

- If the party had an interest in a sole proprietorship or was self-employed on the valuation date, for each of the three years preceding that date,
  - the financial statements of the party's business or professional practice, other than a partnership, and
  - a copy of every personal income tax return filed by the party, including any materials that were filed with the return.

- If the party was a partner in a partnership on the valuation date, a copy of the partnership agreement and, for each of the three years preceding the valuation date,
  - a copy of every personal income tax return filed by the party, including any materials that were filed with the return, and
  - the financial statements of the partnership.

- If the party had an interest in a corporation on the valuation date, documentation showing the number and types of shares of the corporation and any other interests in the corporation that were owned by the party on that date.

- If the corporation in which a party had an interest was privately held, for each of the three years preceding the valuation date,
  - the financial statements for the corporation and its subsidiaries, and
  - if the interest was a majority interest, a copy of every income tax return filed by the corporation.

- If the party was a beneficiary under a trust on the valuation date, a copy of the trust settlement agreement and the trust's financial statements for each of the three years preceding that date.

- Documentation showing the value, on the valuation date, of any property not referred to in paragraphs 1 to 9 in which the party had an interest on that date.
- Documentation that supports a claim, if any, for an exclusion under subsection 4(2) of the *Family Law Act*.
- The statements or invoices issued closest to the valuation date in relation to any mortgage, line of credit, credit card balance or other debt owed by the party on that date.
- Any available documentation showing the value, on the date of marriage, of property that the party owned or in which he or she had an interest on that date, and the amount of any debts owed by the party on that date.

The certificate of disclosure must be filed by the applicant no later than seven days before a case conference, and by the respondent no later than four days before the case conference.

Since Laura's case includes a property claim, she will have thirty days after the delivery of her financial statement to serve her certificate of financial disclosure, with all of the documents attached.

A copy of Form 13A can be found at the end of this chapter.

Form 13B: Net Family Property Statement

Under Rule 13(14) a net family property statement must be served and filed by each party to a property claim under part I of the *Family Law Act*

- not less than seven days before a settlement conference, and
- not more than 30 days and not less than seven days before a trial.

If the party has already served a net family property statement, the party may instead serve and file an affidavit saying that the information on the statement has not changed and is still true.

A copy of Form 13B can be found at the end of this chapter.

This unsworn statement summarizes the contents of Form 13.1 for both spouses in four tables:

- Table 1—Value of assets owned on valuation date,
- Table 2—Value of debts and liabilities on valuation date,
- Table 3—Net value of property (other than a matrimonial home) and debts (other than debts relating to a matrimonial home) on date of marriage, and
- Table 4—value of property excluded under section 4(2) of the *Family Law Act*.

Each table lists the categories and category totals taken from each spouse's financial statement. The table figures are then used to calculate the net family property of both spouses.

Using the information from Laura's Form 13.1, the wife's column of her net family property statement would look like this:

TABLE 1: Value of assets owned on valuation date
(List in the order of the categories in the financial statement.)

ITEM	APPLICANT	RESPONDENT
1. Land	$ 400,000	$
2. General household items and vehicles	$ 27,000	$
3. Bank accounts, savings, securities, and pensions	$ 6,600	$
4. Life and disability insurance	$ 20,000	$
5. Business interests	$ 1,500	$
6. Money owed to you	$ 1,125	$
7. Other property	$ 1,000	$
	$	$
	$	$
	$	$
	$	$
	$	$
	$	$
TOTAL 1	$ 457,225	$

TABLE 2: Value of debts and liabilities on valuation date
(List in the order of the categories in the financial statement.)

ITEM	APPLICANT	RESPONDENT
1. Mortgage	$ 48,500	$
2. Visa	$ 750	$
	$	$
	$	$
	$	$
	$	$
	$	$
	$	$
	$	$
	$	$
	$	$
	$	$
	$	$
TOTAL 2	$ 49,250	$

TABLE 3: Net value on date of marriage of property (other than a matrimonial home) after deducting debts or other liabilities on date of marriage (other than those relating directly to the purchase or significant improvement of a matrimonial home)

(List in the order of the categories in the financial statement.)

3(a) PROPERTY ITEM	APPLICANT	RESPONDENT
Bank accounts, savings, securities, and pensions	$ 5,000	$
Other property	$ 150	$
	$	$
	$	$
	$	$
	$	$
TOTAL OF PROPERTY ITEMS	$ 5,150	$
3(b) DEBT ITEM		
1. Student loan	$ 2,000	$
	$	$
	$	$
	$	$
	$	$
	$	$
TOTAL OF DEBT ITEMS	$ 2,000	$
NET TOTAL 3 *[3(a) minus 3(b)]*	$ 3,150	$

TABLE 4: Value or property excluded under subsection 4(2) of the *Family Law Act* *(List in the order of the categories in the financial statement.)*		
ITEM	**APPLICANT**	**RESPONDENT**
1. Inheritance	$ 3,500	$
	$	$
	$	$
	$	$
	$	$
	$	$
	$	$
	$	$
	$	$
	$	$
	$	$
	$	$
TOTAL 4	$ 3,500	$

TOTAL 2 *(from TABLE 2)*	$ 49,250	$
TOTAL 3 *(from TABLE 3)*	$ 3,150	$
TOTAL 4 *(from TABLE 4)*	$ 3,500	$
TOTAL 5 *([Total 2] + [Total 3] +[Total 4])*	$ 55,900	$

TOTAL 1 *(from TABLE 1)*	$ 457,225	$
TOTAL 5 *(from above)*	$ 55,900	$
TOTAL 6: NET FAMILY PROPERTY *([Total 1] minus [Total 5])*	$ 401,325	$

Form 13C: Comparison of Net Family Property Statements

Under Rules 13(14.2) and 13(14.3), parties who have delivered net family property statements are required to deliver a comparison of net family property statements either jointly or, if the parties can't agree on a joint statement, separately. If a joint comparison is prepared, it is to be filed not later than seven days before the settlement conference. If separate comparisons are prepared, the party requesting the settlement conference must file his or her statement not later than seven days before the conference, and the other party not later than four days before the conference.

The statement is very similar to Form 13B. However, whereas Form 13B simply copies the property information from each party's financial statement, this form asks for the party's position on the assets and debts and their values of the other party, and on the final NFP calculation.

A copy of Form 13C can be found at the end of this chapter.

CHAPTER SUMMARY

In any action for support, exclusive possession of the matrimonial home, and/or equalization of net family properties, both parties must make full financial disclosure of all of their assets, liabilities, income, and expenses. The requirements for financial disclosure are found in the *Family Law Act*, the *Child Support Guidelines*, and the *Family Law Rules*.

If there is a claim for support, but no claim for property or exclusive possession of the matrimonial home, Form 13—Financial Statement (Support Claims)—must be served and filed. Where there is a claim for property and/or exclusive possession of the matrimonial home, whether or not support is also claimed, Form 13.1—Financial Statement (Property and Support Claims)—must be filed. In either case, the parties must also serve and file Form 13A—Certificate of Financial Disclosure—attaching the

documents relied on in the preparation of the financial statement. In an action for equalization of net family properties, Forms 13B—Net Family Property Statement—and 13C—Comparison of Net Family Property Statements—is also required.

Rule 13 of the *Family Law Rules* sets out who must file a financial statement and when this must be done. The lawyer (or an articling student, law clerk, or secretary) usually completes the statement from information provided by the client. The client must provide information that is as complete, accurate, and current as possible. If cross-examined on the financial statement, the client will likely to be asked how various amounts were calculated. Therefore, it is important to maintain notes on how the calculations were made.

KEY TERMS

contingent liability, 191
costs of disposition, 185
encumbrances, 185

REVIEW QUESTIONS

1. What are the requirements for financial disclosure under the *Family Law Act*?

2. What are the requirements for financial disclosure under the *Child Support Guidelines*?

3. Under the *Family Law Rules*, when must Form 13 be served and filed?

4. Under the *Family Law Rules*, when must Form 13.1 be served and filed?

5. Under the *Family Law Rules*, under what circumstances is the court directed not to accept a financial statement for filing?

6. In a support claim, what financial documents must a party include with the certificate of financial disclosure (Form 13A)?

7. Under the *Family Law Rules*, what is the responsibility of the parties to update their financial statements as the proceeding progresses?

8. Under the *Family Law Rules*, when must the parties serve and file a net family property statement?

9. What are the forms required under Rule 13 of the *Family Law Rules*?

10. Why is it important to make and keep notes on the calculations used in completing a financial statement?

EXERCISES

1. You are completing a financial statement (Form 13.1) under the *Family Law Rules* for a client. Working with a blank financial statement form, set out the following information in the appropriate places:

   a. The client is paid a gross salary of $1,346.15 every two weeks.

   b. The client spends $150 every week on groceries.

   c. The client pays property insurance premiums of $1,200 per year.

   d. The client and her husband jointly own the matrimonial home, located at 10579 Canarsie Avenue, Toronto. They bought the home during the marriage for $200,000. When they separated the property was worth $350,000. At the time the financial statement is prepared, the property is worth $380,000.

   e. The matrimonial home is subject to a first mortgage held by the Bank of Montreal. The original amount of the mortgage was $150,000. When they separated, the outstanding balance was $100,000. At the time the statement is prepared, the balance is $98,000.

2. Prepare Form 13.1 for our client Alicia Florrick. We are representing her in her divorce from Peter Florrick. She is also claiming equalization of NFP, custody, child support and spousal support.

   Alicia resides at 123 Manhattan Road, Toronto M2K 1Y3. She is employed as a law clerk by Stern, Lockhart & Gardner, located at 369 Bay Street, Toronto M4G 2X5. Peter resides at 555 Yonge Street, Apt. 2215, Toronto M3X 2Y7. There are three children of the marriage, namely: Thomas, born March 3, 2005; Rachel, born September 16, 2008; and Matthew, born February 21, 2012. The parties were married on June 5, 2003 and separated on the 15th of last month.

Alicia has given you the following information with respect to her income and expenses:

Current income

Salary	$2,000 every two weeks
Actual child support from Peter	$900/mo. (pursuant to Guidelines)

DEDUCTIONS (per pay):

Income tax	$300.00
C.P.P.	$92.34 (assume annual maximum is $2,564.10)
E.I.	$32.60 (assume annual maximum is $836.19)

Current expenses

Mortgage	$1,250/mo. (being paid by husband)
Property taxes	$5,200/yr. (being paid by husband)
Home insurance	$1,500/yr.
Repairs and maintenance	$1,750/yr.
Water	$900/yr.
Heat	$150/mo.
Hydro	$175 every 2 mos.
Phone	$60/mo.
Cable T.V.	$50/mo.
Internet	$35/mo.
Car loan	$250/mo.
Car insurance	$100/mo.
Licence	$90/yr.
Car maintenance	$480/yr.
Gas	$50/wk.
Parking	$10/wk.
Dental	
(self)	$100/yr.
(children)	$300/yr.
Hair (self)	$75/mo.
Hair (kids)	$150/yr.
Entertainment	$50/wk.
Vacation	$3,000/yr.
Children's activities	$300/yr.
Savings (RRSP)	$10/wk.

Alicia also gives you the attached information with respect to her expenses for food, clothing, and gifts:

FOOD (Weekly):	
1. One major grocery order weekly at supermarket:	$150.00
2. Twice weekly to corner store for bread and milk:	15.00
3. Fresh fruits and vegetables (per week):	18.00
4. Miscellaneous small food items:	10.00
	$193.00

CLOTHING (Yearly):	
1. Children	$1,200.00
2. Self	800.00
	$2,000.00

GIFTS (Yearly):	
1. Children's birthdays (3 @ $50.00)	$ 150.00
2. Children's friends' birthdays (12 @ $20.00)	240.00
3. Children's Christmas (3 @ $100.00)	300.00
4. Friends' and relatives' birthdays (8 @ $25.00)	400.00
5. Weddings (2 @ $100.00)	200.00
	$1,290.00

Alicia has given you the following information with respect to her property:

She and Peter jointly own the matrimonial home located at 123 Manhattan Road, Toronto, (purchased during the marriage). She estimates its value to be $650,000. There is a mortgage with CIBC in the amount of $190,000. She also has a 2012 Civic with a book value of $12,000. She is not sure of the value of their furniture and household goods, but figures it is about $2,500. She has a diamond ring, which she inherited from her mother in 2001 (before their marriage on June 5, 2003), which was recently appraised at $10,000. She also has a fur coat that was a gift from Peter's mother last year worth $2,000.

She and Peter have a joint bank account (account no. 12345) at CIBC, 400 Yonge Street, Toronto, containing $2,000. She has an RRSP (account no. 23456) with Toronto-Dominion Securities, 345 Bay Street, Toronto, worth $16,000. She has a term life insurance policy (no. 54321) with Canada Life; it has a face value of $120,000, but no cash surrender value, and Peter is the beneficiary. Her sister, Jane Duncan, owes her $500, which Jane borrowed last year. Alicia owes $2,500 on her CIBC VISA, and has $2,200 outstanding on her car loan, also with CIBC.

At the time of her marriage in 2003, she had a car worth $2,000, a bank account containing $3,000, her mother's diamond ring then worth $6,500, and some furniture worth about $500, which she still has today. She also had a student loan of $3,500.

Figure 11.1 Form 13: Financial Statement (Support Claims)

ONTARIO

Court File Number

_____
(Name of Court)

at _____
Court office address

**Form 13: Financial
Statement (Support Claims)
sworn/affirmed**

Applicant(s)

Full legal name & address for service — street & number, municipality, postal code, telephone & fax numbers and e-mail address (if any).	Lawyer's name & address — street & number, municipality, postal code, telephone & fax numbers and e-mail address (if any).

Respondent(s)

Full legal name & address for service — street & number, municipality, postal code, telephone & fax numbers and e-mail address (if any).	Lawyer's name & address — street & number, municipality, postal code, telephone & fax numbers and e-mail address (if any).

INSTRUCTIONS

You must complete this form if you are making or responding to a claim for child or spousal support or a claim to change support, unless your only claim for support is a claim for child support in the table amount under the *Child Support Guidelines*.

You may also be required to complete and attach additional schedules based on the claims that have been made in your case or your financial circumstances:

- If you have income that is not shown in Part I of the financial statement (for example, partnership income, dividends, rental income, capital gains or RRSP income), you must also complete **Schedule A**.

- If you have made or responded to a claim for child support that involves undue hardship or a claim for spousal support, you must also complete **Schedule B**.

- If you or the other party has sought a contribution towards special or extraordinary expenses for the child(ren), you must also complete **Schedule C**.

*NOTES: You must **fully and truthfully** complete this financial statement, including any applicable schedules. You must also provide the other party with documents relating to support and a Certificate of Financial Disclosure (Form 13A) as required by Rule 13 of the Family Law Rules.*

If you are making or responding to a claim for property, an equalization payment or the matrimonial home, you must complete Form 13.1: Financial Statement (Property and Support Claims) instead of this form.

1. **My name is** *(full legal name)* _____

    I live in *(municipality & province)* _____

    and I swear/affirm that the following is true:

PART 1: INCOME

2. I am currently

    ☐ employed by *(name and address of employer)*

    ☐ self-employed, carrying on business under the name of *(name and address of business)*

    ☐ unemployed since *(date when last employed)*

Figure 11.1   Form 13: Financial Statement (Support Claims) Continued

---

Form 13:   **Financial Statement (Support Claims)   (page 2)**

Court file number

---

3. I attach proof of my year-to-date income from all sources, including my most recent *(attach all that are applicable)*:

☐ pay cheque stub   ☐ social assistance stub   ☐ pension stub   ☐ workers' compensation stub

☐ employment insurance stub and last Record of Employment

☐ statement of income and expenses/ professional activities (for self-employed individuals)

☐ other (e.g. a letter from your employer confirming all income received to date this year)

4. Last year, my gross income from all sources was $ _____ *(do not subtract any taxes that have been deducted from this income)*.

5. ☐ I am attaching all of the following required documents to this financial statement as proof of my income over the past three years, if they have not already been provided:

. a copy of my personal income tax returns for each of the past three taxation years, including any materials that were filed with the returns. *(Income tax returns must be served but should NOT be filed in the continuing record, unless they are filed with a motion to refrain a driver's license suspension.)*

. a copy of my notices of assessment and any notices of reassessment for each of the past three taxation years;

. where my notices of assessment and reassessment are unavailable for any of the past three taxation years or where I have not filed a return for any of the past three taxation years, an Income and Deductions printout from the Canada Revenue Agency for each of those years, whether or not I filed an income tax return.

Note: An Income and Deductions printout is available from Canada Revenue Agency. Please call customer service at 1-800-959-8281.

OR

☐ I am an Indian within the meaning of the *Indian Act* (Canada) and I have chosen not to file income tax returns for the past three years. I am attaching the following proof of income for the last three years *(list documents you have provided)*:

(In this table you must show all of the income that you are currently receiving whether taxable or not.)

	Income Source	Amount Received/Month
1.	Employment income (before deductions)	$
2.	Commissions, tips and bonuses	$
3.	Self-employment income (Monthly amount before expenses: $)	$
4.	Employment Insurance benefits	$
5.	Workers' compensation benefits	$
6.	Social assistance income (including ODSP payments)	$
7.	Interest and investment income	$
8.	Pension income (including CPP and OAS)	$
9.	Spousal support received from a former spouse/partner	$
10.	Child Tax Benefits or Tax Rebates (e.g. GST)	$
11.	Other sources of income (e.g. RRSP withdrawals, capital gains) *(*attach Schedule A and divide annual amount by 12)*	$
12.	**Total monthly income from all sources:**	$
13.	**Total monthly income X 12 = Total annual income:**	$

FLR 13 (January 6, 2015)   Page 2 of 8

Figure 11.1   Form 13: Financial Statement (Support Claims) Continued

Form 13:	Financial Statement (Support Claims)	(page 3)	Court file number

14. Other Benefits

Provide details of any non-cash benefits that your employer provides to you or are paid for by your business such as medical insurance coverage, the use of a company car, or room and board.

Item	Details	Yearly Market Value
		$
		$
		$
		$

PART 2: EXPENSES

Expense	Monthly Amount	Expense	Monthly Amount
Automatic Deductions		**Transportation**	
CPP contributions	$	Public transit, taxis	$
EI premiums	$	Gas and oil	$
Income taxes	$	Car insurance and license	$
Employee pension contributions	$	Repairs and maintenance	$
Union dues	$	Parking	$
SUBTOTAL	$	Car Loan or Lease Payments	$
Housing		**SUBTOTAL**	$
Rent or mortgage	$	**Health**	
Property taxes	$	Health insurance premiums	$
Property insurance	$	Dental expenses	$
Condominium fees	$	Medicine and drugs	$
Repairs and maintenance	$	Eye care	$
SUBTOTAL	$	**SUBTOTAL**	$
Utilities		**Personal**	
Water	$	Clothing	$
Heat	$	Hair care and beauty	$
Electricity	$	Alcohol and tobacco	$

FLR 13 (January 6, 2015)

Figure 11.1 Form 13: Financial Statement (Support Claims) Continued

---

Form 13:	Financial Statement (Support Claims)	(page 4)	Court file number

Utilities, continued		Personal, continued	
Telephone	$	Education (*specify*)	$
Cell phone	$	Entertainment/recreation (including children)	$
Cable	$	Gifts	$
Internet	$	**SUBTOTAL**	$
SUBTOTAL	$	**Other expenses**	
Household Expenses		Life Insurance premiums	$
Groceries	$	RRSP/RESP withdrawals	$
Household supplies	$	Vacations	$
Meals outside the home	$	School fees and supplies	$
Pet care	$	Clothing for children	$
Laundry and Dry Cleaning	$	Children's activities	$
SUBTOTAL	$	Summer camp expenses	$
Childcare Costs		Debt payments	$
Daycare expense	$	Support paid for other children	$
Babysitting costs	$	Other expenses not shown above (*specify*)	$
SUBTOTAL	$	**SUBTOTAL**	$

Total Amount of Monthly Expenses	$
Total Amount of Yearly Expenses	$

PART 3: ASSETS

Type		Details	Value or Amount
		State Address of Each Property and Nature of Ownership	
Real Estate	1		$
	2		$
	3		$
		Year and Make	
Cars, Boats, Vehicles	1		$
	2		$
	3		$

Figure 11.1   Form 13: Financial Statement (Support Claims)   Continued

Form 13:   **Financial Statement (Support Claims)   (page 5)**

Court file number

		Address Where Located	
Other Possessions of Value (e.g. computers, jewellery, collections)	1		$
	2		$
	3		$
		Type – Issuer – Due Date – Number of Shares	
Investments (e.g. bonds, shares, term deposits and mutual funds)	1		$
	2		$
	3		$
		Name and Address of Institution Account Number	
Bank Accounts	1		$
	2		$
	3		$
		Type and Issuer Account Number	
Savings Plans R.R.S.P.s Pension Plans R.E.S.P.s	1		$
	2		$
	3		$
		Type – Beneficiary – Face Amount Cash Surrender Value	
Life Insurance	1		$
	2		$
	3		$
		Name and Address of Business	
Interest in Business (*attach separate year-end statement for each business)	1		$
	2		$
	3		$
		Name and Address of Debtors	
Money Owed to You (for example, any court judgments in your favour, estate money and income tax refunds)	1		$
	2		$
	3		$
		Description	
Other Assets	1		$
	2		$
	3		$

Total Value of All Property	$

FLR 13 (January 6, 2015)

Figure 11.1   Form 13: Financial Statement (Support Claims) Continued

Form 13:   **Financial Statement (Support Claims)**   **(page 6)**

Court file number

PART 4: DEBTS

Type of Debt	Creditor *(name and address)*	Full Amount Now Owing	Monthly Payments	Are Payments Being Made?
Mortgages, Lines of Credits or other Loans from a Bank, Trust or Finance Company		$	$	☐ Yes ☐ No
		$	$	☐ Yes ☐ No
		$	$	☐ Yes ☐ No
Outstanding Credit Card Balances		$	$	☐ Yes ☐ No
		$	$	☐ Yes ☐ No
		$	$	☐ Yes ☐ No
Unpaid Support Amounts		$	$	☐ Yes ☐ No
		$	$	☐ Yes ☐ No
		$	$	☐ Yes ☐ No
Other Debts		$	$	☐ Yes ☐ No
		$	$	☐ Yes ☐ No
		$	$	☐ Yes ☐ No

Total Amount of Debts Outstanding	$

PART 5: SUMMARY OF ASSETS AND LIABILITIES

Total Assets	$
Subtract Total Debts	$
Net Worth	$

NOTE: This financial statement must be updated no more than 30 days before any court event by either completing and filing:

- *a new financial statement with updated information, or*
- *an affidavit in Form 14A setting out the details of any minor changes or confirming that the information contained in this statement remains correct.*

Sworn/Affirmed before me at _____
                                                         municipality

in _____
                          province, state or country

on _____   _____
         date   *Commissioner for taking affidavits*
                          (Type or print name below if signature is illegible.)

_____
Signature
(This form is to be signed in front of a lawyer, justice of the peace, notary public or commissioner for taking affidavits.)

Figure 11.1   Form 13: Financial Statement (Support Claims) Continued

Schedule A
Additional Sources of Income

Line	Income Source	Annual Amount
1.	Net partnership income	$
2.	Net rental income (Gross annual rental income of $)	$
3.	Total amount of dividends received from taxable Canadian corporations	$
4.	Total capital gains ($) less capital losses ($)	$
5.	Registered retirement savings plan withdrawals	$
6.	Income from a Registered Retirement Income Fund or Annuity	$
7.	Any other income *(specify source)*	$

Subtotal:	$

Schedule B
Other Income Earners in the Home

Complete this part only if you are making or responding to a claim for undue hardship or spousal support. Check and complete all sections that apply to your circumstances.

1. ☐ I live alone.

2. ☐ I am living with *(full legal name of person you are married to or cohabiting with)*

    _____

3. ☐ I/we live with the following other adult(s):

    _____

4. ☐ I/we have *(give number)* _____ child(ren) who live(s) in the home.

5. My spouse/partner   ☐ works at *(place of work or business)* _____ .
                         ☐ does not work outside the home.

6. My spouse/partner   ☐ earns *(give amount)* $ _____ per _____ .
                         ☐ does not earn any income.

7. ☐ My spouse/partner or other adult residing in the home contributes about $ _____ per
       _____ towards the household expenses.

Figure 11.1 Form 13: Financial Statement (Support Claims) Concluded

Schedule C
Special or Extraordinary Expenses for the Child(ren)

Child's Name	Expense	Amount/yr.	Available Tax Credits or Deductions*
1.		$	$
2.		$	$
3.		$	$
4.		$	$
5.		$	$
6.		$	$
7.		$	$
8.		$	$
9.		$	$
10.		$	$

Total Net Annual Amount	$
Total Net Monthly Amount	$

* Some of these expenses can be claimed in a parent's income tax return in relation to a tax credit or deduction (for example childcare costs). These credits or deductions must be shown in the above chart.

☐   I earn $ _____ per year which should be used to determine my share of the above expenses.

NOTE:

Pursuant to the Child Support Guidelines, a court can order that the parents of a child share the costs of the following expenses for the child:

.   Necessary childcare expenses;

.   Medical insurance premiums and certain health-related expenses for the child that cost more than $100 annually;

.   Extraordinary expenses for the child's education;

.   Post-secondary school expenses; and,

.   Extraordinary expenses for extracurricular activities.

Figure 11.2 Form 13.1: Financial Statement (Property and Support Claims)

ONTARIO

Court File Number

_____

(Name of court)

at _____

Court office address

Form 13.1: Financial Statement (Property and Support Claims) sworn/affirmed

Applicant(s)

Full legal name & address for service — street & number, municipality, postal code, telephone & fax numbers and e-mail address (if any).	*Lawyer's name & address — street & number, municipality, postal code, telephone & fax numbers and e-mail address (if any).*

Respondent(s)

Full legal name & address for service — street & number, municipality, postal code, telephone & fax numbers and e-mail address (if any).	*Lawyer's name & address — street & number, municipality, postal code, telephone & fax numbers and e-mail address (if any).*

INSTRUCTIONS

1. USE THIS FORM IF:
   - you are making or responding to a claim for property or exclusive possession of the matrimonial home and its contents; or
   - you are making or responding to a claim for property or exclusive possession of the matrimonial home and its contents together with other claims for relief.

2. USE FORM 13 INSTEAD OF THIS FORM IF:
   - you are making or responding to a claim for support but NOT making or responding to a claim for property or exclusive possession of the matrimonial home and its contents.

3. If you have income that is not shown in Part I of the financial statement (for example, partnership income, dividends, rental income, capital gains or RRSP income), you must also complete **Schedule A**.

4. If you or the other party has sought a contribution towards special or extraordinary expenses for the child(ren), you must also complete **Schedule B**.

*NOTE: You must **fully and truthfully** complete this financial statement, including any applicable schedules. You must also provide the other party with documents relating to support and property and a Certificate of Financial Disclosure (Form 13A) as required by Rule 13 of the Family Law Rules.*

1. **My name is** *(full legal name)* _____

   I live in *(municipality & province)* _____

   and I swear/affirm that the following is true:

PART 1: INCOME

2. I am currently

   ☐ employed by *(name and address of employer)*

   ☐ self-employed, carrying on business under the name of *(name and address of business)*

   ☐ unemployed since *(date when last employed)*

Figure 11.2   Form 13.1: Financial Statement (Property and Support Claims)   Continued

Form 13.1:	Financial Statement (Property and Support Claims)	(page 2)	Court file number

3. I attach proof of my year-to-date income from all sources, including my most recent *(attach all that are applicable)*:

☐ pay cheque stub   ☐ social assistance stub   ☐ pension stub   ☐ workers' compensation stub

☐ employment insurance stub and last Record of Employment

☐ statement of income and expenses/ professional activities (for self-employed individuals)

☐ other (e.g. a letter from your employer confirming all income received to date this year)

4. Last year, my gross income from all sources was $ _____ *(do not subtract any taxes that have been deducted from this income).*

5. ☐ I am attaching all of the following required documents to this financial statement as proof of my income over the past three years, if they have not already been provided:

.   a copy of my personal income tax returns for each of the past three taxation years, including any materials that were filed with the returns. *(Income tax returns must be served but should NOT be filed in the continuing record, unless they are filed with a motion to refrain a driver's license suspension.)*

.   a copy of my notices of assessment and any notices of reassessment for each of the past three taxation years;

.   where my notices of assessment and reassessment are unavailable for any of the past three taxation years or where I have not filed a return for any of the past three taxation years, an Income and Deductions printout from the Canada Revenue Agency for each of those years, whether or not I filed an income tax return.

Note: An Income and Deductions printout is available from Canada Revenue Agency. Please call customer service at 1-800-959-8281.

OR

☐ I am an Indian within the meaning of the *Indian Act* (Canada) and I have chosen not to file income tax returns for the past three years. I am attaching the following proof of income for the last three years *(list documents you have provided)*:

(In this table you must show all of the income that you are currently receiving whether taxable or not.)

	Income Source	Amount Received/Month
1.	Employment income (before deductions)	$
2.	Commissions, tips and bonuses	$
3.	Self-employment income (Monthly amount before expenses: $)	$
4.	Employment Insurance benefits	$
5.	Workers' compensation benefits	$
6.	Social assistance income (including ODSP payments)	$
7.	Interest and investment income	$
8.	Pension income (including CPP and OAS)	$
9.	Spousal support received from a former spouse/partner	$
10.	Child Tax Benefits or Tax Rebates (e.g. GST)	$
11.	Other sources of income (e.g. RRSP withdrawals, capital gains) *(*attach Schedule A and divide annual amount by 12)*	$
12.	**Total monthly income from all sources:**	$
13.	**Total monthly income X 12 = Total annual income:**	$

Figure 11.2   Form 13.1: Financial Statement (Property and Support Claims)   Continued

Form 13.1:	Financial Statement (Property and Support Claims)	(page 3)	Court file number

14. Other Benefits

Provide details of any non-cash benefits that your employer provides to you or are paid for by your business such as medical insurance coverage, the use of a company car, or room and board.

Item	Details	Yearly Market Value
		$
		$
		$
		$

PART 2: EXPENSES

Expense	Monthly Amount	Expense	Monthly Amount
Automatic Deductions		**Transportation**	
CPP contributions	$	Public transit, taxis	$
EI premiums	$	Gas and oil	$
Income taxes	$	Car insurance and license	$
Employee pension contributions	$	Repairs and maintenance	$
Union dues	$	Parking	$
SUBTOTAL	$	Car Loan or Lease Payments	$
Housing		**SUBTOTAL**	$
Rent or mortgage	$	**Health**	
Property taxes	$	Health insurance premiums	$
Property insurance	$	Dental expenses	$
Condominium fees	$	Medicine and drugs	$
Repairs and maintenance	$	Eye care	$
SUBTOTAL	$	**SUBTOTAL**	$
Utilities		**Personal**	
Water	$	Clothing	$
Heat	$	Hair care and beauty	$
Electricity	$	Alcohol and tobacco	$

Figure 11.2   Form 13.1: Financial Statement (Property and Support Claims)   Continued

Form 13.1:   **Financial Statement (Property and**   (page 4)   Court file number
Support Claims)

Utilities, continued		Personal, continued	
Telephone	$	Education (*specify*)	$
Cell phone	$	Entertainment/recreation (including children)	$
Cable	$	Gifts	$
Internet	$	**SUBTOTAL**	$
SUBTOTAL	$	**Other expenses**	
Household Expenses		Life Insurance premiums	$
Groceries	$	RRSP/RESP withdrawals	$
Household supplies	$	Vacations	$
Meals outside the home	$	School fees and supplies	$
Pet care	$	Clothing for children	$
Laundry and Dry Cleaning	$	Children's activities	$
SUBTOTAL	$	Summer camp expenses	$
Childcare Costs		Debt payments	$
Daycare expense	$	Support paid for other children	$
Babysitting costs	$	Other expenses not shown above (*specify*)	$
SUBTOTAL	$	**SUBTOTAL**	$

Total Amount of Monthly Expenses	$
Total Amount of Yearly Expenses	$

PART 3: OTHER INCOME EARNERS IN THE HOME

Complete this part only if you are making or responding to a claim for undue hardship or spousal support. Check and complete all sections that apply to your circumstances.

1. ☐ I live alone.
2. ☐ I am living with (*full legal name of person you are married to or cohabiting with*) _____ .
3. ☐ I/we live with the following other adult(s): _____
4. ☐ I/we have (*give number*) _____ child(ren) who live(s) in the home.
5. My spouse/partner   ☐ works at (*place of work or business*) _____ .
   ☐ does not work outside the home.
6. My spouse/partner   ☐ earns (*give amount*) $ _____ per _____ .
   ☐ does not earn any income.
7. My spouse/partner or other adult residing in the home contributes about $ _____ per _____
   towards the household expenses.

Figure 11.2   Form 13.1: Financial Statement (Property and Support Claims)   Continued

Form 13.1:   **Financial Statement (Property and**   **(page 5)**   Court file number
                       Support Claims)

PART 4: ASSETS IN AND OUT OF ONTARIO

If any sections of Parts 4 to 9 do not apply, do not leave blank, print "NONE" in the section.

The date of marriage is: *(give date)* _____

The valuation date is: *(give date)* _____

The date of commencement of cohabitation is (if different from date of marriage): *(give date)* _____

PART 4(a): LAND

*Include any interest in land **owned** on the dates in each of the columns below, including leasehold interests and mortgages. Show estimated market value of your interest, but do not deduct encumbrances or costs of disposition; these encumbrances and costs should be shown under Part 5, "Debts and Other Liabilities".*

Nature & Type of Ownership *(Give your percentage interest where relevant.)*	Address of Property	Estimated Market Value of YOUR Interest		
		on date of marriage	on valuation date	today
		$	$	$
15. TOTAL VALUE OF LAND		$		$

PART 4(b): GENERAL HOUSEHOLD ITEMS AND VEHICLES

Show estimated market value, not the cost of replacement for these items owned on the dates in each of the columns below. Do not deduct encumbrances or costs of disposition; these encumbrances and costs should be shown under Part 5, "Debts and Other Liabilities".

Item	Description	Indicate if NOT in your possession	Estimated Market Value of YOUR Interest		
			on date of marriage	on valuation date	today
Household goods & furniture			$	$	$
Cars, boats, vehicles			$	$	$
Jewellery, art, electronics, tools, sports & hobby equipment			$	$	$
Other special items			$	$	$
16. TOTAL VALUE OF GENERAL HOUSEHOLD ITEMS AND VEHICLES			$		$

Figure 11.2 Form 13.1: Financial Statement (Property and Support Claims) Continued

Form 13.1:	Financial Statement (Property and Support Claims)	(page 6)	Court file number

PART 4(c): BANK ACCOUNTS, SAVINGS, SECURITIES AND PENSIONS

Show the items owned on the dates in each of the columns below by category, for example, cash, accounts in financial institutions, pensions, registered retirement or other savings plans, deposit receipts, any other savings, bonds, warrants, options, notes and other securities. Give your best estimate of the market value of the securities if the items were to be sold on the open market.

Category	INSTITUTION *(including location)/* DESCRIPTION *(including issuer and date)*	Account number	Amount/Estimated Market Value		
			on date of marriage	on valuation date	today
			$	$	$
17. TOTAL VALUE OF ACCOUNTS, SAVINGS, SECURITIES AND PENSIONS			$		$

PART 4(d): LIFE AND DISABILITY INSURANCE

List all policies in existence on the dates in each of the columns below.

Company, Type & Policy No.	Owner	Beneficiary	Face Amount	Cash Surrender Value		
				on date of marriage	on valuation date	today
				$	$	$
18. TOTAL CASH SURRENDER VALUE OF INSURANCE POLICIES				$		$

PART 4(e): BUSINESS INTERESTS

Show any interest in an unincorporated business owned on the dates in each of the columns below. An interest in an incorporated business may be shown here or under "BANK ACCOUNTS, SAVINGS, SECURITIES, AND PENSIONS" in Part 4(c). Give your best estimate of the market value of your interest.

Name of Firm or Company	Interest	Estimated Market Value of YOUR Interest		
		on date of marriage	on valuation date	today
		$	$	$
19. TOTAL VALUE OF BUSINESS INTERESTS		$		$

Figure 11.2   Form 13.1: Financial Statement (Property and Support Claims) Continued

Form 13.1:	Financial Statement (Property and Support Claims)	(page 7)	Court file number

PART 4(f): MONEY OWED TO YOU

Give details of all money that other persons owe to you on the dates in each of the columns below, whether because of business or from personal dealings. Include any court judgments in your favour, any estate money and any income tax refunds owed to you.

Details	Amount Owed to You		
	on date of marriage	on valuation date	today
	$	$	$
20. TOTAL OF MONEY OWED TO YOU	$		$

PART 4(g): OTHER PROPERTY

Show other property or assets owned on the dates in each of the columns below. Include property of any kind not listed above. Give your best estimate of market value.

Category	Details	Estimated Market Value of YOUR interest		
		on date of marriage	on valuation date	today
		$	$	$
	21. TOTAL VALUE OF OTHER PROPERTY	$		$
	22. VALUE OF ALL PROPERTY OWNED ON THE VALUATION DATE *(Add items [15] to [21].)*	$		$

PART 5: DEBTS AND OTHER LIABILITIES

Show your debts and other liabilities on the dates in each of the columns below. List them by category such as mortgages, charges, liens, notes, credit cards, and accounts payable. Don't forget to include:
- *any money owed to the Canada Revenue Agency;*
- *contingent liabilities such as guarantees or warranties given by you (but indicate that they are contingent); and*
- *any unpaid legal or professional bills as a result of this case.*

Category	Details	Amount Owing		
		on date of marriage	on valuation date	today
		$	$	$
	23. TOTAL OF DEBTS AND OTHER LIABILITIES	$		$

Figure 11.2   Form 13.1: Financial Statement (Property and Support Claims) Continued

Form 13.1:	Financial Statement (Property and Support Claims)	(page 8)	Court file number

PART 6: PROPERTY, DEBTS AND OTHER LIABILITIES ON DATE OF MARRIAGE

Show by category the value of your property, debts and other liabilities, calculated as of the date of your marriage. (In this part, do not include the value of a matrimonial home or debts or other liabilities directly related to its purchase or significant improvement, if you and your spouse ordinarily occupied this property as your family residence at the time of separation.)

Category and details	Value on date of marriage	
	Assets	**Liabilities**
Land	$	$
General household items & vehicles	$	$
Bank accounts, savings, securities & pensions	$	$
Life & disability insurance	$	$
Business interests	$	$
Money owed to you	$	$
Other property *(Specify.)*	$	$
Debts and other liabilities *(Specify.)*	$	$
TOTALS	$	$
24. NET VALUE OF PROPERTY OWNED ON DATE OF MARRIAGE *(From the total of the "Assets" column, subtract the total of the "Liabilities" column.)*	$	$
25. VALUE OF ALL DEDUCTIONS *(Add items* **[23]** *and* **[24]**.)	$	$

PART 7: EXCLUDED PROPERTY

Show by category the value of property owned on the valuation date that is excluded from the definition of "net family property" (such as gifts or inheritances received after marriage).

Category	Details	Value on valuation date
		$
26. TOTAL VALUE OF EXCLUDED PROPERTY		$

Figure 11.2   Form 13.1: Financial Statement (Property and Support Claims) Continued

Form 13.1:	**Financial Statement (Property and Support Claims)**	**(page 9)**	Court file number

PART 8: DISPOSED-OF PROPERTY

Show by category the value of all property that you disposed of during the two years immediately preceding the making of this statement, or during the marriage, whichever period is shorter.

Category	Details	Value
		$
	27. TOTAL VALUE OF DISPOSED-OF PROPERTY	$

PART 9: CALCULATION OF NET FAMILY PROPERTY

	Deductions	BALANCE
Value of all property owned on valuation date *(from item [22] above)*		$
Subtract value of all deductions *(from item [25] above)*	$	$
Subtract total value of excluded property *(from item [26] above)*	$	$
28. NET FAMILY PROPERTY		$

NOTE: *This financial statement must be updated no more than 30 days before any court event by either completing and filing:*

- *a new financial statement with updated information, or*

- *an affidavit in Form 14A setting out the details of any minor changes or confirming that the information contained in this statement remains correct.*

Sworn/Affirmed before me at _____
                                                                municipality

in _____
                                    province, state or country

on _____   _____
              date   *Commissioner for taking affidavits*
                              (Type or print name below if signature is illegible.)

_____
                        Signature
(This form is to be signed in front of a lawyer, justice of the peace, notary public or commissioner for taking affidavits.)

Figure 11.2 Form 13.1: Financial Statement (Property and Support Claims) Concluded

Schedule A: Additional Sources of Income

Line	Income Source	Annual Amount
1.	Net partnership income	$
2.	Net rental income (Gross annual rental income of $)	$
3.	Total amount of dividends received from taxable Canadian corporations	$
4.	Total capital gains ($) less capital losses ($)	$
5.	Registered retirement savings plan withdrawals	$
6.	Income from a Registered Retirement Income Fund or Annuity	$
7.	Any other income *(specify source)*	$

	Subtotal:	$

Schedule B: Special or Extraordinary Expenses for the Child(ren)

	Child's Name	Expense	Amount/yr.	Available Tax Credits or Deductions*
1.			$	$
2.			$	$
3.			$	$
4.			$	$
5.			$	$
6.			$	$
7.			$	$
8.			$	$
9.			$	$
10.			$	$

	Total Net Annual Amount	$
	Total Net Monthly Amount	$

* Some of these expenses can be claimed in a parent's income tax return in relation to a tax credit or deduction (for example childcare costs). These credits or deductions **must be shown in the above chart.**

☐ I earn $ _____ per year which should be used to determine my share of the above expenses.

NOTE: Pursuant to the Child Support Guidelines, a court can order that the parents of a child share the costs of the following expenses for the child:

. Necessary childcare expenses;

. Medical insurance premiums and certain health-related expenses for the child that cost more than $100 annually;

. Extraordinary expenses for the child's education;

. Post-secondary school expenses; and,

. Extraordinary expenses for extracurricular activities.

Figure 11.3   Form 13A: Certificate of Financial Disclosure

ONTARIO

	Court File Number

_____
(Name of court)

at _____
Court office address

**Form 13A: Certificate of
Financial Disclosure**

Applicant(s)

Full legal name & address for service — street & number, municipality, postal code, telephone & fax numbers and e-mail address (if any).	*Lawyer's name & address — street & number, municipality, postal code, telephone & fax numbers and e-mail address (if any).*

Respondent(s)

Full legal name & address for service — street & number, municipality, postal code, telephone & fax numbers and e-mail address (if any).	*Lawyer's name & address — street & number, municipality, postal code, telephone & fax numbers and e-mail address (if any).*

TO THE PARTIES

You must provide complete financial disclosure to the other parties in your case. A list of the documents you must provide to the other party is set out in Rule 13 of the Family Law Rules. You must list in this form all of the documents that you are providing to the other party in support of the information set out in your financial statement.

Once you have completed this form,

- if your case includes support with or without special expenses but does not include a claim under Part I of the Family Law Act (Family Property), you must:

  - attach all required documentation to the completed certificate.

  - serve this certificate (with attached documentation) on the other party with your completed Financial Statement.

- if your case includes a claim under Part I of the Family Law Act (Family Property) with or without a claim for support, you must:

  - attach all required documentation to the completed certificate.

  - serve this certificate (with attached documentation) on the other party within 30 days of the day that your Financial Statement was due to be served.

If you do not provide financial disclosure as required, a court may make an order against you.

You must file a copy of this certificate with the court. The documentation is not filed with the court. If you are the applicant or moving party in your case, you must file this certificate seven days before the case conference. If you are the respondent, you must serve it four days before the case conference.

If you have served any additional or updated financial disclosure before the settlement conference, you must prepare, serve and file an updated Certificate of Financial Disclosure.

Figure 11.3   Form 13A: Certificate of Financial Disclosure   Continued

Form 13A:	Certificate of Financial Disclosure	(page 2)	Court file number

Document Number	Document Description	Date of Document *(yyyy/mm/dd)*
Part A: Sources of Income		
Personal Income Tax Returns		
.		
.		
.		
.		
.		
Notices of Assessment and Reassessment		
.		
.		
.		
.		
.		
Employment Income		
.		
.		
.		
.		
.		
Self-Employment Income		
.		
.		
.		
.		
.		
Partnership Income and Interests in a Partnership		
.		
.		
.		
.		
.		

Figure 11.3 Form 13A: Certificate of Financial Disclosure Continued

Form 13A:	Certificate of Financial Disclosure	(page 3)	Court file number

Document Number	Document Description	Date of Document (yyyy/mm/dd)
Income from a Privately Held Corporation		
.		
.		
.		
.		
.		
Beneficial Income from, and Interest in, a Trust		
.		
.		
.		
.		
.		
Income from Employment Insurance or Social Assistance		
.		
.		
.		
.		
.		
Pensions and Annuities		
.		
.		
.		
.		
.		
Income from Spousal Support		
.		
.		
.		
.		

FLR 13A (January 6, 2015) CSD

Figure 11.3　Form 13A: Certificate of Financial Disclosure　Continued

Form 13A:　**Certificate of Financial Disclosure**　(page 4)

Court file number

Document Number	Document Description	Date of Document *(yyyy/mm/dd)*
Tax Benefits or Rebates		
.		
.		
.		
.		
.		
Investment and Interest Income		
.		
.		
.		
.		
.		
Rental Income		
.		
.		
.		
.		
.		
Other Income		
.		
.		
.		
.		
.		
Part B: Special and Extraordinary Expenses		
.		
.		
.		
.		
.		

Figure 11.3 Form 13A: Certificate of Financial Disclosure Continued

| Form 13A: | Certificate of Financial Disclosure | (page 5) | Court file number |

Document Number	Document Description	Date of Document *(yyyy/mm/dd)*
Part C: Claim for Equalization of Net Family Property		
Assets and Liabilities at Valuation Date		
Real Estate		
.		
.		
.		
.		
.		
Savings and Investments		
.		
.		
.		
.		
Pensions		
.		
.		
.		
.		
Life Insurance Policies		
.		
.		
.		
.		
Interest in a Sole Proprietorship		
.		
.		
.		
.		

Figure 11.3   Form 13A: Certificate of Financial Disclosure Continued

Form 13A:	Certificate of Financial Disclosure	(page 6)	Court file number

Document Number	Document Description	Date of Document *(yyyy/mm/dd)*
Interest in a Partnership		
.		
.		
.		
.		
.		
Interest in a Publically Held Corporation		
.		
.		
.		
.		
.		
Interest in a Privately Held Corporation		
.		
.		
.		
.		
.		
Trust Interests		
.		
.		
.		
.		
.		
Property I own which does not belong in any of the other categories		
.		
.		
.		
.		
.		

Figure 11.3 Form 13A: Certificate of Financial Disclosure Concluded

| Form 13A: | Certificate of Financial Disclosure | (page 7) | Court file number |

Document Number	Document Description	Date of Document *(yyyy/mm/dd)*
Liabilities		
.		
.		
.		
.		
.		
Assets and Liabilities at Marriage Date		
Assets		
.		
.		
.		
.		
Liabilities		
.		
.		
.		
.		
Excluded Property		
.		
.		
.		
.		

I am the Applicant/Respondent in this case. I certify that I have provided the opposing party with all of the documents that I have identified in this checklist.

Certified at _____ on _____

                  (City)   *(Date)*

_____

             (Signature of Party)

FLR 13A (January 6, 2015) CSD   Page 7 of 7

Source: <http://ontariocourtforms.on.ca/en/family-law-rules-forms/13a/>

Figure 11.4   Form 13B: Net Family Property Statement

ONTARIO

_____
(Name of court)

at _____
Court office address

Court File Number

Form 13B: Net Family Property Statement

Applicant(s)

Full legal name & address for service — street & number, municipality, postal code, telephone & fax numbers and e-mail address (if any).	Lawyer's name & address — street & number, municipality, postal code, telephone & fax numbers and e-mail address (if any).

Respondent(s)

Full legal name & address for service — street & number, municipality, postal code, telephone & fax numbers and e-mail address (if any).	Lawyer's name & address — street & number, municipality, postal code, telephone & fax numbers and e-mail address (if any).

My name is *(full legal name)* _____

The valuation date for the following material is *(date)*

(Complete the tables by filling in the columns for both parties, showing your assets, debts, etc., and those of your spouse.)

TABLE 1: Value of assets owned on valuation date		
(List in the order of the categories in the financial statement.)		
ITEM	APPLICANT	RESPONDENT
1.	$	$
	$	$
	$	$
	$	$
	$	$
	$	$
	$	$
	$	$
	$	$
	$	$
	$	$
	$	$
	$	$
TOTAL 1	$	$

Figure 11.4 Form 13B: Net Family Property Statement Continued

Form 13B: Net Family Property Statement (page 2)

Court File Number

TABLE 2: Value of debts and liabilities on valuation date
(List in the order of the categories in the financial statement.)

ITEM	APPLICANT	RESPONDENT
1.	$	$
	$	$
	$	$
	$	$
	$	$
	$	$
	$	$
	$	$
	$	$
	$	$
	$	$
	$	$
	$	$
TOTAL 2	$	$

TABLE 3: Net value on date of marriage of property (other than a matrimonial home) after deducting debts or other liabilities on date of marriage (other than those relating directly to the purchase or significant improvement of a matrimonial home)
(List in the order of the categories in the financial statement.)

3(a) PROPERTY ITEM	APPLICANT	RESPONDENT
	$	$
	$	$
	$	$
	$	$
	$	$
	$	$
TOTAL OF PROPERTY ITEMS	$	$

3(b) DEBT ITEM		
	$	$
	$	$
	$	$
	$	$
	$	$
	$	$
TOTAL OF DEBT ITEMS	$	$
NET TOTAL 3 *[3(a) minus 3(b)]*	$	$

Figure 11.4 Form 13B: Net Family Property Statement Concluded

Form 13B: Net Family Property Statement (page 3)

Court File Number

TABLE 4: Value or property excluded under subsection 4(2) of the *Family Law Act*		
(List in the order of the categories in the financial statement.)		
ITEM	APPLICANT	RESPONDENT
	$	$
	$	$
	$	$
	$	$
	$	$
	$	$
	$	$
	$	$
	$	$
	$	$
	$	$
	$	$
	$	$
TOTAL 4	$	$

	APPLICANT	RESPONDENT
TOTAL 2 *(from page 2)*	$	$
TOTAL 3 *(from page 2)*	$	$
TOTAL 4 *(from page 3)*	$	$
TOTAL 5 ([Total 2] + [Total 3] +[Total 4])	$	$

	APPLICANT	RESPONDENT
TOTAL 1 *(from page 1)*	$	$
TOTAL 5 *(from above)*	$	$
TOTAL 6: NET FAMILY PROPERTY ([Total 1] *minus* [Total 5])	$	$

_____
Date of signature

_____
Signature

Figure 11.5 Form 13C: Comparison of Net Family Property Statements

ONTARIO

_____
(Name of Court)

Court File Number [ ]

at _____
(Court office address)

Form 13C: Comparison of
Net Family Property Statements

This document must be completed once both parties have completed and exchanged Net Family Property Statements (Form 13B). This document can be completed jointly by the parties and filed with the court seven days before the settlement conference. If you and the other party are not able to agree on this document, then you each must prepare one, and serve it on the other party and file it with the court before the settlement conference. If you requested the settlement conference, you must serve and file the document seven days before the settlement conference, even if it is a joint statement. If no joint statement has been filed, the other party must serve and file the document four days before the settlement conference.

This form is being prepared by
☐ the Applicant
☐ the Respondent
☐ the Applicant and Respondent jointly

Applicant(s)

Full legal name & address for service — street & number, municipality, postal code, telephone & fax numbers and e-mail address (if any).	Lawyer's name & address — street & number, municipality, postal code, telephone & fax numbers and e-mail address (if any).

Respondent(s)

Full legal name & address for service — street & number, municipality, postal code, telephone & fax numbers and e-mail address (if any).	Lawyer's name & address — street & number, municipality, postal code, telephone & fax numbers and e-mail address (if any).

Valuation Date: _____   Statement Date: _____

1.   VALUE OF ASSETS OWNED ON VALUATION DATE

(a) LAND

NATURE & TYPE OF OWNERSHIP (State percentage interest where relevant)	NATURE & ADDRESS OF OWNERSHIP	COMMENTS	Document Number*	Applicant's Position		Respondent's Position	
				APPLICANT	RESPONDENT	APPLICANT	RESPONDENT
Matrimonial Home				$	$	$	$
				$	$	$	$
				$	$	$	$
(A) TOTALS: Value of Land				$	$	$	$

* Please use the number that you used for the document in your Certificate of Financial Disclosure (Form 13A)

FLR 13C (January 6, 2015) CSD

Page 1 of 5

Figure 11.5 Form 13C: Comparison of Net Family Property Statements *Continued*

Comparison of Net Family Property Statements (Page 2)

Court file number

(b) GENERAL HOUSEHOLD ITEMS AND VEHICLES

ITEM	DESCRIPTION	COMMENTS	Document Number	Applicant's Position		Respondent's Position	
				APPLICANT	RESPONDENT	APPLICANT	RESPONDENT
Household goods & furniture				$	$	$	$
Cars, boats, vehicles				$	$	$	$
Jewellery, art, electronics, tools, sports & hobby, equipment				$	$	$	$
Other special items				$	$	$	$
(B) TOTALS: Value of General Household Items and Vehicles				$	$	$	$

(c) BANK ACCOUNTS AND SAVINGS, SECURITIES AND PENSIONS

CATEGORY *(Savings, Checking, GIC, RRSP, Pensions, etc.)*	INSTITUTION	ACCOUNT NUMBER	COMMENTS	Document Number	Applicant's Position		Respondent's Position	
					APPLICANT	RESPONDENT	APPLICANT	RESPONDENT
					$	$	$	$
					$	$	$	$
					$	$	$	$
(C) TOTALS: Value of Accounts and Savings					$	$	$	$

(d) LIFE AND DISABILITY INSURANCE

COMPANY TYPE & POLICY NO.	OWNER	BENEFICIARY	FACE AMOUNT ($)	COMMENTS	Document Number	Applicant's Position		Respondent's Position	
						APPLICANT	RESPONDENT	APPLICANT	RESPONDENT
			$			$	$	$	$
			$			$	$	$	$
			$			$	$	$	$
(D) TOTALS: Cash Surrender Value of Insurance Policies						$	$	$	$

(e) BUSINESS INTERESTS

NAME OF FIRM OR COMPANY	INTERESTS	COMMENTS	Document Number	Applicant's Position		Respondent's Position	
				APPLICANT	RESPONDENT	APPLICANT	RESPONDENT
				$	$	$	$

Figure 11.5   Form 13C: Comparison of Net Family Property Statements   Continued

Comparison of Net Family Property Statements (Page 3)

Court file number _____

DETAILS		Applicant's Position		Respondent's Position	
		APPLICANT	RESPONDENT	APPLICANT	RESPONDENT
		$	$	$	$
		$	$	$	$
(E) TOTALS: Value of Business Interests		$	$	$	$

(f) MONEY OWED TO YOU

CATEGORY	DETAILS	COMMENTS	Document Number	Applicant's Position		Respondent's Position	
				APPLICANT	RESPONDENT	APPLICANT	RESPONDENT
				$	$	$	$
				$	$	$	$
(F) TOTALS: Money Owed to You				$	$	$	$

(g) OTHER PROPERTY

CATEGORY	DETAILS	COMMENTS	Document Number	Applicant's Position		Respondent's Position	
				APPLICANT	RESPONDENT	APPLICANT	RESPONDENT
				$	$	$	$
				$	$	$	$
(G) TOTALS: Value of Other Property				$	$	$	$

VALUE OF PROPERTY OWNED ON THE VALUATION DATE, ((TOTAL 1) *(Add: item A to item G inclusive)*	$	$	$	$

2. VALUE OF DEBTS AND OTHER LIABILITIES ON VALUATION DATE

DEBTS AND OTHER LIABILITIES

CATEGORY	DETAILS	COMMENTS	Document Number	Applicant's Position		Respondent's Position	
				APPLICANT	RESPONDENT	APPLICANT	RESPONDENT
				$	$	$	$
				$	$	$	$
TOTALS: Value of Debts and Other Liabilities, (TOTAL 2)				$	$	$	$

Figure 11.5   Form 13C: Comparison of Net Family Property Statements   Continued

Comparison of Net Family Property Statements (Page 4)   Court file number _____

3.   NET VALUE OF PROPERTY (Other than a Matrimonial Home) AND DEBTS ON DATE OF MARRIAGE

PROPERTY, DEBTS AND OTHER LIABILITIES ON DATE OF MARRIAGE

CATEGORY AND DETAILS	COMMENTS	Document Number	Applicant's Position		Respondent's Position	
			APPLICANT	RESPONDENT	APPLICANT	RESPONDENT
Assets			$	$	$	$
			$	$	$	$
TOTAL OF PROPERTY ITEMS			$	$	$	$
Debts and other liabilities			$	$	$	$
			$	$	$	$
TOTAL OF DEBTS ITEMS			$	$	$	$
NET VALUE OF PROPERTY OWNED ON DATE OF MARRIAGE (NET TOTAL 3)			$	$	$	$

4.   VALUE OF PROPERTY EXCLUDED UNDER SUBS. 4(2) OF "FAMILY LAW ACT"

ITEM	COMMENTS	Document Number	Applicant's Position		Respondent's Position	
			APPLICANT	RESPONDENT	APPLICANT	RESPONDENT
			$	$	$	$
			$	$	$	$
			$	$	$	$
			$	$	$	$
			$	$	$	$
TOTALS: Value of Excluded Property (TOTAL 4)			$	$	$	$

FLR 13C (January 6, 2015) CSD   Page 4 of 5

Figure 11.5   Form 13C: Comparison of Net Family Property Statements   Concluded

Comparison of Net Family Property Statements (Page 5)   Court file number _____

TOTAL 2: Debts and Other Liabilities	$	$
TOTAL 3: Value of Property Owned on the Date of Marriage	$	$
TOTAL 4: Value of Excluded Property	$	$
TOTAL 5: (TOTAL 2 + TOTAL 3 + TOTAL 4)	$	$

TOTAL 1: Value of Property Owned on Valuation Date	$	$
TOTAL 5: (from above)	$	$
TOTAL 6: NET FAMILY PROPERTY (Subtract: TOTAL 1 minus TOTAL 5)	$	$

EQUALIZATION PAYMENTS

Applicant's Position		Respondent's Position	
Applicant Pays To Respondent	Respondent Pays To Applicant	Applicant Pays To Respondent	Respondent Pays To Applicant
$	$	$	$

FLR 13C (January 6, 2015) CSD   Page 5 of 5

Source: <http://ontariocourtforms.on.ca/en/family-law-rules-forms/13c/>

Divorce Procedure

12

LEARNING OUTCOMES

After completing this chapter, you should be able to:

- Explain the difference between a defended divorce and an undefended divorce.

- Describe the steps in a simple undefended divorce.

- Complete the documents required in a simple undefended divorce.

Introduction

A spouse who wishes to terminate his or her marriage must start a divorce proceeding. While seeking the divorce, the party may also ask the court to deal with issues of support and/or custody under the *Divorce Act*[1] as well as property claims under the *Family Law Act*.[2] If the parties have already settled these issues by way of a separation agreement, the applicant may ask the court to make an order that incorporates the terms of the parties' settlement, or the applicant may ask for a divorce only.

In Chapter 5, we looked at the substantive law of divorce. In this chapter, we look at the procedure for obtaining a divorce, including

- an overview of divorce procedure,
- defended and undefended divorces, and
- the steps and documents required in a simple undefended divorce.

Overview of Divorce Procedure

Divorce procedure in Ontario is governed by the *Family Law Rules*[3] generally and by Rule 36 specifically.

Starting a Divorce Case

Under Rule 5, a divorce case should be started in the municipality where either party resides or, if the application claims custody or access, in the municipality where the children reside. Alternatively, with the consent of the court, it may be started in a municipality chosen by both parties.

If a case is started in a municipality where the Family Court of the Superior Court of Justice does not operate, the case must be started in the Superior Court of Justice.

Under Rule 36(1), either spouse may start a divorce case by filing an application naming the other spouse as a respondent, or by filing a joint application with no respondent, using

- Form 8A if the applicant is asking for a divorce only or if the application is a joint application, and
- Form 8 if the applicant is seeking other relief.

Pursuant to Rule 7(3), the parties to a divorce case are the applicant and the respondent. If the divorce application claims that the respondent committed adultery with another person, under Rule 36(3) that person does not need to be named.

---

1 RSC 1985, c 3 (2d Supp).
2 RSO 1990, c F.3.
3 O Reg 114/99.

Under Rule 13, if the application includes a claim for support, property, or exclusive possession, the applicant is also required to serve and file a financial statement (Form 13 or 13.1).[4]

Pursuant to Rule 9, the applicant is also required to prepare a continuing record for the case.

Service of the Application

Under Rule 8(5), the applicant must immediately serve the application, any financial statement, and the continuing record on the respondent. The applicant must use special service as defined in Rule 6(3). The applicant must then file the application, any financial statement, and the continuing record (after adding the affidavit of service to the continuing record) with the court.

Defended Divorce

Under Rule 10, a respondent who wants to defend a divorce case has 30 days if served in Canada or the United States (60 days if served elsewhere) to serve and file an answer (Form 10). The answer may include a claim by the respondent against the applicant such as divorce, custody, support, or equalization of property.

The applicant then has the right, within 10 days, to serve and file a reply (Form 10A) in response to any claim made by the respondent in the answer.

A divorce case is a standard track case[5] under Rule 39. Accordingly, if the case is defended, the next step is a case conference, which will be scheduled by the court on the request of either party.

Undefended Divorce

Pursuant to Rule 36(4), the court will not grant a divorce until the applicant files:

- a marriage certificate or marriage registration certificate, unless the application states that it is impractical to obtain a certificate and explains why; and

- a report on earlier divorce cases started by either spouse, issued under the *Central Registry of Divorce Proceedings Regulations*[6] (Canada).[7]

---

4 If the only additional claim is for child support in the table amount under the *Child Support Guidelines*, no financial statement is required by the applicant. However, the respondent must file a statement. In addition, parties to a claim for spousal support under the *Divorce Act* do not need to serve and file financial statements if they file a consent agreeing not to serve and file financial statements or agreeing to a specified amount of support.

5 As discussed in Chapter 10, all cases in the Family Court of the Superior Court of Justice are placed on either a fast track or a standard track.

6 SOR/86-600.

7 The Central Registry of Divorce Proceedings (CRDP) prevents duplicate proceedings for divorce in different courts across Canada. Courts handling divorce proceedings submit a registration of divorce proceedings form to the CRDP, where it is recorded in a database. All divorce files are then checked to detect any duplication of proceedings. If there is no duplication, a clearance certificate is issued, which allows the case to proceed.

Under Rule 36(5), if the respondent does not defend the divorce, no court appearance is necessary, and the court decides the divorce case on the basis of affidavit evidence in Form 36. Under Rule 36(6), the applicant must also file:

- three copies of a draft divorce order (Form 25A or A-25A);
- a stamped envelope addressed to each party; and
- if the divorce order contains a support order,
  - an extra copy of the order for filing with the director of the Family Responsibility Office, and
  - two copies of a draft support deduction order.

Pursuant to Rule 36(7), the clerk reviews the documents, prepares a certificate (Form 36A), and presents the documents to a judge who may

- grant the divorce as set out in the draft order,
- have the clerk return the documents to the applicant to make any corrections that are necessary, or
- grant the divorce but make changes to the draft order, or refuse to grant the divorce, after giving the applicant a chance to file an additional affidavit or come to court to explain why the order should be made without change.

Divorce Certificate

Under the provisions of section 12 of the *Divorce Act*, generally a divorce takes effect on the 31st day after the divorce judgment is granted.

Rule 36(8) requires the clerk to issue a divorce certificate (Form 36B) on either party's request.

Defended and Undefended Divorces

As stated above, a divorce proceeding may be either defended (contested) or undefended (uncontested). Usually, an applicant knows before the divorce is started whether or not the case will be defended by his or her spouse.

A divorce will almost certainly be defended if the applicant claims not only a divorce but also custody and/or support and/or an equalization of net family property for the first time. A divorce is likely to be undefended if these issues were dealt with previously in a separation agreement or an action under the *Family Law Act* and/or *Children's Law Reform Act*.[8]

If the parties have settled these issues by way of a separation agreement, the applicant may ask the court to make an order that incorporates the terms of their settlement. Alternatively, the applicant may ask for a divorce only and continue to rely on the terms of the agreement.

---

8 RSO 1990, c C.12.

Steps in a Simple Undefended Divorce

Let's use the case of Brad and Jenny Pitts to illustrate the steps in a simple un-defended divorce.

Our client, Jenny Pitts, is married to Brad Pitts. They separated on September 4, 2016, when Brad left Jenny for Angelina Jolly, a woman he met at work. On January 15, 2017, Jenny and Brad signed a separation agreement that settles all outstanding issues between them. They have agreed that Jenny will start a divorce case based on Brad's adultery, which Brad will not defend. Brad is willing to sign an affidavit admitting to the adultery.

Jenny was born on May 1, 1978, in Richmond Hill, Ontario, and Brad was born on April 6, 1975, also in Richmond Hill. They have lived in Richmond Hill all of their lives. They were married on June 6, 2003, in Thornhill, Ontario. It was Jenny's first marriage, but Brad was married briefly before to Lisa Cujo. That marriage ended in divorce on December 1, 2001.

Brad and Jenny have two children, Matthew Joseph, born on July 4, 2005, and Courtney Monica, born on February 14, 2007. They are living with Jenny at 4 Friendship Street, Richmond Hill, ON L3P 4N2. Brad moved in with Angelina at 15 Central Perk Place, Richmond Hill, ON L5K 1H3 when he left Jenny.

The separation agreement includes provisions as follows:

1. Jenny will have custody of the children, and Brad will have reasonable access.
2. Brad will pay child support, in accordance with the *Child Support Guidelines*, of $892 per month based on his annual income of $60,000.

Jenny does not want to incorporate any of the provisions in the divorce order. Assume that Jenny's application for divorce is being prepared on November 10, 2017.

Step 1: Get Supporting Documents

Before starting a divorce application for Jenny, you should have copies of the following documents:

- *Marriage certificate.* You must file the marriage certificate under Rule 36(4), and it is helpful to have the certificate before you prepare the application to make sure that you name the parties properly.

- *Separation agreement.* It is helpful to have a copy of the agreement before you prepare the application to make sure that you have the correct details about the agreement (and you would have to attach a copy of the separation agreement to Jenny's affidavit if she wanted to incorporate any of its provisions into the order).

As it turns out, Jenny has the original marriage certificate issued by the minister who performed the ceremony (see Figure 12.1 at the end of the chapter).

If Jenny did not have the marriage certificate, you would need to get a certificate of the registration of the marriage.

You may obtain a certified copy of a marriage certificate or a certificate of the registration of a marriage from the government of the jurisdiction in which the parties were married. If the parties were married in Ontario, as Jenny and Brad were, you order the certificate by mail from the Office of the Registrar General in Thunder Bay. You can apply online at the government of Ontario's website at <http://www.ontario.ca>.

If Jenny and Brad had been married outside Ontario, you would also need a copy of the divorce certificate for Brad's divorce from Lisa Cujo to file with the court in order to prove that his marriage to Jenny is valid.[9] You get a certificate of divorce from the court office of the court that granted the divorce.

Step 2: Complete the Forms

You must prepare three forms:

- an application,
- a continuing record, and
- a registration of divorce proceedings form from the Central Registry of Divorce Proceedings.

Application

The application used for a simple divorce is Form 8A—Application (Divorce). Figure 12.2 at the end of the chapter sets out Jenny's completed application.

Page 1

- Insert the name of the court, in this case, the Superior Court of Justice Family Branch, and the address of the appropriate court office. Under Rule 5, Jenny's divorce should be commenced in Newmarket, the location of the court in York Region (where Richmond Hill is located). If you don't know the address of the court office, you can find it on the website for the Ministry of the Attorney General at <http://www.attorneygeneral.jus.gov.on.ca> (follow the links to Court Addresses). The address of the Family Court in Newmarket is 50 Eagle Street West, Newmarket, ON L3Y 6B1.
- Check the box indicating that this is a simple (divorce only) application.
- Insert the names and addresses of the applicant and the respondent. Use the names of the parties as they appear on the marriage certificate. Note that Jenny's full name is Jennifer Elizabeth Pitts,[10] and Brad's full name is Bradley David Pitts.

---

9 Because Jenny and Brad were married in Ontario, you do not need Brad's certificate of divorce ending his marriage with Lisa. The Ontario courts are satisfied that an Ontario marriage licence would not have been issued without proof that Brad's earlier marriage was properly terminated.

10 After the marriage, Jenny assumed Brad's surname.

- Insert the name and address of the applicant's lawyer, if any. In this case, Jenny is represented by your law firm.
- Check the box that indicates that the applicant is claiming a divorce only.

Page 2

- Leave the second page of the form blank. This is not a joint application, so do not check the box in the frame. The court clerk will sign and date the application when it is issued.

Page 3

- Insert the required information under the heading "Family History."
- Insert the required information under the heading "Previous Cases or Agreements." In this case, the parties have not been in a court case before, but they have made a written agreement. You must insert the date of the agreement: January 15, 2017. No terms of the agreement are in dispute. There have been no notices issued by the online Child Support Service.

Page 4

- *Claims.* In a simple divorce that is not a joint application, the applicant may claim a divorce only. In this case, complete the second frame only.
- *Supporting Facts.* Under the heading "Important Facts Supporting the Claim for Divorce," the applicant gives details of the grounds for divorce. Check the box next to the appropriate ground, and then provide the requested details.

In this case, Jenny can proceed on either the ground of separation or the ground of adultery, and has decided to proceed on the ground of adultery. As a result, you have to check the adultery box and provide details of the adultery. Under Rule 36, you do not need to name the other person involved. If you do name another person, he or she will have to be served with the application.

If Jenny were to proceed on the ground of separation, you would check the separation box and fill in the appropriate dates. For the purposes of illustration, Jenny's application is completed for the grounds of both separation and adultery. However, Jenny would complete only the adultery section.

Page 5

- *Joint applications.* In a joint application for divorce, the top frame must be completed to set out details of the other orders that are being sought, and facts that support those claims. Since this is not a joint application, do not complete this frame.
- *Signatures.* Jenny must sign the application and date it. She should use her usual signature. If you know when your client will be coming in to sign the application, insert the date. In this case, Jenny is coming in to sign on November 13, 2017.

- *Lawyer's certificate.* Complete this part of the application by inserting the name of the applicant's lawyer and the name of the client. The lawyer must then sign the certificate. If you know when the lawyer will be signing the application, insert the date; in this case, November 13, 2017.

Continuing Record

Under Rule 9(1), Jenny must prepare and serve a continuing record on Brad when she serves the application. The continuing record cover in this case appears as Figure 12.3, and the continuing record table of contents appears as Figure 12.4, both at the end of the chapter.

Central Divorce Registry Form

You must complete a registration of divorce proceedings form and file it with the court so that the court can get a report from the Central Registry of Divorce Proceedings. This is a federal government form, which can be obtained online at <http://www.justice.gc.ca/eng/fl-df/divorce/crdp-bead.html>.

Step 3: File the Application

You or someone from your law firm must file Jenny's application with the court. You will need

- the original and two copies of the application (the original for the court, one copy for the respondent, and one copy for your file);
- the marriage certificate;
- the registration of divorce proceedings form; and
- the court filing fee.

At the court, the court staff assigns a court file number to the case and puts a seal on the original application. The person filing the application must write the court file number in the upper right-hand corner of the original and all copies of the forms.

Step 4: Serve the Respondent

Your law firm must arrange to serve the respondent with a copy of the application and the continuing record. The documents must be served by special service as defined in Rule 6(3). The person who serves the application must then complete and swear an affidavit of service (Form 6B).

If your firm's process server, Matt LeBlank, served the documents on Brad by personal service on November 28, 2017, the affidavit of service would be as set out in Figure 12.5 at the end of the chapter.

Step 5: File the Application, Continuing Record, and Proof of Service

Once the application and continuing record have been served, your law firm must arrange for someone to file the documents with the court. The continuing record table of contents must be updated to include the affidavit of service. This step is usually combined with Step 7. In other words, the documents are not filed with the court until 30 days have passed and the affidavit and divorce order have been prepared.

Step 6: Complete the Affidavit(s) and Divorce Order

Brad has 30 days to defend the divorce case by serving and filing an answer. Even though he and Jenny have agreed that the divorce will proceed on an undefended basis, the 30-day period must pass before the court will grant the divorce without a court appearance.

The court requires

- an affidavit in Form 36 sworn by Jenny,
- proof of the adultery (in this case, an affidavit in Form 14A sworn by Brad), and
- a draft divorce order (Form A-25A).[11]

You must also update the continuing record table of contents to include the affidavits.

Have a look at Jenny's affidavit, which appears as Figure 12.6 at the end of the chapter. In particular, note the following:

- *Paragraph 5.* Jenny states that the legal basis for the divorce is that Brad "has committed adultery," but does not give any details of the adultery. An affidavit is a document that contains evidence sworn to under oath and should include only matters about which Jenny has personal knowledge. Jenny's only information about the adultery comes from what Brad has told her. All she can swear to is that Brad has admitted to her that the adultery has taken place. Under the law of evidence, a divorce cannot be granted solely on the basis of such an admission. What is required is an admission by Brad sworn to under oath.

- *Paragraph 5a.* When a divorce is sought on the ground of adultery, the court has a duty under section 11 of the *Divorce Act* to satisfy itself that there has been no condonation or connivance on the part of the applicant. The information in this paragraph denying condonation or connivance constitutes "other information necessary for the court to grant the divorce" within the meaning of Rule 36(5). (See Chapter 5 for a more complete discussion of condonation and connivance.)

The court requires evidence of Brad's adultery. As stated above, Jenny cannot give that evidence because she does not have personal knowledge of the adultery. As a result, Jenny needs to file an affidavit from Brad in which he admits to the adultery under oath.

---

11   In this case, it is appropriate to use the one-page divorce order, Form A-25A.

Brad's affidavit appears as Figure 12.7 at the end of the chapter. Note that paragraph 2 contains Brad's sworn evidence that he has committed adultery. The paragraph starts with Brad's acknowledgment of his willingness to give this evidence even though he is not required by law to do so. This statement is included because of the provisions of section 10 of the Ontario *Evidence Act*.[12]

Figure 12.8 at the end of the chapter sets out a draft divorce order. Note that the judge's name and the date of the order are left blank on page 1 because you don't know when or by whom the application will be considered. The court will fill in this information. The date of signature is left blank for the same reason.

Step 7: File the Documents with the Court

Under Rules 36(5) and 36(6), you must file the following documents with the court:

- the original of Jenny's affidavit;
- the original of Brad's affidavit;
- three copies of the draft divorce order; and
- two stamped envelopes, one addressed to Jenny in care of your law firm, and the other addressed to Brad.

Be sure to keep copies of all documents for your file.

Step 8: Obtain the Divorce Order

The court clerk reviews the documents and presents them to a judge for review. If the judge is satisfied with the material, he or she will grant the divorce order. If the judge needs more information, the court will contact your law firm.

Step 9: Obtain a Certificate of Divorce

The divorce order will not take effect until the 31st day after the order is made. Either party can ask the court to issue a certificate of divorce as proof that the divorce has taken effect. The court clerk will check the file to make sure that the required time has passed and that neither party has appealed the order. There is a fee for the certificate.

---

12 Section 10 of the *Evidence Act*, RSO 1990, c E.23, reads as follows: "The parties to a proceeding instituted in consequence of adultery and the spouses of such parties are competent to give evidence in such proceedings, but no witness in any such proceeding, whether a party to the suit or not, is liable to be asked or bound to answer any question tending to show that he or she is guilty of adultery, unless such witness has already given evidence in the same proceeding in disproof of his or her alleged adultery."

CHAPTER SUMMARY

Divorce procedure in Ontario is governed by the *Family Law Rules* generally and by Rule 36 specifically.

A spouse who wishes to terminate his or her marriage must start a divorce proceeding. This party may ask the court to deal with issues of support and/or custody under the *Divorce Act*, and/or property claims under the *Family Law Act*. If these issues are agreed upon through a separation agreement, the applicant may request an order that incorporates the settlement's terms, or he or she may ask for a divorce only.

A divorce proceeding may be either defended (contested) or undefended (uncontested). A divorce will most likely be defended if the applicant claims custody, support, and/or an equalization of net family property. A divorce is likely to be undefended if these issues were dealt with previously in a separation agreement or an action under the *Family Law Act*.

A law firm starting a divorce case must start by acquiring supporting documents such as the marriage certificate and/or separation agreement. After completing the necessary forms, the application is filed with the court and then served on the respondent. If the respondent does not defend within 30 days after being served, the divorce will proceed on an undefended basis. The applicant prepares an affidavit and a draft order and files those documents with the court along with the application, continuing record, and proof of service. The documents will be presented to a judge for review. If the judge is satisfied with the material, he or she will grant the divorce order. The divorce takes effect on the 31st day after the order is made. Either party can ask the court to issue a certificate of divorce as proof that the divorce has taken effect.

REVIEW QUESTIONS

1. Generally speaking, where should a divorce case be started?

2. How may a spouse start a divorce case?

3. Who are the parties to a divorce case?

4. What must the applicant serve on the respondent? When? How?

5. If a respondent wants to defend a divorce case, what must he or she do? When?

6. What will the court do if the respondent does not defend the divorce?

7. Generally speaking, when does a divorce take effect?

8. When is a divorce likely to be defended? When is it likely to be undefended?

9. What forms must the applicant complete to start a divorce case?

10. What documents will the court require in order to grant a divorce in an undefended divorce case?

DRAFTING QUESTION

Jennifer Garnet and Ben Affect were married for only a short time when they realized that they were totally incompatible. They have been separated since August 16, 2017, and Jennifer now wants to get a divorce. Jennifer, who kept her own surname following the marriage, was born in Newmarket on January 1, 1980, and Ben was born, also in Newmarket, on September 15, 1982. They have lived in Newmarket all of their lives and were married there on February 14, 2011. It was the first marriage for both of them. They have no children. Jennifer is now living at 123 Foley Drive, Newmarket, ON L3P 1J4. Ben is living at 215 Paltrow Court, Newmarket, ON L4X 2K6. Prepare a divorce application to be signed by Jennifer, an affidavit (Form 36) to be signed by Jennifer, and a draft divorce order. Assume that a marriage registration certificate is filed with the application.

FIGURE 12.1 Jenny and Brad's Marriage Certificate

Certificate of Marriage

This is to certify that, on the ___sixth___ day of ___June___ 20 _03_

at ___Thornhill United Church___ in the Province of Ontario

the marriage of ___Jennifer Elizabeth Annistone___ and

___Bradley David Pitts___ was solemnized under marriage

Licence No.

C No. 322155

issued on the ___6th___ day of ___June___ 20 _03_

___Rev. Chandler Byng___
Signature of person solemnizing marriage

___135 John Street, Thornhill, Ontario___
Address

___United Church___ ___12345___
Clergy denomination **Clergy registration certificate No.**

Witnesses to marriage:

___Ross Geller___

___Monica Geller___

FIGURE 12.2 Jenny's Application

ONTARIO

SEAL	Court File Number

Superior Court of Justice Family Branch
(Name of court)

at **50 Eagle Street West, Newmarket, ON L3Y 6B1**
Court office address

**Form 8A: Application
(Divorce)**
☒ **Simple (divorce only)**
☐ **Joint**

Applicant(s)

Full legal name & address for service – street & number, municipality, postal code, telephone & fax numbers and e-mail address (if any).	*Lawyer's name & address – street & number, municipality, postal code, telephone & fax numbers and e-mail address (if any).*
Jennifer Elizabeth Pitts **4 Friendship Street** **Richmond Hill, ON L3P 4N2**	**JoAnn Kurtz** **123 College Street** **Toronto, ON ON M2K 1Y3** **Tel: 416-555-1234** **Fax: 416-555-1235**

Respondent(s)

Full legal name & address for service – street & number, municipality, postal code, telephone & fax numbers and e-mail address (if any).	*Lawyer's name & address – street & number, municipality, postal code, telephone & fax numbers and e-mail address (if any).*
Bradley David Pitts **15 Central Perk Place** **Richmond Hill, ON L5K 1H3**	

☒   **IN THIS CASE, THE APPLICANT IS CLAIMING DIVORCE ONLY.**

TO THE RESPONDENT(S): A COURT CASE FOR DIVORCE HAS BEEN STARTED AGAINST YOU IN THIS COURT. THE DETAILS ARE SET OUT ON THE ATTACHED PAGES.

THIS CASE IS ON THE STANDARD TRACK OF THE CASE MANAGEMENT SYSTEM. No court date has been set for this case but, if you have been served with a notice of motion, it has a court date and you or your lawyer should come to court for the motion. A case management judge will not be assigned until one of the parties asks the clerk of the court to schedule a case conference or until a motion is scheduled, whichever comes first.

IF, AFTER 365 DAYS, THE CASE HAS NOT BEEN SCHEDULED FOR TRIAL, the clerk of the court will send out a warning that the case will be dismissed within 60 days unless the parties file proof that the case has been settled or one of the parties asks for a case or a settlement conference.

IF YOU WANT TO OPPOSE ANY CLAIM IN THIS CASE, you or your lawyer must prepare an Answer (Form 10 – a blank copy should be attached), serve a copy on the applicant and file a copy in the court office with an Affidavit of Service (Form 6B). **YOU HAVE ONLY 30 DAYS AFTER THIS APPLICATION IS SERVED ON YOU (60 DAYS IF THIS APPLICATION IS SERVED ON YOU OUTSIDE CANADA OR THE UNITED STATES) TO SERVE AND FILE AN ANSWER. IF YOU DO NOT, THE CASE WILL GO AHEAD WITHOUT YOU AND THE COURT MAY MAKE AN ORDER AND ENFORCE IT AGAINST YOU.**

IF YOU WANT TO MAKE A CLAIM OF YOUR OWN, you or your lawyer must fill out the claim portion in the Answer, serve a copy on the applicant(s) and file a copy in the court office with an Affidavit of Service.

- If you want to make a claim for support but do not want to make a claim for property or exclusive possession of the matrimonial home and its contents, you **MUST** fill out a Financial Statement (Form 13), serve a copy on the applicant(s) and file a copy in the court office.
- However, if your only claim for support is for child support in the table amount specified under the Child Support Guidelines, you do not need to fill out, serve or file a Financial Statement.
- If you want to make a claim for property or exclusive possession of the matrimonial home and its contents, whether or not it includes a claim for support, you **MUST** fill out a Financial Statement (Form 13.1, not Form 13), serve a copy on the applicant(s), and file a copy in the court office.

YOU SHOULD GET LEGAL ADVICE ABOUT THIS CASE RIGHT AWAY. If you cannot afford a lawyer, you may be able to get help from your local Legal Aid Ontario office. *(See your telephone directory under LEGAL AID.)*

FIGURE 12.2   Jenny's Application Continued

Form 8A: **Application (Divorce)**	(page 2)	Court File Number

☐   **THIS CASE IS A JOINT APPLICATION FOR DIVORCE. THE DETAILS ARE SET OUT ON THE ATTACHED PAGES.** The application and affidavits in support of the application will be presented to a judge when the materials have been checked for completeness.

If you are requesting anything other than a simple divorce, such as support or property or exclusive possession of the matrimonial home and its contents, then refer to page 1 for instructions regarding the Financial Statement you should file.

_____   _____
Date of issue   *Clerk of the court*

FIGURE 12.2   Jenny's Application Continued

Form 8A: **Application (Divorce)**	**(page 3)**	Court file number

FAMILY HISTORY

APPLICANT: Age: 39   Birthdate: *(d, m, y)* **1 May 1978**

Resident in *(municipality & province)*   **Richmond Hill, Ontario**

since *(date)*   **1 May 1978**

Surname at birth: **Annistone**   Surname just before marriage: **Annistone**

Divorced before?   ☒ No   ☐ Yes *(Place and date of previous divorce)*

RESPONDENT/JOINT APPLICANT: Age: **42**   Birthdate: *(d, m, y)* **6 April 1975**

Resident in *(municipality & province)*   **Richmond Hill, Ontario**

since *(date)*   **6 April 1975**

Surname at birth: **Pitts**   Surname just before marriage: **Pitts**

Divorced before?   ☐ No   ☒ Yes *(Place and date of previous divorce)*

Toronto, Ontario - 1 December 2001

RELATIONSHIP DATES:

☒ Married on *(date)* **6 June 2003**   ☐ Started living together on *(date)*

☒ Separated on *(date)* **4 September 2016**   ☐ Never lived together

---

THE CHILD(REN)
List all children involved in this case, even if no claim is made for these children.

Full legal name	Age	Birthdate *(d,m,y)*	Resident in *(municipality & province)*	Now Living With *(name of person and relationship to child)*
Matthew Joseph Pitts	12	4 July 2005	Richmond Hill, Ontario	Jennifer Pitts – Mother
Courtney Monica Pitts	10	14 February 2007	Richmond Hill, Ontario	Jennifer Pitts – Mother

PREVIOUS CASES OR AGREEMENTS

Have the parties or the children been in a court case before?

      ☒ No   ☐ Yes

Have the parties made a written agreement dealing with any matter involved in this case?

      ☐ No   ☒ Yes *(Give date of agreement. Indicate which of its terms are in dispute. Attach an additional page if you need more space.)*
          15 January 2017. No terms are in dispute.

FIGURE 12.2   Jenny's Application   Continued

Form 8A: Application (Divorce)   (page 4) | Court file number |

Has a Notice of Calculation and/or a Notice of Recalculation been issued by the online Child Support Service in this case?

☒ No   ☐ Yes *(Give date(s) of Notice(s) of Calculation or Recalculation.)*

If yes, are you asking the court to make an order for a child support that is different from the amount set out in the Notice?

☐ No   ☐ Yes *(Provide an explanation.)*

CLAIMS

USE THIS FRAME ONLY IF THIS CASE IS A JOINT APPLICATION FOR DIVORCE

WE JOINTLY ASK THE COURT FOR THE FOLLOWING:

Claims under the *Divorce Act*

- 00 ☐ a divorce
- 01 ☐ spousal support
- 02 ☐ support for child(ren) – table amount
- 03 ☐ support for child(ren) – other than table amount
- 04 ☐ custody of child(ren)
- 05 ☐ access to child(ren)

Claims under the *Family Law Act* or *Children's Law Reform Act*

- 10 ☐ spousal support
- 11 ☐ support for child(ren) – table amount
- 12 ☐ support for child(ren) – other than table amount
- 13 ☐ custody of child(ren)
- 14 ☐ access to child(ren)
- 15 ☐ restraining/non-harassment order
- 16 ☐ indexing spousal support
- 17 ☐ declaration of parentage
- 18 ☐ guardianship over child's property

Claims relating to property

- 20 ☐ equalization of net family properties
- 21 ☐ exclusive possession of matrimonial home
- 22 ☐ exclusive possession of contents of matrimonial home
- 23 ☐ freezing assets
- 24 ☐ sale of family property

Other claims

- 30 ☐ costs
- 31 ☐ annulment of marriage
- 32 ☐ prejudgment interest
- 50 ☐ Other *(Specify)*

USE THIS FRAME ONLY IF THE APPLICANT'S ONLY CLAIM IN THIS CASE IS FOR DIVORCE.

I ASK THE COURT FOR:
(Check if applicable.)

00 ☒ a divorce   30 ☐ costs

IMPORTANT FACTS SUPPORTING THE CLAIM FOR DIVORCE

☒ **Separation:** The spouses have lived separate and apart since *(date)*   4 September 2016   and

   ☒ have not lived together again since that date in an unsuccessful attempt to reconcile.
   ☐ have lived together again during the following periods(s) in an unsuccessful attempt to reconcile: *(Give dates.)*

☒ **Adultery:** *(Name of spouse)*   Bradley David Pitts   has committed adultery.
   (Give details. It is not necessary to name any other person involved but if you do name the other person, then you must serve this application on the other person.)

   The respondent has resided with another person in a conjugal relationship at 15 Central Perk Place in Richmond Hill, Ontario from in or about September 2012 to the date of this application, and during that time has engaged in acts of sexual intercourse with her on numerous occasions.

FIGURE 12.2   Jenny's Application Concluded

Form 8A: Application (Divorce) (page 5)	Court File Number

☐ **Cruelty:** *(Name of spouse)* _____ has treated *(name of spouse)* _____ with physical or mental cruelty of such a kind as to make continued cohabitation intolerable. *(Give details.)*

USE THIS FRAME ONLY IF THIS CASE IS A JOINT APPLICATION FOR DIVORCE.

The details of the other order(s) that we jointly ask the court to make are as follows: *(Include any amounts of support and the names of the children for whom support, custody or access is to be ordered.)*

IMPORTANT FACTS SUPPORTING OUR CLAIM(S)
(Set out the facts that form the legal basis for your claim(s). Attach an additional page if you need more space.)

Put a line through any blank space left on this page.

Complete this section if your only claim is for a divorce. Your lawyer, if you are represented, must complete the Lawyer's Certificate below.

13 November 2017	
Date of signature	*Signature of applicant*

Complete this section if you are making a joint application for divorce. Your lawyer, if you are represented, must complete the Lawyer's Certificate below.

Date of signature	*Signature of joint applicant*

Date of signature	*Signature of joint applicant*

LAWYER'S CERTIFICATE

My name is: **JoAnn Kurtz**

and I am the lawyer for *(name)* **Jennifer Elizabeth Pitts**   in this divorce case. I certify that I have complied with the requirements of section 9 of the *Divorce Act*.

13 November 2017	
Date	*Signature of Lawyer*

My name is: _____

and I am the lawyer for *(name)* _____ in this divorce case. I certify that I have complied with the requirements of section 9 of the *Divorce Act*.

Date	*Signature of Lawyer*

FLR 8A (April 12, 2016)   Page 5 of 5

FIGURE 12.3   Continuing Record Cover

ONTARIO

_____ Superior Court of Justice Family Court Branch / _____
(Name of court / *Nom du tribunal*)

at / *situé(e) au*   50 Eagle Street West, Newmarket, ON L3Y 6B1
Court office address / *Adresse du greffe*

Court File Number / *Numéro de dossier du greffe*

Volume / *Volume* : 1 _____

Applicant(s) / *Requérant(e)(s)*

Full legal name & address for service — street & number, municipality, postal code, telephone & fax numbers and e-mail address (if any). *Nom et prénom officiels et adresse aux fins de signification — numéro et rue, municipalité, code postal, numéros de téléphone et de télécopieur et adresse électronique (le cas échéant).*	Lawyer's name & address — street & number, municipality, postal code, telephone & fax numbers and e-mail address (if any). *Nom et adresse de l'avocat(e) — numéro et rue, municipalité, code postal, numéros de téléphone et de télécopieur et adresse électronique (le cas échéant).*
Jennifer Elizabeth Pitts **4 Friendship Street** **Richmond Hill, ON L3P 4N2**	**JoAnn Kurtz** **123 College Street** **Toronto, ON M2K 1Y3** **Tel: 416-555-1234** **Fax: 416-555-1235**

Respondent(s) / *Intimé(e)(s)*

Full legal name & address for service — street & number, municipality, postal code, telephone & fax numbers and e-mail address (if any). *Nom et prénom officiels et adresse aux fins de signification — numéro et rue, municipalité, code postal, numéros de téléphone et de télécopieur et adresse électronique (le cas échéant).*	Lawyer's name & address — street & number, municipality, postal code, telephone & fax numbers and e-mail address (if any). *Nom et adresse de l'avocat(e) — numéro et rue, municipalité, code postal, numéros de téléphone et de télécopieur et adresse électronique (le cas échéant).*
Bradley David Pitts **15 Central Perk Place** **Richmond Hill, ON L5K 1H3**	

Children's Lawyer/ *Avocat des enfants*

Name & address of Children's Lawyer's agent for service (street & number, municipality, postal code, telephone & fax numbers and e-mail address (if any)) and name of person represented. *Nom et adresse aux fins de signification de la personne qui représente l'avocat(e) des enfants (numéro et rue, municipalité, code postal, numéros de téléphone et de télécopieur et adresse électronique (le cas échéant)) et nom de la personne représentée.*

Continuing Record /
Dossier continu

FLR-A 9CR (01/07)

FIGURE 12.4   Continuing Record Table of Contents

ONTARIO

Superior Court of Justice Family Court Branch
(Name of court)

Court File Number

**Cumulative Table of Contents
(Continuing Record)**

at   50 Eagle Street West, Newmarket, ON L3Y 6B1
Court office address

Applicant(s)

Full legal name & address for service — street & number, municipality, postal code, telephone & fax numbers and e-mail address (if any).	Lawyer's name & address — street & number, municipality, postal code, telephone & fax numbers and e-mail address (if any).
Jennifer Elizabeth Pitts 4 Friendship Street Richmond Hill, ON L3P 4N2	JoAnn Kurtz 123 College Street Toronto, ON M2K 1Y3 Tel: 416-555-1234 Fax: 416-555-1235

Respondent(s)

Full legal name & address for service — street & number, municipality, postal code, telephone & fax numbers and e-mail address (if any).	Lawyer's name & address — street & number, municipality, postal code, telephone & fax numbers and e-mail address (if any).
Bradley David Pitts 15 Central Perk Place Richmond Hill, ON L5K 1H3	

Document *(For an affidavit or transcript of evidence, include the name of the person who gave the affidavit or the evidence.)*	Filed by *(A = applicant or R = respondent)*	Date of Document *(d, m, y)*	Date of Filing *(d, m, y)*	Volume/Tab
Application	A	11/11/17		Volume 1, Tab 1

☐ *Continued on next sheet*

FIGURE 12.5   Affidavit of Service

ONTARIO

Superior Court of Justice, Family Court	Court File Number
(Name of court)	
at 50 Eagle Street West, Newmarket, ON L3Y 6B1	**Form 6B: Affidavit of Service**
Court office address	**sworn/affirmed**

Applicant(s)

Full legal name & address for service — street & number, municipality, postal code, telephone & fax numbers and e-mail address (if any).	*Lawyer's name & address — street & number, municipality, postal code, telephone & fax numbers and e-mail address (if any).*
Jennifer Elizabeth Pitts **4 Friendship Street** **Richmond Hill, ON L3P 4N2**	**JoAnn Kurtz** **123 College Street** **Toronto, ON M2K 1Y3** **Tel: 416-555-1234** **Fax: 416-555-1235**

Respondent(s)

Full legal name & address for service — street & number, municipality, postal code, telephone & fax numbers and e-mail address (if any).	*Lawyer's name & address — street & number, municipality, postal code, telephone & fax numbers and e-mail address (if any).*
Bradley David Pitts **15 Central Perk Place** **Richmond Hill, ON L5K 1H3**	

My name is *(full legal name)* **Matt LeBlank**

I live in *(municipality & province)* **Toronto, Ontario**

and I swear/affirm that the following is true:

1.   On *(date)* **28 November 2017**   , at *(time)* **3:00 pm**   , I served *(name of person to be served)*

     Bradley David Pitts   with the following document(s) in this case:

	Name of document	Author (if applicable)	Date when document signed, issued, sworn, etc.
List the documents served	**Application** **Continuing Record**	**Jennifer Elizabeth Pitts** **Jennifer Elizabeth Pitts**	**13 November 2017** **13 November 2017**

NOTE: *You can leave out any part of this form that is not applicable.*

2.   I served the documents mentioned in paragraph 1 by:

        ☒ special service. *(Go to paragraph 3 below if you used special service.)*

        ☐ mail. *(Go to paragraph 4 if you used mailed service.)*

        ☐ same day courier. *(Go to paragraph 5 if you used courier.)*

Check one box only and go to indicated paragraph.
        ☐ next day courier. *(Go to paragraph 5 if you used courier.)*

        ☐ deposit at a document exchange. *(Go to paragraph 6 if you used a document exchange.)*

        ☐ an electronic document exchange. *(Go to paragraph 7 if you used an electronic document exchange.)*

        ☐ fax. *(Go to paragraph 8 if you used fax.)*

        ☐ email. *(Go to paragraph 9 if you used email.)*

        ☐ substituted service or advertisement. *(Go to paragraph 10 if you used substituted service or advertisement.)*

FIGURE 12.5   Affidavit of Service Continued

| Form 6B: | Affidavit of Service | (page 2) | Court File Number |
| sworn/affirmed | | | |

3. I carried out special service of the document(s) on the person named in paragraph 1 at *(place or address)*

    15 Central Perk Place, Richmond Hill, Ontario L5K 1H3

    by: ☒ leaving a copy with the person.

    ☐ leaving a copy with *(name)* _____

    Check one box only. Strike out paragraphs 4 to 10 and go to paragraph 11.

    ☐ who is a lawyer who accepted service in writing on a copy of the document.

    ☐ who is the person's lawyer of record.

    ☐ who is the *(office or position)* _____

        of the corporation named in paragraph 1.

    ☐ mailing a copy to the person together with a prepaid return postcard in Form 6 in an envelope bearing the sender's return address. This postcard, in which receipt of the document(s) is acknowledged, was returned and is attached to this affidavit.

    ☐ leaving a copy in a sealed envelope addressed to the person at the person's place of residence with

        (name) _____

        who provided me with identification to show that he/she was an adult person residing at the same address and by mailing another copy of the same document(s) on the same or following day to the person named in paragraph 1 at that place of residence.

    ☐ other *(Specify. See rule 6 for details.)*

4. I mailed the document(s) to be served by addressing the covering envelope to the person named in paragraph 1 at:

    (Set out address.) _____

    which is the address ☐ of the person's place of business.

    Check appropriate paragraph and strike out paragraphs 3, 5, 6, 7, 8, 9 and 10.

    ☐ of a lawyer who accepted service on the person's behalf.

    ☐ of the person's lawyer of record.

    ☐ of the person's home.

    ☐ on the document most recently filed in court by the person.

    ☐ other *(Specify.)* _____

5. The document(s) to be served was/were placed in an envelope that was picked up at _____ a.m./p.m. _____ on

    (date) _____ by *(name of courier service)* _____

    a private courier service, a copy of whose receipt is attached to this affidavit. The envelope was addressed to the person named in paragraph 1 at: *(Set out address.)* _____

    which is the address ☐ of the person's place of business.

    ☐ of a lawyer who accepted service on the person's behalf.

    Check appropriate paragraph and strike out paragraphs 3, 4, 6, 7, 8, 9 and 10.

    ☐ of the person's lawyer of record.

    ☐ of the person's home.

    ☐ on the document most recently filed in court by the person.

    ☐ other *(Specify.)* _____

FIGURE 12.5   Affidavit of Service   Concluded

Form 6B: sworn/affirmed	Affidavit of Service _____	(page 3)	Court File Number

6. The document(s) was/were deposited at a document exchange. The exchange's date stamp on the attached copy shows the date of deposit. *(Strike out paragraphs 3, 4, 5, 7, 8, 9, 10 and 13.)*

7. The documents were served through an electronic document exchange. The record of service from the exchange is attached to this affidavit. *(Strike out paragraphs 3, 4, 5, 6, 8, 9, 10 and 13.)*

8. The document(s) to be served was/were faxed. The fax confirmation is attached to this affidavit. *(Strike out paragraphs 3, 4, 5, 6, 7, 9, 10 and 13.)*

9. The documents were served by email. Attached to this Affidavit is a copy of the email that the document was attached to. *(Strike out paragraphs 3, 4, 5, 6, 7, 8, 10 and 13.)*

10. An order of this court made on *(date)* _____ allowed

    ☐ substituted service.

    ☐ service by advertisement. *(Attach advertisement.)*

    The order was carried out as follows: *(Give details. Then go to paragraph 13 if you had to travel to serve substitutionally or by advertisement.)*

11. My relationship to, or affiliation with, any party in this case is as follows:

    I am a process server employed by JoAnn Kurtz

12. I am at least 18 years of age.

13. To serve the document(s), I had to travel _____**5**_____ kilometres. My fee for service of the document(s) is

    $ **$100.00** _____ including travel.

Sworn/Affirmed before me at   **the City of Toronto**
_____
                                                                  municipality

in   **the Province of Ontario**
_____
                                          province, state, or country

on _____   _____
                      date   *Commissioner for taking affidavits*
                                                  (Type or print name below if
                                                  signature is illegible.)

_____
                      Signature
(This form is to be signed in front of a lawyer, justice of the peace, notary public or commissioner for taking affidavits.)

FIGURE 12.6 Jenny's Affidavit

ONTARIO

Superior Court of Justice Family Court Branch
(Name of court)

| | Court File Number |

at   **50 Eagle Street West, Newmarket, ON L3Y 6B1**
Court office address

Form 36:
Affidavit for Divorce

Applicant(s)

Full legal name & address for service — street & number, municipality, postal code, telephone & fax numbers and e-mail address (if any).	*Lawyer's name & address — street & number, municipality, postal code, telephone & fax numbers and e-mail address (if any).*
Jennifer Elizabeth Pitts **4 Friendship Street** **Richmond Hill, ON L3P 4N2**	**JoAnn Kurtz** **123 College Street** **Toronto, ON M2K 1Y3** **Tel: 416-555-1234** **Fax: 416-555-1235**

Respondent(s)

Full legal name & address for service — street & number, municipality, postal code, telephone & fax numbers and e-mail address (if any).	*Lawyer's name & address — street & number, municipality, postal code, telephone & fax numbers and e-mail address (if any).*
Bradley David Pitts **15 Central Perk Place** **Richmond Hill, ON L5K 1H3**	

My name is *(full legal name)* **Jennifer Elizabeth Pitts**

I live in *(municipality & province)* **Richmond Hill, Ontario**

and I swear/affirm that the following is true:

1. I am the applicant in this divorce case.

2. There is no chance of a reconciliation between the respondent and me.

3. All the information in the application in this case is correct, except:
    (State any corrections or changes to the information in the application. Write "NONE" if there are no corrections or changes.)
    NONE

4. ☒ The certificate or registration of my marriage to the respondent has been signed and sealed by the Registrar General of Ontario and:

    ☒ has been filed with the application.

    ☐ is attached to this affidavit.

    ☐ The certificate of my marriage to the respondent was issued outside Ontario. It is called *(title of certificate)*

    It was issued at *(place of issue)* _____

    on *(date)* _____

    by *(name and title of person who issued certificate)* _____

    and the information in it about my marriage is correct.

    ☐ I have not been able to get a certificate or registration of my marriage. I was married to the respondent on *(date)* _____
    at *(place of marriage)* _____

    The marriage was performed by *(name and title)* _____

    who had the authority to perform marriages in that place.

FIGURE 12.6 Jenny's Affidavit Continued

Form 36:   **Affidavit for Divorce**   **(page 2)**   Court File Number

5.   The legal basis for the divorce is:

☐   that the respondent and I have been separated for at least one year.

We separated on *(date)* _____

☒   Other *(Specify.)*

that the respondent has committed adultery. I have no personal knowledge of the adultery other than what the respondent has told me.

5a. I have not condoned or connived at the respondent's adultery.

6.   I do not know about and I am not involved in any arrangement to make up or to hide evidence or to deceive the court in this divorce case.

Strike out the following paragraphs if they do not apply.

7.   I do not want to make a claim for a division of property in this divorce case, even though I know that it may be legally impossible to make such a claim after the divorce.

8.   I want the divorce order to include the following paragraph numbers of the attached consent, settlement, separation agreement or previous court order: *(List the numbers of the paragraphs that you want included in the divorce order.)*

9.   There are *(number)* 2 _____ children of the marriage. They are:

Full legal name of child	Birth date *(d, m, y)*
Matthew Joseph Pitts	4 July 2005
Courtney Monica Pitts	14 February 2007

10.   The custody and access arrangements for the child(ren) are as follows: *(Give summary.)*
I have custody of the children, and the respondent has reasonable access.

11.   These are the arrangements that have been made for the support of the child(ren) of the marriage:

(a)   The income of the party paying child support is $ 60,000 _____ per year.

(b)   The number of children for whom support is supposed to be paid is *(number)* 2 _____

(c)   The amount of support that should be paid according to the applicable table in the child support guidelines is

$ 892 _____ per month.

(d)   The amount of child support actually being paid is $ 892 _____ per month.
*(**NOTE:** - Where the dollar amounts in clauses [c] and [d] are different, you must fill out the frame on the next page. If the amounts in clauses [c] and [d] are the same, skip the frame and go directly to paragraph 12.)*

FLR 36 (September 1, 2005)   Page 2 of 4

FIGURE 12.6   Jenny's Affidavit   Continued

Form 36:   **Affidavit for Divorce**   **(page 3)**   Court File Number

---

(Paragraph 11 continued.)

Fill out the information in this frame only if the amounts in paragraphs 11(c) and 11(d) are different. If they are the same, go to paragraph 12.

a) Child support is already covered by:

  (i)   ☐ a court order dated *(date)* _____ that was made before the
         child support guidelines came into effect (before 1 May 1997). I attach a copy of the order.

  (ii) ☐ a domestic contract order dated *(date)* _____ that was made before the
         child support guidelines came into effect (before 1 May 1997). I attach a copy of the contract.

  (iii) ☐ a court order or written agreement dated *(date)* _____ made after the
         guidelines came into effect that has some direct or indirect benefits for the child(ren). I attach a copy.

  (iv) ☐ a written consent between the parties dated *(date)* _____ agreeing to the payment
         of an amount different from that set out in the guidelines.

b) The child support clauses of this order or agreement require payment of $ _____ per _____
    in child support.

c) These child support clauses

      ☐ are not indexed for any automatic cost-of-living increases.

      ☐ are indexed according to *(Give indexing formula.)*

d) These child support clauses

      ☐ have not been changed since the day the order or agreement was made.

      ☐ have been changed on *(Give dates and details of changes.)*

e) *(If you ticked off box [i] above, you can go to paragraph 12. If you ticked off boxes [ii], [iii] or [iv] above, then fill out the information
    after box of the corresponding number below. For example, if you ticked off box [iii] above, you would fill out the information
    alongside box [iii] below.)*

  (ii) ☐ The amount being paid under this agreement is a fair and reasonable arrangement for the support of the
         child(ren) because: *(Give reasons.)*

  (iii) ☐ The order or agreement directly or indirectly benefits the child(ren) because: *(Give details or benefits.)*

  (iv) ☐ The amount to which the parties have consented is reasonable for the support of the child(ren) because:
         (Give reasons.)

FLR 36 (September 1, 2005)   **Page 3 of 4**

FIGURE 12.6 Jenny's Affidavit Concluded

Form 36: **Affidavit for Divorce** (page 4)

Court File Number

12. I am claiming costs in this case. The details of this claim are as follows: *(Give details.)*
    N/A

13. The respondent's address last known to me is: *(Give address.)*
    15 Central Perk Place
    Richmond Hill, ON L5K 1H3

Put a line through any blank space left on this page.

Sworn/Affirmed before me at **the City of Toronto**
                               municipality

in **the Province of Ontario**
      province, state or country

on **30 December 2017**
      date   Commissioner for taking affidavits
                                (Type or print name below if signature is illegible.)

Signature
(This form is to be signed in front of a lawyer, justice of the peace, notary public or commissioner for taking affidavits.)

FLR 36 (September 1, 2005)

FIGURE 12.7   Brad's Affidavit

ONTARIO

	Court File Number

Superior Court of Justice Family Court Branch
(Name of court)

**Form 14A: Affidavit
(general) dated**

at   50 Eagle Street West, Newmarket, ON L3Y 6B1
Court office address

_____

Applicant(s)

Full legal name & address for service — street & number, municipality, postal code, telephone & fax numbers and e-mail address (if any).	*Lawyer's name & address — street & number, municipality, postal code, telephone & fax numbers and e-mail address (if any).*
Jennifer Elizabeth Pitts **4 Friendship Street** **Richmond Hill, ON L3P 4N2**	**JoAnn Kurtz,** **123 College Street** **Toronto, ON M2K 1Y3** **Tel: 416-555-1234** **Fax: 416-555-1235**

Respondent(s)

Full legal name & address for service — street & number, municipality, postal code, telephone & fax numbers and e-mail address (if any).	*Lawyer's name & address — street & number, municipality, postal code, telephone & fax numbers and e-mail address (if any).*
Bradley David Pitts **15 Central Perk Place** **Richmond Hill, ON L5K 1H3**	

My name is *(full legal name)*   **Bradley David Pitts**

I live in *(municipality & province)*   **Richmond Hill, Ontario**

and I swear/affirm that the following is true:
Set out the statements of fact in consecutively numbered paragraphs. Where possible, each numbered paragraph should consist of one complete sentence and be limited to a particular statement of fact. If you learned a fact from someone else, you must give that person's name and state that you believe that fact to be true.

1. I am the husband of the applicant.

2. The legal basis for the divorce is adultery. I am aware that I am not obliged to give evidence that I have committed adultery, but I am willing to give that evidence.

3. I have been residing in a conjugal relationship with Angelina Jolly at 15 Central Perk Place in Richmond Hill, Ontario, since September 4, 2016, and I have engaged in sexual intercourse with her on numerous occasions.

4. The applicant has not condoned or connived at my adultery.

5. I do not know about and I am not involved in any arrangement to make up or to hide evidence or to deceive the court in this divorce.

FIGURE 12.7 Brad's Affidavit Concluded

Form 14A: **Affidavit (general) dated**   **(page 2)**

Court File Number

Put a line through any blank space left on this page.

Sworn/Affirmed before me at   **the City of Toronto**

                                              municipality

in   **the Province of Ontario**

                       province, state, or country

on   **30 December 2017**

           date   *Commissioner for taking affidavits*
                                     (Type or print name below if signature is illegible.)

Signature

(This form is to be signed in front of a lawyer, justice of the peace, notary public or commissioner for taking affidavits.)

FLR 14A (September 1, 2005)   Page 2 of 2

FIGURE 12.8 Divorce Order

ONTARIO

Superior Court of Justice Family Court Branch
(Name of court)

SEAL

at   50 Eagle Street West, Newmarket, ON L3Y 6B1
Court office address

Court File Number

Form 25A: Divorce Order

Applicant(s)

Judge (print or type name)

Full legal name & address for service — street & number, municipality, postal code, telephone & fax numbers and e-mail address (if any).	Lawyer's name & address — street & number, municipality, postal code, telephone & fax numbers and e-mail address (if any).
Jennifer Elizabeth Pitts **4 Friendship Street** **Richmond Hill, ON L3P 4N2**	**JoAnn Kurtz** **123 College Street** **Toronto, ON M5Y 1Y3** **Tel: 416-555-1234 Fax: 416-555-1235**

Respondent(s)

Date of order

Full legal name & address for service — street & number, municipality, postal code, telephone & fax numbers and e-mail address (if any).	Lawyer's name & address — street & number, municipality, postal code, telephone & fax numbers and e-mail address (if any).
Bradley David Pitts **15 Central Perk Place** **Richmond Hill, ON L5K 1H3**	

The court considered an application of *(name)*   **Jennifer Elizabeth Pitts**

on *(date)* _____

The following persons were in court *(Give names of parties and lawyers in court. This paragraph may be struck out if the divorce is uncontested.)*

The court received evidence and considered submissions on behalf of *(name or names)*
Jennifer Elizabeth Pitts

THIS COURT ORDERS THAT:

If the court decides that the divorce should take effect earlier, replace "31" with the smaller number.

1. *(full legal names of spouses)*   **Jennifer Elizabeth Pitts and Bradley David Pitts**

who were married at *(place)*   **Thornhill, Ontario**

on *(date)*   **6 June 2003**

be divorced and that the divorce take effect 31 days after the date of this order.

(Add further paragraphs where the court orders other relief.)

Put a line through any blank space left on this page.

_____   _____
Date of signature   *Signature of judge or clerk of the court*

NOTE: Neither spouse is free to remarry until this order takes effect, at which time you can get a **Certificate of Divorce** from the court office.

FLR-A 25A (August 1, 2009)

Support and Custody Claims: A Fast Track Case and a Motion

13

LEARNING OUTCOMES

After completing this chapter, you should be able to:

- Describe the steps, referring to the relevant rules, in a defended support and custody case.

- Complete the documents required to start a support and custody case.

- Describe the steps, referring to the relevant rules, required to bring a motion for temporary custody and support.

- Complete the documents required to bring a motion for temporary custody and support.

Introduction

A spouse who commences a divorce proceeding may ask the court to deal with questions of support and/or custody as part of the divorce case under the *Divorce Act.*[1] All other parties must institute separate proceedings under the *Family Law Act*[2] and the *Children's Law Reform Act.*[3]

We looked at the substantive law of custody and access in Chapter 6, spousal support in Chapter 7, and child support in Chapter 8. In this chapter, we look at the procedure in a support and custody case, including

- an overview of the procedure in a defended support and custody case,
- an examination of the documents required to start a support and custody case, and
- an examination of the steps and documents required to bring a motion for interim support and custody.

Overview of Procedure

The procedure in a support and custody case is governed by the *Family Law Rules*[4] generally and, if the case involves a claim for custody or access, by Rule 35.1 specifically.

Starting a Support and Custody Case

Under Rule 5, a custody case should generally be started in the municipality where the children live, although, with the consent of the court, it may be started in a municipality chosen by both parties.[5] If the case is started in a municipality where the Family Court of the Superior Court of Justice does not operate, the case may be started in either the Superior Court of Justice or the Ontario Court of Justice.

Pursuant to Rule 7, the parties to a support and/or custody case are the applicant and the respondent.

The applicant starts the case by filing an application in Form 8 as required under Rule 8(1). Under Rule 13(1.1), the application must be accompanied by the appropriate financial statement, which is Form 13 in a claim for support without a property claim. However, under Rule 13(1.3) the applicant does not have to file a financial statement if the only claim for support is a claim for child support in

---

1 RSC 1985, c 3 (2d Supp).
2 RSO 1990, c F.3
3 RSO 1990, c C.12
4 O Reg 114/99.
5 If a claim is made for support only, the case may be started in the municipality where either party resides or, with the court's consent, in a municipality chosen by both parties.

the table amount under the *Child Support Guidelines*.[6] Under Rule 13(7), the applicant must attach to the financial statement copies of his or her income tax returns for the previous three years or a copy of the party's Income and Deduction printout provided by the Canada Revenue Agency. According to Rules 13(3.1) and 13(3.2), a party required to serve a financial statement (Form 13) in a support claim is required to serve at the same time a certificate of financial disclosure (Form 13A) along with the following documents:

- the income and financial information referred to in subsection 21(1) of the child support guidelines;
- if the party became unemployed within the last three years, a complete copy of the party's Record of Employment, or other evidence of termination, and a statement of any benefits or income that the party is still entitled to receive from his or her former employer despite or as a result of the termination; and
- in the case of a claim for the support of a child, proof of the amount of any special or extraordinary expenses, within the meaning of section 7 of the *Child Support Guidelines*.

If the case includes a claim for custody, pursuant to the *Children's Law Reform Act* section 21(2) and Rule 35.1, the applicant must also file an affidavit in support of claim for custody or access (Form 35.1). A non-parent applicant must also provide a police records check (under the *Children's Law Reform Act* section 21.1 and Rule 35.1(3)) and a report from the Children's Aid Society stating whether the Society has any records relating to the applicant (under the *Children's Law Reform Act* section 21.2 and Rule 35.1(5)).

The applicant must also prepare the continuing record of the case in accordance with Rule 9. The continuing record is the court's record of all documents in the case. The general rule is that any document that is served and filed must be put into the continuing record. The applicant's law firm is responsible for the initial preparation of the continuing record. See Chapter 10 for a detailed discussion of the continuing record.

If a case is started in the Family Court of the Superior Court of Justice, it will be a fast track case under Rule 39(4). As a result, the court will set a first court date in accordance with Rule 8(4), when the application is filed. If the case is started in the Ontario Court of Justice, that court will also set a first court date in accordance with Rule 8(4). However, if the case is started in the Superior Court of Justice, under Rule 41(4) the court does not set a first court date.

Service of the Application

The applicant must immediately serve the respondent with the application, financial statement, certificate of financial disclosure and supporting documents, and, in

---

6 See Rules 8(5), 9(1), 13(1), and 35.1(2).

a custody case, an affidavit in support of claim for custody or access, along with the continuing record, using special service as defined in Rule 6(3).

The applicant must then file the documents with the court,[7] after adding the affidavit of service or other proof of service to the continuing record.

Subsequent Pleadings

Under Rule 10, the respondent has 30 days if served in Canada or the United States (60 days if served elsewhere) to defend the case by serving and filing an answer (Form 10) and financial statement (Form 13), along with a certificate of financial disclosure and supporting documents (Form 13A).

If the respondent's answer makes a claim against the applicant under Rule 10(6), the applicant may serve and file a reply (Form 10A) within 10 days.

First Court Date and Case Conference

If the case is started in either the Family Court of the Superior Court of Justice or the Ontario Court of Justice, the court will schedule a first court date when the application is filed.

If the respondent does not serve and file an answer, the applicant may file an affidavit for an uncontested trial (Form 23C) and ask the clerk to schedule the matter before a judge for a decision on the basis of the affidavit evidence.[8]

If the respondent serves and files an answer, the applicant may ask the clerk to schedule the case conference to be held at the same time as the first court date. If the case is started in the Superior Court of Justice, the case conference will be scheduled when either party requests it. The party who requests the case conference must serve and file a case conference brief (Form 17A) along with an updated continuing record table of contents no later than seven days before the case conference date.[9] Under Rule 17(14), each party must confirm his or her attendance at the case conference by filing a confirmation (Form 14C) no later than 2 p.m. two days before the conference date.

Other Conferences and Trial

If a case does not settle at the case conference, the judge may schedule another case conference, a settlement conference, and/or a trial management conference. If the case still does not settle, the court will schedule a trial at which a final order will be made concerning the issues.

Motion for Temporary Custody and Support

If a case does not settle, a final determination on the issues will not be made until the case comes to trial. Since it may be some time before the trial takes place, it is

---

7 Documents other than the certificate of financial disclosure, which does not have to be filed until seven days before a case conference.

8 See Rules 39(5) and 23(22).

9 If the applicant's financial statement is more than 30 days old, under Rule 13(12) the applicant must update the financial statement by serving and filing either a new financial statement or an affidavit stating that the information in the financial statement has not changed.

necessary to decide who will have custody of the children until the trial. In addition, one party may have a need for support for himself or herself and/or the children until a final decision is made. If the parties cannot agree on any of these issues, either of them may bring a motion for an order for temporary custody and/or support.

A motion may also be brought for other temporary relief, depending on the claims made in the application—for example, temporary exclusive possession of the matrimonial home, or for directions on how to carry on the case.

The *Family Law Rules* discourage parties from bringing motions before a conference is held. Under Rules 14(4) and 14(4.2), except in situations of urgency or hardship, no notice of motion or supporting evidence may be served and no motion may be heard before a conference dealing with the substantive issues in the case has been completed.

The **moving party** (the party who makes the motion) must get a date from the court office and complete a notice of motion (Form 14) and an affidavit (Form 14A). Pursuant to Rule 14(11), the moving party must serve the notice of motion, affidavit, and an updated continuing record table of contents on the other party no later than four days before the motion date, and must file the documents with the court by no later than two days before the motion date. The moving party must also file a confirmation (Form 14C) no later than 2 p.m. two days before the motion date.

moving party
the party who makes the motion

Documents Required to Start a Custody and Support Case

Let's use the case of Lucille Bell and her husband Dizzy Arnaz, to illustrate the documents required in a custody and support case.

Our client, Lucille Bell, married Dizzy Arnaz on May 31, 2005, and the couple separated on July 4, 2017. It was the first marriage for both of them. Lucille was born on March 5, 1979, and Dizzy was born on June 11, 1978. They were both born in Ottawa and have lived there all of their lives.

Luci and Dizzy have two children: Rita Arnaz-Bell, born on August 30, 2007, and Ricky Arnaz-Bell, born on April 12, 2010. The children live with Lucille in the matrimonial home at 45 Lovett Court, Ottawa, ON K1V 9X4. Dizzy lives at 23 Leavit Place, Ottawa, ON K2W 8Y3.

Lucille has not worked outside the home since Rita's birth. Dizzy is employed as a high school teacher with the Ottawa-Carleton School Board and earns $75,000 annually.

Lucille wants custody of the children, subject to reasonable access by Dizzy, and monthly child support in the amount of $1,105 (the table amount under the *Child Support Guidelines*). She also wants spousal support in the amount of $750 per month.

Assume that Lucille's application is prepared on November 17, 2017.

Application

The application used for a support and custody claim is Form 8. Lucille's application appears as Figure 13.1 at the end of the chapter.

Page 1

- Insert the name of the court, in this case, the Superior Court of Justice Family Branch, and the address of the appropriate court office. Under Rule 5, Lucille's case should be commenced in Ottawa. The address of the Family Court in Ottawa is 161 Elgin Street, Ottawa, ON K2P 2K1.
- Insert the names and addresses of the parties.
- Insert the names and addresses of the parties' lawyers, if any. In this case, Lucille Bell is represented by your law firm, and Dizzy does not yet have a lawyer.
- The court will assign the first court date when the application is filed, so check the box indicating that a first court date is set.
- This case will be on the fast track of the case management system, so check that box.

Page 2

- This case includes a claim for support only. As a result, the required financial statement is Form 13. Check the first box.

Page 3

- Insert the required information under the heading "Family History."
- Insert the date of marriage and the date of separation under the heading "Relationship Dates."
- Insert the names, birthdates, and living arrangements of the children under the heading "The Child(ren)."
- Under the heading "Previous Cases or Agreements," indicate that there have been no court cases, agreements, arbitrations, or notices issued by the online Child Support Service.

Page 4

This page sets out the applicant's claims.

- Lucille's claims for support are being made under the *Family Law Act*,[10] and her claim for custody is being made under the *Children's Law Reform Act*. She is also claiming costs. Check boxes 10, 11, 13, 16, and 30. It is routine to ask to have spousal support payments indexed.

---

10   RSO 1990, c F.3.

- Give details of the orders asked for. It is necessary to advise the court that Lucille is seeking custody of both children and to set out the amount of support that she is seeking for herself.

Page 5

This page sets out the facts on which Lucille relies in support of her claims. As you draft the allegations of fact, keep in mind the substantive law requirements for a valid **cause of action** for each of her claims.

cause of action
the basis for a legal action

- Lucille's claim for custody is based on the fact that she has always been the children's primary caregiver, the children have lived with her since the separation, and it is therefore in the children's best interests to remain in her custody.
- Lucille's claim for spousal support is based on her need and Dizzy's ability to pay.
- Child support will be determined in accordance with the table amounts in the *Child Support Guidelines*. The amount will be based on Dizzy's income, which should be disclosed by him in the financial statement he is required to file. The application gives information about Dizzy's income in case he does not file a financial statement.
- Lucille will sign and date the application.
- Because this is not a divorce case, no lawyer's certificate is required.

Financial Statement

Lucille must serve a financial statement in Form 13 and a certificate of financial disclosure (Form 13A), with supporting documents, because of her claim for spousal support. She would not have to file a financial statement if she were claiming support for the children only in the table amount under the *Child Support Guidelines*. Lucille must then file the documents with the court.[11]

See Chapter 11 for a discussion of financial statements.

Affidavit in Support of Claim for Custody or Access—Form 35.1

Under the *Children's Law Reform Act* section 21(2) and Rule 35.1, Lucille is required to prepare an affidavit in support of claim for custody or access (Form 35.1). Because she is the parent of the children, neither a police records check nor a Children's Aid Society report is required. Lucille's Form 35.1 is attached as Figure 13.2.

For the purposes of this affidavit we are assuming that the children attend Pierre Elliott Trudeau Elementary School and that Lucille will have the support of her parents, Arlene and Kent Bell.

---

11 Other than the certificate of financial disclosure, which does not have to be filed until seven days before a case conference.

Continuing Record

Under Rule 9(1), Lucille must prepare and serve a continuing record on Dizzy when she serves the application, financial statement, certificate of financial disclosure and supporting documents, and the affidavit in support of claim for custody or access. The continuing record cover in this case appears as Figure 13.3 and the continuing record table of contents[12] appears as Figure 13.4, both at the end of the chapter.

Steps and Documents in a Motion for Temporary Custody and Support

Let's assume that Dizzy Arnaz, acting on his own behalf, defends the proceeding by delivering an answer. Lucille and Dizzy attend the case conference and still cannot agree on the issues of support and custody pending the trial. Lucille decides to make a motion for temporary custody and support.

Step 1: Schedule the Motion

Contact the court office to get a date for the motion to be heard.

Step 2: Complete the Forms

You must prepare the following forms:

- a notice of motion,
- an affidavit,
- an updated continuing record table of contents, and
- if Lucille's financial statement is more than 30 days old, a new financial statement or an affidavit stating that the information in the financial statement has not changed.

Notice of Motion

The purpose of a notice of motion (Form 14) is to inform the responding party of the date and time of the motion and the orders that the moving party is asking the court to make.

- Insert the court file number in the upper right-hand corner.
- Insert the names and addresses of the parties and their lawyers.
- Insert the motion date obtained from the court.
- Check off the box indicating that you are serving an affidavit in support of the motion.

---

12   It assumes that Lucille has filed the certificate of financial disclosure at the same time as the other documents.

- List the additional documents from the continuing record being relied on (in this case, the financial statements of the parties and Lucille's affidavit in support of claim for custody or access).
- State the orders being requested on the motion (in this case, orders for temporary custody, temporary child support, and temporary spousal support).

Lucille's notice of motion appears as Figure 13.5 at the end of the chapter.

Affidavit

The purpose of the affidavit (Form 14A) is to provide the court with the evidence on which to make a decision on the motion. An affidavit is a statement of evidence sworn to under oath by the person making the affidavit.

Have a look at Lucille's affidavit, which appears as Figure 13.6 at the end of the chapter and sets out the following:

- *Parties' relationship.* Paragraph 1 states that Lucille and Dizzy were married and have now separated.
- *Information about the children.* Paragraphs 3 to 6 set out information about the children and the reasons why it would be in the best interests of the children for the moving party to be granted custody. Lucille is relying on the fact that she has always been the primary caregiver, that giving her custody would maintain the status quo, and that she is willing to encourage an ongoing relationship between the children and the respondent.
- *Information to support a claim for child support.* Paragraphs 2 and 7 provide information to support a claim for child support under the *Child Support Guidelines*. Lucille gives information about the number of children and the respondent's income.
- *Information to support her claim for spousal support.* In paragraphs 4 and 8, Lucille indicates that she needs support because she is not employed, has not worked outside the home since Rita's birth, and proposes to continue to stay at home to care for the children. Dizzy earns $75,000 per year and is therefore able to pay support.

Updated Table of Contents

The continuing record table of contents must be updated to include the motion documents.

Step 3: Serve the Motion Documents

Pursuant to Rule 14(11), Dizzy must be served with the following documents no later than four days before the scheduled motion date:

- a notice of motion,
- an affidavit,

- an updated financial statement if necessary, and
- an updated continuing record table of contents.

Dizzy may be served by **regular service** under Rule 6 by:

- mailing a copy to Dizzy since Dizzy has no lawyer, in which case service is effective on the fifth day after mailing;
- sending a copy by courier to Dizzy since Dizzy has no lawyer, in which case service is effective on the day after the courier picks the documents up; or
- faxing a copy to Dizzy since Dizzy has no lawyer, in which case service must be carried out before 4 p.m. on a day when the court offices are open.

The person who serves the document must complete and swear an affidavit of service (Form 6B).

Step 4: File the Motion Documents with the Court

No later than two days before the scheduled motion date, someone from your law firm must file the motion documents in the documents section of the continuing record. In addition, the continuing record table of contents must be updated.

Step 5: File a Confirmation with the Court

No later than 2 p.m. two days before the scheduled motion, your firm must file a confirmation (Form 14C) with the court to let the court know that the moving party will be present for the motion.

Respondent

If Dizzy wants to present his own evidence to the court, he must swear an affidavit, serve it on Lucille, and file it with the court as soon as possible before the day of the motion, along with an updated financial statement, if necessary, and an updated continuing record table of contents. The responding party on a motion does not have to file a confirmation with the court.

Order

Under Rule 25, the party in whose favour an order is made is required to prepare a draft of the order. An order reflecting Lucille's success on her motion appears as Figure 13.7 at the end of the chapter. Paragraph 5 of the order is required by the *Family Responsibility and Support Arrears Enforcement Act, 1996*,[13] which is discussed in Chapter 17.

---

13 SO 1996, c 31.

CHAPTER SUMMARY

The procedure in a support and custody case is governed by the *Family Law Rules* generally and, if the case involves a claim for custody or access, by Rule 35.1 specifically.

Under Rule 5, a case involving a claim for custody should be started in the municipality where the child lives, although, with the consent of the court, it may be started in a municipality chosen by both parties. If custody is not claimed, the case can be started in the municipality where either party resides. The applicant begins by filing an application, the appropriate financial statements and, in a custody case, an affidavit in support of a claim for custody or access along with the continuing record. There is no need to file a financial statement if the only claim made is one for child support in the table amount in the *Child Support Guidelines*. A non-parent applying for custody must also provide a police records check and a Children's Aid Society report.

A custody and/or support case started in the Family Court of the Superior Court of Justice will be a fast track case. A case started in either the Family Court of the Superior Court of Justice or the Ontario Court of Justice has its first court date set by the court.

The applicant must immediately serve the respondent with the application, financial statement (if any), affidavit in support of claim for custody or access (if any), and continuing record. The respondent then has 30 days to serve and file an answer. If the respondent makes a claim against the applicant, the applicant may file a reply in 10 days. If the respondent does not file an answer, the applicant may file an affidavit for an uncontested trial.

If the respondent files an answer, the applicant may schedule a case conference. If the case does not settle at the case conference, the judge may schedule additional conferences. If the case still does not settle, the court will schedule a trial.

Since it may take considerable time before the trial takes place, decisions on interim custody and support must be made. If the parties cannot agree on these issues, either of them may bring a motion. The *Family Law Rules* discourage parties from bringing motions before a conference is held, except in urgent situations.

KEY TERMS

cause of action, 273
moving party, 271

REVIEW QUESTIONS

1. Generally speaking, where should a custody case be started?

2. How is a custody case started?

3. What financial statement must be filed by an applicant if an application includes a claim for support without a property claim?

4. What documents must the applicant serve on the respondent? When? How?

5. What must the respondent do if he or she wishes to defend the case? When?

6. When does the court schedule a first court date?

7. What may the applicant do if the respondent does not defend the case?

8. What may the applicant do if the respondent defends the case?

9. What documents must the applicant serve and file before the case conference?

10. Why would a spouse make a motion for temporary custody and/or support?

11. What does a party have to do to make a motion?

DRAFTING QUESTIONS

1. Monica (birth name Geller) and Chandler Byng were married on October 18, 2009, and separated on September 18, 2017. It was the first marriage for both. They were both born in Ottawa and have lived there all their lives. Chandler's birthdate is May 31, 1979. Monica's birthdate is December 22, 1979. They have one child, a son named Joey Byng, who was born in Ottawa on December 22, 2014. Joey lives with Chandler in the matrimonial home at 25 Manhattan Avenue, Ottawa, ON K2S 8B3. Monica lives at 50 York Street, Ottawa, ON K3T 9C4. Chandler has not worked outside the home since Joey's birth. Monica works as a chef at the Central Perk Restaurant and earns $60,000 per year. Chandler wants to start a case claiming custody of Joey, subject to reasonable access by Monica, and monthly child support in the amount of $546 (the table amount under the *Child Support Guidelines*). He also wants to claim spousal support in the amount of $500 per month.

   Prepare an application and affidavit in support of claim for custody or access to be signed by Chandler. For the purposes of the affidavit assume that Chandler looks after Joey full-time, and Joey does not attend school or daycare, and that Chandler will have the support of his parents Ross and Rachel Byng.

2. Using the fact situation in Question 1, assume that Monica has defended the case without a lawyer, and that the parties have attended a case conference. Chandler now wants to make a motion for temporary custody, temporary child support in the amount of $546 per month, and temporary spousal support in the amount of $500 per month.

   Draft the notice of motion and affidavit.

FIGURE 13.1 Lucille's Application

ONTARIO

(SEAL)	Court File Number

Superior Court of Justice Family Branch
(Name of court)

at **161 Elgin Street, Ottawa, ON K2P 2K1**
Court office address

Form 8: Application
(General)

Applicant(s)

Full legal name & address for service – street & number, municipality, postal code, telephone & fax numbers and e-mail address (if any).	*Lawyer's name & address – street & number, municipality, postal code, telephone & fax numbers and e-mail address (if any).*
Lucille Bell **45 Lovett Court** **Ottawa, ON K1F 9X4**	**JoAnn Kurtz** **123 College Street** **Ottawa, ON K3R 3L2** **Tel: 613-555-1234** **Fax: 613-555-2345**

Respondent(s)

Full legal name & address for service – street & number, municipality, postal code, telephone & fax numbers and e-mail address (if any).	*Lawyer's name & address – street & number, municipality, postal code, telephone & fax numbers and e-mail address (if any).*
Dizzy Arnaz **23 Leavit Place** **Ottawa, ON K2W 8Y3**	

TO THE RESPONDENT(S):

A COURT CASE HAS BEEN STARTED AGAINST YOU IN THIS COURT. THE DETAILS ARE SET OUT ON THE ATTACHED PAGES.

☒ **THE FIRST COURT DATE IS** *(date)* _____ **AT** _____ ☐ **a.m.** ☐ **p.m.**

or as soon as possible after that time, at: *(address)*

161 Elgin Street, Ottawa, ON K2P 2K1

NOTE: *If this is a divorce case, no date will be set unless an Answer is filed. If you have also been served with a notice of motion, there may be an earlier court date and you or your lawyer should come to court for the motion.*

☒ **THIS CASE IS ON THE FAST TRACK OF THE CASE MANAGEMENT SYSTEM.** A case management judge will be assigned by the time this case first comes before a judge.

☐ **THIS CASE IS ON THE STANDARD TRACK OF THE CASE MANAGEMENT SYSTEM. No court date has been set for this case** but, if you have been served with a notice of motion, it has a court date and you or your lawyer should come to court for the motion. A case management judge will not be assigned until one of the parties asks the clerk of the court to schedule a case conference or until a motion is scheduled, whichever comes first.

IF, AFTER 365 DAYS, THE CASE HAS NOT BEEN SCHEDULED FOR TRIAL, the clerk of the court will send out a warning that the case will be dismissed within 60 days unless the parties file proof that the case has been settled or one of the parties asks for a case or a settlement conference.

IF YOU WANT TO OPPOSE ANY CLAIM IN THIS CASE, you or your lawyer must prepare an Answer (Form 10 – a blank copy should be attached), serve a copy on the applicant(s) and file a copy in the court office with an Affidavit of Service (Form 6B). **YOU HAVE ONLY 30 DAYS AFTER THIS APPLICATION IS SERVED ON YOU (60 DAYS IF THIS APPLICATION IS SERVED ON YOU OUTSIDE CANADA OR THE UNITED STATES) TO SERVE AND FILE AN ANSWER. IF YOU DO NOT, THE CASE WILL GO AHEAD WITHOUT YOU AND THE COURT MAY MAKE AN ORDER AND ENFORCE IT AGAINST YOU.**

FLR 8 (April 12, 2016)

Page 1 of 5

FIGURE 13.1   Lucille's Application Continued

Form 8:   **Application (General)**   **(page 2)** | Court File Number |

Check the box of the paragraph that applies to your case

☒   This case includes a claim for support. It does not include a claim for property or exclusive possession of the matrimonial home and its contents. You **MUST** fill out a Financial Statement (Form 13 – a blank copy attached), serve a copy on the applicant(s) and file a copy in the court office with an Affidavit of Service even if you do not answer this case.

☐   This case includes a claim for property or exclusive possession of the matrimonial home and its contents. You **MUST** fill out a Financial Statement (Form 13.1 – a blank copy attached), serve a copy on the applicant(s) and file a copy in the court office with an Affidavit of Service even if you do not answer this case.

IF YOU WANT TO MAKE A CLAIM OF YOUR OWN, you or your lawyer must fill out the claim portion in the Answer, serve a copy on the applicant(s) and file a copy in the court office with an Affidavit of Service.

- If you want to make a claim for support but do not want to make a claim for property or exclusive possession of the matrimonial home and its contents, you **MUST** fill out a Financial Statement (Form 13), serve a copy on the applicant(s) and file a copy in the court office.

- However, if your only claim for support is for child support in the table amount specified under the Child Support Guidelines, you do not need to fill out, serve or file a Financial Statement.

- If you want to make a claim for property or exclusive possession of the matrimonial home and its contents, whether or not it includes a claim for support, you **MUST** fill out a Financial Statement (Form 13.1, not Form 13), serve a copy on the applicant(s), and file a copy in the court office.

YOU SHOULD GET LEGAL ADVICE ABOUT THIS CASE RIGHT AWAY. If you cannot afford a lawyer, you may be able to get help from your local Legal Aid Ontario office. *(See your telephone directory under LEGAL AID.)*

_____   _____
                Date of issue   *Clerk of the court*

FLR 8 (April 12, 2016)   Page 2 of 5

FIGURE 13.1 Lucille's Application Continued

Form 8: Application (General) (page 3) Court file number

FAMILY HISTORY

APPLICANT: Age: 38 Birthdate: *(d, m, y)* **5 March 1979**

Resident in *(municipality & province)* **Ottawa, Ontario**

since *(date)* **5 March 1979**

Surname at birth: **Bell** Surname just before marriage: **Bell**

Divorced before? ☐ No ☐ Yes *(Place and date of previous divorce)*

RESPONDENT: Age: 39 Birthdate: *(d, m, y)* **11 June 1978**

Resident in *(municipality & province)* **Ottawa, Ontario**

since *(date)* **11 June 1978**

Surname at birth: **Arnaz** Surname just before marriage: **Arnaz**

Divorced before? ☒ No ☐ Yes *(Place and date of previous divorce)*

RELATIONSHIP DATES:

☒ Married on *(date)* **31 May 2005** ☐ Started living together on *(date)*

☒ Separated on *(date)* **4 July 2017** ☐ Never lived together ☐ Still living together

THE CHILD(REN)
List all children involved in this case, even if no claim is made for these children.

Full legal name	Age	Birthdate *(d, m, y)*	Resident in *(municipality & province)*	Now Living With *(name of person and relationship to child)*
Rita Arnaz-Bell	10	30 August 2007	Ottawa, Ontario	Lucille Bell - mother
Ricky Arnaz-Bell	7	12 April 2010	Ottawa, Ontario	Lucille Bell - mother

PREVIOUS CASES OR AGREEMENTS

Have the parties or the children been in a court case before?

☒ No ☐ Yes

Have the parties made a written agreement dealing with any matter involved in this case?

☒ No ☐ Yes *(Give date of agreement. Indicate which of its terms are in dispute.)*

FIGURE 13.1   Lucille's Application Continued

Form 8:	Application (General)	(page 4)	Court file number

Has a Notice of Calculation and/or a Notice of Recalculation been issued by the online Child Support Service in this case?

☒ No   ☐ Yes *(Give date(s) of Notice(s) of Calculation or Recalculation.)*

If yes, are you asking the court to make an order for a child support that is different from the amount set out in the Notice?

☐ No   ☐ Yes *(Provide an explanation.)*

Have the parties arbitrated or agreed to arbitrate any matter involved in this case?

☒ No   ☐ Yes *(Give date of agreement and family arbitration award, if any.)*

CLAIM BY APPLICANT

I ASK THE COURT FOR THE FOLLOWING:
(Claims below include claims for temporary orders.)

Claims under the *Divorce Act* (Check boxes in this column only if you are asking for a divorce and your case is in the Superior Court of Justice or Family Court of the Superior Court of Justice.)	Claims under the *Family Law Act* or *Children's Law Reform Act*	Claims relating to property (Check boxes in this column only if your case is in the Superior Court of Justice or Family Court of the Superior Court of Justice.)
00 ☐ a divorce 01 ☐ support for me 02 ☐ support for child(ren) – table amount 03 ☐ support for child(ren) – other than table amount 04 ☐ custody of child(ren) 05 ☐ access to child(ren)	10 ☒ support for me 11 ☒ support for child(ren) – table amount 12 ☐ support for child(ren) – other than table amount 13 ☒ custody of child(ren) 14 ☐ access to child(ren) 15 ☐ restraining/non-harassment order 16 ☒ indexing spousal support 17 ☐ declaration of parentage 18 ☐ guardianship over child's property	20 ☐ equalization of net family properties 21 ☐ exclusive possession of matrimonial home 22 ☐ exclusive possession of contents of matrimonial home 23 ☐ freezing assets 24 ☐ sale of family property
Other claims 30 ☒ costs 31 ☐ annulment of marriage 32 ☐ prejudgment interest 33 ☐ claims relating to a family arbitration	50 ☐ Other *(Specify.)*	

Give details of the order that you want the court to make. *(Include any amounts of support (if known) and the names of the children for whom support, custody or access is claimed.)*

1. Custody of the children, Rita Arnaz-Bell, born 30 August 2007, and Ricky Arnaz-Bell, born 12 April 2010;

2. Support for the said children in the table amount in the Child Support Guidelines;

3. Spousal support in the amount of $750 per month;

4. Indexing of the spousal support order in accordance with s. 34(5) of the Family Law Act, RSO 1990, c F.3.

5. Costs

FIGURE 13.1   Lucille's Application Concluded

Form 8:	**Application (General)**	**(page 5)**	Court File Number

IMPORTANT FACTS SUPPORTING MY CLAIM FOR DIVORCE

☐   **Separation:**   The spouses have lived separate and apart since *(date)* _____ and

   ☐   have not lived together again since that date in an unsuccessful attempt to reconcile.

   ☐   have lived together again during the following period(s) in an unsuccessful attempt to reconcile: *(Give dates.)*

☐   **Adultery:**   The respondent has committed adultery. *(Give details. It is not necessary to name any other person involved but, if you do name the other person, then you must serve this application on the other person.)*

☐   **Cruelty:**   The respondent has treated the applicant with physical or mental cruelty of such a kind as to make continued cohabitation intolerable. *(Give details.)*

IMPORTANT FACTS SUPPORTING MY OTHER CLAIM(S)

(Set out below the facts that form the legal basis for your other claim(s). Attach an additional page if you need more space.)

1. The children have resided with the applicant since the separation, and the applicant has always been their primary caregiver. It would be in the best interests of the children to remain in the custody of the applicant.

2. The respondent is employed as a high school teacher with the Ottawa-Carleton School Board and earns $75,000 per year.

3. The applicant is in need of spousal support from the respondent, and the respondent has the ability to pay such support.

Put a line through any blank space left on this page. If additional space is needed, extra pages may be attached.

17 November 2017	
Date of signature	*Signature of applicant*

LAWYER'S CERTIFICATE

For divorce cases only

My name is: _____
and I am the applicant's lawyer in this divorce case. I certify that I have complied with the requirements of section 9 of the *Divorce Act*.

Date	*Signature of Lawyer*

  For information on accessibility of court services for people with disability-related needs, contact:
Telephone: 416-326-2220 / 1-800-518-7901   TTY: 416-326-4012 / 1-877-425-0575

FLR 8 (April 12, 2016)   Page 5 of 5

FIGURE 13.2 Lucille's Affidavit in Support of Claim for Custody or Access

ONTARIO

Superior Court of Justice, Family Court
(Name of court)

at **161 Elgin Street, Ottawa, ON K2P 2K1**
Court office address

Court File Number

Form 35.1: Affidavit in Support of Claim for Custody or Access, dated

Applicant(s)

Full legal name & address for service — street & number, municipality, postal code, telephone & fax numbers and e-mail address (if any).	Lawyer's name & address — street & number, municipality, postal code, telephone & fax numbers and e-mail address (if any).
Lucille Bell **45 Lovett Court** **Ottawa, ON K1F 9X4**	**JoAnn Kurtz** **123 College Street** **Ottawa, ON K3R 3L2** **Tel: 613-555-1234** **Fax: 613-555-2345**

Respondent(s)

Full legal name & address for service — street & number, municipality, postal code, telephone & fax numbers and e-mail address (if any).	Lawyer's name & address — street & number, municipality, postal code, telephone & fax numbers and e-mail address (if any).
Dizzy Arnaz **23 Leavit Place** **Ottawa, ON K2W 8Y3**	

Affidavit in Support of Claim for Custody or Access
(If you need more space, attach extra pages.)

My name is *(full legal name)* **Lucille Bell**

My date of birth is *(d, m, y)* **5 March 1979**

I live in: *(name of city, town or municipality and province, state or country if outside of Ontario)*
Ottawa, Ontario

I swear/affirm that the following is true:

PART A:
TO BE COMPLETED BY ALL PERSONS SEEKING CUSTODY OR ACCESS
(Write "N/A" if any of the paragraphs do not apply to you or the child(ren).)

1. **During my life, I have also used or been known by the following names:**
   N/A

2. **The child(ren) in this case is/are:**

Child's full legal name	Birthdate (d, m, y)	Age	Full legal name(s) of parent(s)	Name(s) of all people the child lives with now *(include address if the child does not live with you)*	My relationship to the child *(specify if parent, grandparent, family friend, etc.)*
Rita Arnaz-Bell	30 August 2007	10	Lucille Bell Dizzy Arnaz	Lucille Bell	parent
Ricky Arnaz-Bell	12 April 2010	7	Lucille Bell Dizzy Arnaz	Lucille Bell	parent

FIGURE 13.2 Lucille's Affidavit in Support of Claim for Custody or Access Continued

Form 35.1: **Affidavit in Support of Claim for** (page 2) | Court File Number
Custody or Access

Child's full legal name	Birthdate (d, m, y)	Age	Full legal name(s) of parent(s)	Name(s) of all people the child lives with now (include address if the child does not live with you)	My relationship to the child (specify if parent, grandparent, family friend, etc.)

3. **I am also the parent of or have acted as a parent (for example, as a step-parent, legal guardian etc.) to the following child(ren):** (include the full legal names and birthdates of any child(ren) not already listed in paragraph 2)

Child's Full Legal Name	Birthdate (d, m, y)	My relationship to the child (specify if parent, step-parent, grandparent, etc.)	Name(s) of the person(s) with whom the child lives now (if the child is under 18 years old)
N/A			

4. **I am or have been a party in the following court case(s) involving custody of or access to any child:** (Including the child(ren) in this case or any other child(ren). Do not include cases involving a children's aid society in this section. Attach a copy of any custody or access court order(s) or endorsement(s) you have.)

Court location	Names of parties in the case	Name(s) of child(ren)	Court orders made (include dates of orders)
N/A			

FIGURE 13.2 Lucille's Affidavit in Support of Claim for Custody or Access Continued

Form 35.1: Affidavit in Support of Claim for (page 3)   Court File Number
Custody or Access

5. I have been a party or person responsible for the care of a child in the following child protection court case(s): *(attach a copy of any relevant court order(s) or endorsement(s) you have)*

Court location	Names of people involved in the case	Name of children's aid society	Court orders made *(include dates of orders)*
N/A			

6. I have been found guilty of the following criminal offence(s) for which I have not received a pardon:

Charge	Approximate date of finding of guilt	Sentence received
N/A		

7. I am now charged with the following criminal offence(s):

Charge	Date of next court appearance	Terms of release while waiting for trial *(attach copy of bail or other release conditions, if any)*
N/A		

8. When the court is assessing a person's ability to act as a parent, s. 24 (4) of the *Children's Law Reform Act* requires the court to consider whether the person has at any time committed violence or abuse against:

- his or her spouse;
- a parent of the child to whom the claim for custody or access relates;
- a member of the person's household; or
- any child.

I am aware of the following violence or abuse the court should consider under s. 24 (4) of the *Children's Law Reform* Act: *(describe incident(s) or episode(s) and provide information about the nature of the violence or abuse, who committed the violence and who the victim(s) was/were)*
N/A

FIGURE 13.2   Lucille's Affidavit in Support of Claim for Custody or Access   Continued

Form 35.1:	Affidavit in Support of Claim for Custody or Access	(page 4)	Court File Number

9. To the best of my knowledge, since birth, the child(ren) in this case has/have lived with the following caregiver(s): *(including a parent, legal guardian, children's aid society etc.)*

Child's Name	Name(s) of Caregiver(s) *(if the child was in the care of a children's aid society, give the name of that children's aid society)*	Period(s) of Time with Caregiver(s) *(d,m,y to d,m,y)*
Rita Arnaz-Bell	Lucille Bell and Dizzy Arnaz Lucille Bell	30 Aug. 2007 - 4 July 2017 4 July 2017 - 17 Nov. 2017
Ricky Arnaz-Bell	Lucille Bell and Dizzy Arnaz Lucille Bell	12 Apr. 2010 - 4 July 2017 4 July 2017 - 17 Nov. 2017

10. My plan for the care and upbringing of the child(ren) is as follows:

  a) I plan to live at the following address: 45 Lovett Court, Ottawa, Ontario K1V 9X4

  b) The following people (other than the child(ren) involved in this case) will be living with me:

Full legal name and other names this person has used	Birthdate *(d, m, y)*	Relationship to you	Has a child of this person ever been in the care of a children's aid society? *(if yes, give details)*	Has this person been found guilty of a criminal offence (for which he/she has not received a pardon) or is he/she currently facing criminal charges? *(if yes, give details)*
N/A				

  c) Decisions for the child(ren) (including education, medical care, religious upbringing, extra-curricular activities, etc.) will be made as follows:

☐ **jointly by me and** *(name(s) of person(s))* _____

☒ **by me**

☐ **by** *(name(s) of person(s))* _____

  (If necessary, provide additional details below.)

FIGURE 13.2 Lucille's Affidavit in Support of Claim for Custody or Access Continued

| Form 35.1: | Affidavit in Support of Claim for Custody or Access | (page 5) | Court File Number |

d) ☒ **I am a stay-at-home parent.**

☐ **I work:** ☐ **full time.** ☐ **part time.**

☐ **I attend school:** ☐ **full time.** ☐ **part time.**

at: *(name of your place of work or school)* _____

☐ **I anticipate that my plans for work and/or school may change as follows:** *(complete if you know or expect that you will be doing something different from what you are doing now))*

e) **The child(ren) will attend school, daycare or be cared for by others on a regular basis as follows:**

The children will attend the neighbourhood elementary school - Pierre-Elliott Trudeau Elementary.

f) **My plan for the child(ren) to have regular contact with others, including the child(ren)'s parent(s) and family members, is as follows:**

I plan for the children to have regular contact with their father as determined by this court.

g) Check the appropriate box:

☒ **The child(ren) does not/do not have any special medical, educational, mental health or developmental needs.**

☐ **The child or one or more of the children has/have the following special needs and will receive support and services for those needs as follows:** *(if a child does not have special needs, you do not have to include information about that child below)*

Name of child	Special need(s)	Description of child's needs	Support or service child will be receiving *(include the names of any doctors, counsellors, treatment centres, etc. that are or will be providing support or services to the child)*
	☐ medical ☐ educational ☐ mental health ☐ developmental ☐ other		
	☐ medical ☐ educational ☐ mental health ☐ developmental ☐ other		
	☐ medical ☐ educational ☐ mental health ☐ developmental ☐ other		
	☐ medical ☐ educational ☐ mental health ☐ developmental ☐ other		
	☐ medical ☐ educational ☐ mental health ☐ developmental ☐ other		

FIGURE 13.2 Lucille's Affidavit in Support of Claim for Custody or Access Continued

---

Form 35.1: **Affidavit in Support of Claim for** **(page 6)** | Court File Number
Custody or Access

   h) **I will have support from the following relatives, friends or community services in caring for the child(ren):**
      My parents, Arlene and Kent Bell, who live nearby.

11. **I acknowledge that the court needs up-to-date and accurate information about my plan in order to make a custody or access order in the best interests of the child(ren) (subrule 35.1 (7)). If, at any time before a final order is made in this case,**

   a) there are any changes in my life or circumstances that affect the information provided in this affidavit; or

   b) I discover that the information in this affidavit is incorrect or incomplete,

  I will immediately serve and file either:

   a) an updated affidavit in support of claim for custody or access (Form 35.1); or,

   b) if the correction or change is minor, an affidavit in Form 14A describing the correction or change and indicating any effect it has on my plan for the care and upbringing of the child(ren).

   _____ *(Initial here to show you have read this paragraph and you understand it.)*

NOTE: If you are not a parent of the child, as determined under the *Children's Law Reform Act*, for whom you are seeking an order of custody, you must complete Part B of this affidavit.

For the purposes of this form and under the *Children's Law Reform Act*, a parent may include:

- **The person who gives birth to a child (a "birth parent").**

- **Where a child is conceived through sexual intercourse, the person who is married to or living with the person who gives birth to the child at the time that the child is born (a "spouse").**

- **The person certified as a parent of the child under the *Vital Statistics Act*.**

- **A person found or recognized by a court as a parent to the child.**

For more information about whether you are a parent for the purposes of this form, see the *Children's Law Reform Act* or talk to a lawyer.

If you are completing Part B, you do not have to swear/affirm the affidavit at this point. You will swear/affirm at the end of Part B.

Sworn/Affirmed before me at Ottawa

                                       municipality

in Ontario

                  province, state, or country

on **17 November 2017** _____
       Date   *Commissioner for taking affidavits*
                (Type or print name below if signature is illegible.)

_____
Signature
(This form is to be signed in front of a lawyer, justice of the peace, notary public or commissioner for taking affidavits.)

FLR 35.1 (April 15, 2017)   Page 6 of 8

FIGURE 13.2   Lucille's Affidavit in Support of Claim for Custody or Access Continued

Form 35.1:	Affidavit in Support of Claim for Custody or Access	(page 7)	Court File Number

PART B
TO BE COMPLETED ONLY BY A NON-PARENT SEEKING A CUSTODY ORDER

If you are a parent of the child, as determined under the *Children's Law Reform Act*, for whom you are seeking an order of custody, you are not required to complete this Part of the form.

Individuals who may <u>not</u> be a parent may include:

- A grandparent, aunt, or uncle.
- A sperm donor.
- A surrogate.
- A step-parent.

For more information about whether you are a parent for the purposes of this form, see the *Children's Law Reform Act* or talk to a lawyer.

NOTICE: If you are a non-parent claiming custody of a child, court staff will conduct a search of the databases maintained by the Ontario courts to identify previous or current family court cases in which you or the child(ren) may have been or may be involved and provide you with a list of those cases. This information will be shared with the court and you must provide a copy to any other party.

If the list contains information about someone other than you, you may swear or affirm an affidavit indicating that you are not the same person as the person named in the list.

In addition to the information in Part A, I swear/affirm that the following is true:

12. **To the best of my knowledge, the child(ren) in this case has/have been involved in the following custody/ access or child protection court cases:** *(do NOT include cases in which the child was charged under the* Youth Criminal Justice Act (Canada)*)*

Child(ren)'s name(s)	Type of Case	Details of Case

13. You must file a police records check with the court. Choose the option below that applies to you:

☐ **I have attached to this affidavit a copy of my police records check, dated** *(date of report from local police force)*

_____ **. Since the date that the attached police records check was completed, I have been found guilty of or charged with the following offence(s):**

☐ **On** *(date)* _____ **, I sent a request to** *(name of local police force)*

_____ **for a police records check.**

I agree to serve and file the police records check with the court within 10 days after the day I receive it. I understand that the court may not make an order for custody of the child(ren) until I have filed the police records check.

FIGURE 13.2   Lucille's Affidavit in Support of Claim for Custody or Access Concluded

Form 35.1:	Affidavit in Support of Claim for Custody or Access	(page 8)	Court File Number

14. Since I turned 18 years old or became a parent, whichever was earlier, I have lived in the following places:

Approximate dates *(month/year to month/year)*	City, town or municipality where you lived *(if outside of Ontario, give name of province, state or country)*

15. I have provided a signed consent form to the court, which authorizes each of the children's aid societies listed below to send a report to me and to the court indicating:

.   whether the society has any records within the meaning of the *Children's Law Reform Act* regulations relating to me; and

.   the date(s) on which any files were opened and/or closed (if applicable).

i)   Name of children's aid society: _____

ii) Name of children's aid society: _____

iii) Name of children's aid society: _____

iv) Name of children's aid society: _____

v)   Name of children's aid society: _____

vi) Name of children's aid society: _____

16. I understand that if any report from a children's aid society indicates that the children's aid society has records related to me, then, unless the court orders otherwise, that report will be shared with:

a) the court;

b) any other parties in this case; and

c) the child(ren)'s lawyer, if there is one in this case.

If I wish to bring a motion asking the court not to release all or part of this report, I understand that I must file my motion with the court no later than **20 days** from the day that the last report is received by the court.

I also understand that any report indicating that a children's aid society has no records relating to me will not be shared with the court, any other party or the child(ren)'s lawyer.

_____ *(Initial here to show that you have read this paragraph and you understand it.)*

Sworn/Affirmed before me at _____
Municipality

in _____
province, state, or country

on _____   _____
  Date   *Commissioner for taking affidavits*
                 (Type or print name below if signature is illegible.)

_____
Signature
(This form is to be signed in front of a lawyer, justice of the peace, notary public or commissioner for taking affidavits.)

FIGURE 13.3   Continuing Record Cover

ONTARIO

Superior Court of Justice Family Court Branch /
(Name of court / Nom du tribunal)

at / *situé(e) au*   161 Elgin Street, Ottawa, ON K2P 2K1
Court office address / Adresse du greffe

Court File Number / *Numéro de dossier du greffe*

Volume / *Volume* : 1

Applicant(s) / *Requérant(e)(s)*

Full legal name & address for service — street & number, municipality, postal code, telephone & fax numbers and e-mail address (if any). *Nom et prénom officiels et adresse aux fins de signification — numéro et rue, municipalité, code postal, numéros de téléphone et de télécopieur et adresse électronique (le cas échéant).*	Lawyer's name & address — street & number, municipality, postal code, telephone & fax numbers and e-mail address (if any). *Nom et adresse de l'avocat(e) — numéro et rue, municipalité, code postal, numéros de téléphone et de télécopieur et adresse électronique (le cas échéant).*
Lucille Bell **45 Lovett Court** **Ottawa, ON K1V 9X4**	**JoAnn Kurtz** **123 College Street** **Ottawa, ON K3R 3L2** **Tel: 613-555-1234** **Fax: 613-555-2345**

Respondent(s) / *Intimé(e)(s)*

Full legal name & address for service — street & number, municipality, postal code, telephone & fax numbers and e-mail address (if any). *Nom et prénom officiels et adresse aux fins de signification — numéro et rue, municipalité, code postal, numéros de téléphone et de télécopieur et adresse électronique (le cas échéant).*	Lawyer's name & address — street & number, municipality, postal code, telephone & fax numbers and e-mail address (if any). *Nom et adresse de l'avocat(e) — numéro et rue, municipalité, code postal, numéros de téléphone et de télécopieur et adresse électronique (le cas échéant).*
Dizzy Arnaz **23 Leavit Place** **Ottawa, ON K2W 8Y3**	

Children's Lawyer/ *Avocat des enfants*

Name & address of Children's Lawyer's agent for service (street & number, municipality, postal code, telephone & fax numbers and e-mail address (if any)) and name of person represented. *Nom et adresse aux fins de signification de la personne qui représente l'avocat(e) des enfants (numéro et rue, municipalité, code postal, numéros de téléphone et de télécopieur et adresse électronique (le cas échéant)) et nom de la personne représentée.*

Continuing Record /
Dossier continu

FLR-A 9CR (01/07)

FIGURE 13.4   Continuing Record Table of Contents

ONTARIO

Superior Court of Justice Family Court Branch
(Name of court)

at _____ 161 Elgin Street, Ottawa, ON K2P 2K1 _____
Court office address

Court File Number

**Cumulative Table of Contents
(Continuing Record)**

Applicant(s)

Full legal name & address for service — street & number, municipality, postal code, telephone & fax numbers and e-mail address (if any).	*Lawyer's name & address — street & number, municipality, postal code, telephone & fax numbers and e-mail address (if any).*
Lucille Bell 45 Lovett Court Ottawa, ON K1V 9X4	JoAnn Kurtz 123 College Street Ottawa, ON K3R 3L2 Tel: 613-555-1234 Fax: 613-555-2345

Respondent(s)

Full legal name & address for service — street & number, municipality, postal code, telephone & fax numbers and e-mail address (if any).	*Lawyer's name & address — street & number, municipality, postal code, telephone & fax numbers and e-mail address (if any).*
Dizzy Arnaz 23 Leavit Place Ottawa, ON K2W 8Y3	

Document *(For an affidavit or transcript of evidence, include the name of the person who gave the affidavit or the evidence.)*	**Filed by** *(A = applicant or R = respondent)*	**Date of Document** *(d, m, y)*	**Date of Filing** *(d, m, y)*	**Volume/Tab**
Application	A	17/11/2017		Volume 1, Tab 1
Financial Statement	A	17/11/2017		Volume 1, Tab 2
Certificate of Financial Disclosure	A	17/11/2017		Volume 1, Tab 3
Affidavit in support of claim for custody or access	A	17/11/2017		Volume 1, Tab 4

☐ *Continued on next sheet*

FLR-A-9B (01/07)

(Français au verso)

FIGURE 13.5 Lucille's Notice of Motion

ONTARIO

	Court File Number

Superior Court of Justice Family Court Branch
(Name of court)

at _____ **161 Elgin Street, Ottawa, ON K2P 2K1** _____
Court office address

**Form 14: Notice of
Motion**

Applicant(s)

Full legal name & address for service — street & number, municipality, postal code, telephone & fax numbers and e-mail address (if any).	*Lawyer's name & address — street & number, municipality, postal code, telephone & fax numbers and e-mail address (if any).*
Lucille Bell **45 Lovett Court** **Ottawa, ON K1V 9X4**	**JoAnn Kurtz** **123 College Street** **Ottawa, ON K3R 3L2** **Tel: 613-555-1234** **Fax: 613-555-2345**

Respondent(s)

Full legal name & address for service — street & number, municipality, postal code, telephone & fax numbers and e-mail address (if any).	*Lawyer's name & address — street & number, municipality, postal code, telephone & fax numbers and e-mail address (if any).*
Dizzy Arnaz **23 Leavit Place** **Ottawa, ON K2W 8Y3**	

The person making this motion or the person's lawyer must contact the clerk of the court by telephone or otherwise to choose a time and date when the court could hear this motion.

TO THE PARTIES:

THE COURT WILL HEAR A MOTION on *(date)* _____

at _____ **, or as soon as possible after that time, at** *(place of hearing)*

161 Elgin Street, Ottawa, ON K2P 2K1

This motion will be made by *(name of person making the motion)* **Lucille Bell** _____
who will be asking the court for an order for the item(s) listed on page 2 of this notice.

☒ A copy of the affidavit(s) in support of this motion is/are served with this notice.

☐ A notice of a case conference is served with this notice to change an order.

If this material is missing, you should talk to the court office immediately.

The person making this motion is also relying on the following documents in the continuing record: *(List documents.)*

1. Financial statement of Lucille Bell sworn on (date)

2. Financial statement of Dizzy Arnaz sworn on (date)

3. Affidavit in support of claim for custody or access of Lucille Bell sworn on November 17, 2013.

If you want to oppose this motion or to give your own views, you should talk to your own lawyer and prepare your own affidavit, serve it on all other parties not later than 4 days before the date above and file it at the court office not later 2 days before that date. Only written and affidavit evidence will be allowed at a motion unless the court gives permission for oral testimony. You may bring your lawyer to the motion.

IF YOU DO NOT COME TO THE MOTION, THE COURT MAY MAKE AN ORDER WITHOUT YOU AND ENFORCE IT AGAINST YOU.

_____ *Date of signature* _____ *Signature of person making this motion or of person's lawyer*	**JoAnn Kurtz** **123 College Street** **Ottawa, ON K3R 3L2** **Tel: 613-555-1234 Fax: 613-555-2345** *Typed or printed name of person or of person's lawyer, address for service, telephone & fax numbers and e-mail address (if any)*

NOTE TO PERSON MAKING THIS MOTION: *You MUST file a confirmation (Form 14C) not later than 2:00 p.m. 2 days before the date set out above.*

If this is a motion to change past and future support payments under an order that has been assigned to a government agency, you must also serve this notice on that agency. If you do not, the agency can ask the court to set aside any order that you may get in this motion and can ask for costs against you.

FLR 14 (June 15, 2007)

Page 1 of 2

FIGURE 13.5 Lucille's Notice of Motion Concluded

| Form 14: | Notice of Motion | (page 2) | Court File Number |

State the order or orders requested on this motion.

1. An order for temporary custody of the children, Rita Arnaz-Bell, born on 30 August 2007, and Ricky Arnaz-Bell, born on 12 April 2010.

2. An order for temporary support for the said children in accordance with the Child Support Guidelines.

3. An order for temporary spousal support in the amount of $750 per month.

4. Costs.

FLR 14 (June 15, 2007)

Page 2 of 2

FIGURE 13.6   Lucille's Affidavit

ONTARIO

Superior Court of Justice Family Court Branch
(Name of court)

	Court File Number

at _____161 Elgin Street, Ottawa, ON K2P 2K1_____
Court office address

**Form 14A: Affidavit
(general) dated**

_____
(date)

Applicant(s)

Full legal name & address for service — street & number, municipality, postal code, telephone & fax numbers and e-mail address (if any).	Lawyer's name & address — street & number, municipality, postal code, telephone & fax numbers and e-mail address (if any).
Lucille Bell **45 Lovett Court** **Ottawa, ON K1V 9X4**	**JoAnn Kurtz** **123 College Street** **Ottawa, ON K3R 3L2** **Tel: 613-555-1234** **Fax: 613-555-2345**

Respondent(s)

Full legal name & address for service — street & number, municipality, postal code, telephone & fax numbers and e-mail address (if any).	Lawyer's name & address — street & number, municipality, postal code, telephone & fax numbers and e-mail address (if any).
Dizzy Arnaz **23 Leavit Place** **Ottawa, ON K2W 8Y3**	

My name is *(full legal name)* **Lucille Bell**

I live in *(municipality & province)* **Ottawa, Ontario**

and I swear/affirm that the following is true:
Set out the statements of fact in consecutively numbered paragraphs. Where possible, each numbered paragraph should consist of one complete sentence and be limited to a particular statement of fact. If you learned a fact from someone else, you must give that person's name and state that you believe that fact to be true.

1. The respondent and I were married on May 31, 2005, and we separated on July 4, 2017.

2. We have two children – Rita Arnaz-Bell, born on August 30, 2007, and Ricky Arnaz-Bell, born on April 12, 2010.

3. The children have been residing with me since the separation in the matrimonial home at 45 Lovett Court in Ottawa. I have always been the children's primary caregiver. I have stayed home with the children full-time since Rita was born.

4. The children are well settled in the neighbourhood. They like their school and have many friends. If I am granted custody of the children, I would continue to reside with them in the matrimonial home and stay at home to look after them full-time.

5. The children have a good relationship with their father, and I would like the children to see him as often as possible.

6. The respondent is employed as a high school teacher with the Ottawa-Carleton School Board and earns $75,000 per year. I am asking for support for the children in the amount of $1,105 per month as set out in the tables in the Child Support Guidelines.

7. I am also in need of support for myself, and the respondent has the ability to pay. I have no employment income, and my other income and expenses are set out in my financial statement filed in this application. I am asking for spousal support for myself in the amount of $750 per month.

FLR 14A (September 1, 2005)   Page 1 of 2

FIGURE 13.6 Lucille's Affidavit Concluded

Form 14A: **Affidavit (general) dated** **(page 2)**
(date)

Court File Number

Put a line through any blank space left on this page.

Sworn/Affirmed before me at **the City of Ottawa**

municipality

in **the Province of Ontario**

province, state, or country

on _____

date

_____
Commissioner for taking affidavits
(Type or print name below if signature is illegible.)

_____
Signature
(This form is to be signed in front of a
lawyer, justice of the peace, notary public
or commissioner for taking affidavits.)

FLR 14A (September 1, 2005)

Page 2 of 2

FIGURE 13.7   Order

ONTARIO

Superior Court of Justice Family Court Branch
(Name of court)

SEAL

at _____ **161 Elgin Street, Ottawa, ON K2P 2K1** _____
Court office address

Court File Number

Form 25: Order (general)
☒ **Temporary**
☐ **Final**

Applicant(s)

Full legal name & address for service — street & number, municipality, postal code, telephone & fax numbers and e-mail address (if any).	*Lawyer's name & address — street & number, municipality, postal code, telephone & fax numbers and e-mail address (if any).*
Lucille Bell **45 Lovett Court** **Ottawa, ON K1V 9X4**	**JoAnn Kurtz** **123 College Street** **Ottawa, ON K3R 3L2** **Tel: 613-555-1234** **Fax: 613-555-2345**

Name of Judge
Judge (print or type name)

Date of Order
Date of order

Respondent(s)

Full legal name & address for service — street & number, municipality, postal code, telephone & fax numbers and e-mail address (if any).	*Lawyer's name & address — street & number, municipality, postal code, telephone & fax numbers and e-mail address (if any).*
Dizzy Arnaz **23 Leavit Place** **Ottawa, ON K2W 8Y3**	

The court heard an application/motion made by *(name of person or persons)* **Lucille Bell**

The following persons were in court *(names of parties and lawyers in court)*
JoAnn Kurtz, for Lucille Bell, and Dizzy Arnaz in person

The court received evidence and heard submissions on behalf of *(name or names)*
Lucille Bell and Dizzy Arnaz

THIS COURT ORDERS THAT:

1. The applicant, Lucille Bell, shall have temporary custody of the children, Rita Arnaz-Bell, born on August 30, 2007, and Ricky Arnaz-Bell, born on April 12, 2010.

2. The respondent, Dizzy Arnaz, shall have reasonable access to the said children.

3. The respondent shall pay temporary child support in accordance with the Child Support Guidelines in the amount of $1,105.00 per month on the 15th day of each month commencing 15 January 2018.

4. The respondent shall pay temporary spousal support in the amount of $750 per month on the 15th day of each month commencing 15 January 2018.

5. Unless the support order is withdrawn from the office of the Director of the Family Responsibility Office, it shall be enforced by the Director and amounts owing under the support order shall be paid to the Director, who shall pay them to the person to whom they are owed.

FIGURE 13.7   Order Concluded

Form 25:   **Order (general)**   **(page 2)**   Court File Number

Put a line through any blank space left on this page. If additional space is needed, extra sheets may be attached.

_____   _____
            Date of signature   *Signature of judge or clerk of the court*

FLR 25 (September 1, 2005)   Page 2 of 2

Property Claims: A Standard Track Case and Conferences

14

LEARNING OUTCOMES

After completing this chapter, you should be able to:

- Describe the steps, referring to the relevant rules, in a defended property case.

- Complete the documents required to start a property case.

- Describe the steps required to schedule a case conference, referring to the relevant rules.

- Complete the documents required to schedule a case conference.

Introduction

Equalization of net family properties (NFP) and other property claims are dealt with under the *Family Law Act*.[1] A spouse may start a case dealing with property claims only, or may combine the property claims with claims for custody and/or support. A spouse may also include property claims in a divorce case.

We looked at the substantive law of property rights in Chapter 9. In this chapter, we look at the procedure in a property case, including

- an overview of the procedure in a defended property case,
- an examination of the documents required to start a property case, and
- an examination of the steps and documents required to schedule a case conference.

Overview of Procedure

The procedure in a property case is governed by the *Family Law Rules*[2] generally. There is no specific rule that deals with property cases.

Starting a Property Case

Under Rule 5, a property case should be started in the municipality where a party lives, or, if the case includes a claim for custody or access, in the municipality where the children live. Alternatively, with the consent of the court, it may be started in a municipality chosen by both parties. If the case is started in a municipality where the Family Court of the Superior Court of Justice does not operate, the case must be started in the Superior Court of Justice.

Pursuant to Rule 7, the parties to a support and/or custody case are the applicant and the respondent.

In accordance with Rule 8(1), the applicant starts the case by filing an application in Form 8. The application must be accompanied by the required financial statements. Under Rule 13(1.2), if the application includes a property claim or a claim for exclusive possession of the matrimonial home or its contents, the financial statement is to be in Form 13.1. Under Rule 13(7), if the application includes a claim for support as well, the applicant must attach to the financial statement copies of his or her income tax returns for the previous three years or, failing that, a copy of the party's Income and Deduction printout provided by the Canada Revenue Agency. Pursuant to Rule 13 (3.4) the applicant will be required to serve a certificate of financial disclosure as well, but has 30 days after the deadline for serving the financial statement to do so.

Rule 9 requires the applicant to prepare the continuing record of the case. The continuing record is the court's record of all documents in the case. The general rule is that any document that is served and filed must be included in the continuing record. See Chapter 10 for a detailed discussion of the continuing record.

---

1 RSO 1990, c F.3.
2 O Reg 114/99.

If the case is started in the Family Court of the Superior Court of Justice, it is a standard track case under Rule 39(7). As a result, the court does not set a court date when the application is filed.[3]

Service of the Application

The applicant must immediately serve the respondent with the application, financial statement, and continuing record, using special service as defined in Rule 6(3).[4]

The applicant must then file the application, financial statement, and continuing record with the court along with the affidavits of service or other documents proving that the continuing record was served.

Subsequent Pleadings

Under Rule 10, the respondent has 30 days if served in Canada or the United States (60 days if served elsewhere) to defend the case by serving and filing an answer (Form 10) and financial statement (Form 13.1).

If the respondent's answer makes a claim against the applicant, the applicant may serve and file a reply (Form 10A) within 10 days in accordance with Rule 10(6).

Case Conference

There is no first court date in a standard track case. The first step in the case is a case conference, which the court schedules under Rule 39(8)(c) when one of the parties requests it.[5]

According to Rule 17, the party who schedules the conference must serve and file a conference notice (Form 17), a case conference brief (Form 17A), and an updated continuing record table of contents no later than seven days before the case conference date.[6] Both parties must confirm their attendance at the case conference by filing a confirmation (Form 14C) no later than 2 p.m. two days before the conference date.

Other Conferences and Trial

If the case does not settle at the case conference, the judge may schedule another case conference, a settlement conference, and/or a trial management conference. If the case still does not settle, the court will schedule a trial at which a final order will be made concerning the issues.

---

3 If the case is started in the Superior Court of Justice, no court date is set under Rule 41(4).

4 See Rules 8(5), 9(1), and 13(1).

5 Rule 41(4) is of the same effect if the case is brought in the Superior Court of Justice.

6 If the parties' financial statements are more than 30 days old, under Rules 13(12) and (13.1) they must also update the statements by serving and filing either new statements or an affidavit stating that the information in the statements has not changed. A party who serves an updated financial statement must serve an updated certificate of financial disclosure as well.

Documents Required to Start a Property Case

Let's use the case of Frasier and Lilith Crane to illustrate the documents required in a property case.

> Our client is Lilith Crane. She and Frasier were married on September 4, 1995, and separated on September 4, 2017, after they had a huge argument while planning their daughter's sweet-sixteen party. They have one child, Charlene Crane, born October 18, 2001. Both Lilith and Frasier have successful careers as psychiatrists. Neither party is claiming support from the other, and they do not want a divorce at this time. Charlene has made it very clear that she wants to live with her mother, so Lilith is claiming custody and child support. The other issues between them are the equalization of their NFP (they have been unable to settle this issue because they cannot agree on the values of their respective medical practices) and exclusive possession of the matrimonial home. Lilith wants exclusive possession until Charlene graduates from high school.
>
> Frasier was born on October 15, 1969, in Oshawa, and Lilith (birth name Stern) was born on January 16, 1971, also in Oshawa. Frasier and Lilith have lived in Oshawa all their lives. It was the first marriage for both of them.
>
> Frasier has moved to 25 Nervosa Place, Oshawa, ON L1H K5J, leaving Lilith and Charlene in the matrimonial home at 933 Seattle Street, Oshawa, ON L2L K4J. Assume that Lilith's application is prepared on October 16, 2017.

Application

The application used for a property claim is Form 8. Lilith's application appears as Figure 14.1 at the end of the chapter.

Page 1

- Insert the name of the court, in this case, the Superior Court of Justice Family Branch, and the address of the appropriate court office. Under Rule 5, Frasier's case should be commenced in Oshawa. The address of the Family Court in Oshawa is 150 Bond Street East, Oshawa, ON L1G 0A2.
- Insert the names and addresses of the parties.
- Insert the names and addresses of the applicant's lawyers. In this case, Lilith is represented by your law firm.
- This case will be on the standard track of the case management system, so check the appropriate box. Because this is a standard track case, no first court date is assigned.

Page 2

- This case includes a claim for property. As a result, the required financial statement is Form 13.1. Check the second box.
- The form will be dated and signed when it is filed at the court.

Page 3

- Insert the required information under the heading "Family History."
- Insert the date of marriage and the date of separation under the heading "Relationship Dates."
- Insert Charlene's name, birthdate, and living arrangements under the heading "The Child(ren)."
- Under the heading "Previous Cases or Agreements," indicate that there have been no court cases, written agreements, notices issued by the online Child Support Service, or arbitrations.

Page 4

This page sets out the applicant's claims.

- Lilith's claim for custody is under the *Children's Law Reform Act*,[7] and her claim for child support is under the *Family Law Act*;[8] her claims for equalization of NFP and exclusive possession are property claims. She is also claiming costs. Therefore, check boxes 11, 13, 20, 21, 22, and 30.
- Give details of the orders asked for.

Page 5

This page sets out the facts on which Lilith relies in support of her claims for custody, child support, an equalization of NFP, and exclusive possession of the matrimonial home under the heading "Important Facts Supporting My Other Claim(s)." Do not complete "Important Facts Supporting My Claim for Divorce" because no claim for divorce is being made. When you draft the allegations of fact, you must keep in mind the substantive law requirements for a valid cause of action for each of her claims:

- Lilith's claim for custody is based on the fact that Charlene has lived with her since the separation, has expressed her desire to continue to live with her, and it is therefore in Charlene's best interests to remain in Lilith's custody.
- Child support is determined in accordance with the table amounts in the *Child Support Guidelines*.[9] The amount will be based on Frasier's income, which should be disclosed by him in the financial statement he is required to file.
- The right to an equalization of NFP applies to married spouses only. It arises when the parties separate and there is no reasonable prospect that they will resume cohabitation.
- As discussed in Chapter 9, exclusive possession of the matrimonial home is most commonly granted when it is in the best interests of a child.

Lilith will have to sign and date the application. If you know when your client will be coming in to sign the application, in this case October 16, 2017, insert the date. No lawyer's certification is required because this is not a divorce case.

---

7 *Children's Law Reform Act*, RSO 1990, c C.12.

8 *Family Law Act*, RSO 1990, c F.3.

9 O Reg 391/97.

Financial Statement

Lilith must serve and file a financial statement in Form 13.1. See Chapter 11 for a discussion of financial statements.

Affidavit in Support of Claim for Custody or Access

Because Lilith's application includes a claim for custody, according to Rule 35.1 she must complete and file an affidavit in support of claim for custody or access (Form 35.1). See Chapter 13 for a discussion of that form.

Continuing Record

Under Rule 9(1), Lilith must prepare and serve a continuing record on Frasier when she serves the application and financial statement. The continuing record cover in this case appears as Figure 14.2 and the continuing record table of contents appears as Figure 14.3, both at the end of the chapter.

Steps and Documents Required for a Case Conference

As discussed in Chapter 10, all cases under the *Family Law Rules* are case managed, and the Rules provide for three types of case management conferences:

- case conferences,
- settlement conferences, and
- trial management conferences.

The purpose of these conferences is to define, narrow, or even settle the issues in dispute.

Under Rule 17, at least one conference must be held in every defended case. The purposes of a case conference are to

- identify the issues that are in dispute and separate them from those that are not in dispute;
- explore ways to resolve the issues that are in dispute or to settle the entire case;
- ensure that the parties disclose all relevant evidence;
- set a date for the next step in the case or, if possible, have the parties agree to a specific timetable for the steps in the case; and
- organize a settlement conference if necessary.

An application in which the applicant makes a property claim is a standard track case under Rule 39. In a standard track case, a case conference is scheduled when either party requests it. A case conference is the first opportunity for the parties to meet with a judge to review the case.

When Lilith wants to schedule a case conference, you must take the steps set out below.

Step 1: Schedule the Conference

Contact the court office to get a date and time for the case conference.

Step 2: Prepare the Necessary Documents

You will need the following documents for a case conference:

- a conference notice (Form 17);
- a case conference brief (Form 17A);
- if the statements are more than 30 days old, an updated financial statement or an affidavit stating that the information in the statement has not changed;[10] and
- an updated continuing record table of contents.

Assume that Lilith's application was issued as Court File no. 17-1267, and that Frasier, representing himself, filed an answer in which he denied Lilith's claims for equalization of net family properties and exclusive possession of their matrimonial home and contents. He did not oppose her claims for custody and child support. On November 16, 2017, Frasier and Lilith signed an interim separation agreement dealing with custody and child support. On December 20, 2017, they attended a mandatory information program at the Oshawa courthouse. Lilith wants to schedule a case conference and wants to ask for the appointment of an independent evaluator to determine the values of their respective medical practices.

Conference Notice

The purpose of this document is to notify the opposing party of the date and time of the case conference that you have scheduled.

Lilith's conference notice appears as Figure 14.4 at the end of the chapter.

Case Conference Brief

The case conference brief (Form 17A) is a lengthy document that is designed to provide the court and the opposing party with detailed information about the case and the filing party's view of the issues in the case.

Lilith's case conference brief appears as Figure 14.5 at the end of the chapter:

- The first page identifies the parties and date of the case conference.
- *Part 1: Family Facts.* This part sets out facts about the parties' relationship.

---

10   If Lilith serves an updated financial statement she must serve an updated certificate of financial disclosure as well.

- *Part 2: Issues.* This part provides information on the issues that have been settled and the issues that have not been settled. Child custody and child support have been settled. Possession of the home and equalization of net family properties have not been settled. Paragraph 9 refers to the interim separation agreement entered into by the parties.
- *Part 3: Issues for This Case Conference.* This part sets out the party's view of the issues and important facts for the case conference. In this case, the outstanding issues are equalization of the parties' net family properties and exclusive possession of the matrimonial home.
- *Part 4: Financial Information.* This part asks for additional financial information in cases of child support.
- *Part 5: Procedural Issues.* This part asks for the party's views on procedural issues. In this case, Lilith would like an order for a valuation of the two medical practices.
- The form must be signed and dated by both the party and the party's lawyer.

Continuing Record Table of Contents

You must update the continuing record table of contents by adding the case conference notice and any updated financial statements or affidavits that you are serving and filing. Under Rule 17(22), case conference briefs do not form part of the continuing record unless the court orders otherwise. If the court orders that a case conference brief is to form part of the continuing record, under Rule 17(22.1), any portion of the brief that deals with settlement is to be deleted.

Step 3: Serve the Documents

The person who has requested the case conference must serve the conference notice, case conference brief, updated financial statements or affidavit, if required, and updated table of contents at least seven days before the case conference. Regular service under Rule 6(2) may be used.

Step 4: File the Documents with the Court

The person who serves the documents must complete an affidavit of service (Form 6B). The original documents and affidavit of service must be filed with the court no later than seven days before the case conference, along with the continuing record table of contents.

No brief or other document for use at the conference may be served on the other party or filed with the court after 2 p.m. two days before the conference.

Step 5: File a Confirmation with the Court

No later than 2 p.m. two days before the case conference, each party must file a confirmation (Form 14C) confirming that he or she will attend the conference.

CHAPTER SUMMARY

The procedure in a property case is governed by the *Family Law Rules* generally.

A property case should be started in the municipality where a party lives, or, if the case includes a claim for custody or access, in the municipality where the children live. Alternatively, with the consent of the court, it may be started in a municipality chosen by both parties. The applicant starts the case by filing an application. The application must be accompanied by a financial statement. The applicant is required to prepare the continuing record of the case, and must immediately serve the respondent with the application, financial statement, and continuing record. The applicant then files the application, financial statement, and continuing record with the court with proof of service. The respondent has 30 days to defend the case. If the respondent's answer makes a claim against the applicant, the applicant may serve and file a reply within 10 days.

A property case is a standard track case. In a standard track case, the court does not set a court date when the application is filed. The first step in the case is a case conference, which can be scheduled by either party. If the case is not settled at the case conference, the judge may schedule another case conference, a settlement conference, and/or a trial management conference. If the case still does not settle, the court will schedule a trial.

The purposes of a case conference include identifying the issues, exploring ways to resolve them, ensuring that the parties disclose all relevant evidence, setting a date for the next step in the case, and, if necessary, organizing a settlement conference. The party who requests the case conference must serve a case conference notice and a case conference brief as well as updated financial statements and an updated continuing record table of contents.

REVIEW QUESTIONS

1. Generally speaking, where should a property case be started?

2. How is a property case started?

3. What financial statement must be filed by an applicant if an application includes a property claim?

4. What documents must the applicant serve on the respondent? When? How?

5. What must the respondent do if he or she wishes to defend the case? By when?

6. When does the court schedule a first court date?

7. Who schedules a case conference? When?

8. What documents must be served by the party who requests a case conference?

DRAFTING QUESTIONS

1. Our client is Ross Geller. Ross and Rachel Geller (birth name Green) were married on December 22, 2010, and separated on September 15, 2017. They have no children. They were both born in Toronto and have lived there all of their lives. Ross' birthday is June 11, 1980, and Rachel's birthday is April 6, 1981. Rachel is living in the matrimonial home at 222 Sumach Street, Toronto, ON M2K 1Y3. Ross has moved out of the matrimonial home and is now living at 333 Yonge Street, Apt. 1216, Toronto, ON M2J 1K7. Ross would like to start a case for equalization of net family properties. Prepare the application for Ross.

2. Using the fact situation in Question 1, assume that your application was issued as court file

no. 17-1525, and was filed in the continuing record as tab number 1, along with Ross's financial statement, which was filed in the continuing record as tab number 2. Rachel, acting for herself, has filed an answer disputing Ross's claim. Ross has requested a case conference, and it has been scheduled for January 8, 2018. He and Rachel have been to a mediator, Mary Mediator, but they were unable to come to an agreement. Assume they attended a mandatory information program held at the courthouse on November 21, 2017. Ross thinks that Mary Mediator might be able to help the parties settle this matter, and he would like to propose that at the case conference. Prepare a case conference brief for Ross.

FIGURE 14.1   Lilith's Application

ONTARIO

SEAL	**Superior Court of Justice Family Branch** *(Name of court)* at **150 Bond Street East, Oshawa, ON L1G 0A2** *Court office address*

Court File Number

Form 8: Application (General)

Applicant(s)

Full legal name & address for service – street & number, municipality, postal code, telephone & fax numbers and e-mail address (if any).	Lawyer's name & address – street & number, municipality, postal code, telephone & fax numbers and e-mail address (if any).
Lilith Crane **933 Seattle Street** **Oshawa, ON L2L K4J**	**JoAnn Kurtz** **123 College Street** **Oshawa, ON L2J 2B2** **Tel: 905-555-1234** **Fax: 905-555-1235**

Respondent(s)

Full legal name & address for service – street & number, municipality, postal code, telephone & fax numbers and e-mail address (if any).	Lawyer's name & address – street & number, municipality, postal code, telephone & fax numbers and e-mail address (if any).
Frasier Crane **25 Nervosa Place** **Oshawa, ON L1H K5J**	

TO THE RESPONDENT(S):

A COURT CASE HAS BEEN STARTED AGAINST YOU IN THIS COURT. THE DETAILS ARE SET OUT ON THE ATTACHED PAGES.

☐ **THE FIRST COURT DATE IS** *(date)* _____ **AT** _____ ☐ **a.m.** ☐ **p.m.**
or as soon as possible after that time, at: *(address)*

NOTE: *If this is a divorce case, no date will be set unless an Answer is filed. If you have also been served with a notice of motion, there may be an earlier court date and you or your lawyer should come to court for the motion.*

☐ **THIS CASE IS ON THE FAST TRACK OF THE CASE MANAGEMENT SYSTEM.** A case management judge will be assigned by the time this case first comes before a judge.

☒ **THIS CASE IS ON THE STANDARD TRACK OF THE CASE MANAGEMENT SYSTEM. No court date has been set for this case** but, if you have been served with a notice of motion, it has a court date and you or your lawyer should come to court for the motion. A case management judge will not be assigned until one of the parties asks the clerk of the court to schedule a case conference or until a motion is scheduled, whichever comes first.

IF, AFTER 365 DAYS, THE CASE HAS NOT BEEN SCHEDULED FOR TRIAL, the clerk of the court will send out a warning that the case will be dismissed within 60 days unless the parties file proof that the case has been settled or one of the parties asks for a case or a settlement conference.

IF YOU WANT TO OPPOSE ANY CLAIM IN THIS CASE, you or your lawyer must prepare an Answer (Form 10 – a blank copy should be attached), serve a copy on the applicant(s) and file a copy in the court office with an Affidavit of Service (Form 6B). **YOU HAVE ONLY 30 DAYS AFTER THIS APPLICATION IS SERVED ON YOU (60 DAYS IF THIS APPLICATION IS SERVED ON YOU OUTSIDE CANADA OR THE UNITED STATES) TO SERVE AND FILE AN ANSWER. IF YOU DO NOT, THE CASE WILL GO AHEAD WITHOUT YOU AND THE COURT MAY MAKE AN ORDER AND ENFORCE IT AGAINST YOU.**

FLR 8 (April 12, 2016)

Page 1 of 5

FIGURE 14.1   Lilith's Application Continued

Form 8:   **Application (General)**   **(page 2)**   Court File Number

---

Check the box of the paragraph that applies to your case

☐   This case includes a claim for support. It does not include a claim for property or exclusive possession of the matrimonial home and its contents. You **MUST** fill out a Financial Statement (Form 13 – a blank copy attached), serve a copy on the applicant(s) and file a copy in the court office with an Affidavit of Service even if you do not answer this case.

☒   This case includes a claim for property or exclusive possession of the matrimonial home and its contents. You **MUST** fill out a Financial Statement (Form 13.1 – a blank copy attached), serve a copy on the applicant(s) and file a copy in the court office with an Affidavit of Service even if you do not answer this case.

IF YOU WANT TO MAKE A CLAIM OF YOUR OWN, you or your lawyer must fill out the claim portion in the Answer, serve a copy on the applicant(s) and file a copy in the court office with an Affidavit of Service.

·   If you want to make a claim for support but do not want to make a claim for property or exclusive possession of the matrimonial home and its contents, you **MUST** fill out a Financial Statement (Form 13), serve a copy on the applicant(s) and file a copy in the court office.

·   However, if your only claim for support is for child support in the table amount specified under the Child Support Guidelines, you do not need to fill out, serve or file a Financial Statement.

·   If you want to make a claim for property or exclusive possession of the matrimonial home and its contents, whether or not it includes a claim for support, you **MUST** fill out a Financial Statement (Form 13.1, not Form 13), serve a copy on the applicant(s), and file a copy in the court office.

YOU SHOULD GET LEGAL ADVICE ABOUT THIS CASE RIGHT AWAY. If you cannot afford a lawyer, you may be able to get help from your local Legal Aid Ontario office. *(See your telephone directory under LEGAL AID.)*

_____   _____
                  Date of issue   *Clerk of the court*

FLR 8 (April 12, 2016)   Page 2 of 5

FIGURE 14.1 Lilith's Application Continued

Form 8:   Application (General)   (page 3)   Court file number

FAMILY HISTORY

APPLICANT: Age: **46**   Birthdate: *(d, m, y)*   **16 January 1971**

Resident in *(municipality & province)*   **Oshawa, Ontario**

since *(date)*   **16 January 1971**

Surname at birth: **Stern**   Surname just before marriage: **Stern**

Divorced before?   ☒ No   ☐ Yes *(Place and date of previous divorce)*

RESPONDENT: Age: **48**   Birthdate: *(d, m, y)*   **15 October 1969**

Resident in *(municipality & province)*   **Oshawa, Ontario**

since *(date)*   **15 October 1969**

Surname at birth: **Crane**   Surname just before marriage: **Crane**

Divorced before?   ☒ No   ☐ Yes *(Place and date of previous divorce)*

RELATIONSHIP DATES:

☒ Married on *(date)* **4 September 1995**   ☐ Started living together on *(date)*

☒ Separated on *(date)* **4 September 2017**   ☐ Never lived together   ☐ Still living together

THE CHILD(REN)
List all children involved in this case, even if no claim is made for these children.

Full legal name	Age	Birthdate *(d, m, y)*	Resident in *(municipality & province)*	Now Living With *(name of person and relationship to child)*
Charlene Crane	16	18 October 2001	Oshawa, Ontario	Lilith Crane - mother

PREVIOUS CASES OR AGREEMENTS

Have the parties or the children been in a court case before?

☒ No   ☐ Yes

Have the parties made a written agreement dealing with any matter involved in this case?

☒ No   ☐ Yes *(Give date of agreement. Indicate which of its terms are in dispute.)*

FLR 8 (April 12, 2016)   Page 3 of 5

FIGURE 14.1   Lilith's Application Continued

Form 8:   **Application (General)**   **(page 4)**   Court file number

---

Has a Notice of Calculation and/or a Notice of Recalculation been issued by the online Child Support Service in this case?

☒ No   ☐ Yes *(Give date(s) of Notice(s) of Calculation or Recalculation.)*

If yes, are you asking the court to make an order for a child support that is different from the amount set out in the Notice?

☐ No   ☐ Yes *(Provide an explanation.)*

Have the parties arbitrated or agreed to arbitrate any matter involved in this case?

☒ No   ☐ Yes *(Give date of agreement and family arbitration award, if any.)*

CLAIM BY APPLICANT

I ASK THE COURT FOR THE FOLLOWING:
(Claims below include claims for temporary orders.)

Claims under the *Divorce Act* *(Check boxes in this column only if you are asking for a divorce and your case is in the Superior Court of Justice or Family Court of the Superior Court of Justice.)*	**Claims under the *Family Law Act* or *Children's Law Reform Act***	**Claims relating to property** *(Check boxes in this column only if your case is in the Superior Court of Justice or Family Court of the Superior Court of Justice.)*
00 ☐ a divorce 01 ☐ support for me 02 ☐ support for child(ren) – table amount 03 ☐ support for child(ren) – other than table amount 04 ☐ custody of child(ren) 05 ☐ access to child(ren)	10 ☐ support for me 11 ☒ support for child(ren) – table amount 12 ☐ support for child(ren) – other than table amount 13 ☒ custody of child(ren) 14 ☐ access to child(ren) 15 ☐ restraining/non-harassment order 16 ☐ indexing spousal support 17 ☐ declaration of parentage 18 ☐ guardianship over child's property	20 ☒ equalization of net family properties 21 ☒ exclusive possession of matrimonial home 22 ☒ exclusive possession of contents of matrimonial home 23 ☐ freezing assets 24 ☐ sale of family property
Other claims 30 ☒ costs 31 ☐ annulment of marriage 32 ☐ prejudgment interest 33 ☐ claims relating to a family arbitration	50 ☐ Other *(Specify.)*	

Give details of the order that you want the court to make. *(Include any amounts of support (if known) and the names of the children for whom support, custody or access is claimed.)*

1. Custody of the child Charlene Crane, born 18 October 2001;

2. Support for the said child in the table amount in the Child Support Guidelines;

3. An equalization of the net family properties of the parties pursuant to s. 5 of the Family Law Act, RSO 1990, c. F.3;

4. Exclusive possession of the matrimonial home and its contents located at 933 Seattle Street, Oshawa, until the child graduates from high school, pursuant to s. 24 of the Family Law Act, RSO 1990, c. F.3;

5. Costs on a substantial indemnity basis.

FIGURE 14.1 Lilith's Application Concluded

Form 8:	Application (General)	(page 5)	Court File Number

IMPORTANT FACTS SUPPORTING MY CLAIM FOR DIVORCE

☐ **Separation:** The spouses have lived separate and apart since *(date)* _____ and

    ☐ have not lived together again since that date in an unsuccessful attempt to reconcile.

    ☐ have lived together again during the following period(s) in an unsuccessful attempt to reconcile: *(Give dates.)*

☐ **Adultery:** The respondent has committed adultery. *(Give details. It is not necessary to name any other person involved but, if you do name the other person, then you must serve this application on the other person.)*

☐ **Cruelty:** The respondent has treated the applicant with physical or mental cruelty of such a kind as to make continued cohabitation intolerable. *(Give details.)*

IMPORTANT FACTS SUPPORTING MY OTHER CLAIM(S)

(Set out below the facts that form the legal basis for your other claim(s). Attach an additional page if you need more space.)

1. The child has resided with the applicant since the separation and has expressed her desire to continue to live with her. It is therefore in the best interests of the child to remain in her custody.
2. The respondent is a psychiatrist and earns in excess of $100,000 per year.
3. The parties were married on September 4, 1995, and separated on September 4, 2017. There is no reasonable prospect that they will resume cohabitation. The applicant therefore seeks an equalization of the net family properties of the parties.
4. It would be in the best interests of the child to remain in the matrimonial home until she graduates from high school. The respondent has moved out of the matrimonial home, and there is no other suitable and affordable alternate accommodation available to the applicant. The applicant therefore seeks an order for exclusive possession of the matrimonial home and its contents.

Put a line through any blank space left on this page. If additional space is needed, extra pages may be attached.

16 October 2017	
Date of signature	*Signature of applicant*

LAWYER'S CERTIFICATE

For divorce cases only

My name is: _____
and I am the applicant's lawyer in this divorce case. I certify that I have complied with the requirements of section 9 of the *Divorce Act*.

_____	_____
Date	*Signature of Lawyer*

For information on accessibility of court services for people with disability-related needs, contact:
Telephone: 416-326-2220 / 1-800-518-7901   TTY: 416-326-4012 / 1-877-425-0575

FIGURE 14.2 Continuing Record Cover

ONTARIO

Court File Number / *Numéro de dossier du greffe*

Superior Court of Justice Family Court Branch

(Name of court / *Nom du tribunal*)

at / *situé(e) au* 150 Bond Street East, Oshawa, ON L1G 0A2

Court office address / *Adresse du greffe*

Volume / *Volume* : 1

Applicant(s) / *Requérant(e)(s)*

Full legal name & address for service — street & number, municipality, postal code, telephone & fax numbers and e-mail address (if any). *Nom et prénom officiels et adresse aux fins de signification — numéro et rue, municipalité, code postal, numéros de téléphone et de télécopieur et adresse électronique (le cas échéant).*	Lawyer's name & address — street & number, municipality, postal code, telephone & fax numbers and e-mail address (if any). *Nom et adresse de l'avocat(e) — numéro et rue, municipalité, code postal, numéros de téléphone et de télécopieur et adresse électronique (le cas échéant).*
Lilith Crane **933 Seattle Street** **Oshawa, ON L2L K4J**	**JoAnn Kurtz** **123 College Street** **Oshawa, ON L2J 2B2** **Tel: 905-555-1234** **Fax: 905-555-1235**

Respondent(s) / *Intimé(e)(s)*

Full legal name & address for service — street & number, municipality, postal code, telephone & fax numbers and e-mail address (if any). *Nom et prénom officiels et adresse aux fins de signification — numéro et rue, municipalité, code postal, numéros de téléphone et de télécopieur et adresse électronique (le cas échéant).*	Lawyer's name & address — street & number, municipality, postal code, telephone & fax numbers and e-mail address (if any). *Nom et adresse de l'avocat(e) — numéro et rue, municipalité, code postal, numéros de téléphone et de télécopieur et adresse électronique (le cas échéant).*
Frasier Crane **25 Nervosa Place** **Oshawa, ON L1H K5J**	

Children's Lawyer/ *Avocat des enfants*

Name & address of Children's Lawyer's agent for service (street & number, municipality, postal code, telephone & fax numbers and e-mail address (if any)) and name of person represented. *Nom et adresse aux fins de signification de la personne qui représente l'avocat(e) des enfants (numéro et rue, municipalité, code postal, numéros de téléphone et de télécopieur et adresse électronique (le cas échéant)) et nom de la personne représentée.*

Continuing Record / *Dossier continu*

FLR-A 9CR (01/07)

FIGURE 14.3 Continuing Record Table of Contents

ONTARIO

Superior Court of Justice Family Court Branch
(Name of court)

Court File Number

Cumulative Table of Contents (Continuing Record)

at _____ **150 Bond Street East, Oshawa, ON L1G 0A2** _____
Court office address

Applicant(s)

Full legal name & address for service — street & number, municipality, postal code, telephone & fax numbers and e-mail address (if any).	*Lawyer's name & address — street & number, municipality, postal code, telephone & fax numbers and e-mail address (if any).*
Lilith Crane **933 Seattle Street** **Oshawa, ON L2L K4J**	**JoAnn Kurtz** **123 College Street** **Oshawa, ON L2J 2B2** **Tel: 905-555-1234** **Fax: 905-555-1235**

Respondent(s)

Full legal name & address for service — street & number, municipality, postal code, telephone & fax numbers and e-mail address (if any).	*Lawyer's name & address — street & number, municipality, postal code, telephone & fax numbers and e-mail address (if any).*
Frasier Crane **25 Nervosa Place** **Oshawa, ON L1H K5J**	

Document *(For an affidavit or transcript of evidence, include the name of the person who gave the affidavit or the evidence.)*	**Filed by** *(A = applicant or R = respondent)*	**Date of Document** *(d, m, y)*	**Date of Filing** *(d, m, y)*	**Volume/Tab**
Application	A	16/10/2017		Volume 1, Tab 1
Financial Statement	A	16/10/2017		Volume 1, Tab 2
Affidavit in support of claim for custody or access	A	16/10/2017		Volume 1, Tab 3

☐ *Continued on next sheet*

FLR-A-9B (01/07)

(Français au verso)

FIGURE 14.4   Lilith's Conference Notice

ONTARIO

	Court File Number
Superior Court of Justice Family Court Branch	17-1267

(Name of court)

at _____ **150 Bond Street East, Oshawa, ON L1G 0A2** _____

Court office address

**Form 17:
Conference
Notice**

Applicant(s)

Full legal name & address for service — street & number, municipality, postal code, telephone & fax numbers and e-mail address (if any).	*Lawyer's name & address — street & number, municipality, postal code, telephone & fax numbers and e-mail address (if any).*
Lilith Crane **933 Seattle Street** **Oshawa, ON L2L K4J**	**JoAnn Kurtz** **123 College Street** **Oshawa, ON L2J 2B2** **Tel: 905-555-1234** **Fax: 905-555-1235**

Respondent(s)

Full legal name & address for service — street & number, municipality, postal code, telephone & fax numbers and e-mail address (if any).	*Lawyer's name & address — street & number, municipality, postal code, telephone & fax numbers and e-mail address (if any).*
Frasier Crane **25 Nervosa Place** **Oshawa, ON L1H K5J**	

Name & address of Children's Lawyer's agent (street & number, municipality, postal code, telephone & fax numbers and e-mail address (if any)) and name of person represented.

TO: *(name of party or parties or lawyer(s))* **Frasier Crane**

A   ☒ **CASE CONFERENCE**   ☐ **SETTLEMENT CONFERENCE**   ☐ **TRIAL MANAGEMENT CONFERENCE**

WILL BE HELD at *(place of conference)* **150 Bond Street East, Oshawa, ON L1G 0A2**

at _____   **on** *(date)* _____

The conference has been arranged at the request of

☒   the applicant   ☐   the respondent
☐   the case management judge   ☐   *(Other; specify.)* _____

to deal with the following issues:

Equalization of net family property and exclusive possession of the matrimonial home.

You must participate at the time and date by
☒   coming to court at the address set out above.
☐   video-conference or telephone at *(location of video terminal or telephone)* _____

as agreed under arrangements already made by *(name of person)* _____

for video/telephone conferencing.

IF YOU DO NOT PARTICIPATE AS SET OUT ABOVE, THE CASE MAY GO ON WITHOUT YOU OR THE COURT MAY DISMISS THE CASE.

_____   _____
Date of signature   *Signature of clerk of the court*

NOTE: *The party requesting the conference (or, if the conference is not requested by a party, the applicant) must serve and file a case conference brief (Form 17A or 17B), settlement conference brief (Form 17C or 17D) or trial management conference brief (Form 17E) not later than seven days before the date scheduled for the conference. The other party must serve and file a brief not later than four days before the conference date. Each party must also file a confirmation (Form 14C) not later than* **2 p.m. two days** *before the conference.*

FLR 17 (September 1, 2005)

FIGURE 14.5   Lilith's Case Conference Brief

ONTARIO

Superior Court of Justice, Family Court

(Name of court)

Court File Number	
17-1267	

at   **150 Bond Street East, Oshawa, ON L1G 0A2**

Court office address

Form 17A:
Case Conference Brief –
General

Name of party filing this brief

Lilith Crane

Date of case conference

Applicant(s)

Full legal name & address for service — street & number, municipality, postal code, telephone & fax numbers and e-mail address (if any).	Lawyer's name & address — street & number, municipality, postal code, telephone & fax numbers and e-mail address (if any).
Lilith Crane **933 Seattle Street** **Oshawa, ON L2L K4J**	**JoAnn Kurtz** **123 College Street** **Oshawa, ON L2J 2B2** **Tel: 905-555-1234** **Fax: 905-555-1235**

Respondent(s)

Full legal name & address for service — street & number, municipality, postal code, telephone & fax numbers and e-mail address (if any).	Lawyer's name & address — street & number, municipality, postal code, telephone & fax numbers and e-mail address (if any).
Frasier Crane **25 Nervosa Place** **Oshawa, ON L1H K5J**	

Name & address of Children's Lawyer's agent (street & number, municipality, postal code, telephone & fax numbers and e-mail address (if any)) and name of person represented.

PART 1: FAMILY FACTS

1.   **APPLICANT:**   Age: **46**   Birthdate: *(d, m, y)* **16 January 1971**

2.   **RESPONDENT:**   Age: **48**   Birthdate: *(d, m, y)* **15 October 1969**

3.   **RELATIONSHIP DATES:**

☒ Married on *(date)* **4 September 1995**

☒ Separated on *(date)* **4 September 2017**

☐ Started living together on *(date)*

☐ Never lived together

☐ Other *(Explain.)*

4.   The basic information about the child(ren) is as follows:

Child's full legal name	Age	Birthdate *(d, m, y)*	Grade/Year and school	Now living with
Charlene Crane	16	18 October 2001	11 Oshawa Secondary	Lilith Crane - mother

FIGURE 14.5 Lilith's Case Conference Brief Continued

Form 17A:	Case Conference Brief - General	(page 2)	Court File Number
			17-1267

PART 2: ISSUES

5. What are the issues in this case that **HAVE** been settled:

- ☒ child custody
- ☐ access
- ☐ restraining order
- ☐ other *(Specify.)* _____

- ☐ spousal support
- ☒ child support
- ☐ ownership of property

- ☐ possession of home
- ☐ equalization of net family property

6. What are the issues in this case that have **NOT** yet been settled:

- ☐ child custody
- ☐ access
- ☐ restraining order
- ☐ other *(Specify.)* _____

- ☐ spousal support
- ☐ child support
- ☐ ownership of property

- ☒ possession of home
- ☒ equalization of net family property
  (Attach Net Family Property Statement, Form 13B)

7. If child or spousal support is an issue, give the income of the parties:

Applicant: $ _____ per year for the year 20____

Respondent: $ _____ per year for the year 20____

8. Have you explored any ways to settle the issues that are still in dispute in this case?

☒ No.   ☐ Yes. *(Give details.)*

9. Have any of the issues that have been settled been turned into a court order or a written agreement?

☐ No.

☒ Yes.   ☐ an order dated _____

          ☒ a written agreement that is attached.

10. Have the parents attended a family law or parenting education session?

☐ No. (Should they attend one? _____)

☒ Yes. *(Give details.)*
Mandatory information program on December 20, 2017.

PART 3: ISSUES FOR THIS CASE CONFERENCE

11. What are the issues for this case conference? What are the important facts for this case conference?
Issues:
1. Equalization of net family properties.
2. Exclusive possession of the matrimonial home and its contents.
Facts:
1. The parties were married on September 4, 1995 and separated on September 4, 2017. There is no reasonable prospect that they will resume cohabitation.
2. It would be in the best interests of the child to remain in the matrimonial home until she graduates from high school. The respondent has moved out of the matrimonial home, and there is no other suitable and affordable alternate accommodation available to the applicant.

FIGURE 14.5 Lilith's Case Conference Brief Continued

Form 17A: **Case Conference Brief - General** (page 3)

Court File Number
17-1267

12. What is your proposal to resolve these issues?
That an independent evaluator be agreed upon or appointed to set a value on the medical practices of the parties;

That I be granted exclusive possession of the matrimonial home until the child of the parties graduates from high school.

13. Do you want the court to make a temporary or final order at the case conference about any of these issues?

☒ No. ☐ Yes. *(Give details.)*

PART 4: FINANCIAL INFORMATION

NOTE: *If a claim for support has been made in this case, you must serve and file a new financial statement (Form 13 or 13.1), if it is different from the one filed in the continuing record or if the one in the continuing record is more than 30 days old. If there are minor changes but no major changes in your financial statement, you can serve and file an affidavit with details of the changes instead of a new financial statement. If you have not yet filed a financial statement in the continuing record, you must do it now. The page/tab number of the financial statement in the continuing record is* _____

14. If a claim is being made for child support and a claim is made for special expenses under the child support guidelines, give details of those expenses or attach additional information.

15. If a claim is made for child support and you claim that the Child Support Guidelines table amount should not be ordered, briefly outline the reasons here or attach an additional page.

FIGURE 14.5   Lilith's Case Conference Brief Concluded

Form 17A:	**Case Conference Brief - General**	(page 4)	Court File Number
			17-1267

PART 5: PROCEDURAL ISSUES

16.   If custody or access issues are not yet settled:

(a)   Is a custody or access assessment needed?

☐ No.   ☐ Yes. *(Give names of possible assessors.)*

(b)   Does a child or a parent under 18 years of age need legal representation from the Office of the Children's Lawyer?

☐ No.   ☐ Yes. *(Give details and reasons.)*

17.   Does any party need an order for the disclosure of documents, the questioning of witnesses, a property valuation or any other matter in this case?

☐ No.   ☒ Yes. *(Give details.)*

An order appointing an independent evaluator to set a value on the medical practices of the parties.

18.   Are any other procedural orders needed?

☒ No.   ☐ Yes. *(Give details.)*

19.   Have all the persons who should be parties in this case been added as parties?

☒ Yes.   ☐ No. *(Who needs to be added?)*

20.   Are there issues that may require expert evidence or a report?

☒ No.   ☐ Yes. *(If yes, provide details such as: the type of expert evidence; whether the parties will be retaining a joint expert; who the expert will be; who will be paying the expert; how long it will take to obtain a report, etc.)*

21.   Are there any other issues that should be reviewed at the case conference?

☒ No.   ☐ Yes. *(Give details.)*

_____   _____
Date of party's signature   *Signature of party*

_____   _____
Date of lawyer's signature   *Signature of party's lawyer*

PART IV

Negotiation, Variation, and Enforcement

Negotiation and Domestic Contracts

15

LEARNING OUTCOMES

After completing this chapter, you should be able to:

- Describe the negotiation process in arriving at the terms of a separation agreement, including mediation and collaborative law.

- Understand the organization and content of a separation agreement.

- Understand the process of working with a precedent separation agreement.

And, under the *Family Law Act*, you should be able to:

- Define a domestic contract.

- Define a marriage contract and discuss the issues that it may deal with.

- Define a cohabitation agreement and discuss the issues that it may deal with.

- Define a separation agreement and discuss the issues that it may deal with.

- Define a paternity agreement and discuss the issues that it may deal with.

- Define a family arbitration agreement and discuss the issues that it may deal with.

- Discuss the formal requirements for domestic contracts.

- Discuss the provisions that limit the freedom of the parties to set the terms of their domestic contract.

Introduction

Most separating couples negotiate a settlement of all their outstanding issues and incorporate the terms of their settlement into a separation agreement. Lawyers usually try to negotiate a settlement before starting court proceedings, and many separating couples settle without ever having started court proceedings. Even in cases where court proceedings are started, negotiations generally continue, and the vast majority of these cases settle before or at trial.

In this chapter we will be looking at

- the law of domestic contracts,
- the negotiation process,
- the organization and content of a separation agreement, and
- how to work with a precedent separation agreement.

The Law of Domestic Contracts

domestic contract
a marriage contract, separation agreement, or cohabitation agreement

Separation agreements are dealt with in part IV of the *Family Law Act*,[1] along with other domestic contracts. **Domestic contract** is the generic term used in the Act, and is defined in section 51 to mean a marriage contract, separation agreement, cohabitation agreement, paternity agreement, or family arbitration agreement.

Part IV of the Act sets out the formal requirements for domestic contracts and the matters with which each of the various domestic contracts may deal.

Marriage Contracts

marriage contract
an agreement between parties who are married or who intend to marry, in which they agree on their respective rights and obligations under the marriage or on separation, annulment, divorce, or death

Marriage contracts are dealt with in section 52. A **marriage contract** is an agreement between two persons who are married to each other or intend to marry in which they agree on their respective rights and obligations under the marriage or on separation, annulment, divorce, or death, including

- property ownership or division,
- support obligations,
- the right to determine the education and moral training of their children, and
- any other matter with regard to the settlement of their affairs.

A marriage contract may *not*

- deal with child custody or access rights (on separation), or
- purport to limit a spouse's right to possession of the matrimonial home under part II of the Act.

---

1 RSO 1990, c F.3.

Cohabitation Agreements

Cohabitation agreements are dealt with in section 53. A **cohabitation agreement** is an agreement between two persons who are cohabiting or intend to cohabit and who are not married to each other in which they agree on their respective rights and obligations during cohabitation, or on ceasing to cohabit or on death, including

- property ownership or division,
- support obligations,
- the right to determine the education and moral training of their children, and
- any other matter with regard to the settlement of their affairs.

A cohabitation agreement may *not* deal with child custody or access rights (on separation).

If parties to a cohabitation agreement marry each other, the agreement is deemed to be a marriage contract.

cohabitation agreement
an agreement between two persons who are cohabiting or intend to cohabit and who are not married to each other in which they agree on their respective rights and obligations during cohabitation, on ceasing to cohabit, or on death

Separation Agreements

Separation agreements are dealt with in section 54. A **separation agreement** is an agreement between parties who cohabited (in or out of marriage) and who have separated,[2] in which they agree on their respective rights and obligations, including

- property ownership or division,
- support obligations,
- the right to determine the education and moral training of their children,
- child custody and access rights, and
- any other matter with regard to the settlement of their affairs.

separation agreement
an agreement between parties who have co-habited, in or out of marriage, and who have separated, in which they agree on their respective rights and obligations

Paternity Agreements

Paternity agreements are dealt with in section 59. A **paternity agreement** is an agreement between a man and a woman who are not spouses for the payment of the expenses of a child's prenatal care and birth, support of a child, or funeral expenses of the child or mother.

On the application of a party, or a children's aid society, to the Ontario Court of Justice or the Family Court of the Superior Court of Justice, the court may incorporate the agreement in an order, and part III of the *Family Law Act* (Support Obligations) applies to the order in the same manner as if it were an order made under that part.[3]

paternity agreement
an agreement between a man and a woman who are not spouses for payments toward various child and/ or mother expenses

---

2   The parties to a separation agreement must be separated at the time the agreement is entered into. An agreement in which parties who are still cohabiting agree to separate in the future is either a cohabitation agreement or a marriage contract; it is not a separation agreement.

3   A court shall not incorporate an agreement for the support of a child in an order unless the court is satisfied that the agreement is reasonable having regard to the child support guidelines, as well as to any other provision relating to support of the child in the agreement.

Family Arbitration Agreements

Family arbitration agreements are dealt with in sections 59.1 to 59.8. A **family arbitration agreement** is an agreement to refer issues to a family arbitration. A **family arbitration** is defined in section 51 to mean an arbitration that deals with matters that could be dealt with in a marriage contract, separation agreement, cohabitation agreement, or paternity agreement, and is conducted exclusively in accordance with the law of Ontario or of another Canadian jurisdiction. A **family arbitration award** is a decision that arises out of a family arbitration.

Pursuant to section 59.1, family arbitrations, family arbitration agreements, and family arbitration awards are governed by the Act and by the *Arbitration Act, 1991*.[4] However, in the event of a conflict between the two statutes, the *Family Law Act* prevails.

A family arbitration award is enforceable only if the arbitration process takes place in accordance with the provisions of the Act, in particular

- Under section 59.2, if a third-party decision is made in a process that is not conducted exclusively in accordance with the law of Ontario or of another Canadian jurisdiction, the process is not a family arbitration, and the decision is not a family arbitration award and has no legal effect.
- Under section 59.4, the family arbitration agreement must have been entered into after the dispute has arisen.
- Under section 59.6, a family arbitration award is enforceable only if,
  - the family arbitration agreement under which the award is made is in writing and complies with any regulations made under the *Arbitration Act, 1991*;
  - each of the parties to the agreement receives independent legal advice before making the agreement;
  - the requirements of section 38 of the *Arbitration Act, 1991* are met (formal requirements, writing, reasons, and delivery to parties); and
  - the arbitrator complies with any regulations made under the *Arbitration Act, 1991*.

Pursuant to section 59.3, the parties cannot vary or exclude any of the above provisions of the Act.

The enforcement procedure is set out in section 59.8.

A **secondary arbitration** is a family arbitration that is conducted in accordance with a separation agreement, a court order, or a family arbitration award that provides for the arbitration of possible future disputes relating to the ongoing management or implementation of the agreement, order, or award. Under section 59.7, the following special provisions apply to secondary arbitrations:

- Despite section 59.4, the award is not unenforceable for the sole reason that the separation agreement was entered into or the court order or earlier award was made before the dispute to be arbitrated in the secondary arbitration had arisen.

---

4 SO 1991, c 17.

- Despite section 59.6(1)(b), it is not necessary for the parties to receive in-dependent legal advice before participating in the secondary arbitration.
- Despite section 59.6(1)(c), the requirements of section 38 of the *Arbitration Act, 1991* need not be met.

Formal Requirements

Pursuant to the provisions of section 55, any domestic contract or agreement to amend or rescind a domestic contract must be in writing, signed by the parties, and witnessed.

Limitations on Freedom of Contract

Section 56 of the Act contains a number of provisions that effectively limit the freedom of the parties to set the terms of their domestic contract:

- Any provisions of a domestic contract dealing with the education, moral training, or custody of or access to a child may be disregarded by a court if they are not in the best interests of the child.
- Any child support provision may be disregarded by a court if it is unreasonable having regard to the child support guidelines (see Chapter 8) and any other child support provisions in the agreement.
- Any provision taking effect on separation that stipulates that any right of a party is dependent upon his or her remaining chaste is unenforceable, although provisions tied to remarriage or cohabitation are enforceable.[5]

In addition, section 56(4) states that a court may set aside a domestic contract or a provision in it

- if one party failed to disclose to the other significant assets, or significant debts or other liabilities, existing when the domestic contract was made;[6]
- if one party did not understand the nature or consequences of the domestic contract; or
- for other reasons that are in accordance with the law of contracts.[7]

---

5   As discussed in Chapter 2, historically a wife receiving alimony lost her right to payments if she had sexual intercourse with a man who was not her husband. Accordingly, it was not uncommon for separation agreements to contain a clause stating that a wife's support payments would continue only as long as she was chaste. These clauses, called *dum casta* clauses, continued to be used until they were declared unenforceable by the *Family Law Reform Act* in 1978. The abolition of *dum casta* clauses does not affect clauses that state that support will end if the recipient remarries or cohabits with another person. These continue to be enforceable.

6   This is the reason that full and complete financial disclosure is so important in the negotiation of a separation agreement.

7   Grounds for setting aside a contract include duress, undue influence, and fraud.

Section 56.1 sets limits on provisions dealing with pension plans, as follows:

- A domestic contract may provide for the immediate transfer of a lump-sum payment out of a pension plan, but, except as set out below, not for any other division of a party's interest in the plan.
- If payment of the first installment of a party's pension under a pension plan is due on or before the family law valuation date, the domestic contract may provide for the division of pension payments, but not for any other division of the party's interest in the plan.
- If the *Pension Benefits Act*[8] applies to the pension plan, the restrictions under sections 67.3 and 67.4 of that Act apply with respect to the division of the party's interest in the plan under a domestic contract.

The Negotiation Process

As stated previously, most separating couples negotiate a settlement of all their outstanding issues.

The Traditional Process

The first step in the negotiation process is the exchange of financial information. The practice is for the parties to exchange the same sworn financial statements that would be filed in a court proceeding, together with supporting documents such as income tax returns, bank statements, investment statements, and credit card statements. It may be necessary to obtain professional evaluations of some of the assets.

Lawyers for the parties negotiate on behalf of their clients by letter, by telephone, and/or in person over a period of time. At some point, the parties may hold a four-way meeting with both lawyers and clients, or the parties may decide to try to resolve certain issues such as custody and access by **mediation** (see below).

While they are collecting the necessary financial information to negotiate a final settlement, the parties may enter into an interim agreement—without prejudice to the rights of either party—on matters such as custody, access, and support.

mediation
a method of dispute resolution in which the parties meet with a neutral third party who will help them try to come to an agreement

Mediation

In mediation, the parties meet with a neutral third party who will help them try to come to an agreement. The mediator's role is to help the parties explore the situation to see whether there is a solution that can satisfy the needs of both parties (and, in custody matters, the needs of the children). It is up to the parties to arrive at a settlement voluntarily. A mediator does not take sides and does not judge who is right or wrong. If the parties cannot come to an agreement, the mediator does not make a

---

8   RSO 1990, c P.8.

decision for the parties. Mediation must be entered into voluntarily and is not appropriate in cases involving domestic violence.

Negotiation Using Collaborative Law

Under the traditional negotiation process, either party is free to institute court proceedings at any time and to continue to be represented by the same lawyer who has been negotiating on his or her behalf. As a result, traditional negotiation is, at least potentially, an adversarial process.

The **collaborative law** negotiation model, however, is non-adversarial in nature. The parties, each working with specially trained collaborative family law lawyers, are encouraged to work toward a settlement cooperatively, in a non-adversarial fashion.

The parties and their lawyers sign a collaborative practice participation agreement. The parties agree, among other things

- to make voluntary disclosure of all financial and other relevant information,
- to treat each other with mutual respect and cooperation, and
- to not institute court proceedings without first providing written notice of the intention to withdraw from the collaborative process, and then waiting 30 days.

The lawyers agree to act for each party only within the collaborative process, and pledge not to represent either party if the collaborative process ends and either party starts a court proceeding.

If appropriate, the parties may agree to use other collaboratively trained professionals such as a neutral child specialist, financial specialist, and/or family professional, each of whom also signs the collaborative practice participation agreement.

When a final settlement is arrived at, whatever the negotiation process, the lawyers for the parties will work on drafting a separation agreement that incorporates the terms of their settlement.

> **collaborative law**
> a non-adversarial, cooperative, collaborative settlement model in which the parties work with specially trained collaborative family law lawyers

The Organization and Content of a Separation Agreement

There is no such thing as a standard separation agreement. There are many issues that arise on the breakdown of a domestic relationship and the facts of each situation are unique. As a result, a separation agreement must be carefully tailored to meet the needs of the particular couple.

Notwithstanding the uniqueness of each separation agreement, most separation agreements contain similar types of clauses, and are organized in a similar fashion.

Title and Identification of the Parties

As is the case with all written contracts, a separation agreement starts with a title and date, and the identification of the parties.

Assume that we are drafting an agreement between Andre Johnson and Rainbow Johnson, to be signed on November 15, 2017. The title, date and identification of the parties would look like this:

THIS IS A SEPARATION AGREEMENT DATED NOVEMBER 15, 2017

Between:

Rainbow Johnson	("Rainbow")
AND	
Andre Johnson	("Andre")

Preliminary Matters

Separation agreements usually start with clauses that set out background matters such as

- the date of the marriage or commencement of cohabitation,
- the date of the separation,
- the names and dates of birth of any children,
- definitions of terms used in the agreement, and
- the agreement of the parties to continue to live separate and apart.

Assume the following facts about Andre and Rainbow:

- They were married on January 1, 1999, and separated on August 1, 2017.
- They have four children: Zoey born on April 15, 2000, Andre Jr. born on October 15, 2012, and twins Jack and Diane born on March 5, 2008.
- They jointly own the matrimonial home at 145 Ellsworth Ave, Toronto.

The preliminary clauses of their separation agreement might look like this:

1.0 BACKGROUND

1.1 Rainbow and Andre were married on January 1, 1999.

1.2 They separated on August 1, 2017. The parties will continue to live separate and apart.

1.3 They have four children, Zoey Johnson ("Zoey"), born April 15, 2000, Andre Johnson Jr. ("Andre Jr."), born October 15, 2012, Jack Johnson ("Jack"), born March 5, 2008, and Diane Johnson ("Diane"), born March 5, 2008.

1.4 They agree to be bound by this agreement which settles all issues between them.

2.0 DEFINITIONS

2.1 In this agreement:

(a) "children" means Zoey, Andre Jr., Jack, and Diane;

(b) "equalization payment" means the payment referred to in section 5(1) of the *Family Law Act*;

(c) "CRA" means Canada Revenue Agency;

(d) "FRO" means the Family Responsibility Office described in the *Family Responsibility and Support Arrears Enforcement Act* or any successor support enforcement agency;

(e) "Guidelines" means the Federal *Child Support Guidelines*, as defined in section 2(1) of the *Divorce Act*,

(f) "matrimonial home" means the property at 145 Ellsworth Avenue in Toronto;

(g) "net family property" means net family property as defined in the *Family Law Act*; and

(h) "property" means property as defined in the *Family Law Act*.

Custody and Access or Parenting

These clauses set out the agreement of the parties with respect to custody of and access to their children, and deal with

- the parent with whom the child will reside,
- how much time the child will spend with the other parent, and
- which parent has the right to make decisions about the child's health, education, and moral upbringing.

The parties may agree that one parent will have sole custody while the other parent will have access rights. In that case, the child will reside with the custodial parent and visit with the access parent. In addition, the custodial parent will have the sole right to make decisions concerning the child. The agreement may set out a strict schedule of access visits, or may simply state that access is to be reasonable or to be as agreed by the parties, depending on the relationship between the parties and how well they expect to be able to cooperate on this matter.

Instead, the parties may agree to shared or joint custody (see Chapter 6). In some shared custody situations, the child will spend equal amounts of time with each parent, while in others the child will reside primarily with one parent and visit with the other parent. In any case, both parents will share the right to make decisions concerning the upbringing of the child.

As part of the child-centred family justice strategy announced by the federal government in December 2002, the government proposed amendments to the *Divorce Act*[9] that would eliminate the terms "custody" and "access" from the Act.

---

9 RSC 1985, c 3 (2d Supp).

It was proposed that the Act instead use the term "parenting arrangements," under which the parties allocate "parenting time" and "decision-making responsibilities," and that the term "parenting order" be used in place of "custody order." The bill containing these proposed amendments died on the order paper. However, some lawyers moved away from using the terms "custody" and "access" in separation agreements. Instead, they use the terms "parenting arrangements," "parenting time," and "decision-making responsibilities."

The custody and access clauses of the agreement may also address related matters such as

- the right of the parties to obtain information with regard to the child,
- the right of the parties to communicate with the child while he or she is spending time with the other parent,
- the right of either party to remove the child from the province, either permanently or during vacations,
- the right to obtain a passport for the child,
- the right to change the name of the child,
- the nature of the child's religious upbringing,
- custody of the child in the event of the death of the parents, and
- a method for resolving disputes that relate to custody and/or access.

Assume that Rainbow and Andre have agreed that she will have custody of the children and Andre will have access according to a set schedule. Their custody and access clause might look like this:

3.0 CUSTODY AND ACCESS

3.1 Rainbow will have custody of the children. Andre will have access to the children (which will include the right to have them stay overnight) as follows:

(a) Every second weekend from Friday after school to Sunday at 8:00 p.m.

(b) During the entire spring holiday and entire Christmas holiday in every odd-numbered year. He will not exercise weekend access during these holidays in even-numbered years.

(c) For one month of his choice during the summer school holiday, and he will advise Rainbow in writing of his choice by no later than the preceding March 1st.

3.2 Rainbow will have the right to have the children with her for a continuous and uninterrupted period of one month during the summer school holiday.

3.3 Andre will have the right to communicate with the children at any reasonable time by telephone and/or email.

3.4 Andre will have the right to be fully advised of the school progress (including the right to have copies of report cards and notices of school events) and the health and general welfare of the children.

Child Support

These clauses set out the agreement of the parties with respect to payment of child support, and they should be drafted to reflect the provisions of the child support guidelines (see Chapter 8). The clauses must take into account the provisions of the guidelines that relate to the particular situation of the parties.

The parties may agree to support in the table amount, in which case:

- if one party has sole custody, the agreement should provide for payment of the table amount and should also address the paying party's share of special or extraordinary expenses;
- if the parties have split custody, the agreement should state how the table amounts for the children are being set off against each other, and how the parties are apportioning special or extraordinary expenses for the children; and
- if the parties have shared custody, the agreement should set out the percentage of the time the children spend with the paying party and state that the parties have set the child support amount taking into account the increased costs of the shared custody arrangement.

If the parties agree to an amount of support that is different from the table amount, the agreement should contain enough information for a court to conclude that the arrangements are reasonable. If the amount of child support is lower than the table amount because of undue hardship, the agreement should set out details of the undue hardship and provide for a review of the hardship issue at a set date in the future.

Whatever the circumstances of the parties, the child support clauses should

- specify the income of the parties,
- provide for ongoing disclosure of income information, and
- identify the events that will terminate child support payments, and, if there is more than one child, state how support for the remaining children will be calculated at that time.

The parties may also wish to include provisions that

- set out their agreement on how insurance claims are to be processed if either or both of the parties have health or dental insurance coverage for the children,
- provide for variation of child support in the event of a material change in circumstances, and
- state that the child support payments will be made by post-dated cheques.

Assume that Andre earns $120,000 per year and agrees to pay $2,659 per month as support for the four children in accordance with the child support guideline tables. There are no special or extraordinary expenses. Andre and Rainbow also agree that support for each child will be paid until the completion of the child's first post-secondary degree up to a maximum age of 22, but that support will end at the age of 18 if the child does not continue in school. The parties agree that the support payments will end if the husband dies because he will be providing life insurance to take the place of the support payments. They also agree that when support for one child ends, they will determine the support for the other children based on the child support guidelines at that time. Their child support clause might look like this:

4.0 CHILD SUPPORT

4.1 Commencing on December 1, 2017, and on the first day of each subsequent month, Andre will pay to Rainbow for the support of the four children the sum of $2,659 in accordance with the child support guideline tables.

4.2 Andre will no longer be obliged to pay support for a child referred to in paragraph 4.1 above when one of the following events occurs:

  (a) the child ceases to reside full time with Rainbow. "Reside full time" includes the child living away from home to attend an educational institution, pursue summer employment, or take a vacation while otherwise maintaining a residence with Rainbow;

  (b) the child becomes 18 years of age and ceases to be in full-time attendance at an educational institution;

  (c) the child obtains his or her first post-secondary degree or diploma;

  (d) the child becomes 22 years of age;

  (e) the child marries;

  (f) the child dies; or

  (g) Andre dies, so long as he has complied with his obligations pursuant to paragraph 12.0 of this agreement to provide life insurance.

4.3 Andre represents that his income (as defined by the child support guidelines) at the date of this agreement is $120,000 per year.

4.4 If Andre's obligation to support a child ends, the parties will determine the support payable for the other children at that time under the child support guidelines.

Spousal Support

These clauses set out the agreement of the parties concerning their responsibility to provide support for each other. The parties may agree that

- neither spouse will pay support to the other,
- one spouse will make a lump-sum payment of support to the other,
- one spouse will make periodic (usually monthly) support payments to the other, but for a limited time only, or
- one spouse will make periodic support payments to the other for an indefinite period of time.

Generally, parties agree that no support will be paid because both parties are financially self-sufficient. If the parties have agreed that neither of them will pay support to the other, the agreement must specifically say so.

The parties may agree that one of them should make a lump-sum payment in satisfaction of his or her obligation to pay spousal support, after which both parties will be financially self-sufficient. If the parties agree that one of them will make a lump-sum payment, the agreement will set out the amount and the date on which the payment is to be made, and will state that the payment is in full satisfaction of the paying party's spousal support obligation.

In both the case of no support and of a lump-sum payment, the agreement will contain a clause in which the parties release each other from any responsibility for future support payments.

In some cases, the parties will agree that one of them requires support for a fixed period of time to enable him or her to become self-sufficient. In that case, the agreement will provide for payment of a specified amount per month, starting on a specific date and ending on a specific date. The support clause will go on to state that the spouse receiving support releases the paying spouse from any claims for support beyond that termination date. The purpose of the release is to prevent the receiving spouse from making a claim for additional spousal support at the end of the fixed term. It is, however, impossible to prevent a court from considering an application for additional support.

If the parties have agreed to support for an indefinite period, the agreement will set out the amount to be paid per month and the date on which the payments are to start. Instead of setting a fixed date for termination, the agreement will set out the circumstances in which support will end, such as the death, cohabitation, or remarriage of the spouse who is receiving support. The support payments may end when the paying spouse dies—if the parties have made arrangements for insurance for the surviving spouse. (See below for a discussion of insurance clauses.) If support payments are not stated to end on the death of the paying spouse, his or her estate will be obligated to continue making the support payments.

The agreement may also provide for variation of the amount of support in the event of a material change in circumstances and/or for the increase of the amount of support in accordance with changes in the cost of living.

Assume that Andre has agreed to pay Rainbow a lump sum of $25,000 in satisfaction of his obligation to pay spousal support, after which both parties will be financially self-sufficient. Their spousal support clause might look like this:

5.0 SPOUSAL SUPPORT

5.1 Andre will pay Rainbow $25,000 on execution of this agreement.

5.2 Upon payment, Andre and Rainbow will each be financially independent of each other and will release his or her right to spousal support from the other forever. Andre and Rainbow intend this agreement to inoculate them from any judicial review.

5.3 Andre and Rainbow know that their financial circumstances, health, employment or the cost of living may all change. They may be unable to work for various reasons, or earn less than they expect. These changes may be catastrophic, unanticipated or beyond imagining. Nevertheless, no change will ever entitle Andre or Rainbow to spousal support from the other.

5.4 Andre and Rainbow do not want any court to order a change which deviates from or overrides the terms of this agreement, especially this release. Andre and Rainbow want the court to uphold this agreement in its entirety because they are basing their future lives upon this release.

5.5 This agreement recognizes all economic advantages or disadvantages to the parties arising from the marriage and its breakdown, has apportioned between them all financial consequences arising from the care of the children in addition to any obligation for the support of the children, relieves any economic hardship arising from the marriage breakdown, and, insofar as is practicable, promotes the economic self-sufficiency of Andre and Rainbow within a reasonable period of time.

5.6 No change in the circumstances of Andre and Rainbow, or both, will be considered a material change justifying any spousal support. All changes will be considered immaterial to their rights and obligations under this agreement. Andre and Rainbow have either anticipated all changes as possibilities or have decided to take the risk that there will be changes. This agreement meets the objectives under the *Divorce Act* and is fair to both parties. For example, if Rainbow loses her job and for any reason cannot find work and therefore has no income, and Andre's income and financial position have vastly improved from what they are now (or vice versa), these facts will not be a material change justifying any spousal support award. They will be considered and are considered now by Andre and Rainbow to be immaterial.

Finality of Support Release Clauses

Whatever the agreement of the parties on the subject of spousal support, the party who is liable to pay support wants as much finality as possible.

As is the case in Andre's and Rainbow's spousal support clause above, separation agreements often contain a clause in which the parties release each other from any responsibility for future support payments. The purpose of the release clause is to prevent either party from making a claim for spousal support in the future.

Until the Ontario Court of Appeal decision in *Miglin v Miglin*,[10] the courts followed the *Pelech*[11] trilogy of cases,[12] and would not override a release of support in a separation agreement unless there had been a radical and unforeseen change of circumstances that was somehow causally connected to the marriage. In the *Miglin* case, however, the Ontario Court of Appeal held that a simple material change in

---

10 (2001), 53 OR 641 (CA), rev'd 2003 SCC 24, [2003] 1 SCR 303.

11 [1987] 1 SCR 801, 1987 CanLII 57.

12 Named for three cases including *Pelech v Pelech*.

circumstances was all that was necessary to allow a court to override a release of support in a separation agreement.

This case was appealed to the Supreme Court of Canada, which heard the appeal on October 29, 2002, and released its decision on April 17, 2003. The court ruled that it was no longer necessary to prove a radical and unforeseen change in circumstances that was causally connected to the marriage, as required under the *Pelech* trilogy of cases. However, a simple material change in circumstances alone was not enough to justify a variation.

Instead, the court's view was that courts should examine both the circumstances surrounding the negotiation of the agreement and the circumstances at the time of the court application, stating that

[u]nimpeachably negotiated agreements that represent the intentions and expectations of the parties and that substantially comply with the objectives of the *Divorce Act* as a whole should receive considerable weight.

When examining the negotiation,

the court should look at the circumstances in which the agreement was negotiated and executed to determine whether there is any reason to discount it, including any circumstances of oppression, pressure or other vulnerabilities. Circumstances less than "unconscionability" in the commercial law context may be relevant, but a court should not presume an imbalance of power. Further, the degree of professional assistance received by the parties may be sufficient to overcome any systemic imbalances between the parties.

When looking at the circumstances at the time of the court application,

the court must assess whether the agreement still reflects the original intentions of the parties and the extent to which it is still in substantial compliance with the objectives of the Act. Accordingly, the party seeking to set aside the agreement will need to show that these new circumstances were not reasonably anticipated by the parties, and have led to a situation that cannot be condoned.

As a result of the decision of the Supreme Court of Canada in *Miglin*, it has again become more difficult to persuade a court to make an order that varies the spousal support provisions of a separation agreement, but not as difficult as it was previously under the *Pelech* trilogy.

Lawyers are constantly refining the wording of their release clauses in an effort to persuade any court that might consider a future support application that the parties did not want the courts to interfere.

Life Insurance

When a separation agreement provides for the payment of ongoing child and/or spousal support, it is important to consider what will happen to the support payments if the paying party dies.

An agreement to pay child support or spousal support does not end with the death of the paying party, unless the support clause states that it does. Instead, the estate of the paying party is obligated to continue to make the support payments. However, having the estate make support payments may cause problems for both parties. The estate may not have enough money to continue making the support payments, which will cause problems for the dependants. The paying party's estate could be tied up as long as the support payments are owing, which will cause problems for the estate.

There is an alternative to this arrangement, and that is to end support payments on the death of the paying party, while requiring the paying party to provide life insurance to take the place of support payments if he or she dies while still obligated to make payments. The amount of the insurance should be enough to satisfy the support obligation as long as it would otherwise last.

Insurance clauses in separation agreements generally require the paying spouse to take out a policy in the appropriate amount with the recipient spouse or the child (through a trustee) as beneficiary, to maintain the policy or a replacement policy until the obligation to provide support ends, and to provide proof, if requested by the other spouse, of payment of policy premiums. If the paying spouse fails to pay a premium, the other spouse is generally given the right to make the payment and be repaid. The clauses also usually provide that, if the paying party dies without having the insurance in place, the estate is bound to continue to make support payments.

Assume that Andre and Rainbow have agreed that Andre will maintain a $500,000 life insurance policy for as long as he is required to pay child support. The insurance clause might look like this:

6.0 LIFE INSURANCE

6.1 Andre will keep a life insurance policy ("the policy") on his life in the amount of $500,000, naming Rainbow as the irrevocable beneficiary for as long as he is obligated to pay child support.

6.2 Within 14 days of signing this agreement, Andre will provide Rainbow with a copy of the policy and the irrevocable beneficiary designation.

6.3 Andre will pay all policy premiums when due. If he does not and Rainbow pays any premiums, interest or penalties to prevent the policy from lapsing, Andre will reimburse Rainbow for such payments. If the policy lapses because Andre failed to pay the premiums, Andre will also pay Rainbow all necessary costs incurred by her to reinstate the policy.

6.4 When Andre's obligation to pay child support ends, Andre's obligation to maintain the policy ends. When it does, Rainbow will provide Andre's insurer with a direction to withdraw the policy's irrevocable designation. If she does not, Andre may obtain a court order directing the insurer to do so. Rainbow will be responsible for the costs Andre incurs in obtaining the order.

Health Insurance

Often, at least one party has medical and/or dental insurance through his or her place of employment. It is customary to require that party to maintain coverage for the other party and children as long as the coverage is available. The obligation to provide coverage will end when the insured party no longer has the insurance or when the other party and/or children no longer qualify as beneficiaries under the policy.[13]

Assume that Andre has health insurance through his employer, and has agreed to continue coverage for Rainbow and the children as long it is available. The health insurance clause might look like this:

7.0 MEDICAL AND DENTAL BENEFITS

7.1 Andre will maintain his medical, extended health and dental coverage through his employment for Rainbow and the children for as long as it is available to him for their benefit. He will immediately reimburse Rainbow for all amounts recovered by him for expenses incurred by her for herself or the children.

Matrimonial Home

If the parties own a matrimonial home, the agreement will identify the property and confirm how title is currently held—either by one spouse alone or by both spouses, either as joint tenants or as **tenants in common**—and then state what is to happen to the property. The parties may agree that

- the home, which is owned by one spouse only, will stay in the name of the registered owner;
- the home, which is owned by one or both spouses, will be transferred to the name of one spouse only; or
- the home, which is owned by both spouses, will be sold, either immediately or after a period of exclusive possession by one spouse.

If the parties agree that the sole current owner of the house will retain sole ownership, the separation agreement will state that the other spouse releases any claim to ownership or possession of the property.

If the parties agree that the matrimonial home will be transferred into the name of one spouse only, the agreement will set out the obligation of the transferring spouse to sign the transfer document, and state which of the spouses is to pay the cost of preparation and registration of the transfer. If there are any outstanding mortgages, the agreement must state whether the mortgages are to be discharged or assumed by the new owner.

If the parties agree that the matrimonial home is to be sold, the agreement must set out all of the mechanics of the sale, including the choice of a real estate agent and the determination of a listing price. The agreement must also set out how the proceeds of sale are to be applied—for example, to pay any taxes, encumbrances, lawyers' fees, and real estate commission—and then how the balance of the proceeds is to be

tenants in common
two or more people who own property and on the death of one owner the owner's share passes to the other's estate

---

13 When the parties have been married, coverage is usually available for the separated spouse until the parties divorce. A former spouse can sometimes continue to be covered until the insured party adds a new spouse to the policy. For unmarried couples (whether same- or opposite-sex), coverage will depend on the terms of the individual policy.

divided between the spouses. The agreement should state which spouse has the right to occupy the home until its sale, and who is to pay the costs of the home until sale.

If the parties agree that the house should not be sold immediately, but that one spouse is to have exclusive possession of the matrimonial home for an extended period of time, the agreement should specify when the right to exclusive possession ends, and that the house is to be sold at that time.

If the home is owned in joint tenancy, and will continue to be owned by both parties for some time, the parties may want to sever the joint tenancy so that, in the event that one spouse dies, the ownership does not pass by right of survivorship to the other spouse.

Assume that Andre and Rainbow own the matrimonial home as joint tenants, that it is mortgage-free, and Andre agrees to transfer his interest in the home to Rainbow. Their matrimonial home clause might look like this:

8.0 MATRIMONIAL HOME

8.1 Andre and Rainbow own the matrimonial home[14] jointly.

8.2 Andre hereby transfers all of his right, title, and interest in the matrimonial home to Rainbow.

8.3 Concurrently with the signing of this agreement, Andre will sign a transfer of the matrimonial home.

8.4 Rainbow will pay the cost of the preparation and registration of the transfer.

Other Property

The agreement should specify how all of the parties' property is to be divided. Depending on the property they own, there may be clauses dealing with

- other real estate,
- the contents of the matrimonial home,
- bank accounts,
- corporate securities,
- RRSPs,
- pensions,
- cars,
- boats,
- Air Miles, etc.

Assume that Rainbow and Andre have agreed
- that their household contents have already been divided, and
- to share any accumulated airline points equally.

---

14 It isn't necessary to set out the address of the matrimonial home in this clause, since the address has been set out in clause 2, Definitions.

Their property clause might look like this:

9.0 OTHER PROPERTY

9.1 Andre and Rainbow have divided their household contents.

9.2 Andre and Rainbow will share equally their accumulated Aeroplan points. Andre will transfer 75,000 points to Rainbow's plan.

On the breakdown of a marriage, either spouse is entitled to apply for a division of the Canada Pension Plan credits of the two spouses. The parties cannot contract out of this right.

Their Canada Pension Plan clause might look like this:

10.0 CANADA PENSION PLAN

10.1 Either party may apply for a division of Canada Pension Plan credits.

Equalization of Net Family Properties

The agreement may state that one spouse will make an equalization payment to the other spouse, or it may state that the transfers of property in the agreement are made in satisfaction of the right of either party to an equalization payment.

Assume that the parties have agreed that Andre will make an equalization payment to Rainbow of $25,000. Their equalization clause might look like this:

11.0 EQUALIZATION OF NET FAMILY PROPERTIES

11.1 Concurrently with the signing of this agreement, Andre will make an equalization payment to Rainbow of $25,000 by certified cheque.

Income Tax Implications

In Chapter 9, we discussed the income tax implications of property transfers between spouses. The separation agreement should contain clauses that address these implications.

The parties should consider whether or not they wish the automatic spousal rollover provisions of the *Income Tax Act*[15] to apply to the transfer of various properties. If they do not want the provisions to apply, they must specifically opt out of the provisions and the transferring spouse must agree to file the appropriate election with his income tax return for that year. If the automatic rollover provisions do apply, the parties should take steps to protect each other from possible capital gains attribution by agreeing to sign and file the appropriate joint election with their income tax returns.

---

15   RSC 1985, c 1 (5th Supp).

If the parties own more than one property that could qualify for the principal residence exemption, they should agree on which property will be designated as their principal residence for each of the relevant taxation years.

No special income tax clauses are required in Andre's and Rainbow's agreement.

Debts

The separation agreement should list the debts of the parties and state who will be responsible for the payment of each debt. The parties should agree to cancel any joint credit cards. They should also agree to indemnify each other if called on to pay a debt that the other party has agreed to pay.

Assume that Andre and Rainbow have no joint debts and no joint credit cards. They each have a credit card account and a car loan. Their debts clause might look like this:

12.0 DEBTS

12.1 Andre and Rainbow will each be solely responsible for payment of their own personal debts and liabilities, which include

(a) Andre's American Express bill,

(b) Andre's car loan with BMO Bank of Montreal,

(c) Rainbow's MasterCard bill, and

(d) Rainbow's car loan with Scotiabank,

and will indemnify the other from any expense or liability with respect to his or her own debts.

Releases

Separation agreements ordinarily contain several clauses by which the parties release each other from any future claims arising out of their relationship, including property claims and claims to a share in each other's estates.

Assuming that all property and other issues have been dealt with in their agreement, Andre's and Rainbow's release clause might look like this:

13.0 RELEASES

13.1 Except as otherwise provided in this agreement, Andre and Rainbow release each other from all claims either may have against the other now or in the future under the terms of any statute or the common law, including all claims under the *Divorce Act*, the *Family Law Act*, and the *Succession Law Reform Act*, for:

(a) possession of property,

(b) ownership of property,

(c) division of property,

(d) compensation for contributions to property, and

(e) an equalization payment.

13.2 Except as otherwise provided in this agreement, Andre and Rainbow release each other from all claims either may have against the other now or in the future under the terms of any statute or the common law, including claims for:

(a) a share in the other's estate,

(b) a payment as a dependant from the other's estate under the *Succession Law Reform Act*,

(c) an entitlement under the *Family Law Act*,

(d) an appointment as an attorney or guardian of the other's personal care or property under the *Substitute Decisions Act*, and

(e) participation in decisions about the other's medical care or treatment under the *Health Care Consent Act*.

13.3 Except as otherwise provided in this agreement, on the death of either party, the surviving party will not:

(a) share in any testate or intestate benefit from the estate, or

(b) act as personal representative of the deceased; and,

(c) the estate of the deceased party will be distributed as if the surviving party had died first.

Dispute Resolution

Parties often agree to a method of dispute resolution if they cannot agree on any matters—such as custody and access provisions and child support—that are subject to change under the agreement. They may wish to have these matters arbitrated or mediated rather than decided by a court.

Assume that Andre and Rainbow do not require a dispute resolution clause.

General Terms

The agreement usually concludes with a number of general clauses, including the parties' acknowledgment that

- they have made and received adequate financial disclosure,
- they have received or have had the opportunity to receive independent legal advice,
- they understand the nature and consequences of the agreement,
- the agreement is fair and reasonable, and
- the agreement is being entered into voluntarily and without duress or undue influence.

The general terms in Andre's and Rainbow's agreement might look like this:

14.0 GENERAL TERMS

14.1 The interpretation of this agreement is governed by the laws of Ontario.

14.2 This agreement binds Andre's and Rainbow's heirs, executors, administrators, and assigns.

14.3 Andre and Rainbow will each sign any documents necessary to give effect to this agreement.

14.4 Andre and Rainbow have each disclosed his or her income, assets, and other liabilities existing at the date of marriage, separation, and the date of this agreement.

14.5 Andre and Rainbow have both had independent legal advice.

14.6 Andre and Rainbow each

    (a) understands his or her rights and obligations under this agreement and its nature and consequences,

    (b) acknowledges that this agreement is fair and reasonable,

    (c) acknowledges that he or she are not under any undue influence or duress, and

    (d) acknowledges that both are signing this agreement voluntarily.

Execution

A separation agreement must be signed and witnessed. The execution page of Andre's and Rainbow's agreement might look like this:

TO EVIDENCE THEIR AGREEMENT ANDRE AND RAIINBOW HAVE SIGNED THIS AGREEMENT BEFORE A WITNESS.

DATE:

_____   _____

Witness   Andre Johnson

DATE:

_____   _____

Witness   Rainbow Johnson

You can find Andre's and Rainbow's complete separation agreement in Figure 15.1 at the end of this chapter.

Working with a Precedent Separation Agreement

Because of the length and complexity of separation agreements, lawyers usually work with a precedent agreement when they prepare a separation agreement for a client. Lawyers often also use checklists to make sure that they have addressed all relevant matters, or they may use their precedent agreement as a checklist.

In 2002, the Law Society of Ontario published a new precedent separation agreement. The agreement was prepared with the assistance of an editorial board made up of senior family law lawyers, and contains clauses to cover most situations and issues together with commentary and explanations. That precedent agreement, as updated, forms the basis of the separation agreement precedent available through the DivorceMate software package. Precedent separation agreements are also available from other legal publishers, such as Carswell.

When working with a precedent separation agreement, use a checklist or the precedent itself to determine which issues need to be addressed. Then choose the most appropriate paragraph or combination of paragraphs from the precedent for each issue. Keep in mind that the paragraphs in the precedent may require modification to reflect the agreement arrived at by the parties to your agreement.

It is important to carefully proofread the document you create—even clauses that have been computer-generated—to make sure that the precedent clause has been reprinted correctly.

CHAPTER SUMMARY

Most separating couples negotiate a settlement of all of their outstanding issues and incorporate the terms of their settlement into a separation agreement.

Under the *Family Law Act*, domestic contracts include marriage contracts, cohabitation agreements, separation agreements, paternity agreements, and family arbitration agreements. Marriage contracts are made between two persons who are married to each other or intend to marry, by which they agree on their respective rights and obligations on marriage, separation, annulment, divorce, or death. Cohabitation agreements are made between two unmarried individuals who live together or intend to live together, and deal with many of the same rights and obligations as marriage contracts. A separation agreement is made between two parties who were living together and have separated, by which they agree on their respective rights and obligations on separation. A paternity agreement is between a man and woman (not

spouses) for payment of expenses relating to the child and mother. A family arbitration agreement is an agreement to refer issues to a family arbitration, resulting in a family arbitration award. A family arbitration award is not enforceable unless the family arbitration takes place in accordance with the Act.

Separating couples may negotiate to settle their outstanding issues using traditional methods, mediation, or collaborative law.

There is no such thing as a standard separation agreement. The facts of each situation are unique and a separation agreement must be carefully tailored to meet the needs of the particular couple. However, most separation agreements contain similar types of clauses and are organized in a similar fashion. Because of the length and complexity of separation agreements, lawyers usually work with a precedent agreement in preparing a separation agreement for a client.

KEY TERMS

cohabitation agreement, 327
collaborative law, 331
domestic contract, 326
family arbitration, 328
family arbitration agreement, 328
family arbitration award, 328

marriage contract, 326
mediation, 330
paternity agreement, 327
secondary arbitration, 328
separation agreement, 327
tenants in common, 341

REVIEW QUESTIONS

1. What part of the *Family Law Act* deals with separation agreements?

2. What is the definition of a "domestic contract"?

3. What is the definition of a "marriage contract"?

4. What may a marriage contract *not* do?

5. What is the definition of a "cohabitation agreement"?

6. What may a cohabitation agreement *not* do?

7. What are the formal requirements for domestic contracts?

8. In what ways do the provisions of the *Family Law Act* limit the freedom of the parties to set the terms of their domestic contract?

9. What is the first step in the process when lawyers try to negotiate a separation agreement for their clients?

10. What preliminary matters are usually dealt with in a separation agreement?

11. What issues do the custody and access clauses of a separation agreement deal with?

12. What should be included in the child support clauses of a separation agreement?

13. Under what circumstances, generally, will the parties agree that they will provide no spousal support for each other?

14. Under what circumstances, generally, will the parties agree that spousal support should be paid in a lump sum?

15. What is the purpose of a spousal support release clause?

16. Why do separation agreements contain life insurance clauses?

17. If the parties wish to transfer title of the matrimonial home from both spouses to one spouse, what matters should the matrimonial home clause of a separation agreement address?

18. If the parties wish the matrimonial home to be sold, what matters should the matrimonial home clause of a separation agreement address?

19. What should a separation agreement specify with respect to the other property of the parties?

20. What should a separation agreement specify with respect to an equalization of net family property?

21. What should a separation agreement specify with respect to the debts of the parties?

DRAFTING QUESTIONS

1. The husband has agreed to pay $1,000 per month for the support of the wife for a period of five years, whether or not the wife remarries or cohabits with another person. The parties agree that the support payments will end if the husband dies because he will be providing life insurance to take the place of the support payments. Working with a precedent separation agreement, draft the support clauses. What other clauses should the agreement contain?

2. A husband and wife jointly own a matrimonial home at 25 Lyndhurst Avenue in Toronto. The parties have agreed that the matrimonial home is to be sold as soon as possible. They have agreed to accept the first reasonable offer they receive, and to split the proceeds of sale equally after paying off the mortgage on the property and any costs of the sale. They have also agreed that the wife will have exclusive possession of the home until it is sold. During that time, the wife will be responsible for the utilities, mortgage, and insurance payments, and both parties will be equally responsible for the realty taxes and any repairs. Working with a precedent separation agreement, draft the matrimonial home clauses. What tax clauses should this agreement contain?

DISCUSSION QUESTIONS

1. Look at clause 3.0—Custody and Access—of Andre's and Rainbow's separation agreement, and answer the following questions:

   a. When will the children be with each parent on a weekly basis?

   b. Which parent has the children for the Christmas holiday this school year?

   c. Which parent has the children for the spring break holiday this school year?

2. Look at clause 4.0—Child Support—of Andre's and Rainbow's separation agreement, and answer the following questions:

   a. Does child support end if the child is 21 and in full-time attendance at UBC living in residence?

   b. Does child support end if the child is 23 and in full-time attendance at York University, living at home?

   c. Does child support end if the child is 19, living at home, and not in school?

   d. Does child support end if the child is 21, living at home, and has just obtained a diploma from Seneca college?

FIGURE 15.1 Sample Separation Agreement

THIS IS A SEPARATION AGREEMENT DATED NOVEMBER 15, 2017

Between:

Rainbow Johnson	("Rainbow")
AND	
Andre Johnson	("Andre")

1.0 BACKGROUND

1.1 Rainbow and Andre were married on January 1, 1999.

1.2 They separated on August 1, 2017. The parties will continue to live separate and apart.

1.3 They have four children, Zoey Johnson ("Zoey"), born April 15, 2000, Andre Johnson Jr. ("Andre Jr."), born October 15, 2012, Jack Johnson ("Jack"), born March 5, 2008, and Diane Johnson ("Diane"), born March 5, 2008.

1.4 They agree to be bound by his agreement which settles all issues between them.

2.0 DEFINITIONS

2.1 In this agreement:
  (a) "children" means Zoey, Andre Jr., Jack, and Diane;
  (b) "equalization payment" means the payment referred to in section 5(1) of the *Family Law Act*;
  (c) "CRA" means Canada Revenue Agency;
  (d) "FRO" means the Family Responsibility Office described in the *Family Responsibility and Support Arrears Enforcement Act*, or any successor support enforcement agency;
  (e) "Guidelines" means the Federal *Child Support Guidelines*, as defined in section 2(1) of the *Divorce Act*,
  (f) "matrimonial home" means the property at 145 Ellsworth Avenue in Toronto;
  (g) "net family property" means net family property as defined in the *Family Law Act*; and
  (h) "property" means property as defined in the *Family Law Act*.

3.0 CUSTODY AND ACCESS

3.1 Rainbow will have custody of the children. Andre will have access to the children (which will include the right to have them stay overnight) as follows:
  (a) Every second weekend from Friday after school to Sunday at 8:00 p.m.
  (b) During the entire spring holiday and entire Christmas holiday in every odd-numbered year. He will not exercise weekend access during these holidays in even-numbered years.
  (c) For one month of his choice during the summer school holiday, and he will advise Rainbow in writing of his choice by no later than the preceding March 1st.

3.2 Rainbow will have the right to have the children with her for a continuous and uninterrupted period of one month during the summer school holiday.

FIGURE 15.1   Sample Separation Agreement   Continued

3.3   Andre will have the right to communicate with the children at any reasonable time by telephone and/or email.

3.4   Andre will have the right to be fully advised of the school progress (including the right to have copies of report cards and notices of school events) and the health and general welfare of the children.

4.0   CHILD SUPPORT

4.1   Commencing on December 1, 2017, and on the first day of each subsequent month, Andre will pay to Rainbow for the support of the four children the sum of $2,659 in accordance with the child support guideline tables.

4.2   Andre will no longer be obliged to pay support for a child referred to in paragraph 4.1 above when one of the following events occurs:

(a)   the child ceases to reside full time with Rainbow. "Reside full time" includes the child living away from home to attend an educational institution, pursue summer employment, or take a vacation while otherwise maintaining a residence with Rainbow;

(b)   the child becomes 18 years of age and ceases to be in full-time attendance at an educational institution;

(c)   the child obtains his or her first post-secondary degree or diploma;

(d)   the child becomes 22 years of age;

(e)   the child marries;

(f)   the child dies; or

(g)   Andre dies, so long as he has complied with his obligations pursuant to paragraph 6.0 of this agreement to provide life insurance.

4.3   Andre represents that his income (as defined by the child support guidelines) at the date of this agreement is $120,000 per year.

4.4   If Andre's obligation to support a child ends, the parties will determine the support payable for the other children at that time under the child support guidelines.

5.0   SPOUSAL SUPPORT

5.1   Andre will pay Rainbow $25,000 on execution of this agreement.

5.2   Upon payment, Andre and Rainbow will each be financially independent of each other and will release his or her right to spousal support from the other forever. Andre and Rainbow intend this agreement to inoculate them from any judicial review.

5.3   Andre and Rainbow know that their financial circumstances, health, employment or the cost of living may all change. They may be unable to work for various reasons, or earn less than they expect. These changes may be catastrophic, unanticipated or beyond imagining. Nevertheless, no change will ever entitle Andre or Rainbow to spousal support from the other.

5.4   Andre and Rainbow do not want any court to order a change which deviates from or overrides the terms of this agreement, especially this release. Andre and Rainbow want the court to uphold this agreement in its entirety because they are basing their future lives upon this release.

FIGURE 15.1 Sample Separation Agreement Continued

5.5 This agreement recognizes all economic advantages or disadvantages to the parties aris-ing from the marriage and its breakdown, has apportioned between them all financial consequences arising from the care of the children in addition to any obligation for the support of the children, relieves any economic hardship arising from the marriage break-down and, insofar as is practicable, promotes the economic self-sufficiency of Andre and Rainbow within a reasonable period of time.

5.6 No change in the circumstances of Andre and Rainbow, or both, will be considered a ma-terial change justifying any spousal support. All changes will be considered immaterial to their rights and obligations under this agreement. Andre and Rainbow have either an-ticipated all changes as possibilities or have decided to take the risk that there will be changes. This agreement meets the objectives under the *Divorce Act* and is fair to both parties. For example, if Rainbow loses her job and for any reason cannot find work and therefore has no income, and Andre's income and financial position have vastly improved from what they are now (or vice versa), these facts will not be a material change justify-ing any spousal support award. They will be considered and are considered now by Andre and Rainbow to be immaterial.

6.0 LIFE INSURANCE

6.1 Andre will keep a life insurance policy ("the policy") on his life in the amount of $500,000, naming Rainbow as the irrevocable beneficiary for as long as he is obligated to pay child support.

6.2 Within 14 days of signing this agreement, Andre will provide Rainbow with a copy of the policy and the irrevocable beneficiary designation.

6.3 Andre will pay all policy premiums when due. If he does not and Rainbow pays any premiums, interest or penalties to prevent the policy from lapsing, Andre will reim-burse Rainbow for such payments. If the policy lapses because Andre failed to pay the premiums, Andre will also pay Rainbow all necessary costs incurred by her to reinstate the policy.

6.4 When Andre's obligation to pay child support ends, Andre's obligation to maintain the policy ends. When it does, Rainbow will provide Andre's insurer with a direction to with-draw the policy's irrevocable designation. If she does not, Andre may obtain a court or-der directing the insurer to do so. Rainbow will be responsible for the costs Andre incurs in obtaining the order.

7.0 MEDICAL AND DENTAL BENEFITS

7.1 Andre will maintain his medical, extended health and dental coverage through his em-ployment for Rainbow and the children for as long as it is available to him for their benefit. He will immediately reimburse Rainbow for all amounts recovered by him for expenses incurred by her for herself or the children.

8.0 MATRIMONIAL HOME

8.1 Andre and Rainbow own the matrimonial home jointly.

8.2 Andre hereby transfers all of his right, title, and interest in the matrimonial home to Rainbow.

FIGURE 15.1   Sample Separation Agreement Continued

8.3   Concurrently with the signing of this agreement, Andre will sign a transfer of the matrimonial home.

8.4   Rainbow will pay the cost of the preparation and registration of the transfer.

9.0   OTHER PROPERTY

9.1   Andre and Rainbow have divided their household contents.

9.2   Andre and Rainbow will share equally their accumulated Aeroplan points. Andre will transfer 75,000 points to Rainbow's plan.

10.0   CANADA PENSION PLAN

10.1   Either party may apply for a division of Canada Pension Plan credits.

11.0   EQUALIZATION OF NET FAMILY PROPERTIES

11.1   Concurrently with the signing of this agreement, Andre will make an equalization payment to Rainbow of $25,000 by certified cheque.

12.0   DEBTS

12.1   Andre and Rainbow will each be solely responsible for payment of their own personal debts and liabilities, which include:
(a)   Andre's American Express bill,
(b)   Andre's car loan with BMO Bank of Montreal,
(c)   Rainbow's MasterCard bill, and
(d)   Rainbow's car loan with ScotiaBank, and will indemnify the other from any expense or liability with respect to his or her own debts.

13.0   RELEASES

13.1   Except as otherwise provided in this agreement, Andre and Rainbow release each other from all claims either may have against the other now or in the future under the terms of any statute or the common law, including all claims under the *Divorce Act*, the *Family Law Act*, and the *Succession Law Reform Act*, for:
(a)   possession of property,
(b)   ownership of property,
(c)   division of property,
(d)   compensation for contributions to property, and
(e)   an equalization payment.

13.2   Except as otherwise provided in this agreement, Andre and Rainbow release each other from all claims either may have against the other now or in the future under the terms of any statute or the common law, including claims for:
(a)   a share in the other's estate,
(b)   a payment as a dependant from the other's estate under the *Succession Law Reform Act*,
(c)   an entitlement under the *Family Law Act*,
(d)   an appointment as an attorney or guardian of the other's personal care or property under the *Substitute Decisions Act*, and
(e)   participation in decisions about the other's medical care or treatment under the *Health Care Consent Act*.

FIGURE 15.1 Sample Separation Agreement **Concluded**

13.3 Except as otherwise provided in this agreement, on the death of either party, the surviving party will not:

(a) share in any testate or intestate benefit from the estate, or

(b) act as personal representative of the deceased; and,

(c) the estate of the deceased party will be distributed as if the surviving party had died first.

14.0 GENERAL TERMS

14.1 The interpretation of this agreement is governed by the laws of Ontario.

14.2 This agreement binds Andre's and Rainbow's heirs, executors, administrators, and assigns.

14.3 Andre and Rainbow will each sign any documents necessary to give effect to this agreement.

14.4 Andre and Rainbow have each disclosed his or her income, assets, and other liabilities existing at the date of marriage, separation, and the date of this agreement.

14.5 Andre and Rainbow have both had independent legal advice.

14.6 Andre and Rainbow each:

(a) understands his or her rights and obligations under this agreement and its nature and consequences,

(b) acknowledges that this agreement is fair and reasonable,

(c) acknowledges that he or she are not under any undue influence or duress, and

(d) acknowledges that both are signing this agreement voluntarily.

TO EVIDENCE THEIR AGREEMENT ANDRE AND RAINBOW HAVE SIGNED THIS AGREEMENT BEFORE A WITNESS.

DATE:

_____   _____
Witness   Andre Johnson

DATE:

_____   _____
Witness   Rainbow Johnson

Variation and Indexing of Orders and Agreements

16

LEARNING OUTCOMES

After completing this chapter, you should be able to:

■ Discuss variation of custody orders under both the *Divorce Act* and the *Children's Law Reform Act*.

■ Discuss variation of spousal support orders under both the *Divorce Act* and the *Family Law Act*.

■ Discuss variation of child support orders under both the *Divorce Act* and the *Family Law Act*.

■ Explain the procedure on a variation application.

■ Explain what is meant by "indexing" of support orders.

■ State the circumstances under which spousal support provisions may be indexed.

■ Calculate the annual increase in a spousal support order under the *Family Law Act*.

■ Calculate the annual increase in a spousal support provision under a domestic contract.

Introduction

A custody or access order, whether made under the *Divorce Act*[1] or the *Family Law Act*,[2] is never final. It is always subject to variation if the circumstances of the parties and/or the children change. Orders for spousal and child support under both the *Divorce Act* and the *Family Law Act* may also be varied by the court if there has been a change in circumstances of any of the parties. In addition, orders for spousal support may be indexed to the cost of living.

In this chapter we will look at

- variation of custody orders,
- variation of spousal support orders,
- variation of child support orders,
- administrative recalculation of child support orders,
- procedure on a variation application, and
- indexing of spousal support.

Variation of Custody Orders

Custody orders under both the *Divorce Act* and the *Children's Law Reform Act*[3] may be varied. A custody order made under the *Divorce Act* must be varied under the *Divorce Act*. A custody order made under the *Children's Law Reform Act* must be varied under the *Children's Law Reform Act*.

Variation Under the Divorce Act

Variation of custody (and support) orders is dealt with under section 17 of the Act.

A variation proceeding may be commenced by either or both former spouses or by any other person, although a person other than a former spouse requires leave of the court. The court has the power to vary, rescind, or suspend a custody order or any provision thereof. The court may include in a variation order any provisions that could be included in a custody order.

Section 17(5) sets out the factors the court is to consider in a variation proceeding. It states that before the court makes a variation order, the court must satisfy itself that there has been a change in the condition, means, needs, or other circumstances of the child that occurred since the making of the custody order. The section also states that, in making the variation order, the court must take into consideration only the best interests of the child as determined by reference to that change. Section 17(5.1) states that for the purposes of subsection (5), a former spouse's terminal illness or critical condition shall be considered a change of circumstances of the child of the marriage, and the court shall make a variation order in respect of access that is in the best interests of the child.

---

1   RSC 1985, c 3 (2d Supp).
2   RSO 1990, c F.3.
3   RSO 1990, c C.12.

As when making a custody order, pursuant to section 17(6), the court is not to take into consideration the past conduct of any person unless the conduct is relevant to the ability of that person to act as a parent of the child. The court is also directed, in section 17(9), to give effect to the principle that a child of the marriage should have as much contact with each former spouse as is consistent with the best interests of the child. For that purpose, where the variation order would grant custody of the child to a person who does not currently have custody, the court is directed to take into consideration the willingness of the person seeking custody to facilitate that contact.

Variation Under the Children's Law Reform Act

Variation of custody orders is dealt with under section 29. According to that section, a court must not make an order that varies a custody or access order unless there has been a material change in circumstances that affects or is likely to affect the best interests of the child.

Principles Applied in Varying Custody Orders

While the language of the statutes differs, a court will apply the same principles whether a case is decided under the *Children's Law Reform Act* or the *Divorce Act*.

Under either statute, the party applying to vary the original order must show that there has been a *material change* in circumstances since the original order was made that affects the best interests of the child. If this threshold test is met, then the court will consider whether a variation in the existing order is necessary to meet the best interests of the child under these changed circumstances.

A variation application is not an appeal. It is not designed to correct an error made by the trial judge. Rather, it is assumed that the original order was correctly made.

Variation of Spousal Support Orders

Spousal support orders under both the *Divorce Act* and the *Family Law Act* may be varied. A support order made under the *Divorce Act* must be varied under the *Divorce Act*. A support order made under the *Family Law Act* must be varied under the *Family Law Act*.

Under section 17(4.1) of the *Divorce Act*, the court must be satisfied that there has been a change in the condition, means, needs, or other circumstances of either former spouse since the making of the spousal support order. Under section 37(2) of the *Family Law Act*, the court must be satisfied that there has been a material change in the dependant's or respondent's circumstances, or that evidence not available on the previous hearing has become available.

Variation of Child Support Orders

Child support orders under both the *Divorce Act* and the *Family Law Act* may be varied. A support order made under the *Divorce Act* must be varied under the *Divorce Act*. A support order made under the *Family Law Act* must be varied under the *Family Law Act*.

Both the *Divorce Act* (in section 17(4)) and the *Family Law Act* (in section 37(2.1)) provide for variation of child support orders in the event of a change of circumstances as provided for in the *Child Support Guidelines*.[4] In addition, the *Family Law Act* allows for variation if evidence not available on the previous hearing has become available.

Section 14 of the guidelines sets out the changes in circumstances that would justify a variation:

- if child support was previously determined in accordance with the tables, any change in circumstances that would result in a different child support order; or
- if child support was previously determined without reference to the tables, any change in the condition, means, needs, or other circumstances of either parent or spouse or of any child who is entitled to support.

Administrative Recalculation of Child Support

Instead of court proceedings, the parent seeking a variation in child support may be able to use the online Child Support Calculation Service to vary the existing support payments by a process known as "recalculation." Please refer back to Chapter 8 for a detailed discussion of administrative recalculation of child support.

Procedure on a Variation Application

Rule 15 of the *Family Law Rules*[5] governs variation proceedings, which are called "motions to change a final order or agreement." A variation proceeding is brought by way of a motion in the proceeding in which the order was made.

According to Rule 15(4), Rule 5 governs where the case is to be started as if the motion were a new case.

Under Rule 15(5), the party seeking the variation must serve a motion to change (Form 15) and a change information form (Form 15A) with all required attachments. Under Rule 15(5.1), if the motion includes a claim for custody of or access to a child, the party seeking the variation must also serve an affidavit in support of claim for custody or access (Form 35.1). The party making the motion is also required under Rule 15(6) to serve a blank response to motion to change (Form 15B) and a blank consent motion to change (Form 15C). Under Rule 15(7), these documents must be served by special service.

Under Rule 15(9) the responding party may either dispute or consent to the motion. If disputing, the responding party must serve and file a response to motion to change (Form 15B); if consenting, the respondent party must complete and return to the moving party a consent motion to change (Form 15C). Under Rule 15(10)

---

4   O Reg 391/97.

5   O Reg 114/99.

those documents must be served and filed or returned within 30 days if the party resides in Canada or the United States, and 60 days if the party resides elsewhere.

Rules 15(16) through 15(19) set out the procedure to be followed where the parties consent to the change. Rule 15(21) sets out the procedure to be followed where the moving party is seeking a change to child support that is not in accordance with the child support guidelines.

Rule 15(22) gives the moving party the right to file an affidavit instead of a change information form. Rule 15(23) gives the responding party the right to file an affidavit instead of a response to motion to change.

Our client is Phil Dunphy. He and his former wife, Claire Dunphy, were divorced on December 15, 2015. The divorce order, made by Mr. Justice Smart, gave Claire custody of their three children: Hayley Dunphy, born 31 May 2003, Alex Dunphy, born 22 December 2005, and Luke Dunphy, born 18 October 2007, subject to reasonable access by Phil. Phil was ordered to pay child support of $1,845 per month and spousal support of $750 per month. At the time, Claire, a full-time mother, was not employed outside the home. However, she recently returned to work and is now earning $60,000 per year. Phil now wants the divorce order varied to terminate Claire's spousal support since she is now self-supporting. He is not seeking any other changes to the order.

The parties were married on October 25, 2001, in Newmarket. The original divorce proceeding was commenced by Claire, as applicant, in Newmarket as action number 13579-15. Claire was born on April 6, 1975, and lives at 307 Gloria Road, Newmarket, L3K 2Y7. Phil was born on June 11, 1973, and lives at 2745 Cameron Court, Newmarket, L1S 3H5.

Phil's motion to change will be a motion in the original proceeding—13579-15. Because the parties and the children all reside in Newmarket, the motion will be brought in the Superior Court of Justice, Family Branch, in Newmarket.

Step 1: Schedule the Motion

Contact the court office to get a date for the motion to be heard.

Step 2: Complete the Forms

You must prepare the following forms:

- a motion to change (Form 15),
- a change information form (Form 15A),
- a financial statement (Form 13), and
- a continuing record.

Phil's motion to change form is found in Figure 16.1 at the end of this chapter, and his change information form is found in Figure 16.2 at the end of this chapter.

Step 3: Serve the Documents

According to Rule 15(7), the documents must be served on Claire by special service, along with a blank response to motion to change (Form 15B) and a blank consent motion to change (Form 15C). A blank response to motion to change is found at the end of this chapter as Figure 16.3, and a blank consent motion to change as Figure 16.4.

Step 4: Wait for Claire to Defend

According to rule 15(10), Claire will have 30 days to respond. If she disputes the motion, she must serve and file a response to motion to change (Form 15B); if she consents to the motion, she must complete and return to the moving party a consent motion to change (Form 15C).

If Claire defends, the motion will proceed like a regular motion. See Chapter 13.

Indexing Spousal Support

The amount of spousal support, whether set by order or agreement, is determined on the basis of the recipient's need and the payor's ability to pay. The need of the recipient is calculated on the basis of his or her expenses at the time the order is made or the agreement is entered into.

If the cost of living goes up after the support amount is set, the recipient's expenses will also go up. Over time, the support payment will no longer be adequate to meet the needs of the recipient.

Historically, a recipient whose support payments became inadequate as a result of inflation would have to bring a proceeding to vary the support order or separation agreement based on a change in circumstances. These applications were expensive, and the recipient would have to wait until the inflationary change was large enough to constitute a "material" change in circumstances.

Now, courts have the power to order that spousal support orders be "indexed" to changes in the cost of living so that they rise automatically. It is also customary for support payments in separation agreements to be similarly indexed. The clauses that provide for indexing are called "cost of living adjustment (COLA) clauses."

Power to Index Spousal Support

Spousal support may be indexed in the following circumstances:

- *A new order under the Family Law Act.* Section 34(5) of the Act gives the court the power to order that periodic support payments be indexed to the cost of living at the time the support order is made.

- *An existing order under the Family Law Act.* Sections 38 and 39 of the Act give the court the power to index a support order that was not indexed at the time it was made. Indexing in this situation is not automatic. Pursuant to section 38(3), the court has discretion to refuse to index the support payments, although the presumption is in favour of indexing.

- *Orders under the Divorce Act.* Although the *Divorce Act* does not contain a provision that specifically authorizes indexing, the Supreme Court of Canada in *Richardson v Richardson*[6] held that the court has the power to order indexing under the Act.

- *New domestic contracts.* The parties may agree in a domestic contract to index support payments. If they do so, the parties may fashion their own rules for indexing, which are binding on both parties.

- *Existing domestic contracts.* A domestic contract that is silent on the issue of indexing may be filed with the Ontario Court of Justice under section 35 of the *Family Law Act*. It is then treated as if it were a court order for the purposes of indexing under section 38 of the Act. A domestic contract that bars variation of spousal support generally, or indexing specifically, may not be indexed.[7]

Measuring Inflation

The government of Canada, through its central statistical agency, Statistics Canada, maintains statistics to track changes in consumer prices and thus measure changes in the cost of living and the rate of inflation.[8]

The consumer price index (CPI) is an indicator of the changes in consumer prices. It is obtained by comparing, over a period of time, the cost of selected goods and services. This "basket" of goods is priced at 100 as of a specific date, which acts as the time base or base period of the index. The current CPI time base or base period is 2002. It is standard practice when quoting an index level to note the base year.

The same basket of goods is then priced every month, and the increase (or, rarely, decrease) in prices compared with that base period cost of 100 can be measured.

If the cost of the basket of goods in the first year after the base year is 125, the increase is 25 points. The percentage change over the base year is

$$\frac{25}{100} = 25\%$$

If the cost of the basket of goods goes up to 150 in the second year, the percentage change for that year over the base year is another 25/100 or another 25 percent. The total change in the two years since the base year is 50 points, for a total percentage change from the base year of 50 percent.

What is the percentage change between the prices at the end of the first year and the end of the second year?

Absolute change in CPI:

CPI year 2 of 150 − CPI year 1 of 125 = 25 points

---

6   [1987] 1 SCR 857, 1987 CanLII 58 (SCC).

7   See section 35(4).

8   The Statistics Canada website is <http://www.statcan.ca>.

Percentage change in CPI:

$$\frac{\text{Absolute change } 25}{\text{CPI year 1 of } 125} = 20\%$$

Statistics Canada maintains a number of different consumer price indexes for different items and locations. For example, there is a CPI for all items for Canada, and a CPI for all items for the City of Toronto. The CPI is published monthly and is available at the Statistics Canada website at <http://www.statcan.gc.ca>. More "user-friendly" CPI tables may be found at the Bank of Canada website (<http://www.bankofcanada.ca>).

How Indexing Works

All indexing formulas, whether in support orders or separation agreements, have the following ingredients in common:

1. *Payment change date.* This is the date on which the amount of the payment changes. The change occurs at regular intervals, usually annually.
2. *Indexing factor.* This is a method of measuring the change in the cost of living together with a formula for increasing payments in proportion to increases in the cost of living.

The CPI is the most commonly used indexing factor. Another common way to index support payments is to tie them to increases in the payor's income.

Indexing Under the Family Law Act

In order to determine the payment change date and the indexing factor, it is necessary to follow the instructions in sections 34(5) and 34(6) of the Act, which read as follows:

(5) In an order made under clause (1)(a), other than an order for the support of a child, the court may provide that the amount payable shall be increased annually on the order's anniversary date by the indexing factor, as defined in subsection (6), for November of the previous year.

(6) The indexing factor for a given month is the percentage change in the Consumer Price Index for Canada for prices of all items since the same month of the previous year, as published by Statistics Canada.

Section 34(5) tells us that the payment change date is the "anniversary date" of the order. The relevant date is the day the order was made, as indicated on the face of the order.

Section 34(6) tells us that the indexing factor is the change in the CPI over a one-year period *ending* in the month of November in the year before the anniversary date.

Assume that a court made an order on April 7, 2015, with support payments of $1,000 to be paid on the 15th of each month, starting with April 15, 2015. The Consumer Price Index for Canada for prices of all items for November 2014 is 120, and for November 2015 is 125. Calculate the increase in support in 2016.

Payment change date

The anniversary of the order: April 7, 2016

Indexing factor

Section 34(5) directs us to use the indexing factor for "November of the previous year"—in other words, November of the year before the payment change date, or November 2015.

   The indexing factor for November 2015 is defined in section 34(6) to be the percentage change in the CPI "since the same month of the previous year," or November 2014. Accordingly, we are directed to measure the percentage change in the CPI between November 2014 and November 2015.

   To calculate the increase in CPI and the increase in the amount payable, use the following formula:

$$\frac{\text{CPI end of period}}{\text{CPI beginning of period}} \times \begin{array}{c} \text{Current support} \\ \text{amount} \end{array} = \begin{array}{c} \text{New support} \\ \text{amount} \end{array}$$

$$\frac{\text{CPI November 2015 of 125}}{\text{CPI November 2014 of 120}} \times \$1,000 = \$1,041.67$$

   $1,041.67 is the increased amount of support to be paid on the first payment *after* the anniversary date, in this case April 15, 2016. Note that, as in this case, payment in the increased amount is not necessarily due on the anniversary date, since the date on which payment is due is not necessarily the day on which the order was made.

   For the next anniversary date, the increase would be calculated as follows, assuming that the Consumer Price Index for Canada for prices of all items for November 2016 is 131.

Payment change date

The next anniversary of the order: April 7, 2017

Indexing factor

Use the indexing factor for November 2016:

$$\frac{\text{CPI November 2016 of 131}}{\text{CPI November 2015 of 125}} \times \$1,041.67 = \$1,091.67$$

Indexing Under Domestic Contracts

It is not unusual for domestic contracts to include a provision for the indexing of spousal support. An example of an indexing clause is as follows (assuming that the husband is paying spousal support and the agreement was signed in 2015):

15.0 COST OF LIVING CLAUSE

15.1 (a) The amount of spousal support payable pursuant to paragraph ___ of this agreement will change at one-year intervals in accordance with the all-items Consumer Price Index for the City of Toronto with base year 2002 equal to 100, as provided by Statistics Canada.

(b) This change in amount will occur on the first day of June of each year in which support is payable, starting with June 1, 2016 [the next following year]. This change will be equal to 100 percent of the percentage change in the Consumer Price Index:

(i) for the June 2016 change, in the period from the month of execution of this agreement to April 2016 and

(ii) for each subsequent change, in the 12-month period from the previous April to the April of the year of the current change.

15.2 (a) In case of an increase in support payments, if in any such year the husband's income for the December to December period before the proposed increase in support payments does not increase at the same or greater percentage than the percentage increase in the cost of living calculated in paragraph 15.1, at the husband's option the increase in support payments will be equal to this percentage increase in the husband's income, so calculated.

(b) For the purpose of paragraph 15.2(a), income means income as defined in the *Income Tax Act*, without reduction of employment expenses or gross up for dividends.

(c) If the husband chooses to rely on paragraph 15.2(a), he will, no later than May 1, produce to the wife a copy of his income tax return for the two immediately preceding years, which will form the basis of the calculation of his percentage increase in income.

This indexing clause gives the payor husband the choice of two methods for calculating the increase in payments, and the right to choose the method most advantageous to him.

The first method uses the CPI[9] to determine the indexing factor and a payment change date chosen by the parties (although it may not be the anniversary of the date on which the contract was signed).

---

9   Note that the agreement uses the CPI for Toronto, not the CPI for Canada, as is used in the *Family Law Act*. Remember to use the appropriate CPI figures when doing your indexing calculations.

In the first year, the indexing factor requires measurement of the CPI from the date of execution of the agreement to April of the year on which the first change occurs, and thereafter from April to April. This provision "catches" increases in the cost of living from the time the agreement is signed.

June 1 is picked as the payment change date even though that is not the anniversary date of the agreement. This date gives the parties enough time to obtain the CPI figures for the April to April interval used to determine the indexing factor. The date also allows the payor to file his income tax return (due by April 30), calculate the increase in taxable income, and decide whether he wants to pay increased support based on the increase in income or the increase in CPI.

Here's how the first CPI increase would be calculated:

Assume that the contract was executed on March 1, 2015, the payment is $1,000 per month, and the CPI for March 2015 is 120 and for April 2016 is 127.

Payment change date
As specified in the agreement: June 1, 2016

Indexing factor
The change in CPI between March 2015 and April 2016:

$$\frac{\text{CPI April 2016 of 127}}{\text{CPI March 2015 of 120}} \times \$1{,}000 = \$1{,}058.33$$

As of June 1, 2016 the payments will increase from $1,000 to $1,058.33.

Here's how the second CPI increase would be calculated:

Assume that the CPI for April 2017 is 131.

Payment change date
As specified in the agreement: June 1, 2017

Indexing factor
The change in CPI between April 2016 and April 2017:

$$\frac{\text{CPI April 2017 of 131}}{\text{CPI April 2016 of 127}} \times \$1{,}058.33 = \$1{,}091.66$$

As of June 1, 2017, the payments will increase from $1,058.33 to $1,091.66.

Before making the increased payment in either year, the husband in this example will want to see whether his income has increased as much as the CPI in order to choose the least expensive mode of calculation.

For the June 2016 increase, use the husband's income reported for the taxation years 2015 and 2014. On April 30, 2016, the payor will have just filed his income tax return for the 2015 taxation year, so the 2015 taxation year information is the most current information available in June 2016.

Assume that the payor's 2014 income was $60,000 and his 2015 income was $72,000.

Payment change date
As specified in the agreement: June 1, 2016

Indexing factor

Percentage change in income from taxation year 2014 to taxation year 2015:

$$\frac{\text{2015 income of \$72,000}}{\text{2014 income of \$60,000}} \times \$1,000 = \$1,200.00$$

Clearly, the payor will elect to use the CPI increase and pay $1,058.33 rather than base the change in payments on the increase in income, which would result in a payment of $1,200.00.

CHAPTER SUMMARY

No custody or access order is ever final. It is always subject to variation if the circumstances of the parties and/or the children change.

A custody order made under the *Divorce Act* must be varied under the *Divorce Act*. The court must be satisfied that there has been a change in the child's situation since the previous order was made. The court must take into consideration only the best interests of the child as determined by reference to that change. A custody order made under the *Children's Law Reform Act* must be varied under the *Children's Law Reform Act*. Under that Act, a court will not make a variation on a custody order unless there has been a material change in circumstances that affects the best interests of the child.

A spousal support order made under the *Divorce Act* must be varied under the *Divorce Act*. The court must be satisfied that there has been a change in the circumstances of either spouse. A spousal support order made under the *Family Law Act* must be varied under the *Family Law Act*. The court must be satisfied that there has been a material change in circumstances or that evidence not available on the previous hearing has become available.

Child support orders under both the *Divorce Act* and the *Family Law Act* may be varied if circumstances change as provided for in the *Child Support Guidelines*.

Variation proceedings are governed by Rule 15 of the *Family Law Rules*. A variation proceeding is brought by way of a motion in the proceeding in which the original order was made. It is started by service of a motion to change.

Under the *Family Law Act*, the court has the power to order that spousal support orders be indexed to changes in the cost of living (inflation) so that they rise automatically. It is also customary for support payments in separation agreements to be similarly indexed. The Consumer Price Index (CPI) is the most commonly used measure of inflation.

REVIEW QUESTIONS

1. What section of the *Divorce Act* deals with variation of custody orders?

2. Under the *Divorce Act*, what factors must the court consider on a proceeding to vary a custody order?

3. What section of the *Children's Law Reform Act* governs variation of custody orders?

4. What must a party show when applying to vary a custody order?

5. How is a variation application different from an appeal?

6. What section of the *Divorce Act* deals with variation of spousal support orders?

7. What section of the *Family Law Act* deals with variation of spousal support orders?

8. Under section 14 of the *Child Support Guidelines*, what changes in circumstances justify a variation in a child support order?

9. What rule governs variation proceedings in the Superior Court of Justice Family Court?

10. What is a cost of living adjustment (COLA) clause?

11. What is the consumer price index?

12. In what circumstances may spousal support be indexed?

13. What is the "payment change date" in an indexing formula?

14. What is the "indexing factor" in an indexing formula?

15. What is the indexing factor under the *Family Law Act*?

EXERCISE

A support order was made on June 19, 2015. The order provides as follows:

> The husband shall pay to the wife for her support the sum of $1,000 per month commencing on the first day of July 2015 and on the first day of every month thereafter.

The order also contains a provision by which it is indexed under the *Family Law Act*.

Assume the following CPI data:

2014:	JAN-101	FEB-101	MAR-101	APR-102	MAY-102	JUN-102
	JUL-103	AUG-103	SEP-103	OCT-103	NOV-104	DEC-105
2015:	JAN-105	FEB-105	MAR-105	APR-106	MAY-106	JUN-106
	JUL-107	AUG-107	SEP-107	OCT-107	NOV-108	DEC-109
2016:	JAN-109	FEB-109	MAR-109	APR-110	MAY-110	JUN-110
	JUL-111	AUG-111	SEP-111	OCT-111	NOV-112	DEC-113

When will the first increase of the order take place? When will it take effect? What will the new support payment be?

When will the next increase of the order take place? When will it take effect? What will the new support payment be?

DRAFTING QUESTION

Our client is Leo Marcus. He and his former wife, Grace Marcus, were divorced on October 15, 2015. The divorce order, made by Mme. Justice Good, gave Grace custody of their two children: Jack Marcus, born 12 January 2005, and Karen Marcus, born 14 November 2007, subject to reasonable access by Leo. Leo was ordered to pay child support of $1,660 per month and spousal support of $1,000 per month. At the time, Grace, a full-time mother, was not employed outside the home. However, she recently returned to work and is now earning $75,000 per year. Leo now wants the divorce order varied to terminate

Grace's spousal support since she is now self-supporting. He is not seeking any other changes to the order.

The parties were married on June 6, 2003, in Toronto. The original divorce proceeding was commenced by Grace, as applicant, in Toronto as action number 24680-15. Grace was born on December 7, 1978, and lives at 350 Truman Road, Toronto, M3K 2Y7. Leo was born on February 14, 1975, and lives at 2300 Walker Court, Toronto, M1S 3H5.

Draft Leo's Motion to Change and Change Information Form.

FIGURE 16.1   Form 15: Motion to Change

ONTARIO

SEAL

Superior Court of Justice, Family Court
(Name of court)

at   **50 Eagle Street West, Newmarket, ON L3Y 6B1**
Court office address

Court File Number
13579-15

Form 15: Motion to Change

☒ **the order of Justice**
Smart ,
dated   15 December 2015

☐ **the agreement for support between the parties, dated**
,

filed with the court on

Applicant(s)

Full legal name & address for service — street & number, municipality, postal code, telephone & fax numbers and e-mail address (if any).	Lawyer's name & address — street & number, municipality, postal code, telephone & fax numbers and e-mail address (if any).
Claire Dunphy **307 Gloria Road** **Newmarket, ON L3K 2Y7**	

Respondent(s)

Full legal name & address for service — street & number, municipality, postal code, telephone & fax numbers and e-mail address (if any).	Lawyer's name & address — street & number, municipality, postal code, telephone & fax numbers and e-mail address (if any).
Phil Dunphy **2745 Cameron Court** **Newmarket, ON L1S 3H5**	**JoAnn Kurtz** **347 Bay Street** **Newmarket, ON L2M 1J2** **Tel: 905-555-1212 Fax: 905-555-2121**

Assignee (if applicable)

Full legal name & address for service — street & number, municipality, postal code, telephone & fax numbers and e-mail address (if any).	Lawyer's name & address — street & number, municipality, postal code, telephone & fax numbers and e-mail address (if any).

NOTE: If you are seeking to change a support term in an agreement that has not already been filed with the court pursuant to s. 35 of the Family Law Act, you must file the agreement and Form 26B (Affidavit for Filing Domestic Contract with Court) before bringing this motion to change.

You may use this form if you are seeking to change an order or agreement that has been recalculated by the online Child Support Service. You must serve a copy of this form on the Family Responsibility Office if the order you recalculated was made under the Divorce Act and the recalculation was completed within the last 35 days.

You may not use this form to change a Notice of Calculation made by the online Child Support Service.

If the order or agreement for support has been assigned to a person or agency, the assignee must be served with this form and the Change Information Form (Form 15A). The assignee's consent to change an order or agreement for support may be necessary. It is the responsibility of the person seeking the change to the order or agreement to determine if the order or agreement has been assigned. You can do this by submitting a Confirmation of Assignment form. The Confirmation of Assignment form is available through the Ministry of the Attorney General website or at the court office.

TO: *(name(s) of party(ies))* **Claire Dunphy**

(Name of party bringing motion) **Phil Dunphy**   has brought a motion to change

☒   the order of Justice **Smart**   , dated **15 December 2015**

☐   recalculated by the online Child Support Service on _____ .

☐   the agreement between you and *(name of party bringing this motion)* _____

       dated _____ ☐ recalculated by the online Child Support Service on _____ .

FIGURE 16.1 Form 15: Motion to Change Continued

Form 15:	Motion to Change Order or Agreement	(page 2)	Court File Number
			13579-15

☒ **THE FIRST COURT DATE IS** _____ , at _____   ☐ a.m.   ☐ p.m.

or as soon as possible after that time, at *(address of court)*

50 Eagle Street West, Newmarket, ON L3Y 6B1

☐ **NO COURT DATE HAS BEEN SET FOR THIS CASE.** A case management judge will not be assigned until one of the parties asks the clerk of the court to schedule a case conference and serves a Conference Notice (Form 17).

IF, AFTER 365 DAYS, THE CASE HAS NOT BEEN SCHEDULED FOR TRIAL, the clerk of the court will send out a warning that the case will be dismissed in 60 days unless the parties file proof that the case has been settled or one of the parties asks for a case or a settlement conference.

(To be completed by the party bringing this motion—check the box of any paragraph that applies to your case:)

☐ This case does not include any claim to change support, and a financial statement is therefore not attached.

☐ The case only includes a claim to change child support in accordance with the table amount specified under the Child Support Guidelines and a financial statement is therefore not attached.

☒ This case includes a claim to change support other than child support in the amount specified in the table of the applicable child support guidelines, and a financial statement is attached. You MUST fill out a Financial Statement (Form 13 or 13.1), serve a copy on the person(s) bringing the motion to change and file a copy in the court office with an Affidavit of Service (Form 6B) even if you do not respond to this case.

IF YOU CONSENT TO THE CHANGES BEING SOUGHT IN THIS MOTION, you or your lawyer must complete the Consent Motion to Change (Form 15C—a blank copy should be attached) and return a copy to the person(s) bringing the motion and any assignee, if applicable, within 30 days of being served (60 days if the motion to change is served on you outside Canada or the United States). The person(s) bringing the motion may then file the consent with the court and may obtain a court order based on the consent. If a first court date has been scheduled, you do not need to attend court on that date unless specifically directed by the court to do so.

IF YOU WANT TO OPPOSE ANY CHANGE BEING SOUGHT IN THIS MOTION OR WANT TO REQUEST A CHANGE OF YOUR OWN, you or your lawyer must complete the Response to Motion to Change (Form 15B—a blank copy should be attached), serve a copy on the person(s) bringing the motion and file a copy in the court office with an Affidavit of Service (Form 6B). **YOU HAVE ONLY 30 DAYS AFTER THIS MOTION TO CHANGE IS SERVED ON YOU (60 DAYS IF THE MOTION TO CHANGE IS SERVED ON YOU OUTSIDE CANADA OR THE UNITED STATES) TO SERVE AND FILE A RESPONSE TO A MOTION TO CHANGE. IF YOU DO NOT, THE CASE WILL GO AHEAD WITHOUT YOU AND THE COURT MAY MAKE AN ORDER AND ENFORCE IT AGAINST YOU.**

NOTE: If you want to make your own claim to change support, you MUST also fill out a Financial Statement (Form 13 or 13.1), serve a copy on the person(s) bringing the motion and file a copy in the court office with an Affidavit of Service (Form 6B) UNLESS your only claim for support is for child support in the table amount specified under the Child Support Guidelines.

YOU SHOULD GET LEGAL ADVICE ABOUT THIS CASE RIGHT AWAY. If you cannot afford a lawyer, you may be able to get help from your local Legal Aid Ontario Office. (See your telephone directory under LEGAL AID.)

_____	_____
Date of issue by the clerk of the court	*Clerk of the court*

FLR 15 (April 12, 2016)   Page 2 of 5

FIGURE 16.1 Form 15: Motion to Change Continued

Form 15: **Motion to Change Order or Agreement** (page 3)

| Court File Number |
| 13579-15 |

CLAIM BY *(name(s) of person(s) bringing motion)* **Phil Dunphy**

I ASK THE COURT TO CHANGE THE EXISTING COURT ORDER OR SUPPORT AGREEMENT BY MAKING AN ORDER AS FOLLOWS: *(complete only those items that affect the terms of the order or agreement that you are seeking to change.)*

☐ **1.** An order that *(name(s) of party(ies) or person(s))* _____

have custody of the following child(ren): *(name(s) and birthdate(s) of child(ren))*

☐ **2.** An order that *(name(s) of party(ies) or person(s))* _____

have access to the following child(ren): *(name(s) and birthdate(s) of child(ren))*

as follows: *(give details of access)*

☐ **3.** An order that *(name(s) of party(ies) and/or person(s))* _____

and _____ have joint custody of the following child(ren):

(name(s) and birthdate(s) of child(ren))

☐ **4.** An order for the following residential/access arrangements for the child(ren): *(name(s) and birthdate(s) of child(ren))*

5. Order(s) dealing with child support as follows:

☐ Since the order/agreement for child support was made, a Notice of Recalculation was issued by the online Child Support Service dated _____ *(please attach)*.

☐ The order/agreement for child support, dated _____ , be terminated for the following child(ren): *(insert name(s) and birthdate(s) of child(ren))*

effective *(date)* _____ .

☐ Based on the payor's annual income of $ _____ , *(name of party)* _____

pay *(name of party)* _____ $ _____ per month for the following child(ren): *(name(s) and birthdate(s) of child(ren))*

with payments to start on *(date)* _____ .

☐ This amount is the table amount listed in the Child Support Guidelines.

☐ This amount is more than the table amount listed in the Child Support Guidelines.

☐ This amount is less than the table amount listed in the Child Support Guidelines.

FIGURE 16.1   Form 15: Motion to Change Continued

Form 15:   **Motion to Change Order or Agreement**   **(page 4)**

Court File Number
13579-15

☐ Starting on *(date)* _____ , *(name of party)* _____

pay to *(name of party)* _____ $ _____

for the following special or extraordinary expenses:

Child's Name	Type of Expense	Total Amount of Expense	Payor's Share	Terms of Payment *(frequency of payment, date due, etc.)*
		$	$	
		$	$	
		$	$	
		$	$	
		$	$	

☐ Other: *(give details)*

6. ☐ Orders dealing with the outstanding child support owed as follows:

　　☐ The child support owed to *(name of recipient)* _____

　　be fixed at $ _____ as of *(date)* _____ .

　　☐ *(Name of payor)* _____ pay to *(name of recipient)*

　　_____ $ _____ per month, with

　　payments to begin on *(date)* _____ until the full amount owing is paid.

　　☐ The child support owed to *(name of agency or other person)* _____

　　be fixed at $ _____ as of *(date)* _____ .

　　☐ *(Name of payor)* _____ pay to *(name of agency or other person)*

　　_____ $ _____ per month, with payments to

　　begin on *(date)* _____ until the full amount owing is paid.

7. ☒ An order that the spousal support be changed as follows:

　　☒ The order/agreement for spousal support, dated **15 December 2015** _____ be terminated effective

　　(date) **1 February 2018** _____ .

　　☐ *(Name of party)* _____ pay spousal support to

　　(name of party) _____ in the amount of

　　$ _____ per month, effective on *(date)* _____ .

　　☐ Other *(give details of the order you want the court to make)*

8. ☐ An order that the outstanding spousal support owed be paid as follows:

　　☐ The spousal support owed to *(name of recipient)* _____

　　be fixed at $ _____ as of *(date)* _____ .

　　☐ *(Name of payor)* _____ pay to *(name of recipient)*

　　_____ $ _____ per month, with

　　payments to begin on *(date)* _____ until the full amount owing is paid.

FIGURE 16.1   Form 15: Motion to Change Concluded

Form 15:   **Motion to Change Order or Agreement**   **(page 5)** | Court File Number
13579-15 |

☐ The spousal support owed to *(name of agency or other person)* _____

be fixed at $ _____ as of *(date)* _____ .

☐ *(Name of payor)* _____ pay to *(name of agency or other person)*

_____ $ _____ per month, with

payments to begin on *(date)* _____ until the full amount owing is paid.

9. ☐ I ask that the term(s) of the order of Justice *(name of judge)* _____ ,

dated _____ , for *(give details)* _____

be changed as follows: *(give details of the order you want the court to make)*

10. ☐ I ask the court for the following order:

The information and facts supporting my motion to change are set out in the Change Information Form (Form 15A) attached.

_____   _____
Date of signature   *Signature of person bringing the motion or person's lawyer*

FIGURE 16.2 Form 15A: Change Information

ONTARIO

Superior Court of Justice, Family Court
(Name of court)

Court File Number
13579-15

at   **50 Eagle Street West, Newmarket, ON L3Y 6B1**
Court office address

**Form 15A: Change
Information Form**

Applicant(s)

Full legal name & address for service — street & number, municipality, postal code, telephone & fax numbers and e-mail address (if any).	Lawyer's name & address — street & number, municipality, postal code, telephone & fax numbers and e-mail address (if any).
Claire Dunphy **307 Gloria Road** **Newmarket, ON L3K 2Y7**	

Respondent(s)

Full legal name & address for service — street & number, municipality, postal code, telephone & fax numbers and e-mail address (if any).	Lawyer's name & address — street & number, municipality, postal code, telephone & fax numbers and e-mail address (if any).
Phil Dunphy **2745 Cameron Court** **Newmarket, ON L1S 3H5**	**JoAnn Kurtz** **347 Bay Street** **Newmarket, ON L2M 1J2** **Tel: 905-555-1212 Fax: 905-555-2121**

Assignee (if applicable)

Full legal name & address for service — street & number, municipality, postal code, telephone & fax numbers and e-mail address (if any).	Lawyer's name & address — street & number, municipality, postal code, telephone & fax numbers and e-mail address (if any).

PART 1 – GENERAL INFORMATION
(This part should be filled out to the best ability of the party asking for a change in an order or support agreement.)

My name is *(full legal name)*   **Phil Dunphy**

I live in *(municipality & province)*   **Newmarket, Ontario**

and I swear/affirm that the following is true:

1. I am the   ☐ applicant   ☒ Respondent

2. The applicant, *(applicant's full legal name)*   **Claire Dunphy**

   was born on *(date of birth)*   **6 April 1975**

   lives in *(municipality & province)*   **Newmarket, Ontario**

   and, at the present time, is   ☐ married   ☐ living in a spousal relationship

            ☐ Separated   ☒ other *(specify)*   **divorced**

   The applicant is the   ☒ support recipient   ☐ support payor

3. The respondent, *(respondent's full legal name)*   **Phil Dunphy**

   was born on *(date of birth)*   **11 June 1973**

   lives in *(municipality & province)*   **Newmarket, Ontario**

   and, at the present time, is   ☐ Married   ☐ living in a spousal relationship

            ☐ Separated   ☒ other *(specify)*   **divorced**

   The respondent is the   ☐ support recipient   ☒ support payor

FIGURE 16.2   Form 15A: Change Information   Continued

Form 15A:	**Change Information Form**	**(page 2)**	Court File Number
			13579-15

4. This order/agreement ☒ has never been assigned

☐ has been assigned to

☐ the Ontario Ministry of Community and Social Services

☐ Ontario Works in *(name of location)* _____

☐ the municipality of *(name)* _____

☐ other *(specify)* _____

The details of the assignment are: *(Give date of assignment, indicate whether it is still in effect, add any other relevant information known to you and attach a copy of the Confirmation of Assignment Form.)*

5. The applicant and the respondent:

☐ started living together on *(date)* _____

☐ were married on *(date)*   **25 October 2001**

☐ never lived together

☐ separated on *(date)* _____

☒ were divorced on *(date)*   **15 December 2015**

6. The following chart gives basic information about the child(ren) in this case:
    (List all child(ren) involved in this case, even those for whom no support is being claimed.)

Child's full legal name	Age	Birthdate *(d, m, y)*	Lives in *(municipality & province)*	Now living with *(name of person and relationship to child)*	Support claimed for child? *(YES or NO)*
Hayley Dunphy	14	31 May 2003	Newmarket, ON	Claire Dunphy-mother	NO
Alex Dunphy	12	22 December 2005	Newmarket, ON	Claire Dunphy-mother	NO
Luke Dunphy	10	18 October 2007	Newmarket, ON	Claire Dunphy-mother	NO

7. I attach a copy of the existing ☒ court order ☐ agreement

that contains the term(s) to be changed.

FIGURE 16.2   Form 15A: Change Information Continued

Form 15A: **Change Information Form**   **(page 3)** | Court File Number
                                                                              | 13579-15

8. The existing custody and access arrangements for the child(ren) are as follows:

Child's name	Custody/Access Arrangement
Hayley Dunphy	applicant has custody/respondent has reasonable access
Alex Dunphy	applicant has custody/respondent has reasonable access
Luke Dunphy	applicant has custody/respondent has reasonable access

9. The details of the existing order/agreement with respect to support are as follows:

Date of order or agreement	Present child support payment	Other terms of child support	Present support payment (if any) for spouse
15 December 2015	$ _____ 1845 *per* month _____		$ _____ 750 *per* month _____

10. The payment status of the existing order/agreement as of today is as follows:

☒ all payments have been made

☐ arrears are owing as follows:

Child support owed to recipient	Child support owed to other(s) *(such as Ministry of Community and Social Services)*	Spousal support owed to recipient	Spousal support owed to other(s) *(such as Ministry of Community and Social Services)*
$ _____	$ _____	$ _____	$ _____

CUSTODY/ACCESS
(Complete only if you are asking for a change in an order for custody or access.)

11. I ask that *(name(s) of party(ies) and/or person(s))* _____ have custody of the

following child(ren) *(name(s) and birthdate(s) of child(ren))* _____

12. I ask that *(name of party)* _____ have access to the following child(ren)

(name(s) and birthdate(s) of child(ren)) _____

as follows: *(give details of access)*

OR

13. I ask that *(name(s) of party(ies) and/or person(s))* _____ and

_____ have joint custody of the following child(ren)

(name(s) and birthdate(s) of child(ren)) _____

14. I ask for the following residential/access arrangements for the child(ren):

(name(s) and birthdate(s) of child(ren)) _____

FIGURE 16.2   Form 15A: Change Information Continued

Form 15A: **Change Information Form**   **(page 4)**   Court File Number
                                                                              13579-15

15. The order I am asking the court to make is in the best interests of the child(ren) for the following reasons: *(give details)*

CHILD SUPPORT
(Complete this section only if you are asking for a change in child support.)

16. I am asking to change the child support in the order/agreement because:

☐ The order/agreement was made before the applicable Child Support Guidelines came into effect.

☐ The following change in circumstances has taken place: *(Give details of change in circumstances.)*

☐ The parties agree to the termination of the support order/agreement, dated _____ ,
   for the following child(ren): *(name(s) and birthdate(s) of child(ren))*

   _____ ,

   as of *(date)* _____ .

☐ Other: *(give details)*

17. I ask that the child support be changed as follows:

☐ Since the order/agreement for child support was made, a Notice of Recalculation was issued by the online
   Child Support Service dated _____ *(please attach).*

☐ The order/agreement for child support dated _____ be terminated for the following
   child(ren): *(insert name(s) and birthdate(s) of child(ren))* _____
   effective *(date)* _____ .

☐ Based on the payor's income of $ _____ per year, *(name of party)* _____
   pay child support to *(name of party)* _____
   in the amount of $ _____ per month for the following child(ren) *(name(s) and birthdate(s) of child(ren))*

   _____

   with payments to start on *(date)* _____ .

   ☐ This amount is the table amount listed in the Child Support Guidelines.

   ☐ This amount is more than the table amount listed in the Child Support Guidelines.

   ☐ This amount is less than the table amount listed in the Child Support Guidelines. *(If this box is checked, you
      must complete paragraph 18.)*

☐ Starting on *(date)* _____ , *(name of party)* _____
   pay to *(name of party)* _____ $ _____ for the following
   special or extraordinary expenses:

Child's Name	Type of Expense	Total Amount of Expense	Payor's Share	Terms of Payment *(frequency of payment, date due, etc.)*
		$	$	
		$	$	
		$	$	
		$	$	
		$	$	
		$	$	

FIGURE 16.2   Form 15A: Change Information   Continued

Form 15A:	Change Information Form	(page 5)	Court File Number
			13579-15

☐ Other: *(give details)*

18. ☐ I am asking that child support be changed to an amount that is less than the table amount listed in the Child Support Guidelines. The reason(s) for my request is/are that:

    ☐ The parties agree to a different amount.

        ☐ I have attached a separate sheet to this form that explains why this is an appropriate amount of child support.

        ☐ The recipient is getting social assistance payments from a public agency whose consent to this arrangement is needed. I am attaching the agency's consent to this form.

    ☐ As can be seen from paragraphs 6 and 8 above, the parties have shared custody of the child(ren) *(the payor has a child at least 40% of the time).*

        ☐ I have attached a separate sheet to this form that compares the table amounts from the Child Support Guidelines for each of the parties, shows the increased cost of the shared custody arrangement, the financial circumstances of each party and of each child for whom support is claimed.

        ☐ The parties are agreeing to this arrangement and I have attached a separate sheet to this form that explains why this is an appropriate amount of child support.

    ☐ As can be seen from paragraphs 6 and 8 above, custody of the children is split between the parties. I have attached a separate sheet to this form that calculates the difference between the amount that each party would otherwise pay to the other under the Child Support Guidelines.

    ☐ A child is 18 or more years old and I attach to this form a separate sheet that calculates the amount of support for this child.

    ☐ A child contributes to his/her own support and I attach to this form a separate sheet showing the amount of the child's own income and/or assets.

☐ The payor's annual income is over $150,000 and I have attached to this form a separate sheet that calculates the amount of support that I want to be put in an order.

☐ Under the order/agreement, *(name(s) of child(ren))* _____

is/are the subject of special provisions that I have detailed on a separate sheet that I have attached to this form.

☐ The payor stands in the place of a parent to *(name(s) of child(ren))* _____

and I attach to this form a separate sheet that gives the details of another parent's duty to pay support for this/these child(ren), as well as the details of the calculation of the amount of support requested.

☐ The amount listed in the Child Support Guidelines would cause undue hardship to me or to the child(ren) for whom support is claimed. I attach to this form a separate sheet that compares the standards of living of the parties and calculates the amount of support that should be paid.

19. I ask that the outstanding child support owed be paid as follows:

    ☐ The child support owed to *(name of recipient)* _____

    be fixed at $ _____ as of *(date)* _____ .

    ☐ *(Name of payor)* _____ pay to *(name of recipient)*

_____ $ _____ per month, with payments to begin on *(date)*

_____ until the full amount owing is paid.

    ☐ The child support owed to *(name of agency or other person)* _____

    be fixed at $ _____ as of *(date)* _____ .

FIGURE 16.2   Form 15A: Change Information Continued

Form 15A: **Change Information Form**   **(page 6)**   Court File Number
                                                                                13579-15

☐ *(Name of payor)* _____ pay to *(name of agency or other person)*

_____ $ _____ per month, with payments to begin on *(date)*

_____ until the full amount owing is paid.

SPOUSAL SUPPORT
(Complete only if you are asking for a change in spousal support.)

20. I am asking to change the spousal support in the order/agreement because:

   ☒ The following change in circumstances has taken place: *(give details of change in circumstances.)*
   The applicant was unemployed at the time of the order but now has a fulltime job and is earning $60,000 per year.

   ☒ Spousal support should no longer be paid as of *(date)*   **1 February 2018**   for the following reasons:
   (give details)
   The applicant is now self-supporting.

   ☐ The parties consent to the termination of the spousal support order/agreement, dated _____ ,
   as of *(date)* _____ .

   ☐ Other *(give details)*:

21. I ask that the spousal support be changed as follows:

   ☒ The order/agreement for spousal support, dated **15 December 2015**   , be terminated
   effective *(date)* **1 February 2018**   .

   ☐ *(Name of party)* _____ pay spousal support to
   (name of party) _____ in the amount of $ _____ per month,
   effective on *(date)* _____ .

   ☐ Other *(give details of the order you want the court to make)*

22. I ask that the outstanding spousal support owed be paid as follows:

   ☐ The spousal support owed to *(name of recipient)* _____
   be fixed at $ _____ as of *(date)* _____ .

   ☐ *(Name of payor)* _____ pay to *(name of recipient)*
   _____ $ _____ per month, with payments
   to begin on *(date)* _____ until the full amount owing is paid.

   ☐ The spousal support owed to *(name of agency or other person)* _____
   be fixed at $ _____ as of *(date)* _____ .

   ☐ *(Name of payor)* _____ pay to *(name of agency or other person)*
   _____ $ _____ per month, with payments
   to begin on *(date)* _____ until the full amount owing is paid.

FLR 15A (April 12, 2016)   Page 6 of 9

FIGURE 16.2   Form 15A: Change Information   Continued

Form 15A: **Change Information Form**   (page 7) | Court File Number
                                                                        | **13579-15**

OTHER
(Complete if applicable.)

23.   I ask that the term(s) of the order of Justice *(name of judge)* _____ ,

dated _____ , for *(give details)* _____

be changed as follows: *(give details of the order you want the court to make)*

24.   I ask that the court make this order for the following reasons:

Sworn/Affirmed before me at **the Town of Newmarket**	
municipality	
in **the Province of Ontario** _____	_____
province, state or country	*Signature*
	(This form is to be signed in front of a
on _____	*lawyer, justice of the peace, notary public or*
date *Commissioner for taking affidavits*	*commissioner for taking affidavits.)*
(Type or print name below	
if signature is illegible.)	

FIGURE 16.2   Form 15A: Change Information   Continued

Form 15A: **Change Information Form**   **(page 8)** | Court File Number |
|---|
| **13579-15** |

PART 2 – INFORMATION FROM SUPPORT PAYOR

DO NOT COMPLETE THIS PART IF THE PARTIES ARE ONLY CONSENTING TO TERMINATE A SUPPORT OBLIGATION OR IF THE MOTION TO CHANGE DOES NOT INCLUDE A CLAIM TO CHANGE CHILD SUPPORT.

My name is *(full legal name)* _____

I live in *(municipality & province)* _____

and I swear/affirm that the following is true:

25. I am the support payor in this case.

26. I attach the following financial information about myself:

    (a) a copy of every personal income tax return that I filed with Canada Revenue Agency for the 3 most recent taxation years;

    (b) a copy of every notice of assessment or re-assessment from Canada Revenue Agency of those returns; and

    (c) ☐ *(applies only if you are an employee)* proof of this year's earnings from my employer as required by clause 21(1)(c) of the Child Support Guidelines.

       ☐ *(applies only if you are self-employed, or you are a partner in a partnership or you control a corporation or are a beneficiary under a trust)* the documents listed in clauses 21(1)(d), (e), (f) or (g) of the Child Support Guidelines.

27. My total income

    ☐ will be $ _____ for this year;

    ☐ was $ _____ for last year; and

    ☐ was $ _____ for the year before that.

28. On the basis of my annual income, the table amount from the Child Support Guidelines for *(number of child(ren))* _____ child(ren) is $ _____ per month.

29. My financial statement   ☐ is attached.   ☐ is not attached.

Sworn/Affirmed before me at _____

                               municipality

in _____

                     province, state or country

on _____

    date   *Commissioner for taking affidavits*
                    (Type or print name below
                      if signature is illegible.)

_____
Signature
(This form is to be signed in front of a lawyer, justice of the peace, notary public or commissioner for taking affidavits.)

FIGURE 16.2 Form 15A: Change Information Concluded

Form 15A: **Change Information Form**	**(page 9)**	Court File Number
		13579-15

PART 3 – INFORMATION FROM SUPPORT RECIPIENT

DO NOT COMPLETE THIS PART IF THE PARTIES ARE ONLY CONSENTING TO TERMINATE A SUPPORT OBLIGATION OR IF THE MOTION TO CHANGE DOES NOT INCLUDE A CLAIM TO CHANGE CHILD SUPPORT.

My name is *(full legal name)* _____

I live in *(municipality & province)* _____

and I swear/affirm that the following is true:

30. I am the support recipient in this case.

Fill in paragraphs 31 and 32 only if:

- *the change for which you are asking is for an amount that is different from the Child Support Guidelines;*
- *the change for which you are asking relates to a child*
  - *over the age of 18 years,*
  - *for whom the payor stands in the place of a parent, or*
  - *with respect to whom the payor has access or physical custody not less than 40% of the time over the course of the year;*
- *each party has custody of one or more children;*
- *the payor's annual income as determined under the guidelines is more than $150,000;*
- *either party claims that an order according to the guidelines would result in undue hardship; or*
- *there is a claim for special or extraordinary expenses.*

31. I attach the following financial information about myself:

(a) a copy of every personal income tax return that I filed with Canada Revenue Agency for the 3 most recent taxation years;

(b) a copy of every notice of assessment or re-assessment from Canada Revenue Agency of those returns; and

(c) ☐ *(applies only if you are an employee)* proof of this year's earnings from my employer as required by clause 21(1)(c) of the Child Support Guidelines.

☐ *(applies only if you are self-employed, or you are a partner in a partnership or you control a corporation or are a beneficiary under a trust)* the documents listed in clauses 21(1)(d), (e), (f) or (g) of the Child Support Guidelines.

32. My total income

☐ will be $ _____ for this year;

☐ was $ _____ for last year; and

☐ was $ _____ for the year before that.

33. My financial statement ☐ is attached. ☐ is not attached.

Sworn/Affirmed before me at _____

in _____
     province, state or country

on _____ _____
   date   *Commissioner for taking affidavits*
     (Type or print name below
     if signature is illegible.)

   municipality

_____
Signature
(This form is to be signed in front of a lawyer,
justice of the peace, notary public or
commissioner for taking affidavits.)

FLR 15A (April 12, 2016)

Page 9 of 9

FIGURE 16.3   Form 15B: Response to Motion to Change

ONTARIO

	Court File Number

_____
(Name of court)

at _____
Court office address

**Form 15B: Response to
Motion to Change**

Applicant(s)

Full legal name & address for service — street & number, municipality, postal code, telephone & fax numbers and e-mail address (if any).	Lawyer's name & address — street & number, municipality, postal code, telephone & fax numbers and e-mail address (if any).

Respondent(s)

Full legal name & address for service — street & number, municipality, postal code, telephone & fax numbers and e-mail address (if any).	Lawyer's name & address — street & number, municipality, postal code, telephone & fax numbers and e-mail address (if any).

Assignee (if applicable)

Full legal name & address for service — street & number, municipality, postal code, telephone & fax numbers and e-mail address (if any).	Lawyer's name & address — street & number, municipality, postal code, telephone & fax numbers and e-mail address (if any).

PART 1 – GENERAL INFORMATION

My name is *(full legal name)* _____

I live in *(municipality and province)* _____

and I swear/affirm that the following is true:

1. I am the   ☐ applicant   ☐ Respondent

2. I am the   ☐ support payor   ☐ support recipient

3. This order/agreement   ☐ has never been assigned

☐ has been assigned to

☐ the Ontario Ministry of Community and Social Services

☐ Ontario Works in *(name of location)* _____

☐ the municipality of *(name)* _____

☐ other *(specify)* _____

The details of the assignment are: *(give date of assignment, indicate whether it is still in effect and add any other relevant information known to you.)*

4. ☐ Since the order/agreement for child support was made, a Notice of Recalculation was issued by the online Child Support Service dated _____ *(please attach).*

5. ☐ I agree with the information set out in paragraphs 1 through 10 of the Change Information Form (Form 15A), dated _____ .

☐ I agree with the information set out in paragraphs 1 through 10 of the Change Information Form (Form 15A), dated _____ EXCEPT as follows: *(give details of the information with which you do not agree and attach any documents that support your position.)*

FIGURE 16.3 Form 15B: Response to Motion to Change **Continued**

Form 15B:	Response to Motion to Change	(page 2)	Court File Number

6. ☐ I agree with the claims made by *(name of person bringing motion to change)* _____

   in paragraphs _____ of the Motion to Change (Form 15), dated _____

   ☐ I disagree with the claims made by *(name of person bringing motion to change)* _____

   in paragraphs _____ of the Motion to Change (Form 15), dated _____

7. ☐ I am asking that the motion to change (except for the parts with which I agree) be dismissed with costs.

CLAIM BY RESPONDING PARTY
(Complete only if you are asking the court to change the existing order or support agreement.)

8. ☐ I am asking the court to make a change of my own, the details of which are set out below.

CUSTODY/ACCESS
(Complete only if you are asking for a change in a custody or access order.)

9. I ask that *(name of party)* _____

   have custody of the following child(ren): *(name(s) and birthdate(s) of child(ren))*

10. I ask that *(name of party)* _____

    have access to the following child(ren): *(name(s) and birthdate(s) of child(ren))*

    as follows: *(give details of access)*

OR

11. I ask that *(name(s) of party(ies) and/or person(s))* _____

    and _____

    have joint custody of the following child(ren): *(name(s) and birthdate(s) of child(ren))*

12. I ask for the following residential/access arrangements for the child(ren): *(include name(s) and birthdate(s) of child(ren))*

13. The order I am asking the court to make is in the best interests of the child(ren) for the following reasons: *(give details)*

CHILD SUPPORT
(Complete this section only if you are asking for a change in child support.)

14. I am asking to change the child support in the order/agreement because:

    ☐ the order/agreement was made before the applicable Child Support Guidelines came into effect.

    ☐ the following change in circumstances has taken place: *(give details of change in circumstances.)*

FIGURE 16.3   Form 15B: Response to Motion to Change   Continued

Form 15B:	**Response to Motion to Change**	(page 3)	Court File Number

☐ the parties agree to the termination of the support order/agreement, dated _____ ,

for the following child(ren): *(name(s) and birthdate(s) of child(ren))*

as of *(date)* _____ .

☐ Other: *(give details)*

15. I ask that the child support be changed as follows:

☐ The order/agreement for child support, dated _____ , be terminated for the

following child(ren): *(name(s) and birthdate(s) of child(ren))*

effective *(date)* _____ .

☐ Based on the payor's annual income of $ _____ , *(name of party)* _____

pay child support to *(name of party)* _____ in the amount of

$ _____ per month for the following child(ren): *(name(s) and birthdate(s) of child(ren))*

with payments to start on *(date)* _____ .

    ☐ This amount is the table amount listed in the Child Support Guidelines.

    ☐ This amount is more than the table amount listed in the Child Support Guidelines.

    ☐ This amount is less than the table amount listed in the Child Support Guidelines. *(If this box is checked, you must complete paragraph 16.)*

☐ Starting on *(date)* _____ , *(name of party)* _____

pay to *(name of party)* _____ $ _____

for the following special or extraordinary expenses:

Child's Name	Type of Expense	Total Amount of Expense	Payor's Share	Terms of payment *(frequency of payment, date due, etc.)*
		$	$	
		$	$	
		$	$	
		$	$	
		$	$	

☐ Other: *(give details)*

16. I am asking that child support be changed to an amount that is less than the table amount listed in the Child Support Guidelines The reason(s) for my request is/are that:

☐ The parties agree to a different amount.

    ☐ I have attached a separate sheet to this form that explains why this is an appropriate amount of child support.

    ☐ The recipient is getting social assistance payments from a public agency whose consent to this arrangement is needed. I am attaching the agency's consent to this form.

FIGURE 16.3   Form 15B: Response to Motion to Change Continued

Form 15B:	Response to Motion to Change	(page 4)	Court File Number

☐ The parties have shared custody to the child(ren) *(the payor has a child at least 40% of the time).*

    ☐ I have attached a separate sheet to this form that compares the table amounts from the Child Support Guidelines for each of the parties, shows the increased cost of the shared custody arrangement, the financial circumstances of each party and of each child for whom support is claimed.

    ☐ The parties are agreeing to this arrangement and I have attached a separate sheet to this form that explains why this is an appropriate amount of child support.

☐ Custody of the children is split between the parties. I have attached a separate sheet to this form that calculates the difference between the amount that each party would otherwise pay to the other under the Child Support Guidelines.

☐ A child is 18 or more years old and I attach to this form a separate sheet that calculates the amount of support for this child.

    ☐ A child contributes to his/her own support and I attach to this form a separate sheet showing the amount of the child's own income and/or assets.

☐ The payor's annual income is over $150,000 and I have attached to this form a separate sheet that calculates the amount of support that I want to be put in an order.

☐ Under the order/agreement, *(name(s) of child(ren))* _____

is/are the subject of special provisions that I have detailed on a separate sheet that I have attached to this form.

☐ The payor stands in the place of a parent to *(name(s) of child(ren)* _____

and I attach to this form a separate sheet that gives the details of another parent's duty to pay support for this/these child(ren), as well as the details of the calculation of the amount of support requested.

☐ The amount listed in the Child Support Guidelines would cause undue hardship to me or to the child(ren) for whom support is claimed. I attach to this form a separate sheet that compares the standards of living of the parties and calculates the amount of support that should be paid.

17. I ask that the outstanding child support owed be paid as follows:

    ☐ The child support owed to *(name of recipient)* _____

    be fixed at $ _____ as of *(date)* _____ and *(name of payor)*

    _____ pay to *(name of recipient)*

    _____ $ _____ per month,

    with payments to begin on *(date)* _____ until the full amount owing is paid.

    ☐ The child support owed to *(name of agency or other person)* _____

    be fixed at $ _____ as of *(date)* _____ and *(name of payor)*

    _____ pay to *(name of agency or other person)*

    _____ $ _____ per month,

    with payments to begin on *(date)* _____ until the full amount owing is paid.

SPOUSAL SUPPORT
(Complete only if you are asking for a change in spousal support.)

18. I am asking to change the spousal support in the order/agreement because:

    ☐ The following change in circumstances has taken place: *(give details of change in circumstances.)*

FIGURE 16.3   Form 15B: Response to Motion to Change   Continued

Form 15B:	**Response to Motion to Change**	(page 5)	Court File Number

☐ Spousal support should no longer be paid as of *(date)* _____ for the following reasons: *(give details)*

☐ The parties consent to the termination of the spousal support order/agreement, dated _____ ,
  as of *(date)* _____ .

☐ Other *(specify)*

19. I ask that the spousal support be changed as follows:

☐ The order/agreement for spousal support, dated _____ , be terminated effective
  (date) _____ .

☐ *(Name of party)* _____ pay spousal support to
  (name of party) _____ in the amount of
  $ _____ per month, effective on *(date)* _____ .

☐ Other: *(give details of the order you want the court to make)*

20. I ask that the outstanding spousal support owed be paid as follows:

☐ The spousal support owed to *(name of recipient)* _____
  be fixed at $ _____ as of *(date)* _____ .

☐ *(Name of payor)* _____ pay to *(name of recipient)*
  _____ $ _____ per month,
  with payments to begin on *(date)* _____ until the full amount owing is paid.

☐ The spousal support owed to *(name of agency or other person)* _____
  be fixed at $ _____ as of *(date)* _____ .

☐ *(Name of payor)* _____ pay to *(name of agency or other person)*
  _____ $ _____ per month,
  with payments to begin on *(date)* _____ until the full amount owing is paid.

OTHER
(Complete if applicable)

21. I ask that the term of the order of Justice *(name of judge)* _____ ,
  dated _____ , for *(give details)* _____
  be changed as follows: *(give details of the order you want the court to make)*

FIGURE 16.3   Form 15B: Response to Motion to Change   Continued

Form 15B: **Response to Motion to Change**	(page 6)	Court File Number

22. I ask that the court make the order set out in paragraph 21 for the following reasons:

23. I ask the court to make the following additional order:

24. I ask the court to make the order set out in paragraph 23 for the following reasons:

Sworn/Affirmed before me at _____

                              municipality

in _____

              province, state or country

on _____   _____

    date   *Commissioner for taking affidavits*
                 (Type or print name below
                 if signature is illegible.)

_____
                Signature
(This form is to be signed in front of a lawyer,
justice of the peace, notary public or
commissioner for taking affidavits.)

FIGURE 16.3   Form 15B: Response to Motion to Change   Continued

Form 15B:	**Response to Motion to Change**	**(page 7)**	Court File Number

---

PART 2 – INFORMATION FROM SUPPORT PAYOR

DO NOT COMPLETE THIS PART IF THE PARTIES ARE ONLY CONSENTING TO TERMINATE A SUPPORT OBLIGATION OR IF THE MOTION TO CHANGE DOES NOT INCLUDE A CLAIM TO CHANGE CHILD SUPPORT.

My name is *(full legal name)* _____

I live in *(municipality and province)* _____

and I swear/affirm that the following is true:

25. I am the support payor in this case.

26. I attach the following financial information about myself:

    (a) a copy of every personal income tax return that I filed with Canada Revenue Agency for the 3 most recent taxation years;

    (b) a copy of every notice of assessment or re-assessment from Canada Revenue Agency of those returns; and

    (c) ☐ *(applies only if you are an employee)* proof of this year's earnings from my employer as required by clause 21(1) (c) of the Child Support Guidelines.

        ☐ *(applies only if you are self-employed, or you are a partner in a partnership or you control a corporation or are a beneficiary under a trust)* the documents listed in clauses 21 (1)(d), (e), (f) or (g) of the Child Support Guidelines.

27. My total income

    ☐ will be $ _____ for this year;

    ☐ was $ _____ for last year; and

    ☐ was $ _____ for the year before that.

28. On the basis of my annual income, the table amount from the Child Support Guidelines for *(number of children)* _____ child(ren) is $ _____ per month.

29. My financial statement   ☐ is attached.   ☐ is not attached.

Sworn/Affirmed before me at _____ *municipality* in _____ *province, state or country* on _____ *date* _____ *Commissioner for taking affidavits* *(Type or print name below* *if signature is illegible.)*	_____ *Signature* *(This form is to be signed in front of a lawyer,* *justice of the peace, notary public or* *commissioner for taking affidavits.)*

FIGURE 16.3   Form 15B: Response to Motion to Change   Concluded

Form 15B: **Response to Motion to Change**	(page 8)	Court File Number

PART 3 – INFORMATION FROM SUPPORT RECIPIENT

DO NOT COMPLETE THIS PART IF THE PARTIES ARE ONLY CONSENTING TO TERMINATE A SUPPORT OBLIGATION OR IF THE MOTION TO CHANGE DOES NOT INCLUDE A CLAIM TO CHANGE CHILD SUPPORT.

My name is *(full legal name)* _____

I live in *(municipality and province)* _____

and I swear/affirm that the following is true:

30. I am the support recipient in this case.

Fill in paragraphs 30 and 31 only if:
- *the change for which you are asking is for an amount that is different from the Child Support Guidelines;*
- *the change for which you are asking relates to a child*
  - *over the age of 18 years,*
  - *for whom the payor stands in the place of a parent, or*
  - *with respect to whom the payor has access or physical custody not less than 40% of the time over the course of the year;*
- *each party has custody of one or more children;*
- *the payor's annual income as determined under the guidelines is more than $150,000;*
- *either party claims that an order according to the guidelines would result in undue hardship; or*
- *there is a claim for special or extraordinary expenses.*

31. I attach the following financial information about myself:

(a) a copy of every personal income tax return that I filed with Canada Revenue Agency for the 3 most recent taxation years;

(b) a copy of every notice of assessment or re-assessment from Canada Revenue Agency of those returns; and

(c) ☐ *(applies only if you are an employee)* proof of this year's earnings from my employer as required by clause 21(1) (c) of the Child Support Guidelines.

☐ *(applies only if you are self-employed, or you are a partner in a partnership or you control a corporation or are a beneficiary under a trust)* the documents listed in clauses 21 (1)(d), (e), (f) or (g) of the Child Support Guidelines.

32. My total income
- ☐ will be $ _____ for this year;
- ☐ was $ _____ for last year; and
- ☐ was $ _____ for the year before that.

33. My financial statement   ☐ is attached.   ☐ is not attached.

Sworn/Affirmed before me at _____
municipality

in _____
province, state or country

on _____
date

_____
Commissioner for taking affidavits
(Type or print name below if signature is illegible.)

_____
Signature
(This form is to be signed in front of a lawyer, justice of the peace, notary public or commissioner for taking affidavits.)

FIGURE 16.4   Form 15C: Consent Motion to Change

ONTARIO

Court File Number

_____
(Name of court)

at _____

Court office address

**Form 15C: Consent
Motion to Change**

Applicant(s)

Full legal name & address for service — street & number, municipality, postal code, telephone & fax numbers and e-mail address (if any).	Lawyer's name & address — street & number, municipality, postal code, telephone & fax numbers and e-mail address (if any).

Respondent(s)

Full legal name & address for service — street & number, municipality, postal code, telephone & fax numbers and e-mail address (if any).	Lawyer's name & address — street & number, municipality, postal code, telephone & fax numbers and e-mail address (if any).

Assignee (if applicable)

Full legal name & address for service — street & number, municipality, postal code, telephone & fax numbers and e-mail address (if any).	Lawyer's name & address — street & number, municipality, postal code, telephone & fax numbers and e-mail address (if any).

YOU MAY USE THIS FORM IF YOU ARE SEEKING TO CHANGE AN ORDER OR AGREEMENT THAT HAS BEEN RECALCULATED BY THE ONLINE CHILD SUPPORT SERVICE. YOU MUST SERVE A COPY OF THIS FORM ON THE FAMILY RESPONSIBILITY OFFICE IF THE ORDER YOU RECALCULATED WAS MADE UNDER THE DIVORCE ACT AND THE RECALCULATION WAS COMPLETED WITHIN THE LAST 35 DAYS.

YOU MAY NOT USE THIS FORM TO CHANGE A NOTICE OF CALCULATION MADE BY THE ONLINE CHILD SUPPORT SERVICE.

EACH OF YOU SHOULD CONSIDER GETTING A LAWYER'S ADVICE BEFORE SIGNING THIS CONSENT.

IF YOU ARE SEEKING TO CHANGE A SUPPORT ORDER OR AGREEMENT THAT HAS BEEN ASSIGNED TO A PERSON OR AGENCY, YOU MUST SERVE ALL DOCUMENTS ON THE ASSIGNEE AND OBTAIN THE ASSIGNEE'S CONSENT TO ANY CHANGE THAT MAY AFFECT THE ASSIGNEE'S FINANCIAL INTEREST. FAILURE TO OBTAIN THE ASSIGNEE'S CONSENT MAY RESULT IN A COURT SETTING ASIDE AN ORDER AND ORDERING COSTS AGAINST THE PARTY WHO DID NOT PROVIDE NOTICE. IT IS THE RESPONSIBILITY OF THE PERSON SEEKING THE CHANGE TO DETERMINE IF THE ORDER HAS BEEN ASSIGNED. YOU CAN DO THIS BY SUBMITTING A CONFIRMATION OF ASSIGNMENT FORM. THE CONFIRMATION OF ASSIGNMENT FORM IS AVAILABLE THROUGH THE MINISTRY OF THE ATTORNEY GENERAL WEBSITE OR AT THE COURT OFFICE.

1.   We know that each of us has the right to get advice from his or her own lawyer about this case and understand that signing this consent may result in a final court order that will be enforced.

2.   ☐   We have filed/are filing Financial Statements (Form 13 or 13.1) with the court.

☐   We have agreed not to file any Financial Statements with the court.

3.   ☐   We have attached the existing final order or support agreement and ask the court to make an order that changes that order or agreement as set out below.

☐   Since the order/agreement for child support was made, a Notice of Recalculation was issued by the

online Child Support Service dated _____ *(please attach).*

CUSTODY/ACCESS *(Complete only if the parties are asking for a change in a custody or access order.)*

4.   ☐   We agree that *(name(s) of person(s) or party(ies))* _____

shall have custody of the following child(ren):

Child's full legal name	Birthdate *(d, m, y)*	Age	Sex

FIGURE 16.4 Form 15C: Consent Motion to Change Continued

Form 15C:	**Consent Motion to Change**	(page 2)	Court File Number

☐ We agree that *(name(s) of person(s) or party(ies))* _____

shall have access to: *(name(s) and birthdate(s) of child(ren))*

_____

as follows: *(give details of access order)*

OR

5. ☐ We agree that *(names of parties or persons)* _____

and _____ shall have joint custody of the following child(ren):

Child's full legal name	Birthdate *(d, m, y)*	Age	Sex

☐ We agree that the residential/access arrangements for the child(ren) *(name(s) and birthdate(s) of child(ren))*

_____

shall be as follows:

CHILD SUPPORT
(Complete only if the parties are asking for a change in child support.)

6. We agree to an order for child support that is:

☐ equal to or more than what is in the Child Support Guidelines.

☐ none (no child support).

☐ less than what is in the Child Support Guidelines for the following reasons:

7. The party receiving support ☐ is ☐ is not receiving social assistance.

8. We agree that child support shall be as follows:

☐ Based on the payor's annual income of $ _____ , *(name of party)* _____

shall pay to *(name of party)* _____ $ _____ per month

for the following child(ren) *(name(s) and birthdate(s) of child(ren))*

_____

with payments to begin on *(date)* _____ .

☐ Starting on *(date)* _____ , *(name of party)* _____

shall pay *(name of party)* _____ $ _____ for the

following special or extraordinary expenses:

FIGURE 16.4   Form 15C: Consent Motion to Change   Continued

Form 15C: **Consent Motion to Change**   **(page 3)** | Court File Number |

Child's name	Type of expense	Total Amount of Expense	Payor's Share	Terms of Payment *(frequency of payment, date due, etc.)*
		$	$	
		$	$	
		$	$	
		$	$	
		$	$	

☐ *(Complete only if the parties are agreeing to special or extraordinary expenses.)* The recipient's total annual income is

  $ _____ .

☐ The order or agreement for child support, with respect to the child(ren) *(name(s) and birthdate(s) of child(ren))*

  _____ ,

  dated _____ , shall be terminated as of *(date)* _____ .

Complete if applicable:

9. We also agree that the outstanding child support owed be paid off as follows:

  ☐ The child support owed to *(name of recipient)* _____ shall be

    fixed at $ _____ as of *(date)* _____ and *(name of payor)*

    _____ shall pay *(name of recipient)* _____

    $ _____ per month, with payments to begin on *(date)* _____ until the

    full amount owing has been paid.

  ☐ The child support owed to *(name of agency or other person)* _____ shall be

    fixed at $ _____ as of *(date)* _____ and *(name of payor)*

    _____ shall pay *(name of agency or other person)* _____

    $ _____ per month, with payments to begin on *(date)* _____ until the

    full amount owing has been paid.

SPOUSAL SUPPORT
(Complete only if the parties are seeking a change in spousal support.)

10. We agree that the spousal support payments should be as follows:

  ☐ *(Name of party)* _____ shall pay to

    (name of party) _____ the amount of

    $ _____ per month, with payments to begin on *(date)* _____ .

  ☐ The order or agreement for spousal support, dated _____ , shall be terminated as of

    (date) _____ .

11. We agree that the outstanding spousal support owed be paid off as follows:

  ☐ The spousal support owed to *(name of recipient)* _____ shall be

    fixed at $ _____ as of *(date)* _____ and *(name of payor)*

    _____ shall pay *(name of recipient)* _____

    $ _____ per month, with payments to begin on *(date)* _____ until the

    full amount owing has been paid.

FLR 15C (April 12, 2016)   Page 3 of 4

FIGURE 16.4   Form 15C: Consent Motion to Change Concluded

Form 15C:	**Consent Motion to Change**	**(page 4)**	Court File Number

☐ The spousal support owed to *(name of agency or other person)* _____

shall be fixed at $ _____ as of *(date)* _____ and *(name of payor)*

_____ shall pay *(name of recipient)* _____

$ _____ per month, with payments to begin on *(date)* _____ until the

full amount owing has been paid.

NOTE: If money is owed to an agency or other person (an assignee), a representative of that agency or the other person must consent to the change in the order.

OTHER
(Complete if applicable.)

12. We agree that paragraph(s) *(specify which paragraphs of the order are to be changed)* _____ of the order

of Justice *(name of judge)* _____ , dated _____ ,

shall be changed as follows: *(give details of the order you want the court to make)*

The parties do not need to sign this consent at the same time. Each party must sign in the presence of his or her witness who shall sign immediately after that party.

NOTE: The witness cannot be one of the parties. If the witness does not know the party, the witness should see identification that proves that the person signing the consent is the same person who is a party to the consent.

_____	_____
Applicant's signature	*Respondent's signature*
_____	_____
Date of applicant's signature	*Date of respondent's signature*
_____	_____
Signature of witness	*Signature of witness*
_____	_____
Type or print name of witness to applicant's signature	*Type or print name of witness to respondent's signature*
_____	_____
Address of witness	*Address of witness*
_____	_____
Telephone number of witness	*Telephone number of witness*

ASSIGNEE'S CONSENT

_____	_____
Signature of person authorized to sign on behalf of assignee	*Date of signature*

_____
Print name and title of person signing the consent

_____	_____
Witness's signature	*Name of witness (type or print legibly)*

Enforcement of Orders and Agreements

17

LEARNING OUTCOMES

After completing this chapter, you should be able to:

■ Explain the role of the Family Responsibility Office in enforcing support orders.

■ Explain the purpose of a support deduction order.

■ Calculate deductions to be made by an income source under a support deduction order.

■ Describe the various other enforcement procedures available to the Family Responsibility Office and to the individual support recipient.

■ Explain how support provisions in a domestic contract may be enforced.

■ Explain how custody orders and agreements may be enforced.

Introduction

In previous chapters, we looked at the law and procedures that apply when seeking various family law orders or negotiating family law settlements. In this chapter, we look at how these orders and settlements are enforced.

This chapter discusses enforcement of

- support orders,
- support provisions in separation agreements, and
- custody orders and agreements.

Enforcement of Support Orders

Historically, support orders were enforced in the same manner as any other order for the payment of money. A party who was owed money under a support order had to collect the arrears by way of garnishment or writ of seizure and sale. Over time, additional enforcement remedies were made available through the Family Court. However, enforcement of an order remained the responsibility of the party to whom support was payable under the order.

By the mid-1980s, approximately 85 percent of all family support orders were in default, and the Ontario government enacted the *Support and Custody Order Enforcement Act* to govern the enforcement of support orders. That statute was replaced in 1992 by the *Family Support Plan Act*, which was in turn replaced by the *Family Responsibility and Support Arrears Enforcement Act, 1996*,[1] which came into force on May 12, 1997. Under these statutes, the government, rather than the party to whom support is payable, is ordinarily responsible for the collection and enforcement of support orders.

These programs have not been completely successful. In his 2003-2004 annual report, the Ontario Ombudsman noted that throughout his five-year term, the Family Responsibility Office "has yielded the second largest number of complaints and enquiries" to his office, with 1,467 complaints and enquiries.[2] According to the report, $1,319.2 million in support arrears were owing in Ontario as of February 2004. In the 2005-2006 report, the Family Responsibility Office ranked fourth, with 858 complaints. In every annual report since then, the Family Responsibility Office has ranked either first or second with between 700 and 1,167 complaints each year.

Overview of the Family Responsibility and Support Arrears Enforcement Act, 1996

Under the *Family Responsibility and Support Arrears Enforcement Act, 1996*, all Ontario support orders[3] are sent to the Family Responsibility Office for collection. The party who is required to make the support payments (the payor) does not make

---

1   SO 1996, c 31.

2   Ontario Ombudsman Annual Reports can be found at <http://www.ombudsman.on.ca/Resources/Annual-Reports.aspx>.

3   The definition of "support order" in the Act includes a notice of calculation under section 39 and an order that has been recalculated under section 39.1 of the *Family Law Act*.

support payments directly to the party who is entitled to support under the order (the recipient). Instead, all payments are made to the Family Responsibility Office, which in turn makes payment to the recipient. The main enforcement tool under the Act is the **support deduction order**, which allows the Family Responsibility Office to arrange for support payments to be deducted automatically from the payor's income sources, such as salaries or pensions. If support is not paid, the Family Responsibility Office has the power to take additional enforcement actions against the payor.

The Act allows the parties to opt out of enforcement by the Family Responsibility Office, unless the court orders otherwise. If payments under the order are up-to-date, both the payor and the recipient must complete a notice of withdrawal form. If the payments are not up-to-date, the recipient alone is required to complete the form. If the parties opt out of the Act, the payor makes support payments directly to the recipient. If payments are not made, the recipient may enforce the support order. Parties who have opted out of the Act may opt back in by written notice signed by either the payor or the recipient.

> **support deduction order**
> an order made under the *Family Responsibility and Support Arrears Enforcement Act, 1996,* that allows the Family Responsibility Office to arrange for support payments to be deducted automatically from the payor's income sources

Support Orders Under the Act

Under section 9(1) of the Act, every support order[4] made by an Ontario court must state in its operative part "that unless the order is withdrawn from the Director's office, it shall be enforced by the Director and that amounts owing under the order shall be paid to the Director, who shall pay them to the person to whom they are owed."[5] See Figure 13.7 in Chapter 13 for an example of the wording used in a support order.

Under section 10(1), every Ontario court that makes a support order[6] must also make a support deduction order. (See Figure 17.1 at the end of the chapter.) Under section 10(2), when a support order is changed, the court shall also make a support deduction order to reflect the change.[7] A support deduction order allows the director to require the payor's income source to deduct support payments from the payor's income. Section 1(1) of the Act defines an income source as "an individual, corporation or other entity that owes or makes any payment, whether periodically or in a lump sum, to or on behalf of a payor."

Under section 12(1), the clerk or registrar of the court that makes the support order is required to file a copy of the support order and the support deduction order with the Family Responsibility Office promptly after it is made. Section 11(2) requires the court, before making a support deduction order, to make inquiries of the parties about the payor's income sources. (The court fulfills this requirement by requiring the parties to complete and file a support deduction order information form when an application for support is filed.) See Figure 17.2.

---

4 Under section 9(2.1), the same wording is required in every support order that is a notice of calculation.

5 "Director" means the director of the Family Responsibility Office.

6 This includes a notice of calculation under section 39 of the *Family Law Act.*

7 A notice of recalculation under section 39.1 of the *Family Law Act* does not require a support deduction order reflecting the recalculation.

Information for the Family Responsibility Office

When the Family Responsibility Office receives the support order and support deduction order from the court, it sends the recipient a registration package, which includes the following:

- *Instructions for recipients of family support.* This sheet sets out the instructions for completing the forms included in the filing package (see Figure 17.3).
- *Recipient information form.* This form provides information about the recipient and the court order (see Figure 17.4).
- *Registration for direct deposit form.* This form authorizes the Family Responsibility Office to deposit payments directly to the recipient's bank (see Figure 17.5).
- *Payor information form.* This form provides information about the payor (see Figure 17.6).
- *Statement of arrears form.* This form, which must be sworn to under oath, is required for the Family Responsibility Office to begin collecting any arrears owed under the order (see Figure 17.7).

The court also sends a payor information form to the payor for completion and return.

Enforcement of the Support Deduction Order

If the payor information form or support deduction order information form shows the payor's employer or other income source, the Family Responsibility Office sends a support deduction notice to the income source, notifying the income source that it is obligated to deduct support payments from the payor's income and forward the deducted amounts to the Family Responsibility Office. A copy of the notice is also sent to the payor.

Under section 22(1) of the Act, an income source that receives a support deduction notice is required to deduct from the money the income source owes to the payor the amount of support owed by the payor or any other amount that is set out in the notice, and to pay that amount to the Family Responsibility Office. Under section 22(2), the income source must make the first payment to the Family Responsibility Office not later than the payor's first payday that falls at least 14 days after service of the notice.

Section 23 of the Act states that the maximum amount that can be deducted by an income source is 50 percent of the *net amount* owed by the income source to the payor. The "net amount" is defined in section 23(5) as the total amount owing by the income source to the payor after deducting

- income tax,
- Canada Pension Plan,
- employment insurance,
- union dues, and
- such other deductions as may be prescribed by the regulations.

Will and Grace separated, and Will obtained an order granting him custody of their son Jack, child support in the amount of $625 per month, and spousal support in the amount of $500 per month, for total support payable of $1,125 per month.

Grace teaches interior design at Ontario University. Her salary is $78,000 per year, and she is paid $3,000 every two weeks. The following amounts are deducted from her salary:

- Income tax $760.10
- Canada Pension Plan $142.05
- Employment insurance $56.40
- Union dues $9.00
- Parking $18.00
- Pension $176.94
- Payroll savings plan $200.00

Grace's total deductions are $1,362.49, leaving her with take-home pay of $1,637.51.

The Family Responsibility Office serves Ontario University with a support deduction notice. Ontario University must now deduct from Grace's pay and send to the Family Responsibility Office the amount of the support payment up to a maximum of 50 percent of her net amount.

Under the Act, not all of Grace's deductions are used in calculating her net amount: only income tax, Canada Pension Plan, employment insurance, and union dues (totalling $967.55) are deducted. Accordingly, while Grace's take-home pay is only $1,637.51, her net amount under the Act is $2,032.45 (50 percent of which is $1,016.23).

Accordingly, Ontario University is required to deduct $1,016.23 from Grace's first paycheque of each month and send it to the Family Responsibility Office. The university must deduct the balance of $108.77 in support from her second paycheque in the month. No further deductions are required until the following month.

Until the income source starts to make the deductions, the payor is required to make support payments directly to the Family Responsibility Office pursuant to section 22(3) of the Act.

Under section 25, if there is an interruption of payments by an income source to the payor—for example, if the payor is fired or laid off—both the income source and the payor must notify the Family Responsibility Office in writing within 10 days. If payments are resumed, both the payor and the income source must notify the Family Responsibility office within 10 days. If the payor instead becomes entitled to income from another income source, the payor must notify the director of the new income source within 10 days.

Under section 26(7), an income source who fails to make the necessary deductions after receiving a support deduction notice is liable to pay to the Family

Responsibility Office the amount it should have deducted. It may also be guilty of an offence pursuant to section 51(2).

A payor who believes that too much money is being deducted under the support deduction order because of a mistake of fact may bring a motion to the court under section 27(1). The support deduction order itself can be varied only by order of the court, and then only if the support order to which it relates is varied pursuant to section 27(7). Under section 28, the court also has the discretion to make an alternative payment order under which the operation of the support deduction order is suspended and the payor instead makes payments directly to the Family Responsibility Office. The court may make an alternative payment order only if

- it would be unconscionable, having regard to all of the circumstances, to have the support obligation paid by way of support deduction; or
- the parties to the support order agree that they do not want support deduction to apply, and the court requires the payor to post security.

Under section 28(6), the following shall *not* be considered by a court in determining whether it would be unconscionable to require a payor to make support payments by means of a support deduction order:

- The fact that the payor has demonstrated a good payment history in respect of his or her debts, including support obligations.
- The fact that the payor has had no opportunity to demonstrate voluntary compliance in respect of support obligations.
- The fact that the parties have agreed to the making of an alternative payment order.
- The fact that there are grounds upon which a court might find that the amount payable under the support order should be changed.

Other Enforcement Procedures

The director of the Family Responsibility Office has the duty to enforce support orders pursuant to section 5(1) and, pursuant to section 6(1), the power to use, in addition to the support deduction order, any other enforcement mechanism, whether or not expressly provided for in the Act. Additional enforcement mechanisms are expressly provided for in parts V and VI of the Act.

Part V of the Act (sections 33-39) deals with suspension of drivers' licences. Under those sections, when a support order is in default, the director may suspend the payor's driver's licence unless, within 30 days of receiving a first notice of a driver's licence suspension, the payor

- makes an arrangement satisfactory to the director to comply with the order and pay the arrears,
- obtains an order that the director refrain from directing suspension of the licence and the payor applies to vary the terms of the support order, or
- pays all the arrears.

The following additional enforcement mechanisms are expressly provided for in part VI the Act when a support order filed with the Family Responsibility Office is in default:

- *Filing of financial statement.* The director may request that the payor complete and file a financial statement with proof of income (see section 40).

- *Default hearing.* The director may require the payor to deliver a financial statement and proof of income, and to appear before the court to explain his or her default. The court has the power to make a variety of orders—for example, that the payor make payments toward the arrears or be jailed for up to 180 days (see section 41).

- *Registration under the Personal Property Security Act.*[8] The director can register the arrears under the *Personal Property Security Act* as a lien or charge on any interest in all the personal property that the payor owns or holds in Ontario at the time of registration, or acquires afterward (see section 43).

- *Garnishment of joint accounts.* The director may issue a notice of garnishment to a bank or other financial institution to seize up to 50 percent of the funds held by the payor in a joint bank account (see section 45).

- *Seizing lottery winnings.* The Ontario Lottery Corporation is required to deduct arrears from any lottery prize of $1,000 or more (see section 46).

- *Reporting to consumer reporting agencies.* The director may report the payor's default to credit-rating bureaus (see section 47).

- *Reporting to a prescribed entity.* The director may report the payor's default to a prescribed entity that is a professional or occupational organization, governing body of a self-governing or regulated profession, or an entity responsible for licensing or registering individuals for occupational purposes (see sections 47.1 and 47.2).

- *Arrest of absconding payor.* The court may issue a warrant for a payor's arrest for the purpose of bringing him or her before the court, if the court is satisfied that the payor is about to leave Ontario and there are reasonable grounds for believing that the payor intends to evade his or her obligations under the support order (see section 49).

The following additional enforcement mechanisms are expressly provided for in part VI the Act whether or not the support order filed with the Family Responsibility Office is in default:

- *Registration of the support order against land.* The director may register the support order in the proper land registry office as a charge against the payor's land that can be enforced by sale of the property (see section 42).

- *Restraining order.* The court may make an order restraining the disposition or wasting of assets that may hinder or defeat the enforcement of a support order or support deduction order (see section 48).

---

8   RSO 1990, c P.10.

When a support order filed with the Family Responsibility Office is in default, the director may also use the following enforcement mechanisms, which are not expressly provided for in the Act:

- *Writ of seizure and sale.* The director may issue and file a writ of seizure and sale for arrears under Rule 28 of the *Family Law Rules.*[9]
- *Garnishment.* The director may use the garnishment procedure under Rule 29 of the *Family Law Rules* to intercept money owing to the payor, such as wages, pensions, bank accounts, rents, and funds from federal sources, such as income tax refunds, employment insurance benefits, and GST refunds.
- *Reporting payor to private collection agencies.* If no payment has been received in over six months, the director may refer a case to its enhanced collection agency project, under which a private collection agent attempts to collect the arrears.
- *Suspend a passport or other federal licence.* The director may ask the federal government to suspend a passport or other federal licence, such as a pilot's licence.

Enforcement Remedies Available to the Individual Recipient

If the support order is withdrawn from the Family Responsibility Office, it is up to the recipient to take steps to enforce the order.

The following remedies are available to a support recipient under the Act:

- registration of the support order against land under section 42,
- registration of arrears under the *Personal Property Security Act* pursuant to section 43,
- a restraining order under section 48, and
- a warrant for the arrest of an absconding payor under section 49.

The following remedies are available to a support recipient under the *Family Law Rules*:

- a request for a financial statement under Rule 27(1),
- a request for a statement of income from an income source of the payor under Rule 27(7),
- a financial examination of the payor under Rule 27(11),
- a writ of seizure and sale under Rule 28,
- garnishment under Rule 29,
- a default hearing under Rule 30, and
- the appointment of a receiver under Rule 26(3).

---

9 O Reg 114/99.

Enforcement of Support Provisions in Domestic Contracts

The support provisions in a domestic contract can be enforced in the same way as any other contract: by suing for breach of contract if payments are not made.

In addition, under section 35 of the *Family Law Act*,[10] either party to a domestic contract may file the contract with the court. The support provision in the contract may then be enforced as if it were an order of the court.

Enforcement of Custody Orders and Agreements

A custody order or agreement requires the ongoing cooperation of the parties whether they share custody or one party has custody and the other access. Underlying the order is an assumption that custodial parents will make children available to access parents, and that access parents will return children to the custodial parents at the end of their access periods. However, sometimes that does not happen, in which case there are a number of enforcement remedies available.

Contempt Proceedings

An order, other than an order for payment of money, may be enforced by contempt proceedings. Contempt involves a willful refusal to comply with the provisions of the order.

Contempt proceedings are governed by Rule 31 of the *Family Law Rules*. A notice of contempt motion must be served by special service. If the court finds a person in contempt, it may order, among other things, that the person

- be imprisoned,
- pay a fine, and
- pay an amount to another party as a penalty.

Under the Children's Law Reform Act

Under section 36 of the *Children's Law Reform Act*,[11] a court may direct the sheriff or the police force to locate, apprehend, and deliver a child to the person lawfully entitled to custody or access if the court is satisfied that someone is unlawfully withholding the child from that person, or is likely to remove the child from Ontario contrary to a separation agreement or court order.

---

10   RSO 1990, c F.3.
11   RSO 1990, c C.12.

Section 37 gives the court the power to make orders with respect to property, support payments, and passports in order to prevent a party from unlawfully removing a child from Ontario. The court may order the party to

- transfer property to a trustee;
- make support payments to a trustee;
- post a bond; or
- deliver the party's passport, the child's passport, and any other travel documents to the court.

Section 38 gives the Ontario Court of Justice powers to punish willful contempt of custody or access orders by fine or imprisonment or both.

Under section 39, the court may make orders requiring any person or public body to provide the court with particulars of the address of the respondent, where the court is of the opinion that the information is necessary for the purpose of bringing a custody or access application or enforcing a custody or access order.

Under the Divorce Act

Pursuant to section 20 of the *Divorce Act*,[12] a custody or access order has legal effect throughout Canada, and may be registered in any court in a province and enforced as an order of that court.

Under the Criminal Code

Abduction of a child by his or her parent or guardian is a crime under sections 282 and 283 of the *Criminal Code*.[13] It is an offence for a parent or guardian to take or keep a child with the intent to deprive another parent of the child, whether or not there is a custody order or agreement.

It is a defence to the charge if the parent or guardian takes the child with the consent of the other parent or guardian or takes or keeps the child in order to protect the child from imminent danger or harm.

---

12 RSC 1985, c 3 (2nd Supp).
13 RSC 1985, c C-46.

CHAPTER SUMMARY

Historically, support orders were enforced in the same manner as any other order for the payment of money. Enforcement was the responsibility of the party to whom support was payable. By the mid-1980s, approximately 85 percent of all family support orders were in default. As a result, the Ontario government enacted legislation to make the government, rather than the party to whom support is payable, responsible for the collection and enforcement of support orders. That legislation was changed several times, and the current statute is the *Family Responsibility and Support Arrears Enforcement Act, 1996*.

Under that statute, support payments are not paid by the payor directly to the recipient, but are instead made to the Family Responsibility Office (FRO), which in turn makes payment to the recipient. The main enforcement tool under the Act is the support deduction order, which allows the FRO to arrange for support payments to be deducted automatically from the payor's income sources, such as salaries or pensions. If support is not paid, the Family Responsibility Office has the power to take additional enforcement actions, such as suspending a driver's licence, or registering the support order against land.

Support provisions in a domestic contract can be enforced by suing for breach of contract, or by filing the contract with the court under section 35 of the *Family Law Act*, upon which the support provision in the contract may be enforced as if it were a court order.

A custody order may be enforced by contempt proceedings under Rule 31 of the *Family Law Rules*. The *Children's Law Reform Act* gives courts a number of tools to prevent the unlawful removal of children from Ontario. Under the *Divorce Act*, a custody or access order has legal effect throughout Canada. Under the *Criminal Code*, abduction of a child by his or her guardian is a crime.

KEY TERM

support deduction order, 397

REVIEW QUESTIONS

1. What statute governs the enforcement of support orders in Ontario?

2. To whom is a support payor required to make support payments?

3. How and when may the parties to a support order opt out of enforcement by the Family Responsibility Office?

4. What must every support order made by an Ontario court include?

5. What must an Ontario court do when making a support order?

6. What action must be taken by the clerk or registrar of the court that makes a support order?

7. What is included in the Family Responsibility Office filing package?

8. What is a support deduction notice?

9. What is the responsibility of an income source that receives a support deduction notice?

10. What is the maximum amount that can be deducted by an income source?

11. What must be done if there is an interruption of payments by an income source to the payor? When? By whom?

12. What is the liability of an income source who fails to make the necessary deductions after receiving a support deduction notice?

13. What action may a payor take if he or she believes that too much money is being deducted under a support deduction order because of a mistake in fact?

14. In addition to the support deduction notice, what enforcement mechanisms are available to the Family Responsibility Office?

15. What enforcement mechanisms are available to an individual support recipient?

16. How may the support provisions in a domestic contract be enforced?

17. What are contempt proceedings? How are they used to enforce custody orders?

18. What provisions for the enforcement of custody orders and agreements are found in the *Children's Law Reform Act*?

19. How may the *Criminal Code* be used to enforce a custody order?

EXERCISE

A support order is made ordering the wife to pay the husband $1,800.00 per month. If the order were to be enforced by the FRO, how much could the wife's employer deduct from her first pay of the month if her pay is as follows:

Gross pay bi-weekly:	$4,500
Deductions:	
Income tax	1,200
Canada Pension Plan	186
E.I.	89
Parking	24
Pension	168
Union dues	25
RRSPs	200

What would be the deduction from her second pay of the month? What would be the deduction from her third pay of the month (if there is one)?

FIGURE 17.1 Support Deduction Order

SUPPORT DEDUCTION ORDER
ORDONNANCE DE RETENUE DES ALIMENTS
Family Responsibility and Support Arrears Enforcement Act, 1996
Loi de 1996 sur les obligations familiales et l'exécution des arriérés d'aliments
Form/Formule 1

Court File No. / *N° de dossier du tribunal*

_____
Name of Court / *Nom du tribunal*

_____
Location / *Lieu*

_____
Judge / *Juge*

_____
Date

Between / *Entre*

Applicant / Petitioner / Plaintiff
Requérant / Demandeur

and / *et*

Respondent / Defendant
Intimé / Défendeur

SUPPORT DEDUCTION ORDER / *ORDONNANCE DE RETENUE DES ALIMENTS*

Upon making an order this day which provides for the payment of support and on making the necessary inquiries required by section 11 of the *Family Responsibility and Support Arrears Enforcement Act, 1996*:

Après avoir rendu ce jour une ordonnance qui prévoit le versement d'aliments et après avoir fait les recherches nécessaires exigées par l'article 11 de la Loi de 1996 sur les obligations familiales et l'exécution des arriérés d'aliments :

1. **THIS COURT ORDERS THAT**
    LE TRIBUNAL ORDONNE QUE

    _____
    (Name of Payor / *nom du payeur*)

    pay support as set out in the attached information form.
    verse des aliments comme le prévoit la formule de renseignements ci-jointe.

2. **THIS COURT ORDERS THAT** any income source that receives notice of this support deduction order make payments to the Director of the Family Responsibility Office in respect of the payor out of money owed to or paid by the income source to the payor.

    LE TRIBUNAL ORDONNE que toute source de revenu qui reçoit avis de la présente ordonnance fasse à l'égard du payeur des versements au directeur du Bureau des obligations familiales à même les sommes qu'elle doit au payeur ou qu'elle lui verse.

    _____
    Signature of Judge, Registrar or Clerk of the Court
    Signature du juge ou du greffier du tribunal

FRO-019 (June 15, 2005 / 15 juin 2005)   © Queen's Printer for Ontario, 2008 / © Imprimeur de la Reine pour l'Ontario, 2008

FIGURE 17.2 Support Deduction Order Information Form

▷ Ontario

SUPPORT DEDUCTION ORDER
INFORMATION FORM
Family Responsibility and Support Arrears Enforcement Act, 1996
Form 2

Court File No.

Name of Court _____

Location _____

NOTE: Please Print. Complete Parts A and B ONLY. Leave Parts C, D, E and F blank to be completed by court.

A. INFORMATION FOR THE FAMILY RESPONSIBILITY OFFICE

INFORMATION ON PARTIES   Family Responsibility Office Case Number *(if known)* _____

Payor

Payor Name	Birthdate (dd/mm/yyyy)	Sex ☐ M ☐ F

Street Number	Unit/Suite/Apt.	Street Name

City/Town	Province	Postal Code

Social Insurance Number	Mother's Maiden Name	Language Preference

Home Telephone Number	Work/Business Telephone Number	Cell Phone Number

Recipient

Recipient Name	Birthdate (dd/mm/yyyy)	Sex ☐ M ☐ F

Street Number	Unit/Suite/Apt.	Street Name

City/Town	Province	Postal Code

Social Insurance Number	Mother's Maiden Name	Language Preference

Home Telephone Number	Work/Business Telephone Number	Cell Phone Number

PAYOR'S EMPLOYMENT

Employer/Income Source Name

Payroll Office Address

Street Number	Unit/Suite/Apt.	Street Name

City/Town	Province	Postal Code

☐ Self employed *(provide legal name of business and address)* _____
☐ Unemployed
☐ Receiving welfare, family benefits or other form of social assistance
☐ Receiving employment insurance benefits
☐ Other (i.e., workers' compensation, pension, etc.) _____
☐ Recipient does not know

SUPPORT ORDER INFORMATION

Is the support order a variation of a previous support order?   ☐ Yes ☐ No   If "Yes", date of previous order _____

FRO-021E (June 15, 2005)   © Queen's Printer for Ontario, 2008   Page 1 of 2

FIGURE 17.2 Support Deduction Order Information Form Concluded

Form 2
(cont'd from page 1)

C, D, E and F to be **COMPLETED BY COURT**

B. The attached support deduction order relates to a support order which says that:

_____ is required to pay support
Payor Name

for the following persons:

Name	Birthdate (dd/mm/yyyy)	Amount Payable	Frequency	Start Date (dd/mm/yyyy)	End Date (if any) (dd/mm/yyyy)
Spouse: a.		$			
Other Dependants b.		$			
c.		$			
d.		$			
e.		$			
f.		$			

C. **TYPE OF SUPPORT ORDER**

☐ Temporary   ☐ Final

D. **SPECIAL EXPENSES**

Name of Child / Children	Birthdate (dd/mm/yyyy)	Amount	Frequency	Start Date (dd/mm/yyyy)	End Date (if any) (dd/mm/yyyy)
		$			
		$			
		$			
		$			
		$			

E. **COST OF LIVING ADJUSTMENTS (DOES NOT APPLY TO CHILD SUPPORT)**

Support is indexed in accordance with s. 34(5) of the _Family Law Act_   ☐ Yes ☐ No

If other indexing, explain method of calculation: _____

F. **ARREARS –** If the order is retroactive, if the order is a variation order or if the order provides for an arrears payment schedule,

are arrears owing as of the date of the order?   ☐ No   ☐ Yes.   If "Yes", the amount of arrears = $ _____

and the arrears are to be paid as follows (if applicable)   _____

PARTS A AND B COMPLETED BY: (please print)

Name	Title (If solicitor for a party, identify which party)	Telephone Number

FIGURE 17.3   Instructions for Recipients of Family Support

 **Ontario**

Ministry of Community
and Social Services

Family Responsibility Office
PO Box 200 Stn A
Oshawa ON L1H 0C5

Family Responsibility Office

Instructions for Recipients of Family Support

This filing package includes forms to be completed and returned to the Family Responsibility Office (FRO) as soon as possible. FRO must have this information for enforcement purposes.

1.   **Recipient Information Form**

   You must provide the requested information that is available to you and indicate where we can contact you by mail and telephone.

   If your order or agreement is not already filed with FRO or if your order or agreement was previously withdrawn from FRO, you must complete this form and **attach a copy of your Order or Agreement**.

   NOTE: If you are filing a Domestic Contract, Separation Agreement, Cohabitation Agreement or Paternity Agreement with FRO, you must first file it with the Ontario Court of Justice or the Superior Court of Justice Family Court. When you file your Contract or Agreement with the court, you will be given an 'Affidavit for Filing Domestic Contract or Paternity Agreement with Court'. This Affidavit, stamped by the court, must be stapled to your Contract or Agreement. The Affidavit, your Contract or Agreement and the completed Registration forms must be submitted to FRO for enforcement purposes.

   YOU MUST SIGN THE RECIPIENT INFORMATION FORM AT THE BOTTOM WHERE SHOWN.

2.   **Registration for Direct Deposit Form**

   Completion of this form authorizes FRO to deposit collected payments directly into your bank account. Funds will be received faster when payments are directly deposited into your bank account.

3.   **Payor Information Form**

   Please answer all the questions as completely as possible and return the form to our office. If you cannot answer a question, write **"DO NOT KNOW"** as your answer, so that we know you saw the question but did not have the information at the time. If there is not enough space provided, please attach a separate sheet of paper including your name and FRO case number.

4.   **Statement of Arrears Form**

   This form must be completed for FRO to begin collecting arrears owed to you prior to FRO enforcement. A copy of this form will be provided to the support payor (Payor) and this form becomes a court document if we take action to enforce support payments. It must therefore be accurate and signed in the presence of a **Commissioner for taking affidavits**, a **Justice of the Peace** or a **Notary Public**.

Check List

☐ **Recipient Information Form** *(Form must be signed)*

☐ **Registration for Direct Deposit** *(Section B must be completed OR void cheque attached)*

☐ **Payor Information Form** *(Provide as much information as possible)*

☐ **Statement of Arrears** *(Form must be signed and your signature witnessed and sworn)*

FIGURE 17.4 Recipient Information Form

Ontario

Ministry of Community
and Social Services

Family Responsibility Office
PO Box 200 Stn A
Oshawa ON L1H 0C5

Recipient Information Form

FRO Case Number

Language Preferred ☐ English ☐ French

| Your Last Name (as written in the order) | Your First Name (as written in the order) | Your Middle Name(s) | ☐ Male ☐ Female |

Address

| Unit/Apt. Number | Street Number | Street Name | Lot, Concession or Township |

| City/Town | Province | Postal Code |

Date of Birth ___ / ___ / ___
Day   Month   Year

Home Telephone Number (incl. area code)

Cellular Telephone Number (incl. area code)

Employer

Social Insurance Number (SIN)

Work Telephone Number (incl. area code)

| Last Name of Payor (Person owing support) (as written in the order) | First Name of Payor (as written in the order) | Middle Name(s) of Payor |

My Support Provisions are contained in a (check one):

☐ Court Order   ☐ Separation Agreement   ☐ Domestic Contract

☐ Cohabitation Agreement   ☐ Paternity Agreement

Date ___ / ___ / ___
Day   Month   Year

(Agreement/Contract must be filed with the Ontario Court of Justice or Superior Court of Justice Family Court)

Are you claiming spousal support for yourself?   ☐ Yes   ☐ No

Are you claiming support for the child(ren) named in the order/agreement?   ☐ Yes   ☐ No

If yes, list the name(s) of the child(ren) you are claiming support for *(use additional sheet if required)*

Last Name, First Name, Middle Name(s)	Date of Birth Day/Month/Year	Sex
		☐ Male ☐ Female
		☐ Male ☐ Female
		☐ Male ☐ Female
		☐ Male ☐ Female

Do you currently receive or have you applied for: ☐ Ontario Works   ☐ Ontario Disability Support   ☐ No

Do you have another case filed with FRO? If yes, please provide the name that the case is filed under and the case number.

| Name case is filed under | **Case Number** |

You must sign this form in order for FRO to enforce the support terms of your order/agreement/contract.

_____
Signature

_____
Date

FIGURE 17.5   Registration for Direct Deposit

Ontario **Ministry of Community** **and Social Services** Family Responsibility Office PO Box 200 Stn A Oshawa ON L1H 0C5	**Registration for Direct Deposit** FRO Case Number

When the Family Responsibility Office (FRO) receives a support payment that is owed to you, these funds will be sent by DIRECT DEPOSIT to your Canadian bank account. To ensure that you receive your money quickly, the following information must be provided. Incorrect information could result in your payment being sent to the wrong account.

Instructions

If you wish to have your support payments deposited into your CHEQUING ACCOUNT, COMPLETE SECTION A and ATTACH A BLANK PERSONAL CHEQUE with "VOID" written on it.

If, however, you wish to designate your SAVINGS ACCOUNT, complete SECTION A, take this form to your bank and ask them to complete SECTION B – Banking Data.

DO NOT FORGET TO SIGN THE BOTTOM OF THE FORM AUTHORIZING THE DIRECT DEPOSIT SERVICE.

Important notes about changing bank accounts

If your account number changes, or if you wish to have your support payments deposited to a different account, you must complete a new DIRECT DEPOSIT FORM and return it to FRO. After the changes have been processed, your support payments will be sent to your new account. DO NOT CLOSE YOUR OLD ACCOUNT UNTIL YOU RECEIVE YOUR FIRST PAYMENT TO THE NEW ACCOUNT.

PLEASE PRINT CLEARLY

Section A – Support Recipient Information

Last Name	First Name	Middle Initial

Address

Unit/Apt. Number	Street Number	Street Name	Lot, Concession or Township

City/Town	Province	Postal Code

Telephone number where you can be reached during the day (incl. area code)

NOTE: If attaching a VOID cheque, please tape the cheque over the Banking Information in Section B.

Section B – Banking Information (Must be completed by your bank if you are not attaching a VOID cheque)

Branch Number	Institution Number	Account Number

Name of Financial Institution

Branch

Branch Address

Place Bank Stamp

Bank Official's Signature and Position

Date (dd/mm/yyyy)

Until further notice, I authorize the direct deposit of my support payments to the account and financial institution designated in this form.

_____
Signature of Recipient

Date

FIGURE 17.6 Payor Information Form

Ontario

Ministry of Community
and Social Services

Family Responsibility Office
PO Box 200 Stn A
Oshawa ON L1H 0C5

Page 1 of 3

Payor Information Form
Information for Recipient to Complete

FRO Case Number

Payor's Last Name (as written in the order)	Payor's First Name (as written in the order)	Payor's Middle Name(s)	☐ Male ☐ Female

Payor's Address

Unit/Apt. Number	Street Number	Street Name	Lot, Concession or Township

City/Town	Province	Postal Code

Home Telephone Number (incl. area code)	Cellular Telephone Number (incl. area code)

Payor's Previous Address

Unit/Apt. Number	Street Number	Street Name	Lot, Concession or Township

City/Town	Province	Postal Code

Payor lived at this address from ___ / ___ / ___ to ___ / ___ / ___
Day Month Year Day Month Year

Does the Payor use an alias or any other name(s)? If so, what name(s)?

Does the Payor have a Driver's Licence? ☐ Yes ☐ No ☐ Unknown

If the Payor has a Driver's Licence

Licence Number	Province

Payor's Social Insurance Number (This may be found on the Payor's tax return or your tax return)	Payor's Date of Birth ___ / ___ / ___ Day Month Year

Payor's mother's name before marriage

Payor's Marital Status

☐ Single ☐ Married ☐ Divorced ☐ Separated ☐ Cohabiting

Income Information

Indicate if the Payor is self-employed ☐ Yes ☐ No

If yes, give details of employment

(e.g. Sole Owner, Partner, Family Business)

Payor's Current Employer/Income Source

Payor's Position	Date Started ___ / ___ / ___ Day Month Year

Employer's Address

Unit/Suite Number	Street Number and Street Name	City/Town

Province	Postal Code	Employer's Telephone Number (incl. area code)

Payor's Previous Employer/Income Source

Payor's Position	Date Started ___ / ___ / ___ Day Month Year

Employer's Address

Unit/Suite Number	Street Number and Street Name	City/Town

Province	Postal Code	Employer's Telephone Number (incl. area code)

FIGURE 17.6 Payor Information Form Continued

Payor Information Form
Information for Recipient to Complete
Page 2 of 3

FRO Case Number

Property Information

Does the Payor own/lease/rent a car, truck, boat, snowmobile, farm equipment or recreational vehicle?

	Vehicle Type	Model	Year	Colour
1.				
	Licence Plate Number	Serial Number	☐ Rent ☐ Own ☐ Lease	
2.	Vehicle Type	Model	Year	Colour
	Licence Plate Number	Serial Number	☐ Rent ☐ Own ☐ Lease	

Does the Payor own (alone or jointly with another person/company) a house, cottage, farm, land, apartment building, office or investment property either in or outside of Canada?

1. Type of Property

Address

Apt. Number	Street Number	Street Name	Lot/Concession/Township

City/Town	Province	Postal Code

What is/are the name(s) of the person(s)/company who also own this property?

2. Type of Property

Address

Apt. Number	Street Number	Street Name	Lot/Concession/Township

City/Town	Province	Postal Code

What is/are the name(s) of the person(s)/company who also own this property?

Please attach additional information on a separate sheet of paper.

Other Information

Do you have the name and addresses of any of the Payor's relatives or friends who may help us locate the Payor if required?

	Name	Relationship to Payor
1.		
	Address: Street Number & Name/Apartment Number/City/Province/Postal Code	Telephone Number (incl. area code)
2.	Name	Relationship to Payor
	Address: Street Number & Name/Apartment Number/City/Province/Postal Code	Telephone Number (incl. area code)

Does the Payor belong to any professional or community groups, associations, clubs, unions that may help us to locate the Payor, if required? (Provide name of organization, address and telephone number if possible.)

FIGURE 17.6 Payor Information Form Concluded

Payor Information Form
Information for Recipient to Complete
Page 3 of 3

FRO Case Number

Does the Payor have other sources of income? *(e.g. Workplace Safety and Insurance Board Benefit, Employment Insurance Benefit, Disability Insurance, Pension Income.)* If yes, provide as much detail as possible, including claim numbers if known.

Please attach additional information *(e.g. business cards, business contacts)* on a separate sheet of paper.

Does the Payor frequently travel outside of Canada? If yes, for ☐ Business   ☐ Pleasure

Passport Number

Does the Payor have any Federal Licences? *(e.g. Pilot Licence, Transport Licence)*

Type of Licence

Licence Number

Physical Description of the Payor (This information is required if we need to serve the Payor with Court Documents.)

If possible, include a current photograph of the Payor. Please attach the photograph to a separate sheet of paper and write the Payor's name, date the photograph was taken and your FRO case number.

Height	Weight	Build	Eye Colour	Eye Glasses	☐ Yes ☐ No

Hair Colour	Complexion (Skin Colour)	Distinguishing Marks or Features (e.g. Tattoos, Scars)

Financial Information

Does the Payor have any Credit Cards?

Card Type	Card Type

Where does the Payor Bank?

1. Name of Financial Institution | Account Number

   Address

2. Name of Financial Institution | Account Number

   Address

List any other assets you are aware of *(e.g. Stocks, Bonds, Term Deposits, Life Insurance, Investment Certificates, RRSP).*
If you require more space, please attach a separate sheet of paper.

Type of Asset	Location	Account/Policy/Serial Number

FIGURE 17.7 Statement of Arrears

Ontario

Ministry of Community and Social Services

Family Responsibility Office
PO Box 200 Stn A
Oshawa ON L1H 0C5

Statement of Arrears

FRO Case Number

Support Recipient's Name

Last Name	First Name	Middle Initial

Support Payor's Name

Last Name	First Name	Middle Initial

1. I am the support recipient under the following:

Order

Date of Order	Court	Court File Number

Agreement filed with the Court

Date of Agreement	Court Agreement Filed With	Court File Number

2. The following amounts due under the order/agreement have not been paid. *(If you need more space, complete Schedule 'A')*

Check if applicable. ☐ See Schedule 'A' attached

Date Payment Due Day/Month/Year	Amount Due	Date Paid Day/Month/Year	Amount Paid	Arrears

If you are entitled to interest on your support, *you must calculate the interest amount.* **Attach a copy of your calculations.**

If you are entitled to a COLA adjustment to your support, *you must include the adjustment in the amount due.* **Attach a copy of your calculations.**

Total Arrears $ _____ (a)

Total Interest to date (if any) $ _____ (b) **Applicable interest rate used** _____ %

My arrears as at: _____ TOTAL $ _____ (c)
      Date   (Add A and B)

You must sign this form in the presence of a lawyer, Justice of the Peace, Notary Public or Commissioner for taking affidavits.

Sworn before me at the _____ of _____

in the _____ of _____

this _____ day of _____ , 20 _____ .

_____   _____
Signature of a commissioner, etc.   Signature of Support Recipient

006-FRO-005E (2015/12) © Queen's Printer for Ontario, 2015   Disponible en français   Page 9 of 10

FIGURE 17.7 Statement of Arrears Concluded

Ontario

Ministry of Community
and Social Services

Family Responsibility Office
PO Box 200 Stn A
Oshawa ON L1H 0C5

Schedule 'A'
To Statement of Arrears Form

FRO Case Number

Date Payment Due Day/Month/Year	Amount Due	Date Paid Day/Month/Year	Amount Paid	Arrears

Enter amount onto Statement of Arrears form.

Clear Form   Print Form

006-FRO-005E (2015/12)   © Queen's Printer for Ontario, 2015   Disponible en français   Page 10 of 10

Glossary

access the right to visit with the child and to obtain information regarding the child's health, education, and welfare

adjusted cost base the cost at which capital property was acquired

adjusted sale price the value at which capital property is transferred

alimony a common law action by a wife for support from her husband

annulment a declaration that the marriage was never valid

as of right without needing the consent of the other party or an order of the court

attribution of capital gains the decision by the Canada Revenue Agency to treat the capital gain of one spouse as the capital gain of the other spouse

capital gain the profit made on the sale or other disposition of capital property

cause of action the basis for a legal action

cohabit to live together in a conjugal relationship within or outside of marriage

cohabitation agreement an agreement between two persons who are cohabiting or intend to cohabit and who are not married to each other in which they agree on their respective rights and obligations during cohabitation, on ceasing to cohabit, or on death

collaborative law a non-adversarial, cooperative, collaborative settlement model in which the parties work with specially trained collaborative family law lawyers

compensatory claim a claim for spousal support based on the recipient spouse's economic loss or disadvantage because of the marriage

condonation forgiveness of a matrimonial offence by continuing or resuming cohabitation with the guilty spouse, with knowledge of the offence

conference brief a case conference brief (Form 17A or Form 17B), a settlement conference brief (Form 17C or Form 17D), or a trial management conference brief (Form 17E)

constructive trust a trust imposed on the legal owner of property in favour of another person who has contributed work, money, or money's worth to the acquisition, preservation, or maintenance of the property

contingent liability a liability that is not fixed and absolute but will become fixed and absolute when a specified event occurs

continuing record the court's records of all the documents in a case

costs of disposition costs of disposing of the property, including real estate commission and legal fees

criminal conversation a tort action by which a husband could claim damages against a man who had sexual intercourse with the husband's wife

custody the rights and responsibilities of a parent, including the right and responsibility to make decisions that will affect the well-being of the child

de facto custody actual custody, or custody in fact

divorce a mensa et thoro an order of the ecclesiastical courts by which the parties to a valid marriage were relieved of their obligation to cohabit, but were still legally married

divorce a vinculo matrimonii an order of the ecclesiastical courts, following a declaration that a marriage was not valid, by which the parties were released from the bonds of marriage

doctrine of constructive desertion a doctrine related to alimony under which it was deemed that the husband had deserted the wife if a wife left her husband because of his misconduct

document exchange a subscription service in which law firms have access to a central facility to deliver and pick up documents

domestic contract a marriage contract, separation agreement, or cohabitation agreement

domicile permanent residence

donor one who makes a gift

duress force or threats that cause a person to do something he or she would not ordinarily do

ecclesiastical courts a system of church courts in England

encumbrances mortgages or other liens registered against the property

equalization of net family properties a process under the *Family Law Act* under which spouses share equally in the value of most property acquired during the marriage

exclusive possession the sole right to reside in the home to the exclusion of the other spouse

family arbitration an arbitration that deals with matters that could be dealt with in a marriage contract, separation agreement, cohabitation agreement, or paternity agreement, and is conducted exclusively in accordance with the law of Ontario or of another Canadian jurisdiction

family arbitration agreement an agreement to refer issues to a family arbitration

family arbitration award a decision that arises out of a family arbitration

joint custody when both parents share care of and decision-making power over the child

joint tenancy property is owned by two or more people and, on the death of one owner, the property passes to the other(s) automatically and not to the estate of the owner who died

jurisdiction shopping the practice of choosing a jurisdiction in which to start a proceeding based on a party's view of his or her chances of success in that jurisdiction rather than on the jurisdiction's connection with the subject matter of the proceeding

legal capacity to marry legal ability to enter into the contract of marriage

legal formalities of marriage the form a marriage ceremony must take

limitation period a certain time allowed by a statute for the commencement of a court proceeding

marriage contract an agreement between parties who are married or who intend to marry, in which they agree on their respective rights and obligations under the marriage or on separation, annulment, divorce, or death

mediation a method of dispute resolution in which the parties meet with a neutral third party who will help them try to come to an agreement

motion for summary judgment a motion for a final order without a trial

moving party the party who makes the motion

non-compensatory claim a claim for spousal support based on need

partition divide

paternity agreement an agreement between a man and a woman who are not spouses for payments toward various child and/or mother expenses

presumption of advancement the presumption, created by the *Married Women's Property Act*, that a husband who placed property in the name of his wife intended to make a gift of the property to her

presumption of resulting trust an equitable principle under which it is presumed that a person who places property in the name of another person intends that person to hold the property in trust for the donor

principal residence under the *Income Tax Act*, a residential property in which the taxpayer or other family member has resided during the taxation year

quantum amount

right of physical chastisement the right of a husband to use physical force to discipline his wife

secondary arbitration a family arbitration that is conducted in accordance with a separation agreement, a court order, or a family arbitration award that provides for the arbitration of possible future disputes relating to the ongoing management or implementation of the agreement, order, or award

separation agreement an agreement between parties who have cohabited, in or out of marriage, and who have separated, in which they agree on their respective rights and obligations

sole custody when one parent has total care of and decision-making power over the child

stayed temporarily stopped or suspended

substituted service service using a method ordered by the court in circumstances when the usual methods of service provided by the court rules are not effective

tenants in common two or more people who own property and on the death of one owner the owner's share passes to his or her estate

testator one who makes a will; one who leaves property to another by will

trial record a document that assembles and organizes documents relevant to the trial to be used by the trial judge

unity of legal personality a doctrine by which a husband and wife were considered to be one person in law

void *ab initio* void, or having no legal force, from the beginning

voidable may be declared void but is otherwise not void

without child support formula the formula used to calculate spousal support under the *Spousal Support Advisory Guidelines* if there are no dependent children and, therefore, no child support obligations

Index